How Did Our Garden Grow?

The History of Hatton Garden

Vivian Watson FGA

The History Press

First published 2022

The History Press
97 St George's Place, Cheltenham,
Gloucestershire, GL50 3QB
www.thehistorypress.co.uk

British Library Cataloguing in Publication Data.
A catalogue record for this book is available from the British Library.

ISBN 978 1 8039 9041 5

Typesetting and origination by The History Press
Printed in Turkey by IMAK

MIX
Paper from responsible sources
FSC® C111584

CONTENTS

INTRODUCTION

HOW DID OUR GARDEN GROW?

The 'Garden', as it is known by those who have worked there in the past or work there today, is a unique area of London. It has been associated with the diamond and gem trade, and the jewellery manufacturing industry for generations.

Originally the site of the garden of Ely Palace, Hatton Garden became known throughout the world as the 'go-to' place for all aspects of the jewellery trade. In a similar way to other London industrial hubs such as Billingsgate for fish, Covent Garden for fruit and vegetables, Smithfield for meat and Fleet Street for the press, Hatton Garden was something of a marketplace. It was also an arena where you could learn about what was going on in the world of diamonds and gems. Unlike the food markets though, with their sights, sounds and smells assaulting the visitor, the true Hatton Garden is a secret world. At a time before mobile phones and modern technology, it was essential to be in close proximity with others, both for trade and for information.

Local street names, such as Saffron Hill, Lily Place, Herbal Hill and Vine Hill, remind us that this area was once rich in horticulture. The palace garden was famed for its roses, fruit and herbs. With a little imagination you can picture the thousands of crocuses growing on the slopes of the River Fleet. A kilo of saffron requires 140,000 flowers and is more valuable than a kilo of gold.

A study of this part of London would not be complete without reference to some of the surrounding landmarks such as St Andrew's Church, Holborn Viaduct, Farringdon Station, the Fleet River, Staple Inn and Furnival's Inn. So, we will step outside the garden walls to explore their part in the local history.

The 'Garden' continues to evolve as one generation makes way for the next. It would not be recognisable, today, to some of those who worked there in years gone by. The strong emphasis on retail jewellery has grown out of its roots in manufacturing and the need to adapt to suit today's market.

In compiling an accurate history of the jewellery and diamond trade in Hatton Garden, one is faced with the reality that in many cases there is very little in the way of a paper trail. Transactions were effected by word of mouth.

'My word is my bond' might well have been written for the diamond trade as much as '*Dictum Meum Pactum*' was for the London Stock Exchange. Many deals were done in secrecy. Many were done illegally. Only inside knowledge can capture some of the remarkable stories of those who have in some way left their footprint in Hatton Garden.

The other major consideration is that of security. Those who work with high-value items need to keep their heads down and not make themselves potential targets for criminals. Many who have contributed to this work have opted for privacy and are not named in these pages.

ABOUT THE AUTHOR

Vivian Watson first came to Hatton Garden as a boy during his school holidays. He enjoyed watching the craftsmen in the workshop of the family's manufacturing jewellery business and was fascinated by the allure of gold and diamonds. He joined his father, Peter Watson, in 1967 and spent over fifty years in the trade before formally retiring in 2017.

Although he is now retired, he continues to take a close interest in the trade and enjoys the freedom and privilege of knowing the 'Garden' better than most. The family business is now in the hands of the next generation and John Watson is now responsible for all operations of PJ Watson Ltd.

The Watson family have the unique claim to having four consecutive generations of qualified gemmologists each holding the coveted FGA diploma (Fellow of the Gemmological Association of Great Britain).

Vivian Watson has been a Liveryman of the Worshipful Company of Goldsmiths since 1995. He has served as Chairman of The Gemmological Association and is an avid collector of trade memorabilia.

His company library contains over 1,000 books on diamonds, gems, precious metals, jewellery and the history of the trade. He lectures on all aspects of the industry to private audiences and acts as a consultant to private clients. His passion beyond the trade is for charity work, which is fronted by The Diamond Trust.

HISTORY

BEFORE THE GARDEN

For many people throughout the world, the name 'Hatton Garden' immediately creates an image of diamonds, jewellery and precious metals or gemstones. For over 150 years, valuable items have been traded by its many dealers and merchants. Manufacturing jewellers and jewellery designers have established themselves here and become an important part of this interdependent neighbourhood. Hatton Garden became, within a generation, an international crossroads and meeting point for anyone connected to the diamond or jewellery trade. In our own time, we have seen a change of emphasis from a market that was almost exclusively trade-focused, to one that is now consumer-targeted. The 'Garden', as it is affectionately known to people in the trade, has evolved and adapted itself to suit the needs of those it serves and those who work there. Those who have known it a long time will tell you it is not what it was. We should, however, not be surprised. In an evolutionary way it has become what it is today and will become what tomorrow's needs dictate.

If we could turn back the clock, we would see a very different place in each of the many generations who have come and gone. Those who remember the Garden in the 1950s and 1960s do so with mixed feelings. Although no one would choose to go back to the smoke-filled streets and the primitive facilities, there is a sense of loss, perhaps more for the people themselves who were once part of this thriving community.

Although significantly damaged by the two world wars, there were more people employed in the trade in the first half of the 20th century than there are today. Real growth began in the latter part of the 19th century, the period when diamonds were found in South Africa and started to become more accessible to a wider circle of people. In wealthy Victorian and Edwardian Britain, there was a healthy appetite for diamond jewellery.

Ely Palace, 18th century.

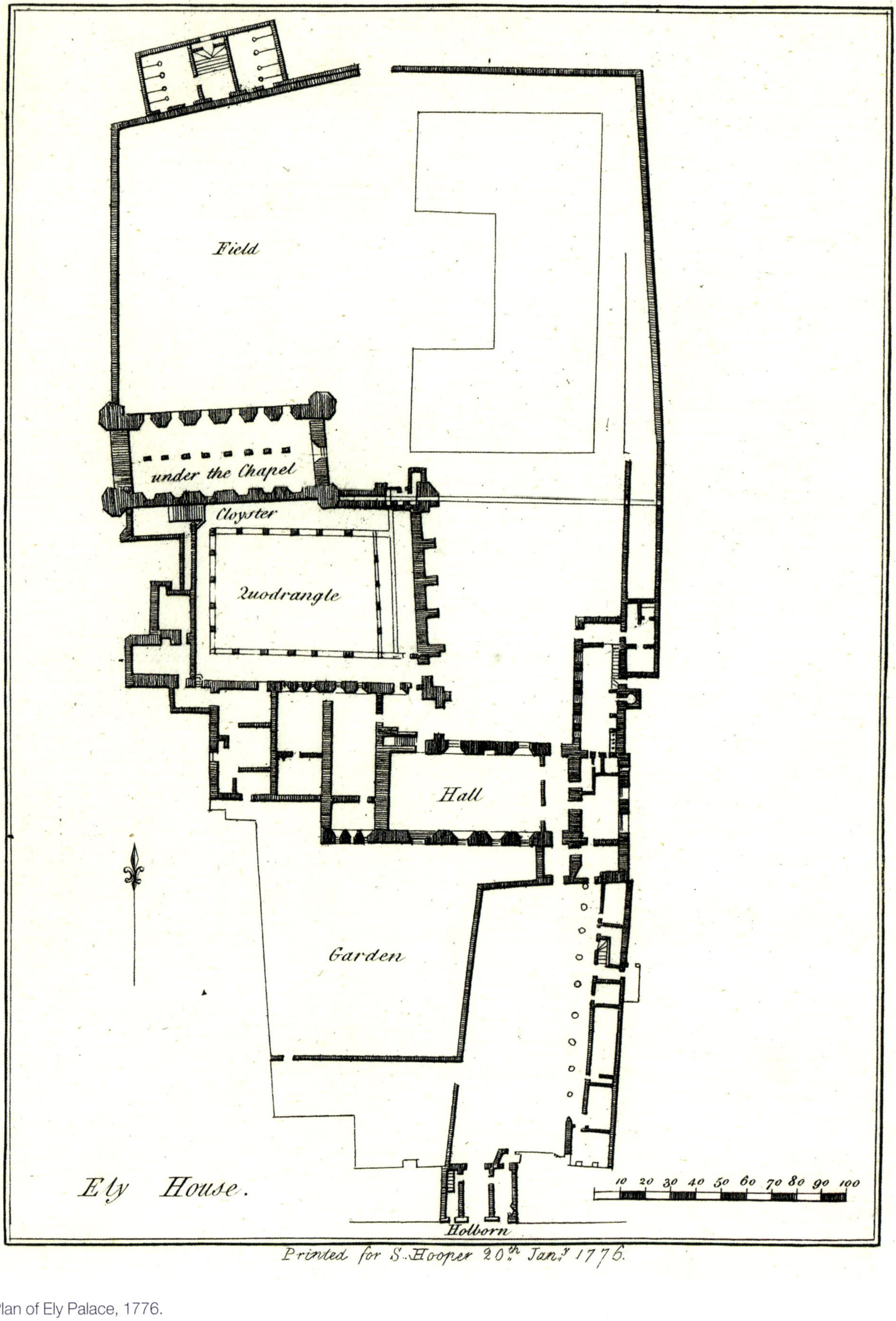

Plan of Ely Palace, 1776.

The story of how Hatton Garden became synonymous with the jewellery trade is an interesting one and to find out the answers we travel back further to its development in the 17th century and beyond to when it was indeed a rather special garden.

Originally known as Hatton Street, the road today runs roughly north–south along the course of what was once a path through the centre of a magnificent garden. The original garden spread to the west where Leather Lane runs today, and to the eastern boundary which is now Saffron Hill. In the north, it went to Hatton Wall and to the south ran along Holborn. Within this area we have other thoroughfares such as Hatton Place, Kirby Street, Greville Street, St Cross Street, Saffron Hill, Bleeding Heart Yard and Ely Place. In total Hatton Garden covers an area of approximately 21 acres.

Although, strictly speaking, Hatton Garden is now one street within an area, the side streets and back alleys are all part of the Garden. With a sense of pride and history, many companies address themselves as Kirby Street, Hatton Garden, or Greville Street, Hatton Garden.

Holborn was the main Roman road west out of Londinium and would have been used by thousands of occupying soldiers. Evidence of graves and human remains were found to the east of Holborn Circus during the construction of the Diamond Trading Company (DTC) building in the 1950s. These were exhumed and reburied on a new site, appropriately named Gravesend in Kent.

For most of its life the area of Hatton Garden would have been quiet woodland and open countryside, a short journey to the west from the City of London. The only feature was the Holborne River that flowed south into the Thames. Literally meaning the bourne or stream in the hollow, the river flowed swiftly through a steeply banked valley just to the east of Hatton Garden. Remains of large fallen trees have been found at great depth in the course of the old stream. Tacitus in his history, *Agricola*, written around AD 98, alludes to the wooded jaws of a narrow inlet from the Thames such as could only have been applicable to the Holbourne. The river had different names and nearer the Thames it was known as the Fleet on account of its fast current. Fleet Street owes its name to the river.

The Romans had arrived in Britain in the first century AD and established Londinium, laying the foundation stones for what was to become the City of London. From the time of the Romans and throughout the first half of the first millennium, Christianity spread throughout the land. Christianity had been made the official religion of the Empire in AD 312 and would have been practised throughout Britain before the Romans departed in AD 410. At the top of the hill above the river a little church was established.

The first mention of St Andrew, Holborn and the Fleet River comes in AD 959. A charter of Westminster Abbey alludes to 'the old wooden church of St Andrew' on the hill above the River Fleet, suggesting that by this point the site was already long established as a place of worship.

St Andrew's Church is the earliest man-made landmark in the area that is still visible today. Although outside Hatton Garden, it is a reference point for later development and can be seen on most maps. The Fleet River is no longer visible, having been buried in a large pipe below Farringdon Road.

During the Anglo-Saxon period that followed the Roman occupation, King Edgar of Wessex, great-grandson of King Alfred, granted five hides of land to Westminster Abbey. The boundaries were defined as running from the Thames along the Tyburn River (Marble Arch) in the west, following the old army road east, believed to be Oxford Street, and turning south again at the church through the London Fen (the Fleet). In the old feudal system, where the land belonged to the king, such a grant was significant. A hide is approximately 30 acres, so five hides would be 150 acres.

In the Norman period, London became the capital city of England, and the area around St Andrew's became the first settlement to the west of London. For a short time, it was the home of the Knights Templar.

In 1086, the Doomsday Book entry states: 'At Holborn the King holds two cottages who pay twenty pence a year to the king's sheriff moreover William, the Chamberlain, pays the king's sheriff six shillings a year for land where he planted his vines.' The Normans introduced viniculture, which became common in the area during the Middle Ages.

A very early manuscript refers to Malcolm, King of Scots, writing to the Monks of Ely (British Museum, Add MS 5811, *Collections of William Cole*) – in about 1100:

> Malcolm, King of Scots, to all his trusty men of his honor of Huntenden and also to his men of his sons in London greeting. Know clergy and laity, present and future, that have granted and, by way of this charter, have confirmed in free and perpetual alms to God and to St Etheldreda and to the Monks of the church of Ely that land which John, the son of Gihaldi, held of me in London and gave to the aforesaid monks, from which land they were wont to return to me 71/2d yearly. Wherefore I will direct that the aforesaid monks may freely and quietly hold and possess that land released from all services and secular taxes in like manner as other alms in land are being held and possessed of me in freedom and in quietness.

As the city grew, more dwellings were built outside the protection of the old city walls. In 1130 the city was permitted to extend its boundaries beyond the walls at Newgate.

Fitzstephen writes of Holborn in 1180: 'On all sides without the houses, are the citizen's gardens and orchards, planted with trees ... On the north side are also pastures, and plain meadows, with brooks running through them turning water mills ... Not far off is a great forest.' There is also a record from about this time that states: 'Geoffrey, son of Arnold, sold his house and garden and quay lying on the water at Holborn to Walter Brunning, a fishmonger. Brunning himself had an orchard nearby and this area lying on the west bank of the river and north of Holborn.' The area was a supplier to the markets of the citizens of London of fruit and vegetables including onions, garlic, beans in the husk, herbs, leeks, parsley and herbage.

The year 1180 is also significant as it is the year in which the Goldsmiths Company is first mentioned. As Britain was coming out of the Dark Ages, there was an increase in population and prosperity along with an increase in learning and the art of keeping of records.

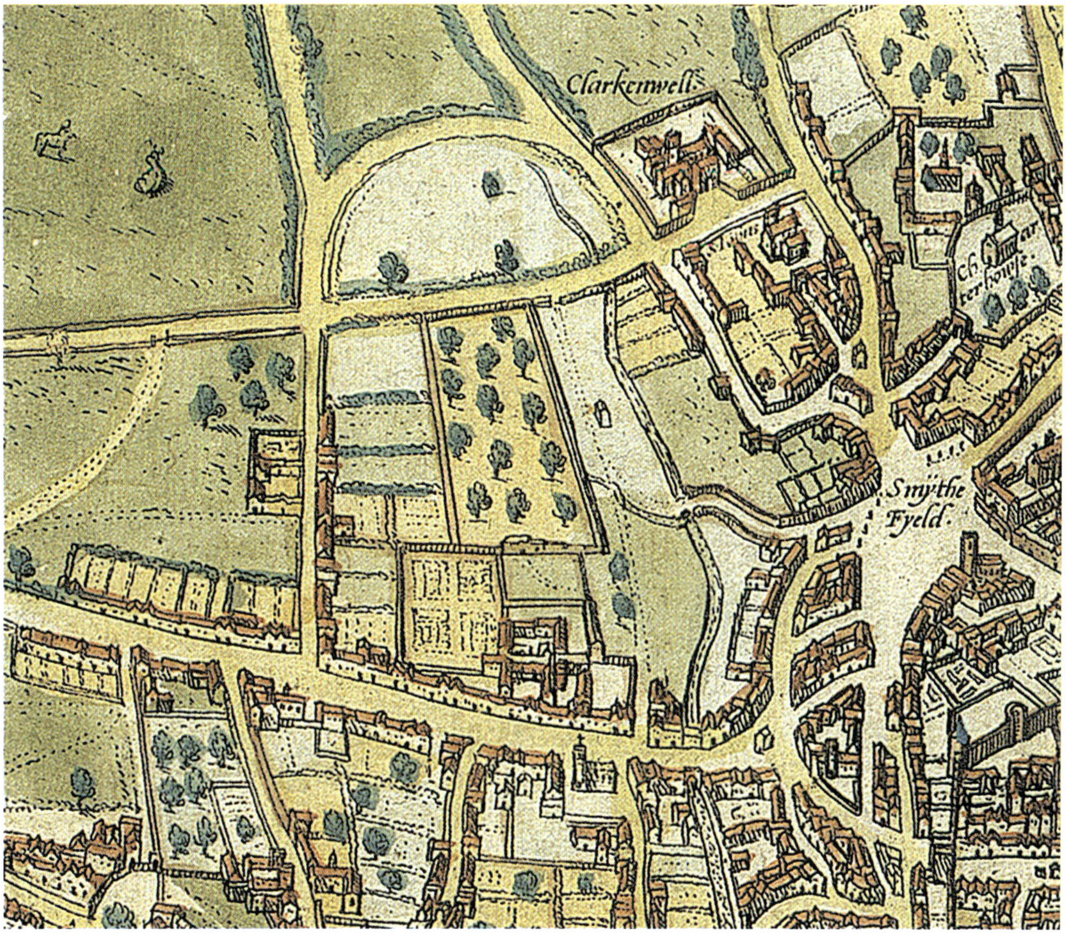

Colour map of a rural life and a well-managed garden belonging to the Bishops of Ely, Braun & Hogenberg, 1572.

In 1223 the city's limit was marked by bars or barriers that were constructed across the road to halt the approaching traffic for tolls. They were also used to keep out undesirables such as lepers. Although originally chains or poles would have been used, these were replaced with a gate and a small hut for the gatekeeper. In Sir Christopher Wren's time there was a stone-built structure. The Holborn Bars were situated towards Chancery Lane near to Staple Inn and markers can still be seen today in the form of ornate dragons outside Chancery Lane station.

In a period of history when travel to London from the country meant more than a day's journey on horseback or by stagecoach it was the privilege of the wealthy, the ruling classes and the Church to have London palaces or large houses. Bishops were also expected to sit in Parliament. Cambridgeshire was particularly wealthy as it was well established in sheep farming and wool production. Education was the responsibility of the Church, so there were strong links between the Church and the ruling classes. The 13th century saw the beginnings of a transformation that led from a totally rural environment to one where a row of small properties lined parts of Holborn. A significant part of the area was owned by the Augustine monks of Missenden.

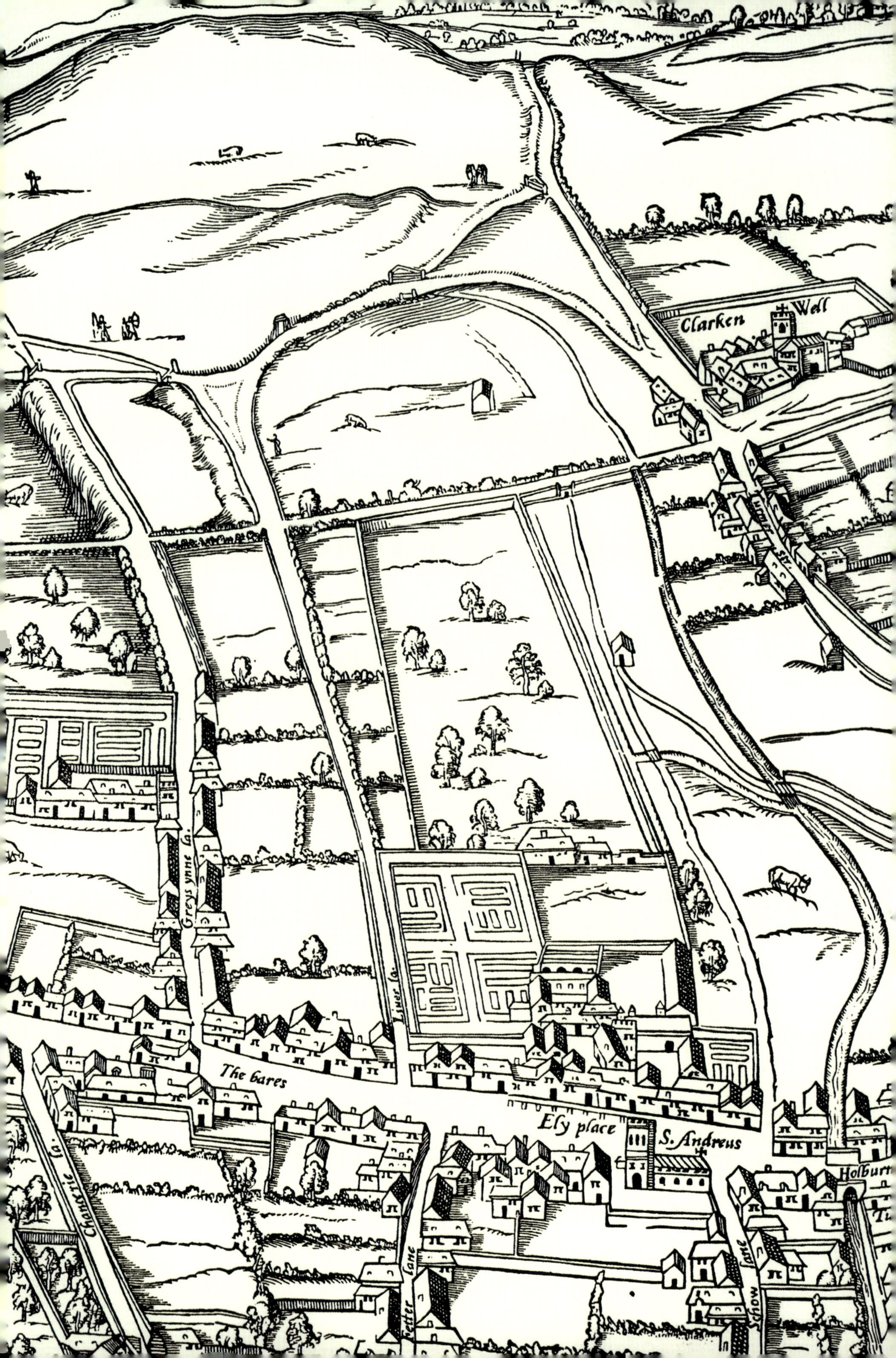
Clarken Well
Cow str.
Greys ynne la.
Liuer la.
The bares
Ely place
S. Andreus
Holburn
Chancerie la.
Fetter lane
Schow lane

In 1251 John le Franceis, a Baron of the Exchequer, was prebendary of Houlbourne and received an income from the prebendary lands abutting the Houlbourne, north of the highway. Before his death in 1268 he had leased land adjoining his court room and built an oratory.

Sir John de Kirkeby, who had become Chancellor of England in 1272, and Bishop of Ely on 22nd September 1286, was the next owner of the land north of Holborn. Kirkeby and his successor, William de Luda, built St Etheldreda's on the site of the oratory and increased the footprint of the existing buildings to form a great complex of halls where he lived. This included a special room dedicated as the Chamber of Receipt where the business of the Chancellor was conducted.

He bequeathed the estate, along with nine cottages, to the Bishopric upon his death on 20th March 1290 for the benefit of his successors. Ely was one of the wealthiest sees in the country: 'The hall with its chambers, the completed Chapel, the stables, Garden and vinery were all in existence at the date of his death.'

The land consisted of 7 acres of vineyards and arable pasture totalling 58 acres. So, the Bishops of Ely established their London home on the high ground above the river, on the site that we know as Ely Place. The boundaries were then the Holbourne River, or later Turnmill Brook, to the east and north and Leather Lane to the west.

Unlike other large houses, which were of timber construction, Ely Palace was built of stone with a cloistered quadrangle and a walled garden, orchard and private chapel.

Subsequent bishops added to the estate. Of particular significance was Thomas Arundel, who later became Archbishop of Canterbury. He built an imposing gatehouse on Holborn.

The area was increased with the acquisition of more land from the Manor, or the Soke, of Portpool. A Soke was an area over which the Lord of the Manor had absolute jurisdiction, including the power to operate his own courts. Originally this stretched eastward beyond Leather Lane, but the Dean and Chapter of St Pauls, as Lord of the Manor, conveyed the eastern part to John de Kirkeby. It was known for a time as 'The Manor in Holborn of Sir John de Kirkeby'. The Manor of Portpool became Gray's Inn and Portpool Lane still connects Gray's Inn Road with Leather Lane.

From the elevated ground on which the buildings stood, fine views could be obtained of the beautiful wooded slopes of Highgate and Hampstead to the north and of the city with its lofty cathedral spire to the east, whilst nearer at hand on the opposite bank of the river might be seen Smithfield, the Hospital of St Bartholomew and the then new buildings of the Charterhouse.

Between Leather Lane and the entrance gates to the Bishop's Palace and fronting the street were the nine shops that had been Sir John de Kirkeby's, standing in their own gardens, and according to the bailiff's rolls, let in 1376 at a uniform rate of 16s a year, afterwards reduced in Henry IV's reign to 13s 4d. Good structures of their class, none

Opposite: Shows Liver Lane for Leather Lane, The Bars in Holborn and Ely Place. Most of the estate is still garden.

of them were thatch covered but all were roofed with tiles, finished off with a crest-end, and also possessing chimneys, although the walls were constructed of timber and plaster. Next to the nine shops was a gatehouse with gates, which were double, each under a separate arch, with rooms over them, and a tower and on one side a postern. The gatehouse was let in 1376 to Adam Vinour, the gardener. To the east there were a further fifteen shops.

Records from the reign of Edward III (1327–1377) are preserved in Ely. They mention names of neighbouring houses such as Farringdon's Inn.

There was enough space in the Bishop's Palace for more than one occupant. In 1327 Philippa of Hainault was a guest for Christmas, while en route to be married to Edward III in York.

In 1357 Edward, the Black Prince, son of Edward III and father of Richard II, stayed there with his followers. Between 1381 and 1399 John of Gaunt, Duke of Lancaster, lived there after his palace (the Savoy) was sacked by Wat Tyler's mob in the Peasant's Revolt. Ely House is where John of Gaunt was when he is quoted in Shakespeare's *Richard II*: 'this sceptred isle, this precious stone set in a silver sea ... this blessed plot, this earth, this realm, this England.' John of Gaunt died at Ely Palace in 1399.

In the 13th century, what was to become Leather Lane was named Lyverslane and in 1329 we see the first mention of Field Lane, which subsequently became Saffron Hill.

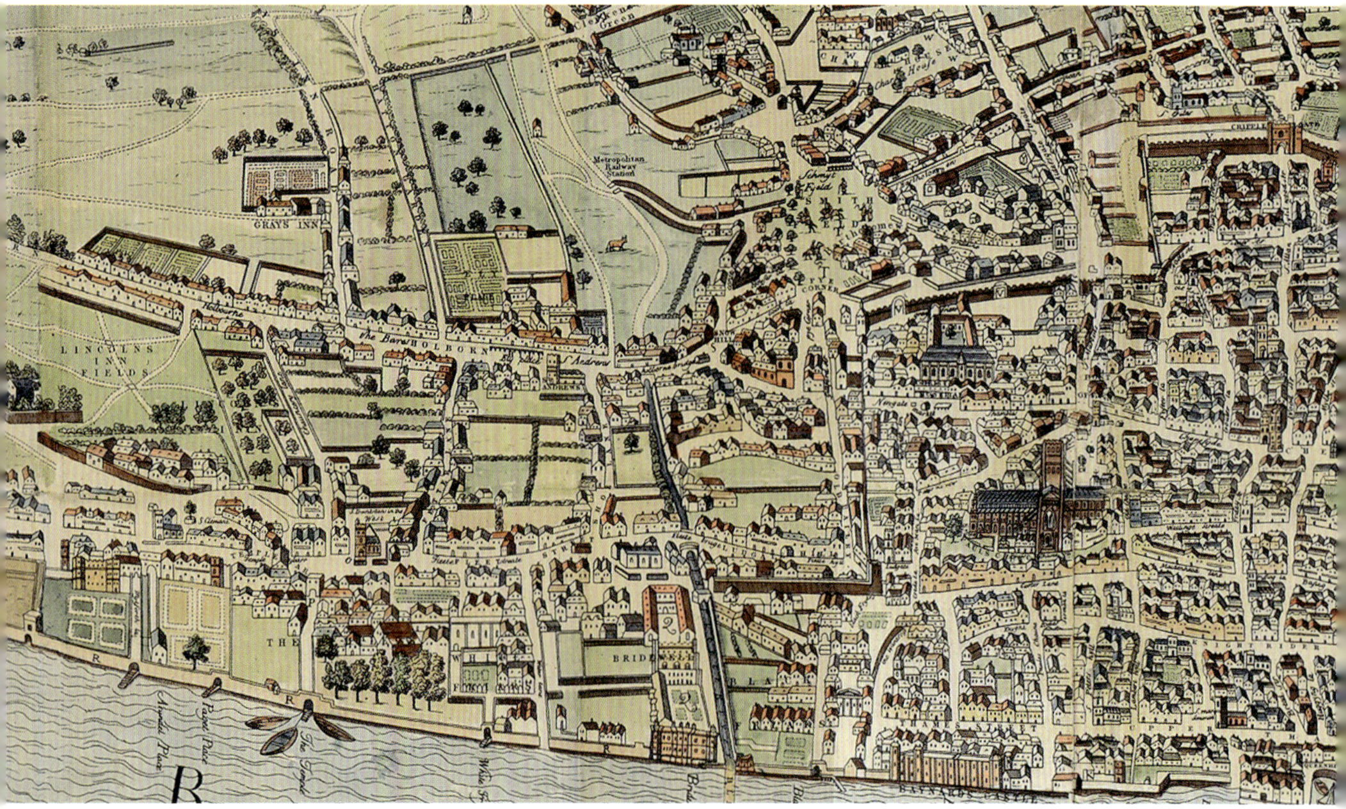

'Ralph Agas'. Panorama from *Civitas Londinium*, 1560.

The grounds of the palace were enclosed by a thorn hedge in which were wooden gates, fitted with locks and keys. Four cart loads of thorns were bought and used for making this hedge. Inner gardens were reserved for the Bishop's private use, and railings and locked doors separated the great garden and the grass yard or meadow from the vineyard. Every year the grass yard was mown, and the grass or hay sold – a tithe of the proceeds being paid to the rector of St Andrew's.

As time went by more land was added and the garden included a vineyard, an orchard and a kitchen garden. In total it occupied an area of about 40 acres. Grape harvest workers were employed at 2d per day. Today, we still have Vine Hill, Herbal Hill and Lily Place to remind us.

Roses would have been the main flower in the garden, and the favourite was the sweet-scented *Rosa gallica*, which became the red rose of England.

In a famous scene of Shakespeare's *Richard III*, Act III.4 (1483–1485), Richard says, 'My Lord of Ely, when I was last in Holborn, I saw good strawberries in your garden there; I do beseech you, send for some of them.' There is still a Strawberry Fayre in Ely Place every June. It is usually held on the Saturday that falls nearest to the 23rd, which is St Etheldreda's Feast Day and the date of her death in AD 679.

Towards the end of the 15th century there was a marked increase in the population of London, which resulted in more and more people living and working outside the walls. There was a stream of 'foreigners' from such places as Hertfordshire, Middlesex and Kent, coming to London for work. Furthermore, there was an increase in immigrants from across Europe. The poorer citizens had to set up shop outside the walls as they couldn't afford to pay city rents.

In 1531 Henry VIII and Catherine of Aragon entertained at Ely Palace. Their lavish hospitality consumed 100 sheep, 51 cows, 91 pigs, 24 oxen, 720 chickens, 444 pigeons, 168 swans and 4,000 larks over a period of five days.

In 1544 Henry VIII's Chancellor, Henry Wriothesley, occupied a large suite of apartments in the building, and it was here that the conspiracy to overthrow the Protector Somerset was hatched. A controversy over whether the Bishop of Ely's Palace in Holborn lay within the jurisdiction of the City of London came to a head in 1567 when the mayor, Sir Roger Martin, attempted to weigh bread that was being sold in a row of shops, part of the property known as Ely Rents. The subsequent arbitration ruled that the shops came under the city's jurisdiction and, in effect, determined from that point on the city's boundary. This is why the boundary is seen on maps as a wavy line.

In 1546 the Mitre was built as a 'pub' for the estate and, although tucked away out of view, still thrives today.

John Gerard, born in 1545, the famous gardener, physician and herbalist who published his *Herbal* in 1597, had a garden at Holborn, on the slope of the hill between Ely Place and the Fleet – a spot surrounded by woods, fields and meadows. Even in those days it was a little country hamlet, not even a village. In this spot he used to gather trefoil, yarrow, lesser hawkweed, red clary, white saxifrage and rocket. He is buried in St Andrew's Churchyard.

The Bishops of Ely continued to enjoy Ely Palace and its beautiful garden for over 300 years. That is, until the arrival of a certain Christopher Hatton in London. His appearance was to mark the beginnings of change in the palace and leads to the next chapter of the story.

HATTON'S GARDEN

The palace remained the London home of the Bishops of Ely until Elizabethan times, when one man entered the story and changed its history in a way no one could have foreseen. Christopher Hatton was born in 1540, the youngest of three sons, to Alice and William Hatton in the Manor House of Holdenby, Northamptonshire. His early education was at the hands of his maternal uncle, William Saunders, who was from a strong Catholic background. In his mid-teens, Hatton was admitted to St Mary's Hall, Oxford, but there is no record of him having attained a degree.

On 26th May 1560, at the age of 20, he enrolled at the Inner Temple to begin a career in the legal profession but once again there is some doubt as to whether he achieved his goals in this direction. On 18th January 1562, he danced before Queen Elizabeth in a play put on by his peers. He caught the eye of the Queen in an entertainment in which he took the role of 'Master of the Game'. This new relationship was of his making but also proved to be his undoing. There is some speculation as to the level of their intimacy but there is considerable proof among the archives of the National State papers that their relationship went way beyond normal protocol.

An aerial view of Ely Palace looking east with Smithfield beyond the Fleet River.

Model of Ely Palace.

The hall and quadrangle of Ely Palace.

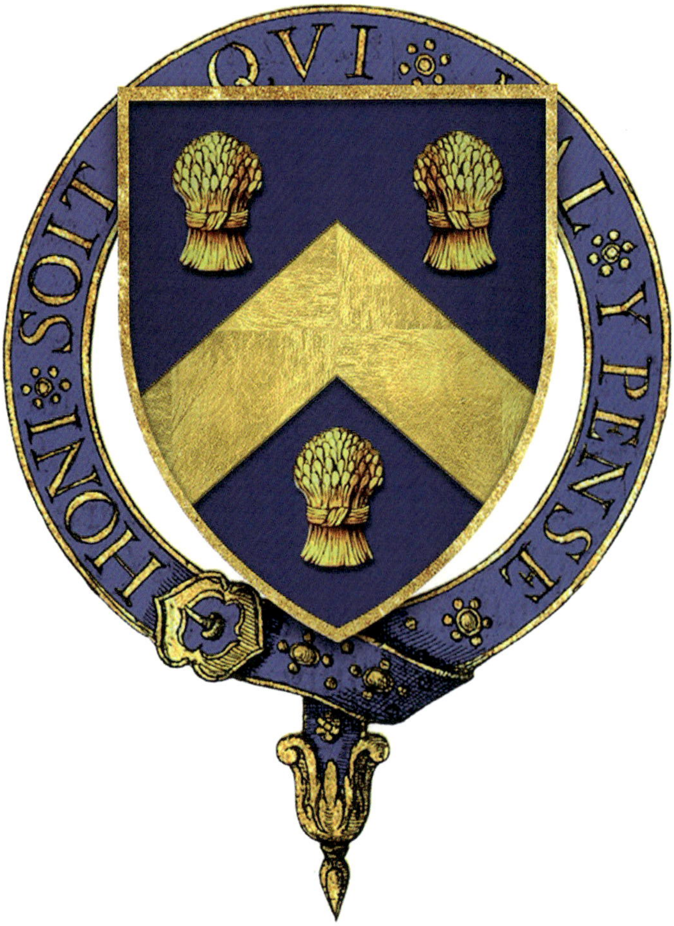

Above: The hall and chapel of Ely Palace.

Left: Coat of arms of Sir Christopher Hatton.

Opposite: Queen Elizabeth.

Sir Christopher Hatton.

Plan of the City of London in the time of Queen Elizabeth. (John Norden, 1593.)

In 1564 he was made 'Gentleman Pensioner', which means that he was part of the Queen's bodyguard. The Gentlemen Pensioners were founded by Henry VIII as a ceremonial bodyguard. Their main weapon was a spear. He served for thirteen years.

In his twenties, he mixed with the finest in the land and entered jousting competitions at Westminster. Clearly, he had developed a taste for the high life. However, this was a strain on his finances even though the Queen gave him a lot of support.

In 1571, now aged 30, he entered the House of Commons as MP for Higham Ferrers, Northamptonshire. His relationship with the Queen deepened and they exchanged gifts. He gave the Queen a 'fairy jewel' with rubies and diamonds. In July 1572, he was made captain of the Yeomen of the Guard. On this occasion, he gave Elizabeth a flower of gold set with an emerald.

It would appear that the Queen was willing to give Hatton what he wanted, and he had set his sights on Ely Palace. Hatton first made a bid for the property in 1575. Alarmed by this approach, the Bishop wrote to Burghley saying that he would be loath to leave the house as it was so convenient for him when he visited London. He firmly believed that he was responsible for maintaining his rights and those of his successors and that he 'must not scatter what his predecessors had gathered'.

Bishop Cox was a well-respected man in his day. He was appointed Bishop of Ely in 1559 by the Queen. He had acquired his DD (Doctor of Divinity) at Cambridge in 1537, having been through both Oxford and Cambridge, and had been Master of Eton College. He had served as tutor to the Prince of Wales, Chaplain to King Edward VI and Archbishop Cranmer. He had sat on the commission that produced the first English Communion Service and Prayer Book in 1549. Elizabeth had chosen him to preach the sermon at the opening of Parliament in January 1559. As a man of integrity, however, he objected to the Queen's scheme of appropriating episcopal lands for the Crown.

At that time Ely Palace consisted of a hall, cloisters, a chapel, nine cottages, a 7-acre vineyard, 5 acres of arable land or meadow, a garden famous for its saffron crocuses, roses and strawberries and an orchard. It was one of the finest cultivated gardens in Tudor England. It was to become Hatton's Garden. It is interesting to reflect that the value of saffron exceeds that of gold and ironic to think that nearly 250 years later the garden would be famous for its gold.

Bishop Cox.

On 20th March 1576, Richard Cox, Bishop of Ely:

> Granted unto our trusty and well-beloved servant Christopher Hatton esquire, Captain of our Guard, for the term of twenty and one years from the Feast of the Annunciation of our Blessed Lady the Virgin (25th March) then next ensuing all and singular those parts and parcels of that his, the said Bishop's, palace or house in Holebourne ... commonly called Ely Palace ... that is to say the gate house, the first courtyard and divers chambers and rooms of the said palace ...

The twenty-one-year lease required the payment of £10 per annum, ten loads of hay and a red rose from the garden on Midsummer's Day. However, the Bishop had needed to be pushed in order to allow Hatton in. It was the Queen who eased him out with a relentless campaign. She is reported as having said to the Bishop: 'Proud prelate, you know what you were before I made you what you are! If you don't immediately comply with my request, by God! I will unfrock you.'

Hatton's tenure of the gatehouse and garden proved to be the thin end of the wedge. Once established in this desirable location, he gradually, with the continuing help of the Queen, displaced the poor bishop entirely. Cox died in 1581, a broken man.

Hatton was responsible for the repairs and renovation of the gatehouse to make it habitable. He quickly took possession and began to improve the big rambling palace, subletting to other interests and allowing servants and others to reside there. He was to use it increasingly in the coming years as the London residence for himself, his servants and friends, for official duties, the holding of trials, the house arrest of political prisoners, and even some commercial enterprises.

In 1576, Francis Flower had lodgings at Hatton's residence, Ely Place. He became MP for Huntingdon in 1584 and for Corfe Castle in 1593. Flower had been a protégé of Hatton, who had helped him in his career. Flower left in his will a diamond worth £50 (several thousand pounds at today's prices) to Hatton's nephew, Sir William Hatton.

The detailed inventory of the repair work to the gatehouse that Hatton initiated in order to make it habitable gives a delightful snapshot of the building tradesmen of the time. The schedule includes the names, places of domicile and money paid to the bricklayers, masons, carpenters, tilers, lime burners, plasterers, turners and smiths who worked on the restoration. The cost of glass, lead, nails, timber lathes, pumps and paving is enumerated in detail using Roman numerals at a time when Arabic numbering was becoming the norm in Elizabethan England.

A legal loophole was discovered in the original lease: faulty wording undermined Hatton's title to the property and it was realised that the successors of the Bishop might be able to claim it back. As Hatton had spent a great deal of money on its improvement, he did not want to lose his investment. On 25th May 1577 under the Privy Seal at Greenwich, it was reported that Hatton's costs on Ely Place had amounted to the sum of £1,880, which should be recompensed to him.

As part of the original agreement, the Bishop had retained certain rights. He had access through the gatehouse and permission to walk in the garden, including the right to gather twenty bushels of roses a year.

The property extended along Holborn, from Leather Lane to Holborn River. The hall measured 72 by 32 feet, and the oak roof was 30 feet high. It was lit by six Gothic windows. At the west end of this building were the chief lodging rooms and apartments. To the north-west was a cloister measuring 95 by 73 feet, built around a garden and topped by rooms and galleries. To the north of the cloister stood the chapel surrounded by a walled garden full of trees.

In Agas's map of London, in 1560, the north side of Holborn consisted only of a single row of houses, with gardens behind them, and Field Lane was a mere opening from the street to the fields between Holborn and Clerkenwell. There was a narrow path, where at present stands Saffron Hill, through a long pasture, bounded by the Turnmill Brook and the wall of Lord Hatton's garden.

On 11th November 1577, Hatton was made vice chamberlain and had a seat on the Privy Council. Hatton usually accompanied the Queen on her annual progresses around the country. He was knighted on 1st December, the same year, at Windsor.

It was in 1578 that Francis Drake set sail in the 'Pelican' on his circumnavigation of the globe. On 20th August 1578, he renamed his boat the 'Golden Hind' in honour of Christopher Hatton, who had sponsored his voyage and whose coat of arms featured a golden hind.

In July 1578, the freehold of the palace was transferred to Hatton by the Queen for £1,897 5s 8d and he began to build Hatton House there, where he lived until his death in 1591. He was the cause of great jealousy among other officials and would-be contenders. He was also the cause of great anxiety to the Church as he converted the crypt of the chapel into a buttery.

On 29th April 1587, Elizabeth presented the Great Seal to Hatton at the Palace of the Archbishop of Canterbury in Croydon where the Court was in residence. The Queen took the Great Seal from its red velvet bag and put it into Hatton's hands, bidding him to use it to seal a writ, and then named him Lord Chancellor.

John Stow recorded in his *Annales of England*, 1601, that on 3rd May 1587 (First day of Trinity):

Coat of arms of the Hatton family, featuring the golden hind.

> A stately procession made its way from Ely Palace in Holborn to Westminster where Hatton took the oath of office. Before him in the procession went forty of his gentlemen in blue livery and chains of gold, plus gentlemen pensioners and other gentlemen on foot. Also, attending him were the officers and clerks of the Court of Chancery. Hatton rode in state behind them, having on his right-hand Lord Treasurer Burghley and on the left the Earl of Leicester. Following him were nobles, judges, and many knights with their retinues.

Elizabeth visited Hatton on various occasions at his new London residence. Philip Gawdy wrote to his father telling him of a royal progress that Hatton hosted from 21st November to 6th December 1587: 'Upon Tuesday at night she came to my Lord Chancellor's where she hath been ever since. Her entertainment hath been very great there both for herself and all her train, which a number of us hath very well tasted of.'

Elizabeth visited again on 19th August 1588, when Hatton's muster of men at arms paraded for her. She dined there with him in May 1589 and stayed there longer the following May, when she stayed with him until 6th June. Later in that year (1590), she met Viscount Turenne, the French Ambassador at Ely House. One year later she was to stay for five days, comforting Hatton during his terminal illness.

However, the relationship between Hatton and the Queen wasn't without its problems. The Queen expected repayment of the debts that he had accrued, and he was not able to honour them. The Queen was insistent, and he couldn't cope with the strain. Before his death he was in debt to the tune of nearly £69,000, mostly to the Queen, including £42,000 from revenues he had collected.

An inventory made before his death showed his assets were approximately £31,000 plus properties including Ely Palace. Without any significant private wealth, Hatton's debts had increased as he enjoyed his life as a member of the royal circle.

In the last years of his life he became the object of derision among some. It was said of Hatton House:

> Sir Christopher Hatton lives here.
> He has a great house, but no cheer,
> A large cellar but no beer.

On 2nd September 1590, at Drayton, and then three days later at Ely Place, Hatton had instructions drawn up for his heir, Sir William Hatton, regarding his estate consequent upon his death.

Hatton suffered with gout. By the latter half of 1591 Hatton's health began a significant decline. Thomas Phelippes (one of Walsingham's agents) wrote: 'The Chancellor is very sick with a strange strangury [severe difficulty in urinating as with cystitis and prostate difficulties] and is not likely to recover.'

Christopher Hatton's House.

The news swept through the Court circles, quickly reaching the ears of the Queen. Realising that Hatton was in the throes of his final illness, she visited him at Ely Palace and on 11th November 1591 'she brought him cordial broths with her own hands, but all would not do ... No pulleys could pull up a heart once cast down, though a Queen herself set her hand thereto.' Elizabeth stayed with him for five days. Hatton died on 20th November 1591, aged 51.

The Queen was broken-hearted at the loss of a 'very close friend' and confidante. A great funeral was arranged for him. He was buried with great pomp in Old St Pauls Cathedral in London on 16th December 1591. The funeral cortège passed through the city with a hundred poor people given caps and gowns for the occasion, preceding the coffin. In the procession were 300 gentlemen and yeomen dressed in gowns, cloaks and coats as well as eighty members of the Queen's Guard and the Lords of the Council.

Hatton's nephew, Sir William (Hatton) Newport, erected a tomb so massive and ornate that it was considered too large even for St Pauls. It was inscribed with copious eulogies in Latin and located between the memorial stones of Sir Philip Sidney and Sir Francis Walsingham. Unfortunately, this grand tomb was destroyed in the Great Fire of 1666.

A somewhat sarcastic epitaph was written for his tomb: 'Philip and Francis have no tomb. For Great Sir Christopher takes all the room.'

Hatton had never married. In the settlement of his estate in 1573, he made his sister's son, William Newport, his adopted heir. Newport took the name Hatton as a tribute to the man who had come from modest beginnings and risen to enviable heights, and thus given lasting recognition. Along with the assets came the debts. William survived his uncle by only six years. Such was the complexity of the estate that it wasn't settled within William's lifetime and went to his successor, another Christopher Hatton, apart from Hatton House. This was inherited by his widow, a granddaughter of the great Lord Burleigh. Lady

Monumental grave of Sir Christopher Hatton in the old St Paul's Cathedral.

Hatton was young and attracted the attention of many would-be suitors, including Sir Francis Bacon and Sir Edward Coke, the latter of whom she married on 5th November 1598. The St Andrew's Parish Church Register has an entry of marriage between Edward Coke 'The Queen's Attorney-General and my Lady Elizabeth Hatton'.

Bacon penned the lines: 'God Almighty first planted a garden, and indeed it is the purest of human pleasures. It is the greatest refreshment to the spirit of man; without which buildings and palaces are but gross handiworks.' It would seem that he was inspired by the garden of Christopher Hatton.

After the death of the second Hatton (Newport), the Bishops tried to repossess what was once theirs. Lady Elizabeth Hatton, who occupied the large house that Hatton had built, would not allow it.

The heirs found it necessary to sell part of the furnishings of Holdenby and later some land. William is said to have sold most of Hatton's jewels to Elizabeth (Bess) Hardwick, Lady Shrewsbury. However, he did keep a blue sapphire, which he wore on his shirt string. She also bought a famous set of tapestries from Holdenby. Eventually, the garden would be sold off too. Fortuitously, it was purchased by a developer, who created Hatton Street, as it was originally known, thus bringing to an end the life of one of the most renowned gardens in London.

During the 16th century the population of London had increased from about 50,000 to 250,000. Many were foreigners escaping Europe; others had come from the shires. Places like Holborn were transformed from rural communities to residential areas. Large family houses took in lodgers, then divided up into smaller units. We have a snapshot of the scene in the record of John Stow's well-known *Survey of London* of 1598:

> On the right hand or north side, at the bottom of Oldebourne Hill is Gold Lane, sometime a passage into the fields, now both sides built with small tenements. Then higher is Lither Lane, turning also to the field, lately replenished with houses built, and so to the bar.

On 28th December 1599, as the century drew to a close, a new Bishop of Ely was appointed. He was able to get back the old palace buildings, now in a state of dilapidation, but not the beautiful grounds, which remained with the Hatton heirs.

During the 16th century, London grew more rapidly than its European counterparts. By 1600 it was the third largest city, with only Paris and Naples being larger. In the middle of the century, three-quarters of London's population lived within the city, but as we move forward to the next century the population starts to spread. The urban sprawl that began at this time has continued ever since to meet the demands for housing and business.

THE END OF THE GARDEN (17TH AND 18TH CENTURIES)

As we leave the Elizabethan period behind with the death of the Queen in 1603, we enter a new chapter in the development of the United Kingdom, including the union with Scotland and the Commonwealth era. The Civil War of 1642–1646 threatened the monarchy but also delivered some positive changes. In London the period is marked by the Great Plague of 1665, the Great Fire of 1666 and the development of Hatton Garden in the wake of Sir Christopher Hatton and his heirs.

Whereas the 16th century had seen a somewhat random development of houses in many of the new thoroughfares leading to the city, the 17th century witnessed a planned development. Initially housing had been needed to cater for all the newcomers to London from far and wide. Now there was an increase of professional people working in London.

During this century London continued its rapid expansion and by 1700 had become the largest city in the world. In the latter half of the 16th century, three-quarters of London's population lived within the city. Fast forward 100 years and now only a quarter of the population live within the bars. The old city walls had become irrelevant and obsolete.

Hatton Garden.

54 Hatton Garden, showing typical fanlight.

The first official census was in 1801, when the population of London was 1,096,000. This represents a five-fold increase over the 200 years from 1600, despite the Great Plague. The consequence of the greater numbers was the demand for housing and the value of land increased to such an extent that all greenfield sites were targets for developers, not least of all was what remained of Hatton's garden.

London had seen an influx of Spanish and Portuguese refugees escaping the inquisition in their own countries. Some of them brought with them their trade in rough diamonds. At that time the only known source of diamonds in the world was India and the overland route was the only option for traders. Venice had become a major crossroads and was the birthplace of Europe's diamond-cutting industry.

Then with the discovery of the sea routes to India, trade was opened up by the Portuguese and the Dutch, making Lisbon and Amsterdam major players throughout the 16th century and until the end of the 17th century, when the English begin to rule the waves and exercise their muscles on trade with the Empire. This early development of the trade in rough diamonds paved the way for the late 19th century, when diamonds were discovered in British-owned South Africa. The East India Company records boast of the diamond trade in the 17th century ... 'formerly driven by the way of Italy and Portugal has become almost a sole English trade'.

Many of the old estates were lost to new accommodation. Some were laid out by their titled owners and others by property developers. Hatton Garden was developed to create houses for the gentry. It has been suggested that 1633 was the beginning of the end for the grand old houses in this part of London.

From 1620 to 1624 Ely Palace was used as the Spanish Embassy. The Count of Gondomar, Diego Sarmiento de Acuna, was the ambassador to England from 1613 to 1622. The fashion for wearing jewels in the hat was universal throughout the courts of Europe at that time. The Spanish Ambassador had his hat stolen while passing over Holborn Bridge, the mob openly encouraging the fellow who made off with it because it was stolen from a Spaniard. The Spanish Armada of 1588 was still within living memory.

Lady Hatton, Sir Christopher's daughter-in-law, continued to rule the roost at Hatton House, in her eccentric way, until her death on 3rd January 1646, although she did try to sell Hatton House to the King (Charles I) in 1638. The sale was blocked by an injunction by the bishops over the disputed title. She had to fight to prevent the Church getting the land back from the Hatton family. Ultimately, her heir, the third Christopher Hatton, Baron Hatton of Kirby, needed to sell off more land and was responsible for carving up the estate and laying out streets where previously there had only been garden paths, flower beds, orchards or lawn.

There is a wonderfully descriptive account that portrays the lifestyle of Lady Hatton in 1626 to be found in *The Ingoldsby Legends*, by Richard Barham, published in 1837. The full poem can be found at the back of this book.

St Andrew's Parochial School, 1920.

A Hatton Garden interior showing the quality finish.

Ely Palace was confiscated early in the Civil War (1641–1652). The Hattons took refuge in France during these turbulent times. Lady Hatton died in Paris and Lord Hatton returned to England in 1656. For a time, their house became a prison and then a hospital for the wounded 'Roundhead' soldiers of Oliver Cromwell.

Journals of the House of Commons leave us the following record:

> 1642–3. Jan. 3. The palace was this day ordered to be converted into a prison, and John Hunt, sergeant-at-arms, appointed keeper during the pleasure of the House. He was at the same time commanded to take care that the gardens, trees, chapel, and its windows, received no injury. A sufficient sum for repairs was granted from the revenues of the see.

Bishop Wren, the uncle of Sir Christopher Wren, was held in prison because of his loyalty to the Crown. Serious damage was done to the palace and it would never be the same again. His demise allowed the Hattons to act without opposition in developing the estate. It is recorded that Lady Hatton sold the lead from the roof of the palace, and sold off the trees for timber, as well as some of her own jewellery to cover her outgoings.

Another consequence of the war was the influx of people who moved to the area to avoid the conflict and battles that broke out like fires around the land. London was considered a safe place to be by the Cromwell sympathisers. In particular there was an influx of weavers from Mortlake. The King had left his Palace of Whitehall on 10th January 1642 and moved away from London.

Christopher Hatton III was made Baron Hatton of Kirby in 1643 and Comptroller of the King's Household in an impoverished Court at Queen's College, Oxford. The Royalists of London abandoned their homes. Some were demolished and others boarded up. Less than a hundred years earlier, Queen Elizabeth had held meetings in Ely Palace.

On 12th June 1654, Christopher Hatton III, short of funds, made over 'the great capital messuage Hatton House ... and all its appurtenances' to one Robert Smythe of Upton for a 200-year lease, for the sum of £1,500 with minute provisos for its speedy redemption.

St Andrew's School building, 1910.

In 1659, the new road, 60 feet wide, was laid out. On 7th June 1659, the famous diarist and admirer of architecture, John Evelyne wrote: 'To London to take leave of my brother and see the foundations now laying for a long street and buildings in Hatton Garden, designed for a little town, lately an ample garden. Approx. 14 acres.'

Fairthorne's map of London from 1658 still shows some of the garden laid out with its knot beds, typical of the era, intersected by paths bordered by box hedges. At the centre there still stood a statue and a fountain. The fountain was still there in September 1672.

When Bishop Wren was released from the Tower in 1660 at the Restoration of the Monarchy, he found half his house demolished. The garden, which every bishop since Elizabeth's day had cherished a hope of regaining, was now in the hands of a speculative builder. The Restoration of the Monarchy led to a building boom. The old medieval style gave way to the neoclassical look.

In State Papers of 1661, there is a record of a petition from Christopher, son and heir of Lord Hatton, to the King, for 'pardon for tenements already erected, and leave to build others on ground already let for the purpose at Hatton House, Holborn, for which, till the restoration, no licence could be obtained.'

The last Lord Hatton proceeded to dismantle Hatton House to make room for more development. By 1661 Hatton House was gone and the new houses continued to be built on Hatton's Garden. Prior to its final demise, the house had fallen into disrepair and became dilapidated – as a result of which, part was demolished. Ironically, it had become a dance academy, which may or may not have been approved by the original Sir Christopher Hatton, who had been renowned for his dancing skills. It was also used as a printing office and at the back there was a small chapel. This was originally used by the congregation of the New Jerusalem Church, and followers of Emanuel Swedenborg. Subsequently, it was used for Calvinistic followers.

The disputed title of the land between the Hatton family and the Church continued. In 1662 Bishop Wren took legal action, but the new building development continued apace. Hatton and his contractors were constantly served with injunctions regardless. To add insult to injury, the new buildings encroached further into the Bishop's domain – so much so that he was forced to bring his horses through the Great Hall of the palace to get to his house. The Bishop died in 1667 and his successor agreed on a rent of £100 per annum for the see. Hatton was able to continue the development without further hindrance.

The plague that hit London in 1665 killed over 100,000 people. In 1665 St Andrew's Church Holborn buried a total of 3,958 people. Of these, 3,103 had succumbed to the plague (over 78%). It was reported that one day in July as many as a hundred houses were shut up in the Parish of St Andrew's. The Worshipful Company of Goldsmiths lost its Prime Warden, Mr Charles Everard, although most of the wealthy people had left the city to escape death. A small committee of Aldermen consisting of Sir William Peake, later Lord Mayor and President of St Thomas' Hospital, and Sir William Turner, a Master of the Merchant Taylors Company, asked the College of Physicians to set up of a committee for the prevention and the cure of the plague within the city and its liberties. They nominated Sir William Turner and Dr Thomas Witherley of Hatton Garden.

Map showing the walled garden with a fountain and gates, 1658.

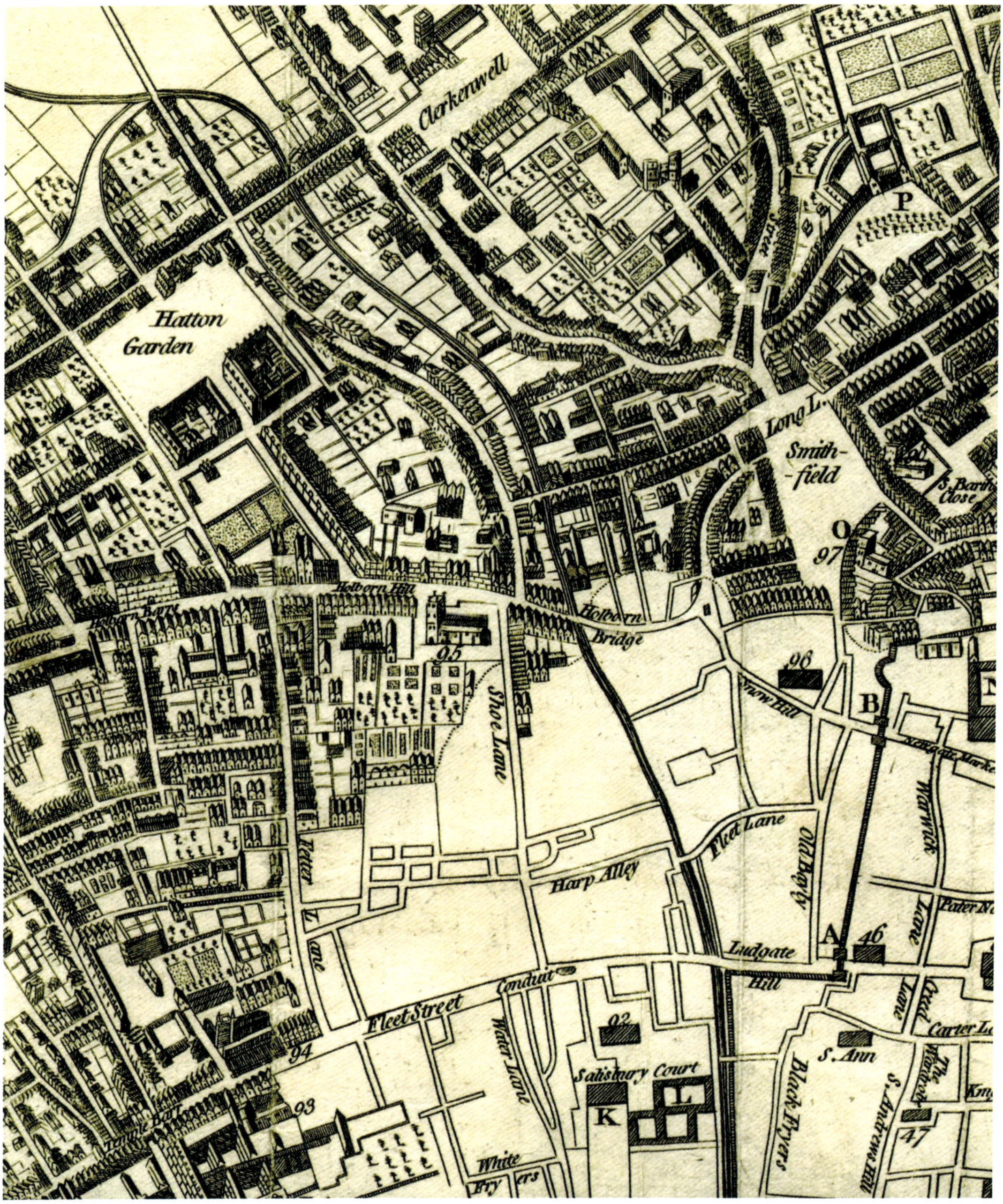

London after the 1666 fire.

Hardly had London recovered from the plague than it was devastated by the Great Fire of 1666. Hatton Garden was spared from the conflagration thanks to a change in the direction of the wind that had driven the fire. The fire had reached Holborn Bridge and was about to leap across Holborn when the wind changed. Not only was Ely Palace and Hatton Garden spared but also the Tudor buildings along Holborn, which are part of Staple Inn. At that time Hatton Garden was largely a building site. It became a refuge for Londoners and their rescued goods. There was an assortment of goods including tapestries, paintings, books, silver and silks all heaped up. Some of the richest houses in the country were destroyed and only a few owners managed to salvage their property. The problem in part had been that there weren't enough carts to transport the goods and the streets were crowded with other people all trying to do the same thing. As the fire subsided, Hatton Garden was left in a thick layer of soot and ash. The residents had a Herculean task in cleaning up the mess.

In the aftermath of the fire there was a large-scale rebuilding of London, which demanded more and more craftsmen and tradespeople. Some of those who were displaced by the fire chose to live in the new houses in Hatton Garden.

We have another snapshot of Hatton Garden from John Evelyn as he wrote on 23rd September 1673:

> I went to see Paradise, a room in Hatton Garden furnished with the representations of all sorts of animals handsomely painted on boards of cloth, and so cut out, and made to stand, move, fly, crawl, roar and make their several cries. The man who showed it made us laugh heartily at his formal poetry.

Paradise was a popular exhibition in the latter part of the 17th century in which models of birds and other animals were made to move and make their natural sounds to the delight of the audience.

One of the best records we have is the detailed map and survey by Abraham Arlidge produced in 1694 for Lord Hatton at the completion of the development begun thirty-five years earlier. It was made on vellum and measured 32 by 26 inches, using a scale of 48 feet to one inch. It shows a total of 372 properties on the 14-acre estate. Each site shows the length of the frontage, the site number and the leaseholder's name.

In 1671, a house with a 22-foot frontage attracted a rent of £6 12s. The graceful and refined architecture and wide street succeeded in attracting gentry and professional people. Hatton Street, which we know as Hatton Garden, was laid down as close to the west side of Ely Palace as possible. The buttresses from St Etheldreda's encroach on 13 and 15 Hatton Garden. The houses originally had gardens, many backing on to open fields, but these were built over as the properties were extended and later redeveloped. No. 51 Hatton Garden was the last to succumb as an old will had forbidden the development of its garden.

Abraham Arlidge had started his career as a carpenter and progressed to be a master builder and property speculator. His map makes it clear how the garden was used for the development as the original footprint of Hatton House is still visible to the west of Hatton Street (Hatton Garden) and the much-reduced ground occupied by Ely Palace also features as a white space. There are still in existence a few documents in the form of leases to the new owners. The earliest is to Robert Smythe from Lord Hatton. Most of the original buildings survived until late Victorian times when some were redeveloped as larger properties. Arlidge succeeded Sir John Cass as Master of the Worshipful Company of Carpenters in 1712.

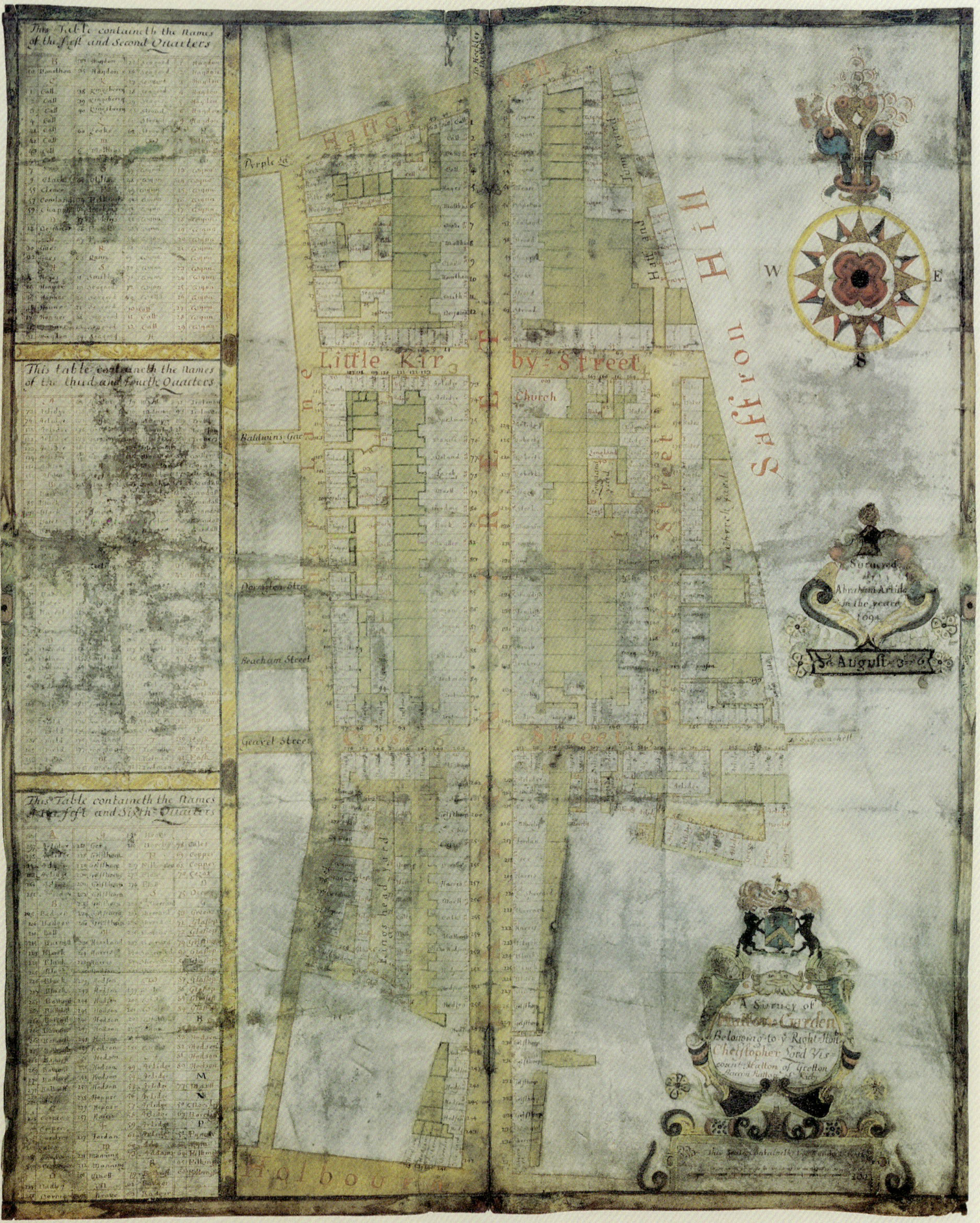

A Survey of Hatton Garden
by
Abraham Arlidge
1694

The white area to the south-east still belonged to the Bishops of Ely and the smaller white area to the south-west shows the footprint of Sir Christopher Hatton's House.

The houses were built of red brick and had two rooms to each of three floors, plus a basement and sometimes an attic, a closet at the back, a wide oak staircase, casement windows and a carved wooden entrance doorway. It is said that the old cisterns contained a high percentage of silver. The rooms were beautifully panelled and when number 27 was pulled down in 1907, the panelling was acquired by the Victoria & Albert Museum and preserved for posterity.

Part of the development was to include a new church building. This was constructed in 1687 on the corner of Hatton Street and Cross Street. However, St Andrew's feared a loss of tithes and objected. The building was only used for a short while but was subsequently put to good use in the form of a schoolhouse.

The new street attracted many notable names of their day. In 1666, Gilbert Thomas Marshall, wrote from Hatton Garden to Lord Arlington. Lord Fanshawe lived there in 1667. The Countess of Drogheda lived there prior to her marriage to the dramatist William Wycherley on 29th September 1679. Sir George Treby MP married Rachel Standish of Hatton Garden on 12th April 1681. Christopher Merret FRS lived and died there on 19th August 1695. George Bate, doctor to Oliver Cromwell, lived and died there in 1669. In a list of London merchants published in 1677, six are named as resident in Hatton Garden and two are still there in Arlidge's survey of 1694.

There is a record of a new playhouse and training school for young actors in Hatton Garden in 1667. It was called the 'Nursery' and a play by James Shirley called 'The Constant Maid' was performed there at that time.

Lord Hatton, Christopher IV, died in 1670.

Ogilby's map of 1677 shows clearly the progress of development at that time. In 1686, a new stone church was built on Holborn Hill to replace the somewhat dilapidated parish church of St Andrew. The architect was Sir Christopher Wren, and this would have increased the desirability of this part of London as a residence. By the end of the century the development was all but complete.

In 1711, Hatton Street was described as a spacious and fashionable place – 'an esteemed place for the gentry'. To the eyes of the connoisseur, Nicholas Hawksmoor, it was 'one of the best streets in London'. It was still the home to professional people, including doctors, solicitors and merchants. In Cross Street lived William Whiston, a famous preacher of his day, from 1712 to 1715. Other residents in the 18th century included such names as Captain Thomas Coram, who started the Foundling Hospital, who lived there in 1741, and John Stanley, the blind composer and organist at St Andrew's Church, who lived there from 1751 and died at his home on 19th May 1786. Mirabeau, the French revolutionary, lodged there in 1784. Mazzini lived at No. 2. Other famous residents included Alderman Daniel Baker and Samuel Wilson, who died in 1766 leaving £20,000 in trust as a loan fund for young men setting up in business in the city. In Kirby Street lived William Bowyer, an 18th-century printer.

In 1720, Richard Blome produced a map that shows progress in the area. John Strype wrote in 1728:

> Hatton Garden is a very large place now containing several streets viz. Hatton Street, Charles Street, Cross St and Kirby Street., all which tract of ground was garden and belonged to Hatton House, now pulled down and built into houses, which streets are very gracefully built, and well inhabited by gentry, especially Hatton Garden which is spacious.

A curious excerpt from the *British Magazine* of 12th February 1747 reports:

> A woman about 40 years of age having poisoned herself was buried in the cross roads at the bottom of Hatton Gardens leading to Hockley in the Hole, and a stake drove through her heart.

Robert and James Dodsley, the writers of *London and its Environs* in 1761, said:

> Hatton Garden, Holborn, a broad straight and long street in which the houses are pretty lofty, but though they are plain and unadorned on the outside, yet there being something like regularity in the buildings they appear to great advantage, and the street affording a fine vista may justly be reckoned among the handsomest within the liberties of the city.

And of Ely Palace:

> The city mansion of the Bishop of Ely [which stands] on a large piece of ground. Before it is a spacious court, and behind it a garden of considerable extent; but it is so ill kept that it scarcely deserves the name. The buildings are very old and consist of a large hall, several spacious rooms, and a good chapel.

The parishioners of St Andrew's in 1778 described the houses of Hatton Garden as:

> very large and spacious ... Formally inhabited by persons of high rank and quality and at present, the same are chiefly inhabited by merchants retired from business, gentlemen of estate and fortunes and, in general, by persons of most respectable character.

The remains of Ely Palace were sold in 1772 to the Crown for £6,500. The government had plans to use the site for a new prison to replace The Fleet, but the scheme was scrapped after strong protest from the residents of Hatton Garden. It was then purchased in 1776 from the Office of Works by a surveyor and property developer, Charles Cole, for £7,600. He cleared the whole site apart from the Chapel, which he was not allowed to touch. He then constructed what we know as Ely Place. The chapel was preserved as a place of worship for the new residents. Brayley in his *Londinium* says: 'This venerable Palace was sold to that eminent surveyor C. Cole who utterly destroyed it and, on its site, erected the present handsome and uniform street with its neat and appropriate gates in 1776.'

In 1786, all the leasehold owners of dwellings were granted their freehold. This proved to be a massive legal exercise, consuming tons of paper and accruing vast sums of legal expenses.

Hatton Garden enjoyed a reputation as an oasis of respectability for a long time. It was featured in the *Fashionable Court Guides* of the period. Throughout this period of history, there was no hint of what was to come by way of the arrival of the diamond and jewellery industry. Until the 19th century shops were not permitted in Hatton Garden. However, some professional people practised their skills from their homes. There is evidence of a Mr John Gray of Field Lane, who was a goldsmith/banker and known to be in this location from 1716 to 1743. In 1730, he advertised in *Fog's Weekly Journal* for the whereabouts of his absconded apprentice. In 1733 he registered for the Poor Rate. In 1735, he insured his household goods, stock in house and shed adjoining, including manufactured and wrought plate, etc. for £200. In 1743, he was involved in a trial at the Old Bailey, concerning the theft of diamonds that had been left with him but were no longer traceable because of his subsequent death.

At that time there was a watchmaker in Hatton Garden – a Mr Joseph Turner. There was also a watch maker in Leather Lane called White. There were no jewellers but there were five pawnbrokers in Saffron Hill. However, many streets in London had similar numbers of goldsmiths, watch makers etc.

SEE HOW THE GARDEN GROWS (19TH CENTURY)

During the 200 years prior to the dawning of the 19th century, the area we know as Hatton Garden changed out of recognition. At the beginning of the period it was mostly green fields, with gardens, orchards and vineyards. At the end of the period it was the new suburban London of its day. Within a generation the population of London trebled from 1 million to 3 million. Before the advent of railways most people lived and worked in the same neighbourhood. London barely spread beyond Regent's Park to the north, so all the inhabitants had to find a home within the boundaries. Poor families had to make do with an overcrowded room within a house for the whole family, usually with little or no sanitation.

The next hundred years would see further change and in particular the arrival and development of the jewellery industry and the diamond trade. In the directory of the Hatton Garden area for 1807, there were a total of eleven entries for those engaged in the trade. There were six in watches and clocks, two jewellers, one wholesale jeweller and two in sundry supplies.

There is a record of Peter Perchard (1729–1806) coming from Guernsey and joining his uncle, Matthew, in Hatton Garden prior to 1779. His uncle was a renowned silversmith of his day and when he died in 1779, he left £30,000 in his estate, a considerable amount at that time. Peter went on to become Prime Warden of the Worshipful Company of Goldsmiths in 1786–7 and became Lord Mayor of the City of London in 1804.

Until the 19th century no shops had been permitted in Hatton Garden. The limited records that are available to us are not always consistent but together they give us a picture of life in Hatton Garden in the late Georgian and Victorian periods.

In 1836, there was only one watch and clock maker, a Mr John Lund, at No. 4 Hatton Garden. There were ten instrument makers, mostly foreign: ten printers and bookbinders, six glass makers and four auctioneers or appraisers.

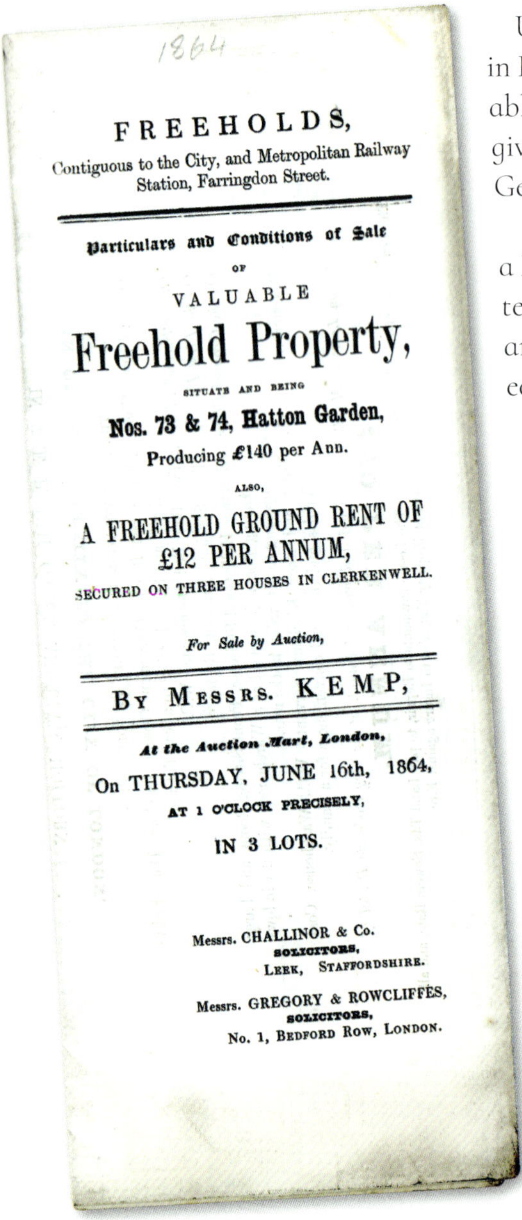

1864

FREEHOLDS,

Contiguous to the City, and Metropolitan Railway Station, Farringdon Street.

Particulars and Conditions of Sale

OF

VALUABLE

Freehold Property,

SITUATE AND BEING

Nos. 73 & 74, Hatton Garden,

Producing £140 per Ann.

ALSO,

A FREEHOLD GROUND RENT OF £12 PER ANNUM,

SECURED ON THREE HOUSES IN CLERKENWELL.

For Sale by Auction,

BY MESSRS. KEMP,

At the Auction Mart, London,

On THURSDAY, JUNE 16th, 1864,

AT 1 O'CLOCK PRECISELY,

IN 3 LOTS.

Messrs. CHALLINOR & Co.
SOLICITORS,
LEEK, STAFFORDSHIRE.

Messrs. GREGORY & ROWCLIFFES,
SOLICITORS,
No. 1, BEDFORD ROW, LONDON.

Above: Auction notice for the freehold of 73 & 74 Hatton Garden, 1864.

Right: 37–38 Hatton Garden from the *Building News*, 4th October 1912.

Opposite page: Hatton Garden.

In that respect Hatton Garden wasn't different to many other streets where the residents worked from their homes in their chosen professions. This remained about the same throughout the next fifty years.

Tallis's Street View of 1840 gives us a wonderful image of how Hatton Garden looked in the first half of the 19th century. The combination of this view with the street in 2020 in this book shows that a large part of the original profile remains.

By the end of the century, according to a directory for 1897, the total number engaged in the trade had risen to 236. Horological workers had increased from six to thirty-five, jewellers from two to seven, wholesale jewellers from one to fourteen, and sundry suppliers from two to eighteen. Furthermore, there were now twenty-seven silversmiths, two goldsmiths, thirty manufacturing jewellers, three refiners or assayers, five dealers in ivory or coral, forty-one diamond merchants, thirty diamond brokers, eight diamond cutters, five dealers in pearls, nine dealers in precious stones and two lapidaries. The Hatton Garden party had begun.

Coach and horses labouring up Holborn Hill.

The opening of Holborn Viaduct.

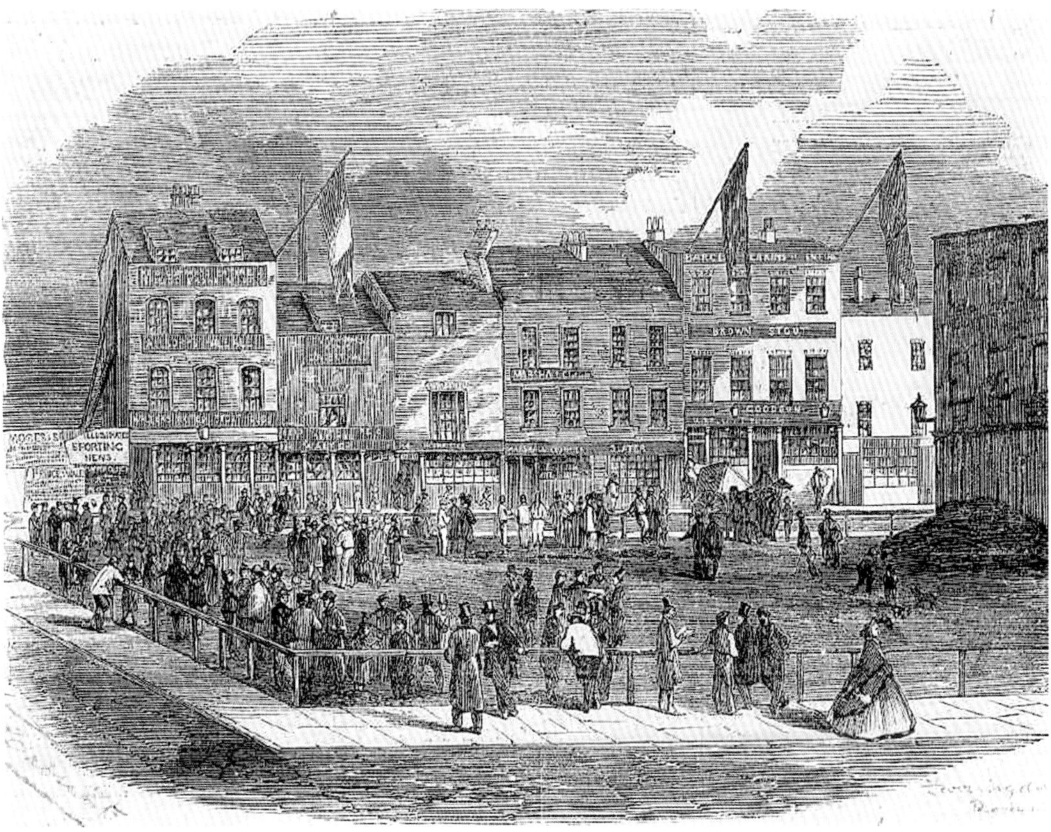

The corner of Farringdon Road and Greville Street in 1863.

View from Holborn Circus looking north, 1895.

104 Hatton Garden. An 1866 letter to J Hasluck, one of the earliest goldsmiths.

Before 1842, Samuel Hasluck, a Jewish gold chain maker and jeweller, had been one of very few established in Hatton Garden. His premises at 104 Hatton Garden is depicted on *Tallis's Street View*. Other Jews in the same trades were operating from Clerkenwell, Whitechapel and Spitalfields. Hatton Garden was occupied mainly by English and Italian traders and there was still some residential housing.

There was never a single day when a decision was made to make Hatton Garden a jewellery quarter. However, it was through mutual needs that trades congregated in the same areas as one another. London, like other large cities, had many districts that became synonymous with their trades. Among the best known are perhaps Billingsgate for fish, Smithfield for meat and poultry, Fleet Street for the press and Covent Garden for flowers, fruit and vegetables. The advantage of working in a close-knit community was that, firstly, information and networking could only be achieved by having a physical presence, unlike modern times when there are better and easier ways to do so. Secondly, there was also a somewhat more parochial supply and distribution chain compared to the global marketplace we now enjoy. Thirdly, there is some comfort in security when you are part of a herd.

The 19th century saw the effects of the Industrial Revolution. Electric lighting replaced the old gas lamps and gave a new source of power for industry. Major changes and continuing improvements became the norm. The world's first underground railway was built with its terminus at Farringdon Street. The Holborn Valley improvement scheme swept away the old slums and Holborn Bridge was replaced with a new viaduct. Large buildings such as the 'Prudential' were constructed, and new church buildings were opened. By the end of the century motor cars were seen on the London streets.

The original buildings in Hatton Garden remained much unchanged. Once, they had been comfortable homes for the gentry, but were now beginning to look a little tired. London had continued to expand and improving transport systems allowed people to live further out. The older buildings were ripe for 'change of use' and light industrial manufacturing started to appear. Previously, it had existed in Clerkenwell where many of the continental artisans had settled. By end of the 19th century, residential use had given way to commercial use. It was now quiet at night once the businesses had closed up for the day.

In his *Journal of Travels 1805 and 1806* Benjamin Silliman of Yale University wrote:

> 6th August – I have been with an English companion to see the manufactory of carpets at Saffron Hill in London. There I had the pleasure of witnessing, on a large scale, the execution of most of the processes, by which these beautiful stuffs are produced, which adorn the floors of our halls and parlours. The weaving is extremely ingenious but eludes my power of description. We went next to Hatton Garden, where is a principal seat of inquiry into offences against the peace. This inquiry is held before a single magistrate, who proceeds in a very summary way, binding over, or dismissing the party, as he thinks proper. We went into the court and heard an examination and decision in course of five minutes. The Police of London must be very good, or the people uncommonly well disposed, for the place is almost as free from turmoil as a village.

At 11 Hatton Garden, in 1810, lived Charles Halsey Johnson, who had carried on his business of gold refining for over twenty years. Charles was the uncle of Percival Johnson, who would subsequently come to Hatton Garden and set up new premises for his business that would later become Johnson Matthey. It may well have been that his uncle was already established here that attracted Percival to choose Hatton Garden.

Throughout the 19th century there was a large exodus of nationals from continental Europe. Many moved to the United States, but some settled in Great Britain. Most established themselves in groups and colonised districts that became enclaves such as 'Little Italy' in Clerkenwell and Saffron Hill. Various reasons contributed to this phenomenon. Famine in Italy was significant, and the population was increasingly leading to overcrowding.

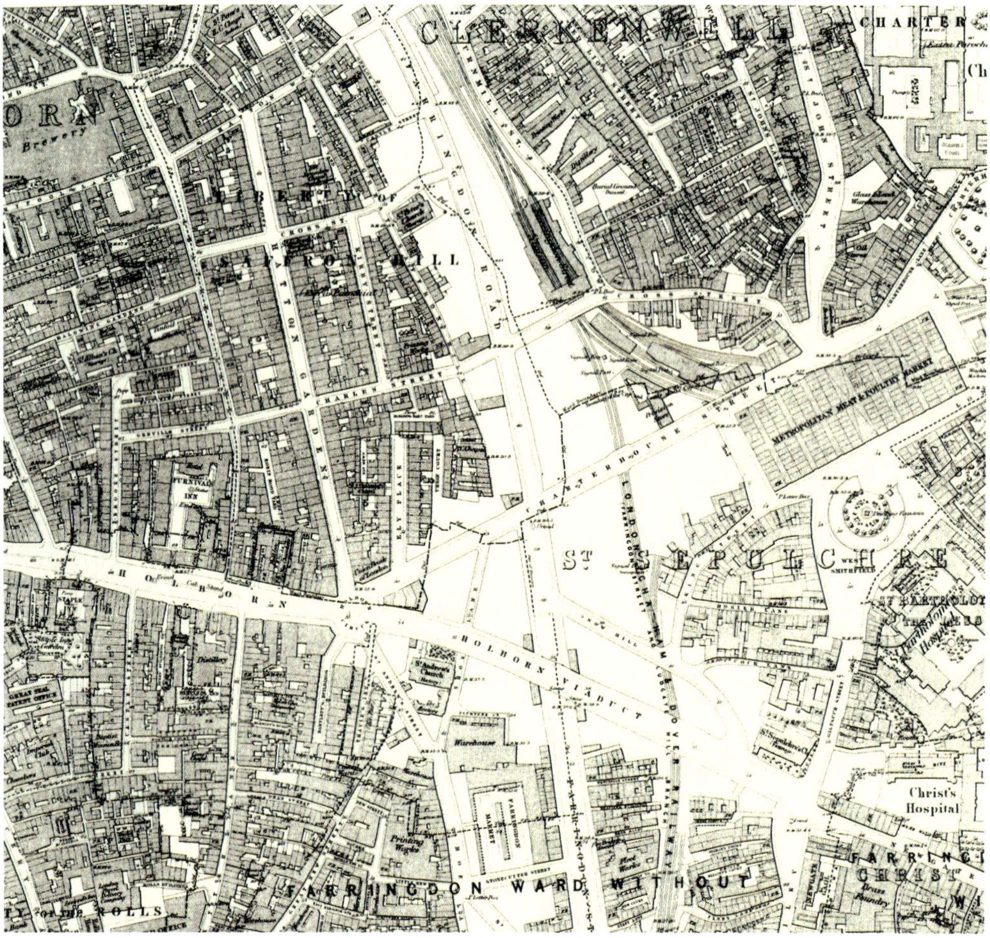

An 1873 Ordnance Survey map showing slum clearance after the creation of Holborn Viaduct and Farringdon Road. Clerkenwell Road had not yet been established. Christopher Street is at the north end of Hatton Garden and is now part of Hatton Garden. Cross Street and Charles Street preceded St Cross Street and Greville Street. The locations of Jerusalem Chapel and Trinity Chapel are behind the houses. Charterhouse Street has truncated the end of Hatton Garden.

Unfortunately, London was probably more crowded than the areas from which the immigrants had come. There were opportunities for manual labour available as new building projects were to be found across the city. The immigrants had to be content to live in the slums such as Saffron Hill and Leather Lane until their clearance took place towards the end of the century. They were famous for organ grinding, knife sharpening and mosaic construction. They sold food on the streets and were renowned for their ice cream in the summer and hot chestnuts in the winter. It was estimated that the ice cream industry employed around 900 people in 1900.

One writer of the time described the Italian Quarter as:

> The gay and noisy Mediterranean atmosphere that pervaded in Saffron Hill, thinly disguised the overcrowded and insanitary conditions. Often there was more than one family to a room. Children were sold as organ grinders.

The area at this time has been described as reminding the visitor of Soho with the appearance of the inhabitants and the many cafés and eating opportunities. An English visitor might feel quite alien and uncomfortable.

> You will hear occasionally the querulous voice of an old woman in a dark interior directing a rattle of abuse toward the street; you can pick your way through swarms of children ugly as monkeys and beautiful as angels; you can see dark girls with full unfashionable figures lounging against doorposts. These and many other impressions you receive, but you will not yourself make the faintest impression on the old woman or the children.
>
> I never heard of an Englishman celebrating Empire Day in Rome, but the Italians of Saffron Hill religiously celebrate their festivals, and those who enjoy a show should visit the quarter on one of these days. They are the only occasions when the residents display themselves.

The more skilful artisans lived in Hatton Garden and Charles Street, where they set up workshops. Their skills produced barometers, picture frames, spectacles, surgical, optical and mathematical instruments and many other products of light engineering. Many were skilled craftsmen and they were, in part, responsible for bringing the manufacturing skills that triggered the growth of the jewellery industry.

Italian ice cream seller in Saffron Hill.

The Italian community in Saffron Hill.

Organ grinders in the Italian Quarter.

"'Would you like to see the organ stables?'"

The Italian Quarter.

In the first half of the century, before the availability of diamonds from South Africa, jewellery was made with far less diamond content.

For the first time in history, British workers received paid annual holiday and made for the seaside. Ice cream sales rocketed and brought financial security to many of the newcomers. The Italian population in Great Britain had trebled by the end of the century. In 1861 the UK population of Italians was estimated to be 4,489, of which approximately half lived in London and close to half of them lived in Holborn and Clerkenwell. It was further estimated that nearly half the Italian men earnt a living as organ grinders until they started to become a public nuisance and a law was passed in 1864 to restrict such music. The large numbers of immigrants, both Italian and others, was seen as a threat by many and led to the first legislation to restrict immigration, the Alien's Act of 1905.

About 1850, two Italians formed the company Negretti and Zambra, which was to become a world-famous brand by the end of the century. Enrico (Henry) Negretti and Joseph Zambra were makers of scientific instruments, optical and photographic equipment and received the Royal warrant from Queen Victoria. They also ran a photographic studio. Their business premises were in Hatton Garden and then moved to Holborn Circus. Their building was destroyed in the Blitz. After the war they relocated to Aylesbury in Buckinghamshire. The company continued until it was taken over in 1981.

NEGOZIO
VINO
Kg

Italian Quarter in Back Hill.

Opposite: Saffron Hill's Italian Quarter, 1900.

MAP1 ITALIAN OCCUPIED HOUSES 1871

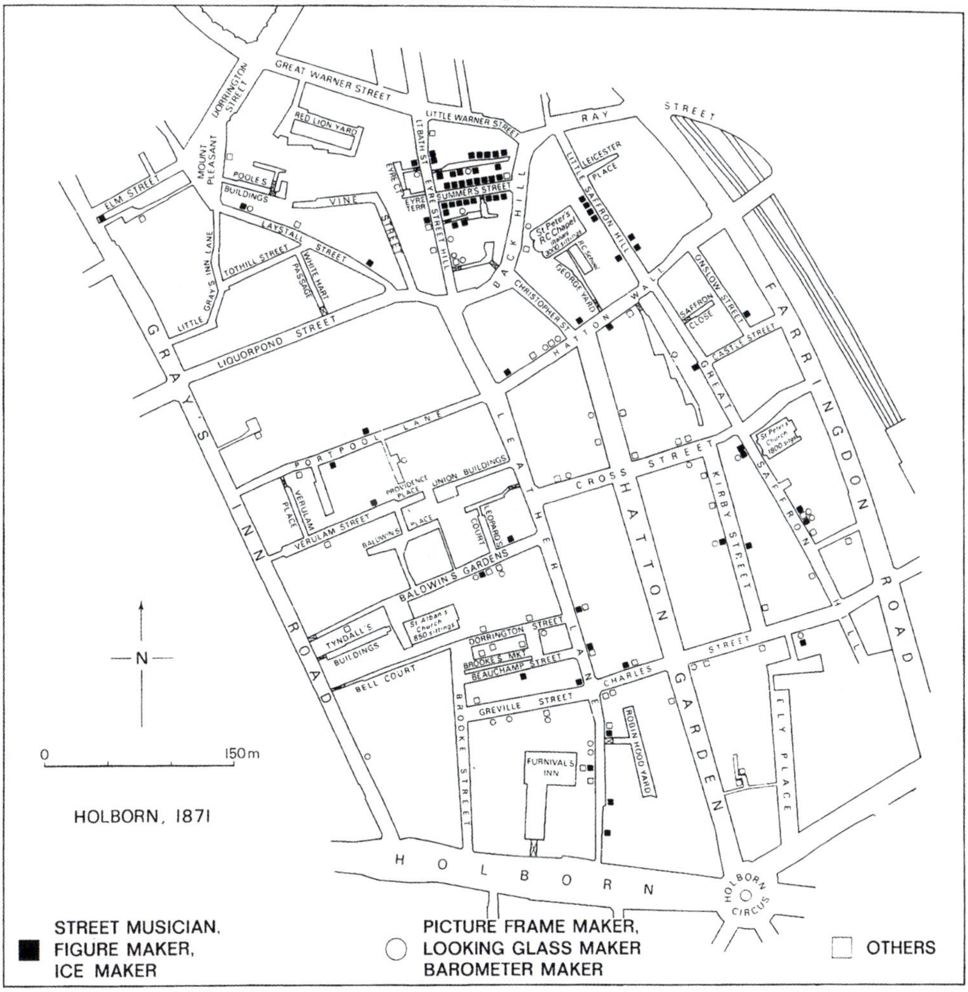

Source: Census Enumerator's Book 1871

Map showing the Italian community.

Negretti & Zambra.

A compass from Negretti & Zambra, 1 Hatton Garden.

Opera glasses from Negretti & Zambra, 1 Hatton Garden.

There can be little doubt that another of the major influences in Hatton Garden becoming a jewellery centre was the arrival of what was to become the major supplier of gold to the jewellery trade, Johnson Matthey.

It was on 23rd February 1822 that Mr Percival Norton Johnson signed a lease for premises at 79 Hatton Garden, which would be both his home and his business address. The building was on the west side of the 'Garden' and midway between Greville Street and St Cross Street. The house had a rear garden with some outbuildings that backed on to the yard of a tenement building in Leather Lane. Although Leather Lane had been built at the same time as Hatton Garden it was occupied by a poorer class of people and was very overcrowded.

THE CORNER OF HATTON GARDEN AND HOLBORN AT THE TIME OF THE DEMOLITION FOR THE CONSTRUCTION OF THE VIADUCT AND CIRCUS, 1866.

Negretti & Zambra were originally located on the corner of Hatton Garden and Holborn, 1866.

Saffron Hill to the east of Hatton Garden was much the same. The landlord of No. 79 was Edward Fane and the rent £70 10s per annum, which is an expression of the desirability of the address. From relatively small beginnings, Johnson acquired further premises in the street and in Leather Lane behind.

In a curious turn of events, it was discovered that an earlier resident of 79 Hatton Garden back in 1798 had been John Newman Coussmaker, who was the great, great uncle of Percival Johnson. He was a Dutch banker and would have been familiar with gold.

The new home occupied a site of 2,000 square feet, including the garden of roughly 1,000 square feet. It was a huge undertaking at the time and although the business had some success, cash flow may have been a problem. There is a family story of how Mrs Johnson gave harp lessons to supplement their income and among her students was the famous novelist Grace Aguilar.

The two ground floor rooms of No. 79 were all used for business. The front parlour was an office where the books were kept and it was also the room for receiving customers. It became known as the front office. The name was used thereafter to describe that part of the premises into which customers were permitted and trade took place.

In 1832 the back parlour was the assay office and laboratory. Three men worked in this room and one in the front room, including Mr Johnson. There were a further four workmen and five boys.

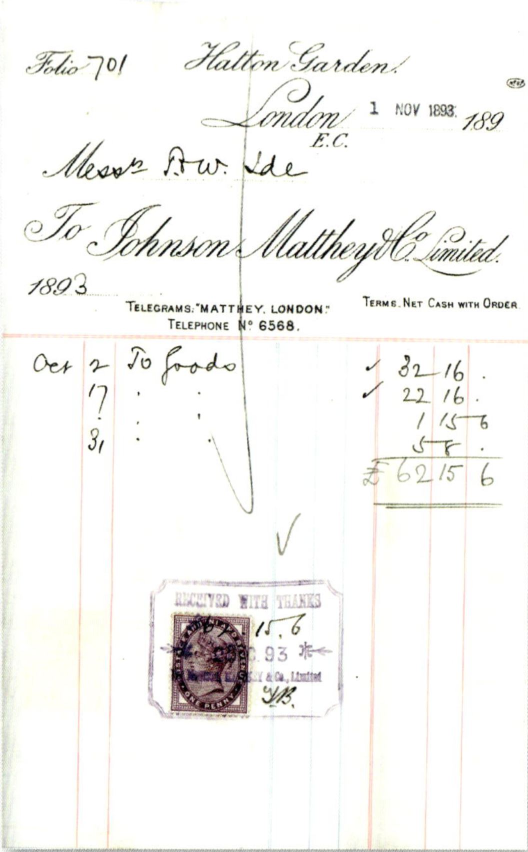
Folio 701 Hatton Garden, London E.C. 1 NOV 1893 189

Messrs A.W. Ide

To Johnson Matthey & Co. Limited.

1893

TELEGRAMS: "MATTHEY, LONDON." TELEPHONE No 6568.

TERMS. NET CASH WITH ORDER

			£	s.	d.
Oct	2	To Goods	32	16	.
	17	" "	22	16	.
		" "	1	15	6
	31	" "	5	8	.
			£62	15	6

RECEIVED WITH THANKS

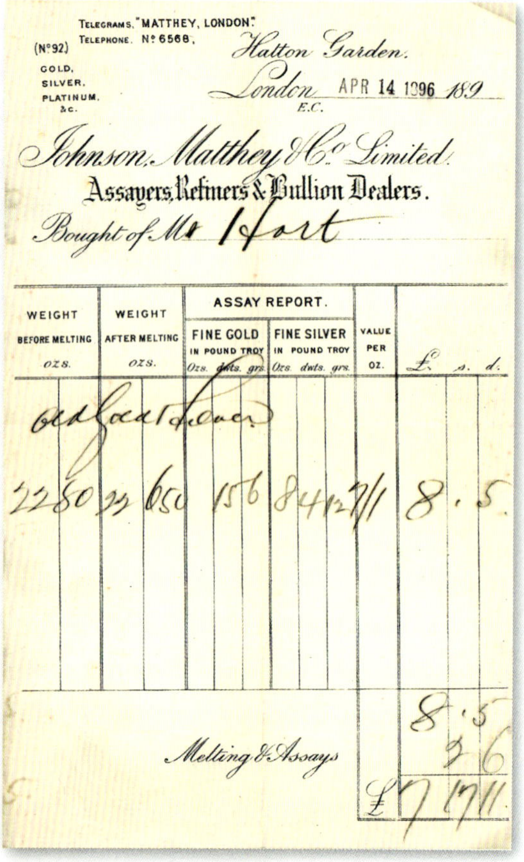
(No92) TELEGRAMS. "MATTHEY, LONDON." TELEPHONE. No 6568.

GOLD, SILVER, PLATINUM, &c.

Hatton Garden, London E.C. APR 14 1896 189

Johnson, Matthey & Co. Limited.

Assayers, Refiners & Bullion Dealers.

Bought of Mr Hort

WEIGHT BEFORE MELTING ozs.	WEIGHT AFTER MELTING ozs.	ASSAY REPORT. FINE GOLD IN POUND TROY Ozs. dwts. grs.	FINE SILVER IN POUND TROY Ozs. dwts. grs.	VALUE PER OZ.	£ s. d.
Old Gold Lower					
22 80	22 65	15 6	8 4 12	7/1	8 . 5

Melting & Assays

£7 17 11

Clockwise from top left: A sales invoice from Johnson Matthey, Hatton Garden, dated 1893; a purchase of scrap gold by Johnson Matthey, Hatton Garden, dated 1896; Percival Norton Johnson, 1829.

Johnson Matthey's premises in Hatton Garden.

View of Johnson Matthey's premises, 1939.

In the biography of Percival Johnson, Donald McDonald writes of an incident that shows the caring side of this pioneering metallurgist:

> On Saturday 26th January 1833, Death stalked in Hatton Garden. Down the road at 103 Hatton Garden were the business and home of Thomas Christian Manley, human hair merchant, a trade not uncommon when so many men wore wigs. Manley himself had died in the previous spring, leaving his young family of eight children and his business in the care of his half-mad wife who had a mania for buying unnecessary furniture at auction sales and throwing knives at people who entered her room. Early in the morning of January 26th, a neighbour becoming aware of fire raised the alarm. Unfortunately, there was a long delay before the turncock could be found, and in the meantime the flames, fed by Mrs. Manley's collection of furniture, obtained a good hold. It was possible to rescue only some of the family, and Mrs. Manley and three of the younger children perished in the flames. Those who were rescued were looked after by neighbours and Eliza aged about seven found herself in the hands of the Johnsons. Tradition says that, 'Someone asked Uncle Percival what he was going to do with the child', and he said, 'get a nurse and take her in'. So, Eliza Manley became a member of the Johnson household.

The McDonald family lived above the shop in so far as their home was the roof apartment above the Johnson Matthey building at 78–80 until 1937, when they moved to the country.

There is some confusion about the way in which the business expanded during its early days in Hatton Garden. In 1836 there was a large building, in excess of 28 by 19 feet in size, abutting Mr Johnson's rear boundary marked on a map as 'melting house', although there is no documentary evidence to support this until 1850. Should it have been 'Meeting House', referring to what was at one time the Trinity Chapel? Or, more likely, Johnson had an informal arrangement with the lessee, a Mr Thomas Green, who among other things was a tallow chandler. Johnson could have well used the additional space. Perhaps this was the so-called stable where he practised his trade.

In 1850, leases were obtained for 78 Hatton Garden, next door, and 23 Leather Lane at the back. This gave the required space for the increasing amount of work that came their way. Then in 1856, leases for 76 Hatton Garden and 25 and 26 Leather Lane increased their footprint further. The Leather Lane properties provided access to a large yard known as Trinity Chapel Yard.

Trinity Chapel had been built in 1667 as a primitive Methodist Chapel. It is said that John Bunyan preached there. Johnson held an annual service there for his staff and families.

This was also the century of the great gold rushes: 1849 California, 1851 Australia, 1861 New Zealand, 1886 South Africa and 1896 the Yukon. The miners shipped their gold back to the Bank of England and Johnson was called upon to refine and assay the new metal. The services he offered were much in demand and he needed to grow.

The *Illustrated London News* of 12th March 1853 featured the promotion of a better life in the 'Land of Plenty', Australia. A room in Hatton Garden was the assembly point for young women, on the brink of starvation, before making the long voyage. Over 1,000

204 THE ILLUSTRATED LONDON NEWS. [March 12, 1853.

THE FEMALE EMIGRANTS' HOME, AT HATTON-GARDEN.—THE CHIEF ROOM.

FEMALE EMIGRATION FUND.

In presenting our readers with two Engravings illustrative of the departure of the thirtieth party of female emigrants, sent out by the Fund for promoting Female Emigration from want and misery in London, to happiness and plenty in Australia, it will be, perhaps the most profitable course, instead of describing the ordinary incidents of farewell embarkation, shortly to state the proceedings of the Society since it commenced its operations, and equally briefly to notice some of their results.

It was in the winter of 1849, that Mr. Sidney Herbert, horrified, with many others, by the fearful revelations then in the process of being made of the condition of the London needlewomen, started the idea of a great emigrational scheme, which was actively taken up in the higher and more opulent branches of society; a large sum was promptly subscribed, and immediate practical measures were adopted. The sum at first received amounted to upwards of £22,000, and some small additions have since dropped in. With this money the promoters of the scheme have sought for, investigated the cases and the characters, organised into bands, fed, lodged, and despatched, in 1850, not less than 409 young women; in 1851, upwards of 228; and in 1852, the greatest number, 434—making a grand total of 1071 young women rescued from the brink of starvation in London; and now—at least the [illegible] of them, comfortable settled in marriage or service amid will amply prove the great success of the experiment. The eager welcome with which girls of good character were received by the various Australian colonies, the rapidity with which one and all were provided with service, and the concurring testimony, not only of their own letters—hundreds of which have been received—but of many of the principal colonists and government functionaries at the Antipodes, leave no doubt of the benefits conferred upon the emigrants themselves, or the advantage afforded by the arrival of so copious a succession of supplies of female labour to the settlements. And yet the demand continues more eagerly—more extensively than ever. The gold fever has attracted a vast male emigration, and the balance of sexes in Australia is more uneven than ever; while in Great Britain the reverse is the case—the number of females, by the last Census, outstripping that of the males of the population by no less than 545,762 individuals. It is evident, therefore, that reasons both of humanity and of policy combine to urge forward a system of female emigration on as great a scale as can be effected.

The tables showing the difference of wages and general position of the emigrants sent by Mr. Sidney Herbert's society are very curious, and contain information which it would be well for the working-classes generally to read. The list of occupations from which women were taken in London is in itself remarkable. There were artificial-flower-makers, box-makers, brush-makers, carpet-bag-makers, gelatine-packers, gold-burnishers, lace-transferrers, and furriers: these are, of course, exceptional employments. The vast proportion of the emi-

Employment in England.	Yearly wages (with rations) in Australia
Servant, £7 per annum	18
Servant, 1s. 6d. per week	20
Servant, no wages	20
Stock-maker, 1s. to 2s. per week	25
Nursemaid, 3s. per week	30
Laundress, 1s. 6d. per week	20
Housemaid, 2s. per week	25
Fancy needleworker, 5s. per week	25
Nurse, 9s. per week	52
Shoebinder, 5s. per week	30
Needlewoman, 2s. 6d. to 3s. per week	18

With the above sums as wages, rations and lodging must not be forgotten. The table from which they were taken relates to forty-nine young women, who landed in March, 1852, at Port Phillip. More recent arrivals present nearly the same results, and offer a cheering picture of the change in the circumstances and prospects of so many of our poorer countrywomen.

On Wednesday (last week) there were dispatched in the *Madagascar* forty emigrants, of ages ranging from seventeen to thirty-two, and who had hitherto been sempstresses, stock-makers, shoebinders, domestic servants, &c. The *Madagascar* (1200 tons burden), Captain Harris, one of the finest ships hitherto engaged in the East India trade, but which has just been transferred by Mr. Green (her owner) to the Australian trade, had been engaged to convey the emigrants to Port Phillip; and a most commodious and convenient cabin had been especially fitted up amidships

No. 76 Hatton Garden. Temporary home for women emigrating to Australia in 1853.

people left London to start a better life between 1850 and 1852. The gold fever that took many men down under had led to an increase in the male population. The arrival of so many young women would have evened up the ratios and perhaps laid the foundation for generations to follow.

On 18th September 1851, Johnson took in a new partner. Originally, he had had Mr Cock but when Cock died, he offered the position to George Matthey. The firm of Johnson & Matthey was born.

At the rear of No. 79, three new rooms had been added on to the garden: the Oxide Room, the Platinum Laboratory and the Gold Refinery. Johnson was a pioneer in the extraction of platinum from its ore and its alloy with gold.

In the latter half of the 19th century Russia changed its coinage from platinum to gold and Johnson & Matthey were able to purchase the unwanted coinage at £1 per ounce.

The new bonanza created by the flow of rough diamonds from South Africa led to many watchmakers and other skilled craftsmen to adapt their skills to suit the opportunities that it brought. The tools and workbenches were easily modified to accommodate the new requirements.

Samuel Cohen, originally a wholesale jeweller (1852), became Cohen & Co. goldsmiths (1869) and diamond merchants (1875). Similarly, Eisman & Tuteur, goldsmiths in 1872 were diamond merchants in 1875. A dramatic increase in the number of importers and merchants also attracted allied trades and crafts – cutters, polishers, etc.

In 1852, Louis Keller and Joseph Price each started a diamond business there. They were typical of the strong presence of Jewish businessmen. In the following fifteen years there was an influx of businesses related to the diamond trade – importers of coloured stones, pearls, jewellery, fancy goods, even leather and furniture.

In 1867 there was only one diamond cutter in London; by 1900 there were twenty-five. In 1875 there were twenty-three diamond merchants in Hatton Garden; by 1880 the number had almost doubled to forty-four. In 1885 there were sixty-seven in Hatton Garden alone and by the end of the century there were at least 100. Workers were brought in from Amsterdam, which had previously been a major cutting centre.

In 1880, three entrepreneurs returned from the diamond fields in South Africa and set up the London office of their firm: Porges, Wernher & Beit. They chose 29 Holborn Viaduct as their address. Julius Porges retired on 31st December 1889 and the firm became Wernher, Beit & Co.

Also in 1880, Barney Barnato and Solly Joel set up a London office at 106 Hatton Garden. Until then there were very few Jewish or foreign members of the trade. Anton Dunkelsbuhler was another, who had opened an office at 97 Hatton Garden, in 1878. Barnato, Dunkelsbuhler and Mosenthal formed a syndicate with a few others to purchase the entire De Beers production.

Hatton Garden quickly became the diamond and precious stone capital of the world. In an interesting extract from *The Randlords* by Geoffrey Wheatcroft, we read:

> With the Joel boys in Kimberley, Harry Barnato spent more and more time in London looking after the family interest there, and with Ludwig Lippert, starting the first informal market in diamond shares on the pavement between Hatton Garden and Holborn Viaduct. Barnato Brothers were going from strength to strength.

This was the eve of the formation of what would become De Beers. Individual claims were the normal way of mining diamonds. Individual mining companies sold their production through various London dealers and brokers, some of whom were destined to become both syndicate members and shareholders in De Beers. However, as the diggings got deeper the sides of the claims would cave in, making it more and more necessary to cooperate with neighbouring claim holders. Wheatcroft also writes:

> In 1886 Louis Oppenheimer had arrived in Kimberley to join his brother Bernard. They were two of the six sons of a cigar merchant, Edward Oppenheimer, and of his wife Nanette Hirschhorn who belonged to the small Jewish community of Friedburg near Frankfurt on Main. They belonged also to the larger network of kinship of German Jewry, which had already played such an important part in the South African mining industry. It was to play its part in the careers of Oppenheimers, cousins of the Dunkelsbuhlers and the Hirschhorns. The two brothers had followed their cousin Anton Dunkelsbuhler. 'Dunkels' was the representative for the Mosenthal's, before starting business on his own account, with offices in Hatton Garden, the London diamond centre, and Kimberley.

De Beers was established in 1888 by Cecil Rhodes with help from MN Rothschild and others. The four deep mines in Kimberley created a focus for the South African side of the business and London became the international home of the diamond trade for at least the next a hundred years. As early as 1894 lists of buyers were established. De Beers was handling over 5 million carats a year, which was most of the global production.

The original 'syndicate' of 1890 was made up of Wernher, Beit & Co. – 23%, Barnato Bros – 20%, Mosenthal & Co. – 15%, A. Dunkelsbuhler – 10%, S. Neuman – 8%, Joseph Bros – 7%, with four smaller companies sharing the remaining 17%.

In 1896, Ernest Oppenheimer joined A Dunkelsbuhler & Co. at the age of 16, as a trainee diamond valuer. Their offices were now at No. 1 St Andrew Street on Holborn Circus. 'Dunkels' had no sons of his own and when Cecil Rhodes insisted that syndicate members have representation in both London and Kimberley, Ernest was sent out to South Africa.

It was, then, the advent of the South African diamonds in Hatton Garden that galvanised the established craftsmen and the gold suppliers into the Hatton Garden that would become known throughout the world as the diamond, gem and jewellery centre. It has been estimated that at its peak, 90% of the world's supply of diamonds were marketed via Hatton Garden.

The century saw continuing change in the area, both in its trade and in its society. Other industries flourished in the area. In the 19th century it was common practice to work a twelve- or thirteen-hour day, 8 a.m. to 9 p.m. from Monday to Friday, and then on Saturday from 8 a.m. to 5 p.m. This made a sixty-nine-hour working week.

OUR GARDEN

The beginning of the 20th century was the high point of changes brought about in Victorian England. Diamonds and gold were being shipped in from the Empire. Great Britain led the world in manufacturing. Queen Victoria died in 1901 and the new Edwardian era enjoyed all the benefits laid down in the previous century. We begin the century in the art nouveau period and progress to art deco in the 1920s and 1930s, which many would argue was the pinnacle of jewellery design.

However, all this was to change. Over the next hundred years there were two world wars, an outbreak of Spanish Flu, which killed more people than had died during the Great War, and a financial roller coaster of boom and bust economic times.

London remained the most populated and influential city in the world. New inventions changed the lives of everyone to a greater or lesser degree: the omnibus powered by a mechanical engine, the telephone and electricity in the home and office.

The houses that defined Hatton Garden would be lost both to German bombs and to developers. The original houses had remained intact until the end of the 1800s. Planning regulations were almost non-existent at that time and the idea of conservation was not yet understood.

Hatton Garden.

Charterhouse Street.

No. 5 Hatton Garden, S.H. Harris. Note the absence of numbers 2, 3 and 4.

The showroom of Wedgwood at Nos 26 & 27 Hatton Garden.

Clockwise from top left: The De Beers building on Holborn Circus; the Stewart Dawson Building; the east side of Hatton Garden; Nos 34–35 Hatton Garden.

Hatton Garden *c.*1908.

Diamond dealers operating on the street in Hatton Garden, 1929.

Life was very different in so many ways. One dealer tells of how Johnson Matthey used to make their deliveries of gold bullion by horse and cart. The gold was carried out from their refinery, placed on the back of the cart and covered with a tarpaulin, before being trotted off to its destination.

Despite the setbacks, Hatton Garden continued to grow. In 1930 the diamond trade alone accounted for eighty names out of some 360 in the directory. There were another eighty in related fields such as gemstones and the associated crafts. There were twelve pearl merchants and forty clockmakers. There were more businesses close by. Anton Dunkelsbuhler and the Barnato Brothers moved from Hatton Garden to 39 Holborn Viaduct, the site of which was to become the London Office of De Beers and the Diamond Trading Co. later in the century.

When the Germans invaded Belgium on 4th August 1914, many of the Antwerp diamond dealers fled to London. This gave new impetus to the significance of London as a trading centre. After the war some returned but many stayed on. Those who returned would never have guessed that in just over twenty years they would have to flee again.

The Wall Street Stock Market Crash of October 1929 heralded a decade of global recession. In 1931, 2.4 million carats of diamonds were imported into England. In 1933 this figure had dropped to 14,000 carats.

In June 1933, Ernest Oppenheimer set up the Diamond Trading Company (DTC) and Central Selling Organization (CSO), which replaced the old Diamond Corporation syndicate. Of the original syndicate, only Barnato Bros and Dunkelsbuhler remained. The role of the DTC was to purchase and sell stones from members of the Diamond Producers Association. The business model was close to a monopoly as a large majority of the diamonds mined found their way to the DTC. Oppenheimer was then able to exercise some serious control of the supply and demand and, therefore, the price. At one time, 90% of world production of diamonds went through the DTC.

The DTC made its home in Charterhouse Street and relocated to St Andrew's House on Holborn Viaduct after being bombed out during the war. The offices and vaults of the DTC have seen unimaginable riches pass through their doors. In one of its better years 7 million carats were received by post.

The uncut stones were sorted into numerous categories and made up into lots, known as sights. Clients were 'by invitation only' and were expected to take the whole selection offered in the sight, paying on the spot. Refusal to accept a sight might jeopardise future invitations.

Part of their role was also to maintain some stability in the market. Mine production could vary, and demand certainly did. This was done by stockpiling goods in times of over-supply and releasing them according to demand. Prior to the war it maintained a minimum stock of $10 million.

Originally many of the DTC clients were based in Antwerp, Amsterdam, Paris and other European cutting centres. However, the First World War put a stop to this for a number of years and even after the war it took a long time to rebuild these damaged industries. In the meantime, the market in the USA was growing. Many exiles had found their way to New York and started cutting there. De Beers were promoting the diamond engagement ring like never before.

Many jewellery workshops at that time were larger than those with which we are familiar today. It was not uncommon for up to 100 people to be employed by one company.

The geography of Europe was still fluid. One Hatton Garden diamond dealer would tell of how his father was born in Austria. When asked which part, he would reply, 'Warsaw'. Poland didn't come into being until 1918.

In 1921 cultured pearls created by Mr K Mikimoto in Japan appeared on the market for the first time. This was a great concern to the many pearl dealers, who saw the bottom fall out of the market almost overnight. To all intents and purposes the man-made product looked just like the real thing. Throughout the millennia natural pearls have been sought by kings and queens and anyone else who was seriously wealthy. Now they could be bought in quantity at a fraction of the price by thousands of people.

A report in *The Star* on 4th May 1921 captures the mood with the headline 'Big London Pearl Swindle – Alarm in Hatton Garden and the West End'.

> A sensation has been created in Hatton Garden and among West End Jewellers by the discovery of a big pearl swindle. The Star learns that thousands of pounds have been paid for faked pearls, which are in fact only worth a few shillings. The discovery was only made by accident. This faked pearl is so like the natural Oriental pearl that it has completely taken in the London pearl merchants and jewellers. The discovery will cause quite a flutter in the dovecotes of Society people who have recently purchased pearl necklaces.
>
> London West End jewellers and pearl merchants are so alarmed over the discovery that at a meeting held this week, all those present were sworn to secrecy. The new faked pearl is the most wonderful imitation of the real article ever produced and has been so cleverly 'planted' on the London market that it has surprised and deceived all the experts. There seems to be no doubt that this faked pearl comes from Japan, but it is not known who has been actually engaged in the swindle.
>
> **The Discovery**
>
> So perfect are these faked pearls, however, that one Hatton Garden merchant was induced to give £10,000 for some, which he proceeded to have made into a necklace. Like the Oriental pearls, these imitations have been sent to this country ready pierced, but one of this £10,000 bunch was so finely pierced that the workman making up the necklace had to slightly enlarge the hole. Whilst the workman was doing this a piece of the outer covering chipped off and disclosed the mother of pearl bead. This happened one day last week, and though every effort was made to keep the matter secret, the news came out. Another merchant discovered that a bunch of small 'pearls' for which he had given £700 were all fakes, and he succeeded in getting back his money from the merchant from whom he made the purchase.

Litigation

There is already talk of litigation against those who decline to return the purchase money. A deputation of jewellers and merchants has visited the Board of Trade and placed the facts before the officials there, and it is probable that an attempt will be made to exclude the import of all pearls till a simple test has been found for disclosing this latest jewel fake. A pearl merchant told a 'Star' reporter that he thought it would be possible to do this by means of some very strong light or an extremely powerful glass, but at the moment the faked pearl has resisted all attempts to disclose its identity without breaking it open – a most expensive method if it should happen to be a genuine gem under suspicion.

There was an urgent need for a method of testing pearls for their authenticity. The London Chamber of Commerce coordinated the establishment of a laboratory in Hatton Garden whose technicians were equipped to carry out the work. There had also been a need to distinguish certain gems from new imitations or synthetics. The laboratory name was 'The Diamond, Pearl and Precious Stone Section of the London Chamber of Commerce'.

So, it was in 1925 that a laboratory opened in Hatton Garden for the testing of pearls. Basil William Anderson became well known as a gemmologist and author. The first premises were in Diamond House, in a small room on the fourth floor.

He travelled to Paris to study how the French were coping with the problem. They had created an instrument that was able to place a small probe into the drilled hole in order to inspect its core. Basil Anderson and his 'endoscope' became the saviour of the pearl trade in Hatton Garden.

The Precious Stone Laboratory at 15 Hatton Garden.

Hatton Garden, 1939.

The volume of work being brought in was more than Anderson could handle as some time was needed for research and experimentation. He was joined in 1928 by CJ Payne, who was also destined to become one of the founding fathers of gemmology in the UK. When the laboratory relocated to 55 Hatton Garden in 1929, an X-ray machine was installed to assist with their work. This enabled work on undrilled pearls, which the endoscope couldn't do. Later the laboratory extended its work to the testing of gemstones.

In the 1930s there was a growing tide of Jewish immigrants from Europe as the prospect of war threatened again and persecution was rife. Prior to 1939 Antwerp was the global hub of the diamond trade.

Diamond cutting became an important part of the UK economy and those involved in it were given preferred occupation status, which meant they couldn't enlist even if they had wanted to. The bulk of production went to the USA and diamonds were now traded in US dollars. The American economy was strong, and many profited from the supply of arms. The exchange rate of the day was $5 to £1.

Some diamond cutting and polishing moved to the provinces. Towns including Bangor, Brighton, Luton, Maidenhead, Welwyn and Wolverhampton had factories of various sizes.

The Italians found themselves in an uncomfortable position in the 1930s. Having fought alongside the British in the First World War and being immensely patriotic, their loyalty was divided. On 10th May 1940, Benito Mussolini declared war against Britain. Italians in the UK were targeted by angry mobs, particularly the ice cream parlours and Italian restaurants. Italian men between the ages of 16 and 60 were placed in internment camps in the Isle of Man. As a result, the catering and hospitality industry was brought to its knees.

Many of those working in the 'Garden' at the time were called up to fight in the war or serve in some other way. The trade rallied round and raised the funds to pay for a Spitfire for the RAF.

1940S

In the 1940s, the government needed to raise funds for the war effort and introduced a 'temporary' tax on manufactured items, called Purchase Tax. It came into force on 21st October 1940 at a rate of 33%. Within eighteen months it was doubled to 66% and then a year later to 100%, where it remained until after the war. Although it was reduced, and the rate set by the government of the day, it rarely went below 50%. It was the responsibility of a manufacturing jeweller to levy the tax on its products when sold. This created a huge black market and cash sales became commonplace. Some companies boasted keeping two sets of books; one for themselves and one for Customs & Excise. Offices and workshops had coal fire heating at that time, and it was not uncommon to find manufacturers burning their records when the inspectors were doing a purge.

Holborn Viaduct and St Andrew's in 1941.

Ruined buildings on Holborn Circus after the Blitz.

Loose stones and second-hand goods were exempt. Some firms would invoice the stones separately from the goldsmithing. Others would make a new ring and knock it about the workshop floor a while to make it look second-hand. Another practice was to remake a customer's 'second-hand' ring in two separate transactions. First the head was made without incurring tax and later the shank was supplied, also free of Purchase Tax. These scams could bring the final owner of the piece into trouble, which was somewhat unfair as many innocent parties were held accountable for the tax and given a fine for a crime that they did not commit. The trade rallied round and hired a QC to fight their case. The day before the case was due to be heard Customs & Excise dropped their ruling, much to the relief of the jewellery manufacturers.

The Negretti & Zambra building at Holborn Circus burns during the Blitz.

Aerial view of Hatton Garden post-war showing the extent of bomb damage, particularly in Kirby Street.

After the bombs in Kirby Street, 1941.

Map showing the extent of damage incurred during the Blitz.

Map showing the extent of damage incurred during the Blitz.

View across Farringdon Road to Greville Street, 1941.

The corner of Kirby Street and St Cross Street looking towards Hatton Place, 1940.

Purchase Tax (PT) inspectors would often arrive for an inspection unannounced and be dreaded by anyone operating in any untoward manner. The inspectors were known to be aggressive and sometimes they needed to be.

The department store on the south side of Holborn Circus was hit by incendiary bombs in the early hours of 17th April 1941. Over 1,000 civilians died that night. The Blitz lasted eleven weeks. In all, 60,595 civilians lost their lives across the country.

The worst night of bombing was 10th May 1941, when 8 Charterhouse Street, then home of the Diamond Trading Company, was destroyed. The safes, which were buried in the rubble, were not found for several days. It has been said that they were also too hot to touch as a result of the inferno, sometimes referred to as 'the second great fire of London'. As a contingency plan, diamond sorting had been moved to Louis Oppenheimer's home in White Waltham, Berkshire. However, 'sights' were held in London and De Beers moved into St Andrew's House on Holborn Viaduct.

Another anecdote associated with the Blitz was of the setter in Greville Street who used to work at the bench on a sawn-off barstool. The stool had come through his window when The Globe pub on the corner of Hatton Garden was hit by a bomb.

The skills applied to manufacturing so prevalent throughout Hatton Garden were seconded during the war and applied to military use. Light industrial applications included instrument making. Ironically, this was where the industry had been in its infancy in the last century.

Until the opening of the London Diamond Bourse in 1940, many dealers didn't have a place of their own. Some were, by their unfortunate circumstances, not able to afford an office and others preferred the freedom of the slightly shady way of operating, which suited their style of business better. Some brokers gave their trading address as 'care of Jo Lyons Tea Shop, Hatton Garden' and received mail there. The characters who traded on the pavement or in the many cafés and bars provided a wonderful cross section of humanity. Their style of dress gave no clues as to their activity. A casual observer would never imagine the extraordinary wealth that was on offer.

It was common practice to trade from doorways and even out on the pavement. On any given day, you might find more than a dozen clusters of men engrossed in conversation. The various conversations may have been diverse but all of them at some point would focus on a small folded paper packet, known as a *brifka*. This may have contained a gem, sometimes of considerable value, that the dealer was offering on behalf of its owner. The gems were inspected and appraised with some care. At that time there were no third-party laboratory reports or certificates, only the opinions of the parties to the transaction. A grey or gloomy day would colour the judgement of a dealer and was to be avoided. The trading day was normally between 10 a.m. and 3 p.m. to get the best of the daylight. Diamonds were viewed away from direct sunlight and whenever possible facing north. Diamonds with strong fluorescence appeared blue-white in the bright sunshine and were made to look more desirable than they would at another time.

The banter between the broker and a potential buyer was invariably a mixture of hard bargaining and good humour – the seller doing his utmost by way of romancing the stone and the buyer nonchalantly acting as if he was not interested. The seller would describe a stone as being 'clean' but when challenged by the buyer would say 'it's clean apart from the inclusion', or in another instance a stone was described as 'D colour /flawless' and when challenged the answer would be 'obviously not the whole stone but part of it'. Jews predominated, as many had escaped from Europe, and an eavesdropper would hear Yiddish, French, Dutch or German being spoken, as well as English and sometimes a mix of more than one language.

The trade of the pavement or café was only the tip of the iceberg. Behind closed doors, others operated in secure environments. Their offices were often a rabbit warren of passages and connecting rooms. The buildings they inhabited were, after all, designed as homes. Any would-be robber would have to run the gauntlet of secure doors and security staff.

It was believed to be safer to open a *brifka* over the tarmacked road surface than over the granite pavements and it was a common sight to see diamond dealers standing beside the road. The original granite paving slabs of the Georgian era were replaced in the 1960s with concrete ones. The local council would have benefitted well from the exercise.

The pavement traders felt some comfort in being part of a herd but inevitably their visibility attracted more and more undesirables, including dubious traders and fences. The allure of diamonds and gems and their ability to be concealed or sold on without trace made them into a currency for the underworld.

London Diamond Bourse in Greville Street, 1940.

The Viennese Café in Greville Street was run by a Mrs Cohen. It was here in 1940 that brokers and dealers would meet in a small, crowded space, over a long coffee break, and conduct business. Those who remember it always talk about the thick atmosphere of smoke and the unpleasant smell of humanity. It became known as 'The Diamond Merchants Restaurant'. This establishment became the first London Diamond Bourse. One regular always made it his business to stay until close of play and then volunteer to sweep the floor. Presumably, he made some gains from doing this. However, the café would also attract some undesirables and the need for a private and secure environment was recognised.

The vast majority of merchants, dealers and brokers were and still are decent, hard-working people. Their integrity and honesty have always been essential to them as these qualities permit them to belong to a very exclusive 'club'. All transactions between members are based upon a mutual trust and respect whereby millions of pounds can change hands with no more than a handshake. There was never any collateral as security and rarely a paper trail; just the traditional way of confirming a deal with the Hebrew words '*Mazal*' and '*Bracha*' and a handshake. This saying translates into English as 'Luck and Blessing' and is fitting for all sorts of reasons. This time-honoured method is used around the world where diamonds are traded. It is believed that its usage goes back to Amsterdam in the late 15th century when Jews were expelled from Spain.

Anyone who considered reneging on a deal would be committing commercial suicide as they would be ostracised from the community, not just in this country but internationally. There was one broker at this time who was blind. He had no way of judging the quality or value of stones, but he made a living out of being a 'runner'. Others would trust him with their goods, and he would trust those to whom he showed them.

However, not everyone was honest. There was an old trick whereby a con merchant would borrow a diamond on approval supposedly to show a client.

He would also source a very similar stone of a slightly lower weight, say .01ct difference, which he would purchase. The smaller stone was returned to the supplier in place of the more valuable one. By repeating this trick, a number of times, the original stone would 'grow' into something far more valuable. Another trick of the trade was to place a 'swimmer' in a parcel of diamonds. A swimmer was a stone that was superior to the rest of the parcel and would lure a buyer into taking the whole parcel.

A further trick was performed by sleight of hand. The fingernails on the little finger were grown beyond their normal length. When looking at a tray of rings, the thief would use his thumb and forefinger to pick up a ring from the far side of the tray while hooking a nearer ring within the palm of his hand using his little finger.

There were more and more refugees from Europe, particularly Belgium, as the Nazis closed in on Antwerp, and they worked from their pockets. There was no welfare state until 1948, so they needed to provide for themselves. Previously, it had been trade practice for someone coming into the industry to do an apprenticeship in diamond cutting or polishing before becoming a trader.

One well-known dealer was Willy Trenner, who had been a furrier at home in Antwerp. He and a close friend, who was a diamond merchant, both saw the need to escape while they still had a chance. However, tickets for the crossing to England were like gold dust and they could only get one between them. It was agreed that Willy should go first, but for peace of mind he agreed to take the stock of diamonds belonging to his friend. It would be safer for the friend to escape later without the diamonds if the Nazis caught up with him. The Germans came the next day. The friend was never seen again. Despite every effort by Willy to make contact during and after the war, it can only be assumed that the friend was shipped to one of the Nazi extermination camps.

Willy was able to set himself up in London as a diamond dealer. Although he had next to no experience, he used his wits and wonderful Jewish ability to 'romance the stone'.

Also in 1940, on 7th November, the London Diamond Club was formed mainly for diamond dealers working in rough. At first it had a base in Ely Place but moved to a more fitting location at 87 Hatton Garden in 1943. This was a listed Georgian property. The initial membership of the club was about seventy. Members mostly dealt in rough, unpolished stones, for which London became a global hub during the war. The early presidents were Mr Edward (Eddie) Goldstein and Mr Paul Hirschfield. They also had an important role in the World Federation of Diamond Bourses, with which the London Bourse was affiliated.

Many of the members were refugees or survivors who had escaped the persecution of Jewish people in Europe. Some were fortunate enough to escape with their goods, often by sewing them into their clothing.

The success of the Bourse and the club was partly due to the increased numbers of Jewish merchants who had come from Europe. There were many personalities and characters who in one way or another contributed to the rich tapestry of everyday life in the Bourse. There was a dealer in the Bourse, sometimes referred to as 'one match a day' as he was a chain smoker. His practice was always to go home with more cash than he started with that morning. So, towards the close of play, bargains would be had as he liquidated his purchases.

A cartoon from the *London Evening Standard* capturing some of the many characters.

There was a big upset one day when a cry went up across the trading floor from Willy Trenner. His brother and business partner, Emile, had purchased a very nice piece from another dealer at the far end of the room. It turned out that Willy had sold that item earlier in the day and his brother bought it back at a higher price.

High Purchase Tax encouraged big business in second-hand jewellery. There were two men in Hatton Garden whose 'sideline' was producing official documents for second-hand items, complete with a 2d stamp.

Graham Tom's father was a well-established dealer in rough diamonds. When he had his kidney stones removed he noticed a similarity to his own stock. He wrapped the stones in a *brifka* and showed them to a client. The client, knowing that Mr Tom was a reliable source, immediately offered on the stones!

Even after 1945 there was a further influx of those who had survived the Nazi occupation or the concentration camps. Some returned to Antwerp and took a role in rebuilding the city's diamond industry. Many, however, chose to remain and became British subjects. These survivors, in many cases, had missed out on an education.

After the war, work at the laboratory picked up again and two new members of staff were appointed: Alec Farn and Robert Webster. Their passion and enthusiasm took the science of gemmology to a new level.

Hatton Garden, 1947.

Hatton Garden, 1947.

In 1942, a Prohibition of Supplies order stated that gold wedding rings must be made in 9ct and weigh less than 2dwts (3.11 grams). Gold standards had varied since their introduction in 1300 when 19.2ct was established; 18ct was introduced in 1478, 22ct in 1576 and then in 1854, 15, 13, and 9ct made their debut. This was changed again in 1932 when 15 and 13 were replaced by 14ct.

The normal working week was forty hours and, in most cases, also included Saturday mornings until 1 p.m. Prior to the war, businesses often worked 8 a.m. to 8 p.m., but the black-out requirements reduced that to 9 a.m. to 5 p.m., which for many has been the standard working day ever since.

One of the lasting legacies of this decade was the creation of the advertising line 'A Diamond is Forever'. De Beers had engaged the advertising agency NW Ayer in New York and their copywriter Frances Geraghty was the one who had the inspiration.

1950S

In the 1950s a change occurred in the manufacturing industry as more jewellery makers started to use centrifugal casting to increase their production. This meant fewer people at the bench and marked the beginning of a change that would impact the jewellery and diamond trade of Hatton Garden.

Buildings were without central heating and a coal fire was the source of warmth in many places. However, for some the cost was prohibitive and when a young trainee complained of being too cold to work, he was told to run around the block. When he returned, he was still cold and had to go around again.

In the mid-1950s the London Diamond Bourse moved to the ground floor of 57 Hatton Garden and a short time later to No. 32, where it occupied the whole of the first floor in a purpose-built environment. There was a reception area for visitors and four or five telephone boxes, to which members would be paged to receive an incoming call. There was also a small kiosk where diamonds could be officially weighed. These were busy times and the Bourse and its membership increased to around 700 people.

Members were offered the freehold of 32 Hatton Garden, which could be acquired for £100 per member. It was a good time to buy in London as confidence in the property market had not yet returned since the war. Dealers such as Max Strassman paid their share to support the proposal but there was opposition from at least two parties. Mr Gordon, who was a committee member, had just opened the safe deposit at Nos 88–90 Hatton Garden and it would not be in his best interest if a competing safe deposit were to be built below the new Bourse. Secondly, there was a very evident and understandable point of view from those who were known as the survivors, those who had escaped Europe. They were either not in a position to contribute or they were not willing, mostly the latter. They caused such dissension that the scheme had to be abandoned.

To supplement the supply of diamonds, there was a big business in second-hand and antique jewellery. Articles had come to the market as older generations died off. Many of these pieces were broken up and the diamonds re-cut as modern brilliants.

One dealer, by the name of Jack Yukutiel, came to Hatton Garden in 1954 at the age of 27. He was tasked by a certain antique dealer called Mr Levy to sell a large jewellery box. He decided that it might be of interest to Garrard & Co. in Regent Street and carried it across London to show their buyer. He was asked to leave it with them for a few days while they mulled it over. Unfortunately, they decided not to make the purchase and Jack had to go and collect it and bring it back to Mr Levy in Hatton Garden. Mr Levy then gave Jack about twenty pieces of second-hand jewellery to sell. The cost price was agreed, and Jack could add a margin at his discretion. He went back to the West End and this time called upon a shop in Bond Street run by two ladies. They asked Jack how they might help him and he said that he had some jewellery to sell. The ladies were delighted with the jewellery and the prices and paid him in cash with the old white £5 notes or blankets, as they were known. His common sense in not being greedy had made him a dealer and he was still operating in Hatton Garden in 2020.

In 1957, Prime Minister Harold Macmillan made a speech in which he coined the phrase 'You have never had it so good'. Post-war manufacturing throughout the land was taking us into a new era. Chris Kochli, a retired diamond mounter, started work in the early sixties on £2 2s a week, which after tax gave him £1 16s 9d for his fares and living expenses. He recalls how the workshop had a problem with mice and rats. The holes in the skirting board were much like those of any *Tom & Jerry* cartoon. Cyanide was left out on a saucer to deal with it. Health and safety considerations and risk assessments were not yet part of life. The overalls worn in the workshop were also full of holes from acid splashes.

Despite the boom time, a large number of diamond-cutting factories closed. Many of the workers returned to Antwerp or moved to Israel. By 1962, there were only two remaining in Hatton Garden.

1960S

In the 1960s international air travel made it possible for dealers to travel to sources for their gemstones. Countries such as India, Thailand, Sri Lanka and Myanmar welcomed stone dealers with offices in Hatton Garden. The sea routes had been time-consuming and laborious.

This was a boom time, not just for Hatton Garden but for the whole of London and beyond. There were no 'To Let' signs in Hatton Garden and if you wanted premises you were likely to have to pay 'key money' to find it. Any walk along the street would be to the sounds of busy workshops as the tapping of hammers on triblets rose from the basement windows. At that time the trade was very much segmented or layered in the form of the supply chain. Stone importers sold to stone dealers, who in turn sold to manufacturing jewellers. Manufacturers sold to wholesalers or retailers. There were also brokers who would act as 'go-betweens'. They would offer a stone on behalf of the merchant who owned it and, where required, negotiate a sale, usually for a 1% commission. This would usually involve getting an offer that would be taken back and submitted to the owner. This legwork was how the broker earned his living as there were not yet any mobile phones. An offer was usually sealed in an envelope and was binding unless the seal was broken. This meant that the stone couldn't be offered to other buyers until the seal was broken. Eventually a broker would build up his own stock and become a merchant. He now had the advantage of knowing the customers and could cut out the middleman.

In the 1960s more Italians came to the UK. They were relatives of those already living here and were granted four-year permits. Many opened cafés and brought Italian cuisine with them. Dishes like spaghetti bolognese had not previously been available as they now were. The much-loved Italian café in St Cross Street known as Dina's was famous for its toasted bacon sandwiches and it was quite common to see a queue of messengers or runners from various workshops with their orders for all the craftsmen. Seating was limited, although they offered a typical 'greasy spoon' full English breakfast. The Formica-topped tables were never empty from early to late. In the days before health and safety it was not uncommon to see the cat up on the table scavenging for food.

In 1965 Holborn became part of Camden as the London County Council (LCC) gave way to the Greater London Council (GLC). Thus, Middlesex quietly left the stage. Another change was that of London phone numbers. Prior to 1968 the first three letters of the local telephone exchange were followed by a four-digit number. So, Holborn was HOL and Chancery Lane was CHA. This was dialled on a mechanical wheel. The new numbers that replaced them were the corresponding digits for the letter. So, HOL became 405 and CHA became 242. Later a seven was added in front of the three digits. Ironically, the Post Office, who introduced the new system, promoted it with an advertising campaign featuring ANN (All figure Numbers Now).

Diamonds were then mostly graded according to the traditional scales; a blue-white colour being the most desirable. Terms, once in common use, like 'Cape' and 'Wesselton' to describe colour, now seem rather quaint. The Gemological Institute of America (GIA) started issuing diamond certificates in 1955 and their system of grading, where D is the top colour, gradually achieved acceptance in the European markets and globally.

1970S

The decade started with the decimalisation of sterling on 15th February 1971. One consequence of this was that a lot of cash had to be moved on as new banknotes replaced the old. Purchase Tax, which had had such a negative effect on the UK jewellery manufacturing industry, was replaced by VAT on 2nd April 1973. Initially it was set at 10%, which came as a great relief. However, within eighteen months it was increased to 25% and has fluctuated between 12.5% and 20% ever since. The advantage for the manufacturer was that he could now offset any tax paid on his materials against the tax he might have to pay on sales.

Prior to the introduction of VAT there was a Purchase Tax concession allowed by Customs & Excise whereby if a manufacturer supplied a product to a retailer the payment of the tax could be delayed until the goods were sold from the shop. The goods were considered to be on consignment but there was no option to return them if not sold. When VAT was introduced there was a large-scale reconciliation of stock on consignment. Some of it had been sold and therefore attracted Purchase Tax. Some was still in stock and therefore attracted VAT.

In 1974, the Chancellor, Denis Healey, introduced in his autumn budget a temporary tax concession known as 'stock relief'. This was a provision for a reduction in corporation tax payable during a period of high inflation. In a straightforward way, a gross profit was calculated by deducting the cost of goods from sales but when the replacement of that stock was significantly higher, any profit could be wiped out, thus making the corporation tax a burden and changing a profit on paper into a loss in reality.

Normal businesses had to adjust to accommodate the 'Postal Strike', which started on 19th January 1971 and ran for two months until 19th March. Deliveries and repairs were sent by registered post and customers' cheques would have been sent by post.

In February the miners went on strike, disrupting fuel supplies, particularly to power stations. On 1st January 1974 businesses were restricted to a three-day working week. This continued until 7th March. During this period all companies in the commercial sector were restricted in the use of electricity to three normal working days. Television finished at 10.30 p.m. to conserve supplies. The Hatton Garden offices and workshops employed candles and 'Camping Gaz' lighting to continue trade. Some put blinds up at the window to hide their clandestine activity. One managed to get a generator and bought fuel with old wartime coupons, which were reintroduced during the crisis.

These were difficult economic times and businesses had to work hard compared to the 1960s. There were only a small handful of shops. The earliest ones had been opened as buying offices for dealers to give public access. There was now a growth in jewellery shops in Hatton Garden. Some were outlets for manufacturers; others were not. Of these, some were very professional, and many were not. In the initial flurry of activity, day-glow stickers were seen everywhere offering huge discounts.

The 'Winter of Discontent', 1978–1979, was when snow and blizzards compounded the problems of fuel shortages caused by the miners' strikes. High inflation forced unions to request unrealistic pay rise demands. The dustmen who were responsible for Hatton

Garden went on strike in January and rubbish started to pile up on the pavements as the offices and workshops cleared their refuse. Bin bags weren't in common use until later, but some people used them to hide the provenance of their contents. The accumulation caused an increase in rat sightings and although in some boroughs, parks were used as a holding area, in Hatton Garden the piles were waist high. The Camden authorities finally gave in to an 11% pay increase.

Another change was the introduction of natural gas to replace the old town gas with its once familiar gas holders. The new gas burned with a hotter flame and initially caused problems with ring sizing as the diamonds in their settings would be burnt if the process was done in the old way. Oxygen cylinders, from British Oxygen, were delivered by a man in a brown coat, who would carry a 5-foot cylinder on his shoulder from the lorry parked in the street up the stairs to the various workshops. The old lorries were recognisable by the sound of the clinking of the cylinders as the lorry approached or drove away.

At the beginning of the decade men wore trousers with turn-ups but by the end of the period they were less fashionable. There are a number of diamond merchants or dealers who thought they had lost a stone, only to discover that it was lodged in the turn-up.

The 1970s saw the boom in oil prices and Arab clients started to visit showrooms in London's West End. Proactive manufacturers were able to visit states in the Middle East and supply jewellery. The demand at this time was fuelled by the requirement for yellow gold.(New Year's Day became a public holiday on 1st January 1974 and May Day was declared a public holiday for the first time on 1st May 1978.)

A new Hallmarking Act was introduced on 2nd January 1975, having received royal assent the previous year. This replaced all previous acts and is largely the system we work to today.

Towards the end of 1979 the price of silver reached an all-time high. It had risen from around £11 an ounce in September to £50 an ounce in January 1980. Suddenly, the family silver that had adorned the shelves and tables of many homes throughout the land was worth selling. Antique works of art and heirlooms went into the same melting pot as old cutlery and dishes. Furthermore, old British coinage still in circulation containing silver was also melted for a higher price than its face value. Hundreds of people made a pilgrimage to the metal refiners and scrap buyers of Hatton Garden and queues were seen up and down the street. 'Best Prices Paid' was an all too familiar sight in shop windows, and touts even worked the queues to get business. It was tragic that so much was lost in such a short time. By March the price was back where it had been before all the speculation had begun.

Selling the family silver, 1979.

Many silversmiths got into trouble as they paid over the top prices for the metal and when the market crashed, they could not sell their stock. It all came about through the activities of one man and his brothers. Nelson Bunker Hunt, a Texan oil executive, had tried to corner the global market in silver by a continuing series of acquisitions. It has been estimated that they made in excess of $2 billion from their activity. At one time they held an estimated 3.1 million kilos of the metal. It all came crashing down on what has become known as Silver Thursday, 27th March 1980. The Hunts had overstretched themselves and as a result declared themselves bankrupt.

1980S

In November 1985, the Chancellor, Nigel Lawson, announced that in future VAT would be payable at the time of importation. This was arguably the beginning of the end, if not the death blow, for the many dealers in precious stones who imported goods from overseas. Not only did this hit the cash flow of regular importers, but it also actively discouraged temporary importations, which had been a great source of business in an international marketplace. In order to fund the VAT payable, a large sum would have to be found. This was allegedly to bring the UK into line with other European countries, although somehow Antwerp was given special dispensation. London lost its status overnight. 'To Let' signs appeared up and down Hatton Garden.

By the end of the decade the Bourse had outgrown its space. At the same time the Gamages department store site was being developed. This involved the whole of the block from Hatton Garden to Leather Lane and Holborn to Greville Street being demolished to make way for a new building. Part of this development, now generally called

The old Gamages site being cleared for development, 1973.

100 Hatton Garden, would be the new home to the London Diamond Bourse as well as offices suitable for those in the trade. The design also included a safe deposit in the basement.

January 1980 saw a spike in the price of gold at $850 an ounce, an increase of over 60% on 1979. This panic was caused by several factors: high, double-digit inflation in the UK; strong oil prices; unrest in Iran; and Soviet intervention in Afghanistan. The price returned to a more normal level later in the year and didn't return to that level until 2008.

The price of diamonds also spiked. There was a plethora of 'pop-up' businesses offering diamonds for 'investment'. Many of them were remote from the trade itself but increased demand caused prices to rise. De Beers tried to curb it by introducing surcharges on their sights. This was intended to suggest that the higher prices were only temporary, but it was construed as being a good investment. Initially the surcharge was 10% and later 40%. A 1ct D colour, flawless stone peaked at around $43,000 per carat and fell back to around £13,000. The market dropped in parallel to the gold market and 'investors' tried to sell, only to realise that they were going to lose money. There are still investment scams today and it is tragic to have to tell a victim that they have been caught.

Within the structure of De Beers and the Diamond Trading Company was a much-loved department known as the Diamond Promotion Service. A small team of highly professional people orchestrated annual campaigns to put diamonds into the spotlight through various media. Television advertising and cinema advertising showed diamond jewellery as a consumer choice. Close cooperation with the trade enabled them to put together collections of diamond jewellery from well-known manufacturers. These were advertised in the glossy magazines, often with a stockists list, which would direct the consumer to their local jeweller. In due course, De Beers lost their market share as other diamond producers increased their output and new sources were discovered. Consequently, advertising budgets on generic advertising were cut. De Beers reinvented themselves as a brand with the opening of their first retail store in 2002.

New postcodes were introduced in January 1980. Most of Hatton Garden became EC1N followed by a three-character suffix.

1990S

Towards the end of the 20th century another change appeared on the horizon that had significant impact on our local manufacturing industry. Manufacturers in Asia were able to offer products at prices lower than those for which the same items could be made in London.

Initially, there were realistic concerns over quality, but as time went by many factories in India, Thailand, Taiwan, China and elsewhere started to become serious competition. Their factories were larger as they were geared up for the global marketplace and were supplying jewellery to the USA, which was the world's biggest consumer market. Some Hatton Garden companies shifted their manufacturing to Asia and just maintained a shell in Hatton Garden for the address. At the same time, some relocated outside London to save costs and improve on their quality of life. Commuting to Hatton Garden, by private car or public transport, had gradually become more tiring.

Relationships are often built over a drink or a meal and the area was rich in choices. The Lema Buttery was located on the corner of Greville Street and Hatton Garden. Further down Greville Street was the Nosherie, arguably one of London's best kosher cafés. Their hot salt beef was a house speciality and there was always a queue around midday as the meat was taken from the oven in the basement and hoisted up in a 'dumb waiter' lift to the counter where it was carved. For something lighter, the Florence Restaurant created fresh home-made sandwiches while you waited.

On the corner of Greville Street and Hatton Garden next to the Safe Deposit was a unique tobacconist who specialised in cigars but also sold single cigarettes.

Messengers were an important part of the working community. Top firms employed commissionaires from the Corps of Commissionaires, who also acted as security. Workshops used the apprentices for their errands. It was common for the older craftsmen to have a laugh at the expense of the young trainees and many false errands were invented: two-legged stools, a diamond magnet or a 'long weight' and tartan paint were just a few. The other prank was to heat a coin and drop it out of the window to the pavement below.

By the end of the 20th century, a number of businesses were into their second or third generation. The family atmosphere that was created was a recognisable feature of trade in the street.

THE GARDEN MAKEOVER AND THE 21ST CENTURY

The start of a new millennium is a perfect opportunity to look back on the past with both sentiment and a pragmatic view of all that has brought us to where we are today. It is also an opportunity to look forward to the future and speculate what the 21st century and beyond may bring. Are we on a mountain top, a plateau or have we started a descent? Nothing remains the same for long. The original garden became a street of smart houses. Then it became an area of light industrial activity that attracted the diamond trade and manufacturing jewellers, among others. Now it has a strong retail presence with far less manufacturing than in its heyday. On looking back there can be a certain satisfaction for all that has been achieved within the 'Garden'. Many, both working and retired, have fond memories of their time in Hatton Garden.

The old NatWest Bank building, 2019.

Those who have been privileged to be part of a family firm, spanning the generations, have a heritage of which they can be justifiably proud.

The story of Hatton Garden has always been one of change and will continue to be so. There are strong opposing views of what the future may hold. Travel for the commuter gets a little harder every year as planners allow developers to create a higher density of people working in the area. On the one hand, the cost of premises are forcing the small workshops to reconsider the need to remain in the area. The Farringdon area of London has become desirable and property owners are able to obtain a better return on their buildings by converting them to residential use. This re-gentrification is taking Hatton Garden back to where it began. The offices and small workshops that remain are increasingly let out to new technology tenants, who seem to be more comfortable with higher rents.

Some of the trade have moved out. The original reasons for the coming together of Hatton Garden no longer apply. Trade is now global and a manufacturer with the right connections can source from anywhere in the world without getting out of bed. There has always been a community spirit within the street and information was exchanged over a coffee or some other drink. Today, the same intelligence is available online. Commuting and overcrowding have made the journey to Hatton Garden increasingly uncomfortable, whether on public transport or by car. The old London markets have all found new homes; some together, like Covent Garden, others dissipated, like Fleet Street. Will Hatton Garden go the same way? In 2017, Brent Council redeveloped their Brent Cross site and a proposal was made to rehouse all of Hatton Garden's trade into a new location with retail units and specialist facilities. This 'New Hatton Garden' didn't happen. We will never know what the opportunity might have offered by way of benefit. Part of the problem is that getting joint decisions is almost impossible when so many people are involved.

The process often goes unnoticed as the gradual erosion of 'leavers' moving to greener pastures continues. One observer remarked, 'There are more safes coming out than going in.'

The situation was summed up recently by a dependable source of all knowledge – a London cab driver – from his own experience. 'People used ter come from all over to 'atton Garden – it doesn't 'appen anymore.'

As we approached the millennium, there was a change in emphasis away from 'British Made' towards goods being manufactured overseas. The cost of labour and premises in the UK made it difficult to compete with Asian countries, which were able to offer high quality at low prices. Many Hatton Garden manufacturers moved at least part of their production to the Far East.

On the other hand, the 'remainers' sincerely believe in the future of Hatton Garden. Some have reinvented themselves as retailers to attract more business. The collective skills and range of opportunities will continue to bring people from all over London for their jewellery.

There can be no doubt that for those who don't want to pay a premium for a branded Bond Street name with its associated packaging and red-carpet treatment, Hatton Garden will offer competitive prices.

The arrival of the new Elizabeth Line at a cost of over £15 billion has led to an increase in property values. More people living and working in this part of London will bring an increase in trade.

In 2006, the London Assay Office opened a facility in Greville Street for the hallmarking of jewellery, thus endorsing its confidence in the future of the area.

There have been several initiatives to put Hatton Garden in the spotlight and create a go-to destination that meets the expectations of tomorrow's consumer. The idea of a visitor and information centre is not new, and approaches have been made to several potential benefactors, so far without success. The future is ultimately, perhaps, a matter of opinion. You might see opportunity in every difficulty, or you might see difficulty in every opportunity.

Those who have taken on this mantle have been frustrated by the lukewarm attitude of many who could benefit from greater exposure and are reluctant to commit to joint expense. This may be because the cost is beyond their budget capability or it may be that working with others is viewed as a surrender of control.

In other European cities, the local authorities provide subsidised rents in order to preserve the history of a district. The possibility of Camden doing this would be of great benefit to the trade.

THE FLEET RIVER

Not far to the east of Hatton Garden is Farringdon Road, which was built in Victorian times during a period of redevelopment and much-needed slum clearance. If you stand in Farringdon Road today, it is difficult to imagine a beautiful, fast-flowing stream in a steep, wooded valley flowing down into the Thames. The river still runs below street level but is now contained in a large pipe that empties out below Blackfriars Bridge. A small section of the pipe is visible over the railway to the north of Farringdon Station. There are a number of so-called 'hidden rivers' below the streets of London, but the Fleet is arguably the best known and with a length of about 4 miles is the longest. It gave its name to Fleet Street, the historic home of the newspaper and press industry in London. Other 'hidden rivers' include the Walbrook, Tyburn and Westbourne.

In the long period before urbanisation it would have been possible to follow the Fleet to its two main sources in the hills to the north of London; one in Hampstead Ponds and the other in Highgate. It is also fed by several springs or wells along its route, notably from 'Clerkenwell'. It was sometimes called the River of Wells.

Its name is derived from the Saxon word 'Fleot', meaning fast, which described the flow of the river. In Norman times it is referred to as the 'Old Bourne', from which we get the name Holborn. There is a spring located under St Andrew's Church near to Holborn Viaduct. This may have been the original source of the name.

In the early days there were two crossing points towards its southerly end before reaching the Thames. Holborn Bridge was built by the Romans to carry the main road to the west, through Newgate, and out of Londinium. The remains of the bridge are still to be found well below Holborn Viaduct and can be seen in the London sewers. Secondly, the Fleet Bridge stood where Ludgate Circus is today at the beginning of Fleet Street.

As more people started to live outside the protection of the city walls the river was used increasingly as a place for rubbish and particularly sewage. The contamination and foul smell were causing problems as early as the 13th century. It is recorded that in 1290

Mouth of the Fleet by Samuel Scott.

the monks of Whitefriars, which was located to the south of what is now Fleet Street and the west of the Fleet, complained to the King in Parliament.

An occasional natural cleansing would occur from time to time when heavy rains caused the river to flood. Perhaps the most notable was in July 1317 when a massive thunderstorm caused the Fleet to burst its banks and people were drowned. Such was the severity of the storms, Holborn Bridge and the Fleet Bridge were both damaged, and homes and mills were carried away by the waters while others were flooded. An ongoing battle ensued as numerous attempts were made to clean up the river, only to be followed by further abuse. In 1343 butchers were given permission to use the river for washing the entrails of their slaughtered animals.

In Tudor times the section north of Holborn Bridge to Kings Cross was known as Turnmill Brook. The river would have been the source of power to several mills. We still have Turnmill Street, which runs from Clerkenwell Road to Farringdon Station, parallel to the course of the river. Another street name that relates to the river is Cowcross Street, which perhaps is where once the cattle owners allowed their cows to cross the river.

In 1589 further work was carried out to improve the flow of the stream. This involved the channelling of other tributaries on Hampstead Heath into the Fleet but with little benefit as the constant dumping of sewage clogged it.

In 1652 a plan was made for the cleansing of the river by the removal of 'the houses of office' that overhung its course, but in 1661 Lord Hatton was permitted to let his new sewer from Hatton House be discharged into the river.

John Fuller writes, in 1662, that the Fleet River was so called 'from its former fleetness, though now it creepeth slow enough, not so much for age as the injection of the City refuse wherewith it is obstructed',

During another flood, in 1679, the wholesale butchers in Cowcross lost their livestock as they were carried away by the floods.

The author of *Gulliver's Travels*, Jonathan Swift, also wrote a famous poem: 'A Description of a City Shower', published in *Tatler Magazine* in 1710. It contains the lines:

> Now from all parts the swelling kennels flow,
> and bear their trophies with them as they go;
> Filths of all hues and odours seem to tell
> What street they sailed from by their sight and smell.
> They, as each torrent drives, with rapid force,
> From Smithfield to St Pulchres shape their course,
> And in huge confluence joined at Snow Hill ridge,
> Fall from the conduit prone to Holborn Bridge;
> Sweepings from butchers' stalls, dung, guts and blood,
> Drowned puppies, stinking sprats, all drenched in mud,
> Dead cats and turnip tops, come tumbling down the flood.

It has been suggested that the expression 'raining cats and dogs' is a picture of such a deluge.

A report in the *Gentleman's Magazine* in 1836 records how on 24th August 1736 a local butcher recovered his lost boar, which had not only survived on the waste from the ditch but flourished on it:

The Fleet River.

> A fatter boar was hardly ever seen than one taken up this day coming out of the Fleet Ditch into The Thames. It proved to be a butcher's near Smithfield Bars, who had missed him five months, all which time he had been in the common sewer and was improved in price from ten shillings to two guineas.

Early records describe how boats used to sail up to Holborn Bridge from the Thames carrying stone for the building of St Paul's between 1110 and 1133.

In 1307, Henry Lacey, Earl of Lincoln, told Parliament that 'whereas in times past the River Fleet has been of such depth and breadth, that ten or twelve ships with merchandise were wont to come to Fleet Bridge, and some of them to Old Bourne Bridge, now the same course, by the filth of the tanneries and such others, and by the raising of wharfs, is stopped up'.

In the 14th and 15th centuries, the tidal section of the river was still navigable by large boats south of Holborn Bridge. There is a record from 1417 that describes two vessels of 20 tons each bringing stones to Holborn Bridge. By the beginning of the 16th century it had silted up and was no longer navigable. Over the next two 200 years it had to be dredged several times, particularly in 1606 at a cost of £28,000 and again in 1652. After the Great Fire of 1666 it was widened to improve the access to barges. It was then known as the 'New Canal' and was 40 feet wide. Unfortunately, the cost of building it, which was in excess of £74,000 caused the tolls to be unrealistic and it silted up again.

Finally, in 1733 it was arched over between Holborn Bridge and the Fleet Bridge. A market was built on the site, which continued until Farringdon Street (now Road) was established in 1829.

In its last days it was known as the 'Fleet Ditch' or 'Town Ditch'. A poetic picture is portrayed for us by John Gay in 'Trivia' in the lines:

> If where Fleet Ditch with muddy current flows,
> You chance to roam; where oyster tubs in rows
> Are ranged beside the posts; there stay thy haste,
> And with the savoury dish indulge thy taste:
> The damsel's knife the gaping shell commands,
> While the salt liquor streams between her hands.

In around 1700, in a letter about London, Daniel Defoe wrote:

> The canal or river, called Fleet-ditch, was a work of great magnificence and expense; but not answering the design, and being now very much neglected, and out of repair, is not much spoken of, yet it has three fine bridges over it, and a fourth, not so fine, yet useful as the rest, and the tide flowing up to the last; the canal is very useful for bringing of coals and timber, and other heavy goods; but the warehouses intended under the streets, on either side, to lay up such goods in, are not made use of, and the wharfs in many places are decay'd and fallen in, which make it all look ruinous.

Left and above: Fleet River.

Prior to the development of Farringdon Road and the final interment of the river, this area had become a home to criminals and prostitutes. Charles Dickens describes it well in works like *Oliver Twist*. The Rookeries, which is where Fagin had his den, was a no-go area for the police at night.

Before it was enclosed in a pipe, the Fleet Ditch was described in 1850 by Beames as:

> a most unsavoury black stream, that is not so much as flow but rush impetuously between the walls of the houses on each side. It carries along with its current all sorts of refuse floating on the water. It is difficult, even in cold weather, to stand a few minutes in the room when the windows looking down upon it are opened. In summer the stench is intolerable.

It was described as 'a wide deep open sewer ... running just under the kitchens of the houses'. Anthony Crosby, the Victorian artist, has left us with this description:

> There are no fewer than four bridges over the River Fleet at the part called Holborn-Bridge. They are joined together at their sides, two of these evidently having been added at different periods to widen the passage of the original bridge; and the additional bridge which was erected by Wren, was introduced not only to secure that object, but to supply a

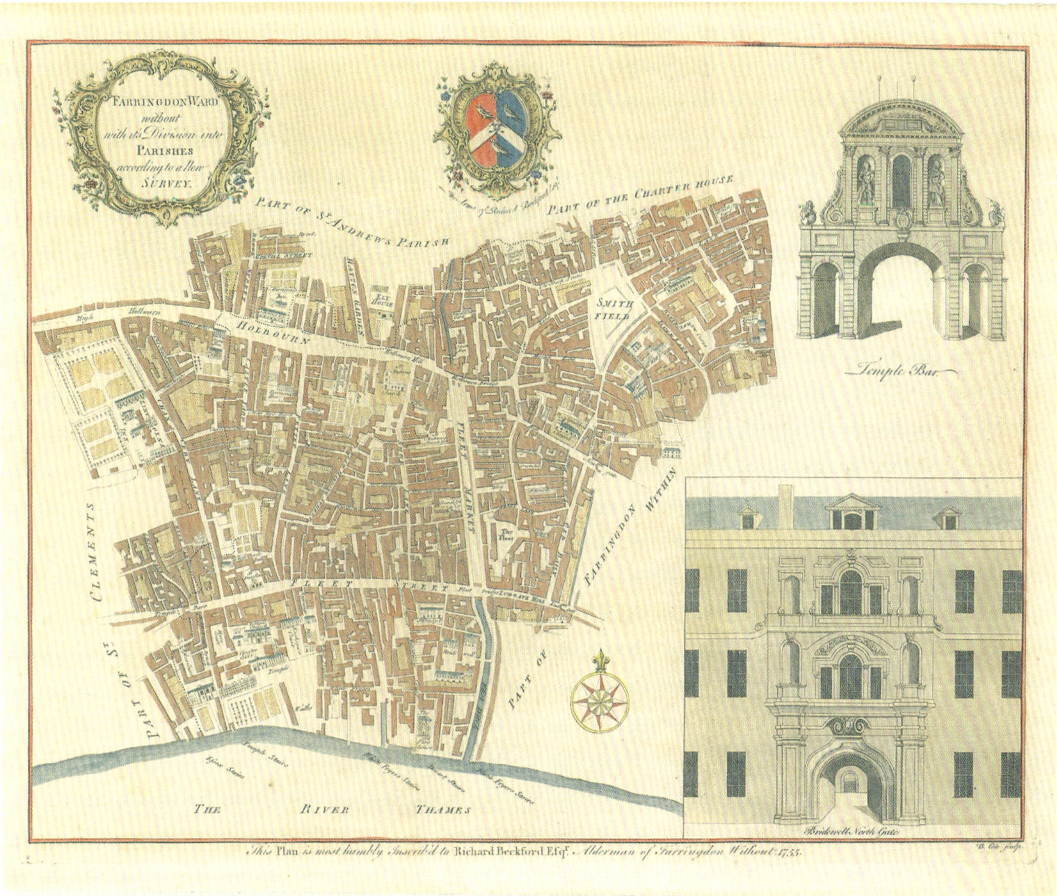

Fleet River south of a section from Holbourn Bridge to the Fleet Bridge, now covered over with Fleet Market in its place, 1755.

> beautiful terminus to the Grand Canal that was formed after the Great Fire of 1666 by the cutting and embanking of the River Fleet from Holborn to the Thames. The whole of these bridges is now hidden … and of the thousands who still daily pass over them perhaps there is scarcely one who has ever heard of their existence.

John Stow, a contemporary of William Shakespeare, in his *Survey of London*, written in 1598, gives us a window into the life of the Fleet in his time:

> Anciently, until the conqueror's time, and two hundred years after, the City of London was watered, besides the famous river of Thames on the south part. With the river of Wells, as it was then called, on the west.
>
> In the west suburbs was also another great water, called oldborne, which had its fall into the river of Wells; then there were three principal fountains, or wells in the other suburbs.
>
> Records show that in 1397, during the reign of Edward 1, Henry Lacey, earl of Lincoln, complained that whereas in times past the course of the water, running at London, under 'Oldborne Bridge' and 'Fleet Bridge' into the Thames, had been of such breadth and depth

Course of the Fleet River and its tributaries.

that ten or twelve ships' navies at once, with merchandise, were wont to come to the foresaid bridge of Fleete, and some of them to Oldborne Bridge: now the same course by filth of the tanners and such others, was sore decayed; also by raising of wharfs; but especially, by diversion of the water made by them of the new Temple for their mills standing without Baynardes Castle, in the first year of King John, and diverse others impediments, so as the said ships could not enter as they were wont, and as they ought: wherefore he desired that the mayor of London with the sheriffs and other discreet Aldermen, might be appointed to view the course of the said water, and that by the oaths of good men, all the aforesaid hindrances might be removed, and it to be made as it was wont of old.

Whereupon Roger le Brabason, the constable of the Tower, with the mayor and sheriffs were assigned to take with them honest and discreet men, and to make diligent search and enquiry, how the said river was in old time, and that they leave nothing that may hurt or stop it but keep it in the same state as it was wont to be.

Whereupon it followed that the said river was at that time cleansed, these mills removed, and other things done for the preservation of the course thereof. Notwithstanding never brought to the old breadth and depth; whereupon the name of the river ceased and it was called a brook, namely Turnmill or Tremill brook, for that divers mills were erected upon it as appeareth by a fair-registerbook.

This brook hath been divers times since cleansed, namely, and last of all to any effect in the year 1502. The whole course of the Fleete Dike, then so called was scowered I say down to the Thames so that boats with fish and fuel were rowed to Fleete Bridge, and to Oldborne Bridge, as they of old time had been accustomed, which was a great commodity to all inhabitants in that part of the City.

CHURCHES

The Anglican Parish of St Andrew included a number of other churches. St Etheldreda's in Ely Place was for most its life a Catholic place of worship. St Peter's in Saffron Hill was established in the 19th century when the parish was divided into two.

St Peter's Church, 1941.

St Peter's Church, Saffron Hill.

ST ANDREW'S CHURCH, HOLBORN

The Church of St Andrew has stood for well over a thousand years in a prominent position next to the old Roman road to the west of the City of London. It is a familiar landmark for us today just to the south of Hatton Garden. When looking for Hatton Garden on an old map or its whereabouts, it is easier to start with the church and work northwards from there.

It is first mentioned in AD 959 in a charter granted by King Edgar. At that time there were very few houses west of London as most people lived within the protection of the city walls. It is most likely that the church was originally built as a wayside chapel or an oratory where travellers could pray for safety as they set out on their journeys. At that time, it was constructed from wooden logs. It wasn't until the 13th century that it was built in stone.

Perhaps one of the most significant dates in its early history was in September 1348 when the church received a large bequest from John Thavie (Tavy) of funds and nearby property. John Thavie was a citizen of London and a well-known armourer. It is recorded that he 'left a considerable Estate towards the support of the fabric forever'.

St Andrew's Church.

St Andrew's Church.

Interior of St Andrew's Church.

THE WEST END OF ST. ANDREW'S, SHOWING THE GOTHIC ARCH.

The west end of St Andrew's Church.

This legacy provided more than enough funding to look after all the foreseeable needs of the church for a long time to come. Somehow, it avoided confiscation during the Reformation. Careful and prudent investment has meant that the fund can still provide for the church today. The name of Thavie can also be found at Thavie's Inn in Holborn but this was named after a different person.

In the mid-15th century the west tower was added, and the church was expanded. The whole church was very nearly destroyed in 1666 when the Great Fire of London swept away all that was before it. It was only a last-minute change in the wind direction that spared it. Sir Christopher Wren had been retained to rebuild most of the city churches destroyed in the fire and in 1686 it was decided to rebuild St Andrew's as it was in such a poor state of repair. Wren built on the original foundations and the vaulted crypt is still visible today. The tower was preserved, and its stone structure can be seen inside the church. This was the largest of his parish churches. The building costs came to £9,000, which would be in excess of £13 million today.

The tower with which we are familiar today came into being when, in 1793, the original was extended to create a bell tower and the Portland stone cladding was added. It is 110 feet tall and has 188 steps within its narrow spiral staircase. From the top it is possible to see Alexandra Palace, about 6 miles to the north.

Soon after this, at the beginning of the 19th century, Joseph Henry Good was employed by the fabric committee to improve the interior. Among other things, he built a new gallery at the west end of the church.

Then towards the end of the century, there was an unprecedented upheaval when the Holborn Valley Improvement scheme was announced. This involved the clearing of hundreds of homes, which were mostly slums, the building of Holborn Viaduct and the new Farringdon Street. The direct impact on St Andrew's was that the Parish Court House and Rectory had to be demolished and furthermore the north churchyard was acquired by the developers. This involved the exhumation and reburial of thousands of human remains. They were all reinterred at the City of London Cemetery in Ilford. The compensation provided enabled the building of a new Court House and facilities in Andrew Street.

St Andrew's had many well-known patrons. In 1618, the leading Elizabethan herbalist and close friend of Shakespeare, John Gerard, was buried here. St Andrew's buried Christopher Merret, too – an English scientist, who was one of the first to study the creation of sparkling wine.

During the Civil War, the Rector, John Hacket, persisted in using the Book of Common Prayer. One day, Roundhead soldiers arrived at the Church and held a pistol to Hacket's head. He simply replied: 'I am doing my duty. Now do yours.' The soldiers departed with Hacket victorious and unscathed. This rebellious spirit must have been passed on to Dr Henry Sacheverell, incumbent 1714–24. He was a prominent High Church Anglican

Left: Interior of St Andrew's Church after the Blitz, 1958. Right: St Andrew's Church before the construction of the viaduct, 1866.

and the bane of the Whig Party. His subversive sermons, in which he undermined the government, led to riots (known as the Sacheverell Riots, which were instrumental in the introduction of the 1714 Riot Act) and eventually earned him impeachment and a trial.

Marc Brunel, father of Isambard Kingdom, was married here in 1799, while Benjamin Disraeli was christened at the church in 1817 at the age of 12, after his father renounced Judaism.

John Stanley (1712–1786) was organist here from the age of 14 and died nearby in Hatton Garden. He became a governor of the Foundling Hospital after George Frederick Handel's death and continued the tradition of performing the Messiah for the Hospital.

The church is also the resting place of Thomas Coram, who established the Foundling Hospital. Charles Dickens mentions St Andrew's in *Oliver Twist*, in which Bill Sykes looks up at St Andrew's tower.

Having escaped the Great Fire, the church sadly succumbed to the German bombing of London in the Second World War. On 16th April 1941, it was hit by an incendiary bomb, which destroyed everything but the exterior walls, crypt and tower. There was discussion as to whether the site should be cleared and used for other purposes, but good sense won through. Perhaps the Thavie legacy helped the decision.

The rebuilding took many years, but the church was finally reconsecrated in 1961. The architects, Seely and Paget, kept as close as possible to the original Wren design. However, life had changed and fewer people lived in the parish. St Andrew's became a City Guild Church with a mission to look after those working in the area instead of those living there. The crypt has recently been cleared with a view to using the space. A small part of it remains a storage area for old furniture and an empty lead coffin dating from 1450.

Visitors to the church might appreciate many of its interesting features but of particular note is the organ, located at the west end. The casing was removed from the chapel of the Foundling Hospital in Bloomsbury, as was the pulpit and the font.

Above the doorway of the west door, below the tower, are two statues of school children in their blue uniforms. These are the originals removed from the St Andrew's Charity School's north entrance carved by one of Wren's craftsmen. The school was located on the corner of St Cross Street and Hatton Garden. Today it is a business premises but still features two similar models over the entrance on Hatton Garden.

William Marsden 1796–1867.

The church also has a close association with the Royal Free Hospital. It was on the steps of the church in 1827 that William Marsden, a newly qualified surgeon, discovered a young destitute woman dying of a malignant disease and exposure. He was unable to get assistance from any hospital as they were selective of their clientele, mostly based on their ability to pay. It would be over a hundred years before the National Health Service would have been able to help.

Marsden was so moved by her death that he set up a new hospital at 16 Greville Street to cater for those who were unable to pay. It was called the 'London General Institution for the Gratuitous Care of Malignant Diseases'. Marsden's founding principle was that he would take in anyone who needed treatment – the first hospital in London to do so and the only London hospital to stay open during the 19th-century cholera epidemics. The hospital received its royal charter from Queen Victoria in 1837 by way of recognition for its painstaking work in the treatment of cholera. The hospital subsequently became known as the Royal Free and is now located in Hampstead.

The significance of St Andrew's on the lives of those who lived nearby is captured in a poem called 'The Bells of St Andrew's Holborn', from *Rambles with an American* by Mills & Boon:

They rang their message of weal or woe
In the days of Romish pride:
They caught a gleam of the fires below,
When the Smithfield martyrs died.
They rang for feast, and they rang for fast:
They rang for the Roses twain,
Ere the Red Rose scattered, and fell at last,
In the mire of the Barnet plain.
And lo, they rang for a mite today,
Who chewed at his fist the while,
Or wriggled about with his arms at play,
And a quaint little toothless smile!
In years to come, you will understand,
And blush at the humour done –
They rang for Warwick the Kingmaker;
And they rang for YOU, my son!

They rang at first over stream and dell
Where the nodding Alder shook,
And toilers bowed to the vesper bell,
As they rowed on Turnmill Brook;
When Ely's lord had a fair demesne
With chapel and gatehouse, too,
And Saffron Hill was an upland green

Where the purple saffron grew.
They rang the obit of bishop and priest:
They rang for his majesty's grace,
When Henry rode to the serjeants' feast
In the Hall of Ely Place.
The same old bells in the same old tower,
Good sooth as records run!
They rang for King Hal and Queen Katherine:
And they rang for YOU my son!

Pealing and tolling from year to year,
They hailed the centuries through,
Hero or sovereign, abbot or peer
Ere ever they rang for you –
You, such an image to favour the joke,
Fidgeting there on your spine,
Such a hot little shrimp in the christening cloak
Your grandmother thinks so fine!
Sucking a fist that is pudgy and soft,
Working your bonnet awry,
Deaf as a post to the clamour aloft,
Though the great bells clash on high:
All Holborn astir with their music:
And you such a figure of fun –
They rang for the Nile and Trafalgar:
And they rang for YOU my son.

ST ETHELDREDA'S

Located in the quiet backwater that is Ely Place, St Etheldreda's Church is rich in history. It is the only surviving part of what was once the Palace of the Bishops of Ely and part of the home of Sir Christopher Hatton. The church continues not only to be a spiritual sanctuary preserving the tradition laid down by centuries of worshippers but also a venue for corporate events or private hire.

For over 300 years Ely House and its chapel were home to a succession of twenty-one Roman Catholic Bishops. It was established about 1250, when John le Franceis obtained a licence from the Dean of St Paul's, who owned the land, to build an oratory. It claims to be the oldest Catholic church in the country and one of only two remaining buildings from the reign of Edward I.

Completed in 1290, it was erected on the site of the oratory, which had been built over an earlier Roman structure, the remains of which have been traced at one end

John Moore, Bishop of Norwich and Ely.

of the crypt. Originally owned by John de Kirkeby, the Bishop of Ely and Treasurer of the Kingdom, the estate was left to the future Bishops of Ely to enjoy and remained outside London for at least another 300 years.

It is said that the crypt and the church above are on slightly different orientations. On St Etheldreda's Day, 6th June, the sun rises in line with the nave.

Bishops had London homes to enable them to attend Parliament and they had jurisdiction within these confines such as they enjoyed at home. As such, they were known as liberties and a felon could escape the civil law by entering the liberty.

The church is named in memory and recognition of St Etheldreda or Aethelfryth, whose name is sometimes known as Audrey. She was a princess and an influential member of the ruling family of East Anglia. She was born around AD 630 and was the daughter of Anna, Saxon King of East Anglia, a devout Catholic and godly man. She aspired to be a nun but was persuaded to marry. However, it was a condition of the marriage that she should remain celibate. Her first marriage in 652 to Tondbert was brief as he died young, but she received as a wedding gift the land that was known as the Isle of Eels. Today it is the City of Ely in Cambridgeshire. Her father then arranged for her to marry Prince Egfrith, heir to the Kingdom of Northumbria. This was a marriage of political convenience and it was agreed that she could remain a virgin. This worked for several years, with Etheldreda living a separate life. However, after he became king, Egfrith wanted his queen to be part of the Court. When she did not respond, he went after her and she managed to escape, travelling south to Ely.

The years spent under the tutelage of St Wilfred and St Cuthbert and her time at Lindisfarne stood her in good stead. She settled in the Isle of Ely as it was then, where she established a religious community, becoming the abbess. She rebuilt the church, originally established by St Augustine, that had been destroyed by war. She was noted for her frugal and exemplary lifestyle and is remembered for liberating the bondsmen on her land.

She died on 23rd June 679, from a tumour in her throat. After her death she was still revered by her people. Many who had been blessed believed that it was her intercession in heaven that had helped them, particularly in matters of chastity and throat complaints.

St Etheldreda's Church, 1815.

Fifteen years after her burial, it was decided to move her body to a more fitting marble tomb in Canterbury Cathedral. Her followers were amazed to discover that her body was still in perfect condition. Her abbey in Ely was destroyed by the Danes in AD 870.

Then, in 1106, the Normans built the present Norman Cathedral in Ely, and her body, still not decomposed, was once again reinterred in an old Roman coffin. The tumour in her neck, reportedly, had been healed. A shrine was built in the cathedral, but it was destroyed at the time of the Reformation in the 16th century by Thomas Goodrich, the first Anglican Archbishop of Canterbury. Her body was lost, but in the 19th century one of her hands was discovered in Arundel Castle, Sussex. This relic is now housed in St Etheldreda's Church, in Ely Place.

There remains a memorial to her in Ely Cathedral today in the form of a stone bearing the inscription:

> HERE STOOD THE SHRINE OF ETHELDREDA,
> SAINT AND QUEEN, WHO FOUNDED THIS HOUSE AD 673

She continues to be held in high esteem by many and pilgrimages are made to her shrine in Ely. Cheap necklaces of silk and lace were sold at St Audrey's Fair as talismans. Our word tawdry is derived from this origin.

The chapel in London survived a troubled period during the Reformation, losing its Catholic status in 1559. The Mass, which had been celebrated in England since the coming of Christianity, was abolished. To participate in the Catholic Mass became punishable by hanging and priests had to hide. The Mass was replaced by the Book of Common Prayer. Those who wanted to see a more puritan look in the churches set about destroying the shrines and the medieval stained-glass windows. The crucifixes were burned in bonfires in Smithfield.

John Houghton was the Carthusian Prior of the London Charterhouse just across the Fleet from Ely Palace and St Etheldreda's. He and his monks were selected by King Henry VIII as an example and as vengeance for their obstruction to his marriage plans. Whether this was because they were devoted to their faith or their monastery was particularly wealthy is not certain. Houghton and two peers, Robert Lawrence and Augustine Webster, were expected to sign an oath of allegiance to the King as head of the Church of England. This Act of Supremacy was designed to put the King in place of the Pope. Despite their appeal and reasoning, they were taken to the Tower and on 4th May 1535 led out to their gruesome execution. They were tied to wicker bundles and dragged to Tyburn. They were hung there in front of a large crowd, wearing their monks' habits, a sight that had not previously been seen. Not yet dead, their organs and intestines were cut out and burned. Their corpses were then beheaded and quartered. John Houghton's arm was nailed to the door of Charterhouse as a warning to others. He and four others are commemorated in the great west window of St Etheldreda's.

The opportunity came when the descendants of Charles Cole, the developer, had to sell off their assets. It took a further twenty years to achieve the task and apart from the architectural restoration the building became a Catholic chapel once again. In December 1873, it was announced that the church was to be sold at public auction.

The auction proved to be a triumph for the 'Rosminians', who were keen to serve the strong Italian community and needy of the area. Against stiff competition from the Welsh Episcopalians, who had the backing of a Welsh steel magnate, they won. Unfortunately for the Welsh, they mistook the agent acting for the Rosminians as their own. They therefore stopped bidding when he had bid £5,400 only to discover their mistake after the hammer fell.

It was recorded that the next day the Welsh clergyman called on Father William Lockhart of the Rosminians and offered him a considerably higher sum than was bid, but he declined. 'Well, Sir,' said the clergyman, 'I'm sorry to have lost the old place but this I will say – I'm glad it has passed into your hands for you will, I have no doubt, restore it in a way that we never could.'

Father Lockhart launched an immediate restoration appeal. Money poured in. He then began years of extensive and costly restoration.

It was Father Lockhart who decided to repair the crypt. First, he had to attend to the floor, which was made of hard earth trampled in over the centuries. And they had to remove about 2½ feet of earth. In the course of digging, they came across eighteen bodies, which were victims of the Fatal Vespers of 1623, and we know that one of those concerned was a priest because he was buried facing west.

The upper church was then restored with all the splendour intended by its medieval builders. The balconies and other 18th-century additions were removed. The plaster ceiling was brought down, amid what was described as 'inconceivable filth', to reveal the original medieval roof surviving virtually intact.

The royal coat of arms, which had been hanging over the main altar since the reign of Charles I, was removed and placed in the cloister. Since Elizabethan times, such royal emblems had been ordered to be hung in churches to repudiate the authority of Rome and the successor of St Peter.

It was on 23rd June 1878 that solemn High Mass was celebrated again, the first time in 200 years. The church continued to thrive under Father Lockhart.

In the Great War of 1914–1918 the church became a Mecca for US servicemen on their way to the battlefields of Europe.

In 1925, it was recognised as an 'Ancient Monument' by the Royal Commission for Ancient Monuments.

Then, in the Second World War of 1939–1945, the crypt was used as an air-raid shelter. An anti-aircraft shell fell at 20 Ely Place, missing the church. On the night of 11th May 1941, however, during one of the worst nights of the Blitz, the roof was hit and the glass in the windows destroyed.

Father Baines was the parish priest at the time, and he kept a parish diary of those years. In November 1940, he wrote:

> During the last half of the year night raids became frequent and much damage was done to property with considerable loss of life. The building opposite St Etheldreda's suffered a direct hit.

An entry in the diary of 10th and 11th May of the following year says:

> On Saturday night another long disastrous raid. St Etheldreda's was hit by an explosive bomb which tore a hole in the original roof about six feet in diameter, stripped a good part of the tiling off the roof and sent three beams hurtling to the floor of the Church. The explosion also blew out what was left of the stained-glass windows ... a number of people were in the Crypt when the bomb fell but mercifully no one was injured.

A new thriving London rose on the bomb sites surrounding St Etheldreda's. Seven years were needed to repair the bomb damage to the ancient Chapel. The great east window made by Joseph Lutyens and completed in 1952 reflects all the original medieval splendour.

THE ITALIAN CATHOLIC CHURCH OF ST PETER

The Italian Catholic Church of St Peter, on Clerkenwell Road, was dedicated on 16th April 1863 by Cardinal Wiseman of Westminster. It was the largest Catholic Church in the country at the time. Westminster Cathedral wasn't completed until 1903.

It was originally conceived as an international church serving all communities, but soon after its opening sermons in English were banned. It took two years of petitioning by interested parties to lift the ban. Confessions were subsequently heard in English, French, German and Spanish for all Catholics. In 1878, Mass in Polish was also offered.

One event in particular has been recorded as it is somewhat bizarre. In January 1880, during the course of Mass, a member of the congregation fired a pistol at the Chaplain, thankfully missing him. The assailant rushed to the security of the sacristy, shutting himself in. Two further shots were fired, both missing their target. In the uproar that followed, candles were knocked over, setting fire to the altar cloth. The gunman was overpowered and disarmed by the congregation, then marched off to Clerkenwell Police Court. The would-be assassin was called Schloss and came from Milan. He lived at No. 37 Great Saffron Hill. On 11th February 1880 he was convicted of premeditated murder and sentenced to life imprisonment.

Apart from its religious function, the church served as a hub for the community, offering a form of labour exchange, especially for the transient population. It also ran a school teaching both English and Italian languages. Italians came from across London either to worship there or to benefit from its social programme.

During the Second World War when Italians were interned the church was used by an Irish group of worshippers but it was returned to the Italian community in 1953.

TIBI·DABO·CLAVES·REGNI·CŒLORVM

The church continues an annual tradition dating back to 1883. On the first Sunday after 16th July they celebrate 'Our Lady of Mount Carmel'. A long procession is held in and around the vicinity of the church. Thousands of Italians come to be part of this great event. When it was instigated, it was the first Roman Catholic festival to be celebrated in the UK since the Reformation.

From the early days of St Peter's, music has been a very important feature of the church's agenda. Concerts designed as fundraisers were held to defray the huge construction costs and subsequently the ongoing maintenance and ministry of the building. The orchestra and choir were made up of distinguished musicians and soloists who were employed in the West End. The high standard of their concerts attracted both Catholic and Protestant audiences. Tickets were often hard to come by and attracted the well-heeled from all over London.

Festival of Our Lady of Mount Carmel.

Opposite: St Peter's Italian Church.

St Peter's Italian Church.

St Peter's Italian Church, *The Builder Magazine*, 1863.

THE HATTON CHAPEL

There were also several Nonconformist churches and chapels. The yards at the back of the houses offered the opportunity for small meeting rooms.The Hatton Chapel or Trinity Chapel was built in 1667 for the Nonconformist minister John Turner. It was located at the rear of 75–77 Hatton Garden and was approached by a narrow passage between 26 and 27 Leather Lane. In the 18th century it became a centre of Calvinistic Methodism. It was later known as the Wesleyan Mission House. William Thomas Brown (1821–1899) entered service here. He cared for Spanish sailors visiting the port of London and learnt Spanish. He subsequently requested the missionary committee to send him to Spain, which they agreed. The building was demolished in the second quarter of the 19th century.

Hatton Chapel.

Hatton Chapel after the fire, 1914.

The reredos from the Hatton Chapel, *c*.1690.

A letter to the Wesleyan Mission House behind 77 Hatton Garden, 1840.

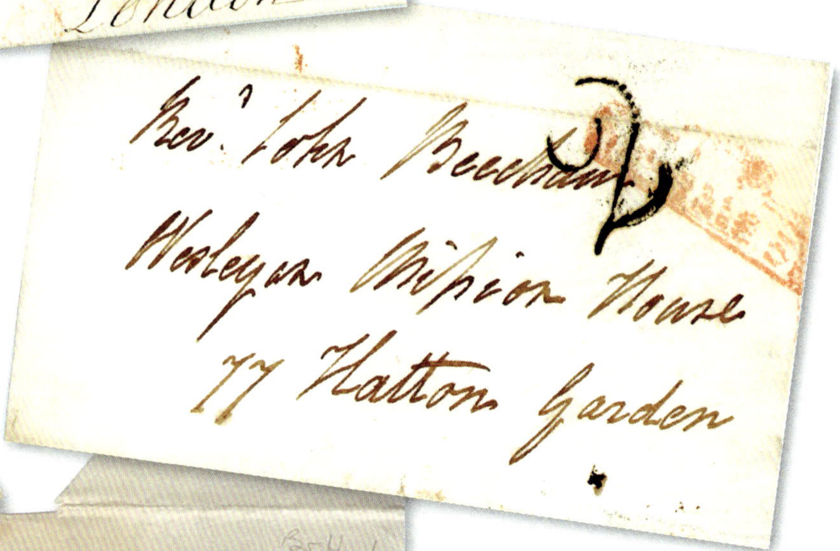

A letter to the Wesleyan Mission House behind 77 Hatton Garden.

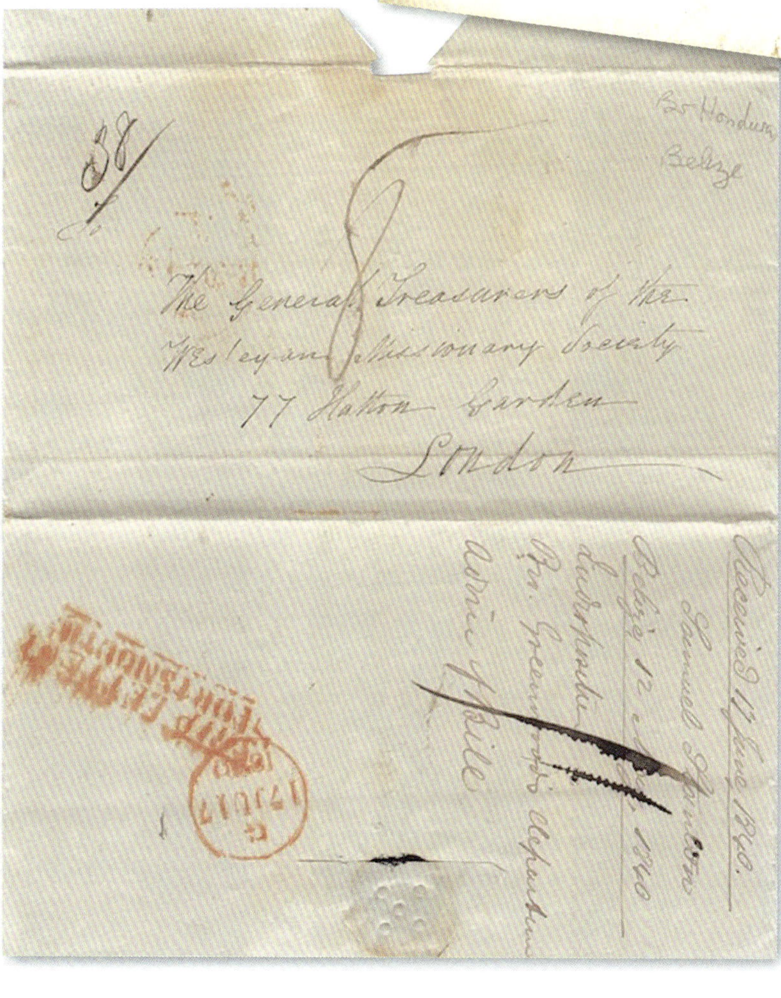

Letter to The Wesleyan Mission House behind 77 Hatton Garden, 1840.

THE NEW JERUSALEM CHAPEL

At the end of the 18th century the 'New Jerusalem Chapel' of Swedenborgian was set up in Cross St, but in 1797 it was licensed to the Independents. The building was used as a warehouse (1930) before being destroyed by a serious fire. Chapel House now stands on the site.

New Jerusalem Chapel.

THE CALEDONIAN CHURCH

The Caledonian Church in Cross Street was led by Reverend Edward Irving (1792–1834), a Scottish clergyman generally regarded as the main figure behind the foundation of the Catholic Apostolic Church. He had little success in converting the Scottish public and was about to give up hope and focus his attention towards missionary labour in the Far East when he suddenly had an invitation from the Caledonian Church in London; over that charge he was ordained in 1822. The church then became very fashionable, with people coming from all over London. His sermons were so popular that tickets were issued.

Other popular preachers of the time were 'Praise God Barebones', who lived on the north side of Holborn, and 'Thankful Owen', who lived in Hatton Garden at the time of his death in 1861.

Until the Education Act of 1870 the churches had a major role in the education of children. St Andrew's Church School has records back to 1609. In 1721, it acquired the lease to a part-finished church building situated on the corner of St Cross Street and Hatton Garden. The rent was £40 per annum. Children of the underprivileged, servants and poor, were admitted at the age of 8 and left at 14. In 1712 there were eighty boys and eighty girls.

The freehold was obtained in 1862 for £1800. On the outside above the entrance are the figures of two charity children, identical to those on the tower of St Andrew's Church. It is now a grade II-listed building, as are its railings. Although now used as offices, a new building has been constructed within the original shell.

THE CHAPEL OF THE HOLY FAMILY

At 141–142 Saffron Hill, the Chapel of the Holy Family was established in 1854. A school was attached but the priest found it almost impossible to attend. Various leisure activities and a guild of the Holy Family were established to try to deter the congregation from the viciousness of the public houses and dancing halls found in the area of Saffron Hill. In 1861 the priest reported that the church was so packed, people were kneeling in the doorway.

RAGGED LONDON

A look at the history of Hatton Garden and this part of London would not be complete without reference to the poverty that blighted the area. From its foundation and throughout the following centuries, destitution has never been far away. Overcrowding had long been a problem, but many other factors contributed to the life of misery and squalor that was the lot for the thousands of people who lived there.

As the city grew and spread itself outside its original Roman walls, tradesmen found it to their advantage to free themselves from the restrictions and regulations imposed upon them by their guilds and Livery Companies. They found cheaper accommodation in areas like Holborn and Clerkenwell, which had become the overspill from the city. There was also migration to the capital from the country and immigration from overseas. Many of the newcomers found themselves having to live in areas like Saffron Hill. Furthermore, the Great Fire of 1666 had displaced many families from within the city, compounding the problem.

Originally constructed in the late 17th century, these so-called 'thieves' houses' attracted all manner of illicit activity from thieves and pickpockets to prostitution. Most inhabitants rented a room or a bed and there was no sense of ownership or the responsibility that goes with it. The cellar was normally used to dispose of the household rubbish and waste and the foul smell would have permeated the floorboards, causing the house to be rank. The sleeping area above would have been accessed by ladder and beds would be packed in side by side, offering nothing but a space to lay down, although in practice many shared a bed with one or two others or even more in the case of children and families. It was said that keepers of the lodging houses bought cheap second-hand furniture that was known to include items from hospitals where people had died of the diseases that were rampant at that time.

The construction of the buildings left much to be desired. Today we would almost call it a 'shanty town'. Maintenance didn't exist. Missing roof tiles, broken windows and crumbling bricks all added to the look of abandonment and dereliction. The narrow, unmade streets would have compounded the poor health and the lack of proper sanitation led to disease. Access was very restricted as there were little or no planning regulations and it was normal to duck and dive through doorways and archways, which is why they were so well suited to felons escaping the law. The trap doors and holes in walls, hidden cellars and loft spaces were used as escape routes.

They were described later by an eyewitness in 1844 as:

> The most ingenious and extraordinary part of the premises, I consider to be the means of escape. If a prisoner once got within their walls, it was almost impossible to capture him, there were so many outlets and communications. The most active officer had scarcely a chance of taking the thief if the latter only got a few minutes start on him.

Criminals found the Rookeries an ideal place to dispose of stolen goods and they were the home of such notorious characters as Jack Sheppard, Jonathan Wild and Dick Turpin in the 18th century.

Such were the appalling conditions in the Saffron Hill area that when in 1801 the Parish Council met to determine the 'poor rate' they seriously considered whether or not it would be possible or even desirable to levy rates upon the inhabitants at all. The Parish Clerk gave notice of the meetings as follows:

> The inhabitants of the Liberty of Saffron Hill, Hatton Garden and Ely Rents in this Parish are desired to meet at the workhouse upon Little Saffron Hill on Thursday next at Three O'clock in the Afternoon precisely to make a rate for relief of the poor of the said liberty.

The above notice was published in the Parish Church of St Andrew, Holborn on the morning of Sunday, 20th December 1801 immediately after Divine Service, by Reverend Perry, the Parish Clerk.

It was decided to impose a 'poor rate' on the unfortunate inhabitants but it proved almost impossible to collect. A notice issued by the Chairman of the Saffron Hill & Ely Place Committee read as follows:

> The Ely Place committee deem it very Essential that you direct your collectors IMMEDIATELY to demand the two rates assessed on the inhabitants of Ely Place, and beg to inform you that it is necessary that such demand be made before Michaelmas Day next, and that you allow him to leave printed notices at each house, stating the said demand.
> I am Gentlemen, On behalf of the said Committee
> Your obedient servant
> BI Armstrong, Chairman, Workhouse Saffron Hill
> 24th September 1829.

Two areas of London were regarded as the worst to live: one was St Giles in the Fields and the other was Saffron Hill. The squalor of these areas was unimaginable. The slums spread from Kirby Street, through Saffron Hill and across the Fleet Ditch towards the east and ranged from Holborn Bridge in the south to Vine Street in the north.

Such places were known as 'Rookeries' because of the overcrowding and the necessity to find your own space between others in small confines already at bursting point. The inhabitants were commonly referred to as 'the great unwashed' as there was next to no facilities for hygiene or sanitation.

Thomas Beames, in *The Rookeries of London, 1850* called it:

> a squalid neighbourhood between HOLBORN and CLERKENWELL, densely inhabited by poor people and thieves. It runs from Field Lane into Vine Street. The Clergymen of St Andrew's, Holborn, have been obliged, when visiting it, to be accompanied by policemen in plain clothes.

Charles Dickens describes the area in *Oliver Twist* (1837):

> Near to the spot on which Saffron Hill and Holborn Hill meet, there opens, upon the right hand as you come out of the City, a narrow and dismal alley leading to Saffron Hill. In its filthy shops are exposed for sale huge bunches of second-hand silk handkerchiefs, of all sizes and patterns, for here reside the traders who purchase them from pickpockets. Confined as the limits of Field Lane are, it has its barber, its coffee shop, its beer shop, and its fried fish warehouse. Here, stores of old iron and bones, and heaps of mildew fragments of woolen stuff and linen, rust and rot in the grimy cellars.

A large number of the fences operating were typically Jewish, according to observers of the time. It is widely believed that the character of Fagin in *Oliver Twist* was based on a real-life character in Saffron Hill, known to Dickens. Characters like Bill Sykes and the Artful Dodger had real-life counterparts in these rookeries.

Towards the middle of the 19th century there was a large influx of Italians. They had an influence on the character of the area and it was mainly for the better. The Italians brought with them their skills in ice cream making, and entertainment.

Opera singers, barrel organists with monkeys, folk singers, clowns and dancers, all brought a new vibrancy to the scene. Their colourful lifestyle and community spirit firmly established this part of London as 'Little Italy' and although most immigrants gradually resettled elsewhere, the identity of the district remained intact until the Second World War.

In some instances, they brought with them skills in instrument making, both musical and optical, some of which would have contributed to the micro-engineering employed in the manufacture of jewellery. Jewellers and opticians have long since been bedfellows and can still be found together in remote parts of the country today.

There were long debates in Victorian times as to the cause and effect of the poverty and crime. Not everyone who lived in this district was a criminal, even though they lived alongside such people. Some had gainful employment and the district became the home to printers, cabmen, dustmen, sellers of fruit and watercress and crossing sweepers.

By the middle of the 19th century, living conditions had reached an all-time low and were about to experience a major transformation with the construction of the Metropolitan Railway from Paddington to Farringdon, and the building of Clerkenwell Road, Farringdon Road and Holborn Viaduct. The demolition of the Rookeries and slum clearance allowed the area to be made safer and perhaps the timing was right to allow the advent of a more legitimate diamond and jewellery trade into the area.

FIELD LANE RAGGED SCHOOL

In the middle of the 19th century, the area to the east of Hatton Garden, which included Saffron Hill, Field Lane and West Street, was one of absolute squalor. The deprivation and poverty led young unschooled children into a life of crime.

Such accommodation that there was, was fearfully overcrowded with several families to a room, no sanitation, rats and cockroaches in profusion. It was said that the police would not go there at night and even in the daytime they would go in pairs.

So, it was with great compassion that a young missionary by the name of Andrew Provan decided that he should do something about it. He had come to this part of London in 1841 and had been horrified by what he saw.

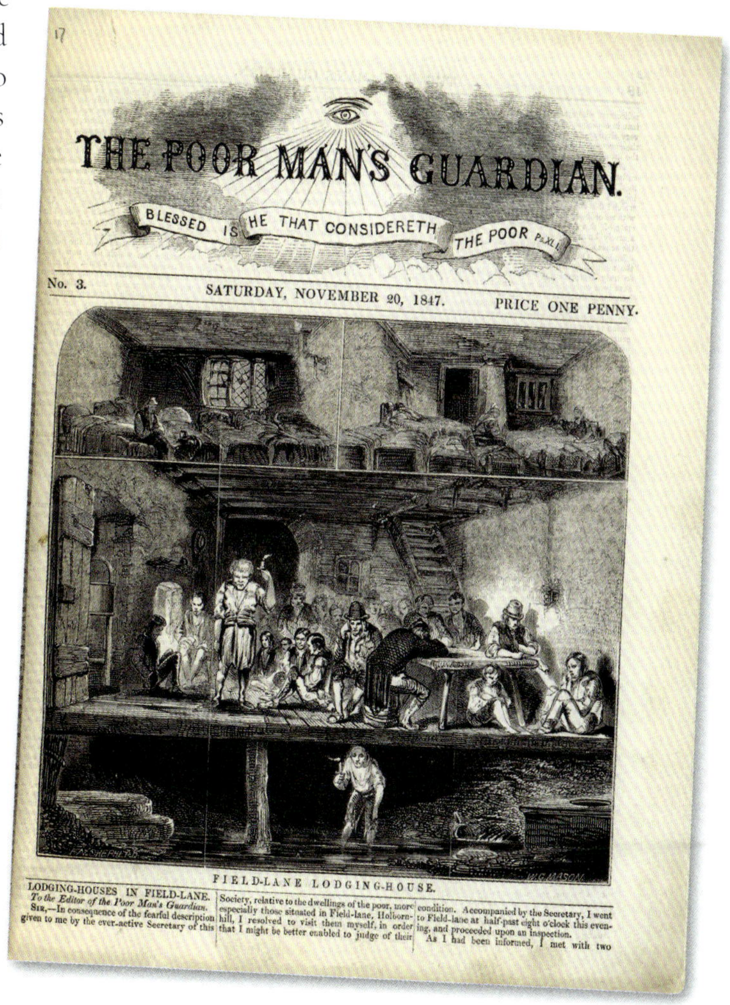
THE POOR MAN'S GUARDIAN.

BLESSED IS HE THAT CONSIDERETH THE POOR Ps. XLI.

No. 3. SATURDAY, NOVEMBER 20, 1847. PRICE ONE PENNY.

FIELD-LANE LODGING-HOUSE.

LODGING-HOUSES IN FIELD-LANE.

To the Editor of the Poor Man's Guardian.

SIR,—In consequence of the fearful description given to me by the ever-active Secretary of this Society, relative to the dwellings of the poor, more especially those situated in Field-lane, Holborn-hill, I resolved to visit them myself, in order that I might be better enabled to judge of their condition. Accompanied by the Secretary, I went to Field-lane at half-past eight o'clock this evening, and proceeded upon an inspection.

As I had been informed, I met with two

Field Lane Ragged School.

Without any education the children were doomed to scraping out an existence in a life of crime as their parents had done before them. However, respectable society would not allow such dirty, ragged children near their schools. Education was then a privilege of the rich and state education wasn't compulsory until the 1880s. The only way to help these unfortunate children was for Provan to teach them himself. So, he hired a room and on the afternoon of Sunday, 7th November 1841 he started the Field Lane Sabbath School. Forty-five children came along, sat on the floor and listened to his teaching.

However, his efforts weren't always well received. He received abuse and hostility from those he was trying to help and was often discouraged. A contemporary and supporter has left us his record of what he saw:

> In the year 1842, I was led to visit the Field Lane Sabbath School, then lately commenced, where I witnessed a scene so foreign to anything I had ever before experienced or heard of that it made an impression on my mind never to be effaced. On opening the door to the school, then housed in a miserable Court in Saffron Hill, a motley group of half-clad youths rushed up the rickety staircase into a small apartment, some 10 feet square and commenced leaping upon and overturning the forms which stood in their way; others showed their daring agility by descending from the first floor window into the yard beneath, whilst the remainder evinced their love of fun and mischief by blowing out the lights and giving ever and anon a specimen of their vocal talents by a shouting chorus of some low and popular song; when however, some order was obtained and the two teachers present endeavoured to impart instruction with candle in hand, they were obliged to keep on their hats for protection from the rotten vegetables and animal refuse which the rebels without were continually throwing through the broken windows.
>
> Such scenes lasted more or less for several months until the following circumstance brought matters to a crisis. The school at this time was open on Tuesday evenings for females, and Thursday for males. One Tuesday evening, being at the school prior to the arrival of the superintendent, I was engaged in admitting the young women and girls, when I was surprised by a woman coming hastily into the passage of the house and beckoning me to close the door. As soon as she had recovered her breath, she informed me that she had overheard a number of young men state that they intended coming to the school that evening to have a lark, and if the teacher interfered, they would 'rip him up'. One having attempted on previous occasion to stab the Superintendent; the threat was deemed no vain one. Ere, however, she had finished her tale, the door was surrounded by men, who, on its being opened civilly asked to be admitted, but the unfairness of the females was pointed out as it would deprive them of their usual night of instruction. Arguments were to no avail; therefore, the door was closed and bolted, and I ascended to the schoolroom on the first floor, which was filled with women and children. I had, however, scarcely entered, when a loud crash and a general rush up the dilapidated stairs, gave note of their triumph, and the room was crammed with the denizens of the neighbouring lane. Fearing the consequences, I determined to send the children away; and whilst so engaged,

at a given signal the lights were extinguished, the window smashed, the forms and tables broken to pieces and a general rush took place to the stairs with the movable articles of the room. Here the screaming, swearing and uproar, as they fell pell-mell over one another, was tremendous. At this time the landlords lay in an adjoining room in a dying state. His wife and two young children, the only other inmates, supplied fresh lights, but these were blown out immediately afterwards. After considerable difficulty the house was cleared, but not before the woman was nearly stripped to the back by the rough usage she received. Three policemen now arrived, having heard the 'row'.

Andrew Provan was not deterred by such hostility and developed the school by having more teachers and assistants. The growth of the school put more and more demands on the limited resources of the teachers. In 1843, an advertisement was placed in *The Times* newspaper seeking support. It caught the eye of Lord Ashley (later known as Lord Shaftesbury). He wrote:

> I never read an advertisement with greater pleasure. It answered exactly what I had been looking and hoping for. I could not regard it as other than a direct answer to my fervent prayer.

Field Lane, 1896.

The Ragged School, Vine Hill, 2019.

He wholeheartedly gave his support to the school for over forty years, becoming its president, an office that he held until his death in 1885. He used his influence to bring about changes in legislation.

By 1851, there were over 500 street children and young people receiving daily lessons, all in one very large classroom. Initially, the lessons had been simple but as time went by, they were specifically designed by offering trade skills that might help the students to find employment. Tailoring and shoemaking were taught and an alliance with other schools was formed from which the 'Shoe-blacks Society' was formed. The enterprise raised £500 during the Great Exhibition of 1851 by cleaning 101,000 pairs of shoes.

Charles Dickens also gives us an insight as to the conditions that surrounded the school in its early days. He wrote:

> I found my first ragged school in an obscene place called West Street, Saffron Hill, pitifully struggling for life under every disadvantage. It had no means; it had no suitable rooms; it derived no power or protection from being recognised by any authority; it attracted within its walls a fluctuating swarm of faces – young in years, but youthful in nothing else – that scowled hope out of countenance. It was held in a low-roofed den, in a sickening atmosphere, in the midst of taint and dirt and pestilence; with all the deadly sins let loose, howling and shrieking at the doors. Zeal did not supply the place of method and training; the teachers knew little of their office; the pupils with an evil sharpness, found them out, got the better of them, derided them, made blasphemous answers to Scriptural questions, sang, fought, danced, robbed each other, seemed possessed by a legion of devils. The place was stormed and carried over and over again; the lights were blown out, the books strewn to the gutters, and the female scholars carried off triumphantly to their old wickedness. With no strength but its purpose, the School stood it all out and made its way. Some two years since I found it quiet and orderly, full, lighted with gas, well white-washed, numerously attended and thoroughly established.

Charles Dickens's first visit to the Field Lane Ragged School in 1843 moved him so much that he wrote *A Christmas Carol*. He kept in touch, making donations, and later wrote about the school and his experience in *Household Words*. Dickens's intimate knowledge of this area caused him to write about Bleeding Heart Yard in *Little Dorrit*. Ely Place was the home of Mr Waterbrook in *David Copperfield*, and Jaggers, the solicitor in *Great Expectations*. Fagin's kitchen was supposedly at 144 Saffron Hill. In *Martin Chuzzlewit*, we find Mr Lewsome being nursed by Mrs Gamp at the Black Bull, which at the time was a popular inn on the site where Gamages was later built. Most famous was the Police Court where Oliver Twist went before the 'beak', which was based on the actual Police Court at 52–53 Hatton Garden.

Andrew Provan's care and compassion was not limited to the classroom. He was well aware that many of the problems experienced by the children were as a result of their environment and their family situations. Family breakdown, sickness, unemployment, overcrowding and crime all condemned a young person to an existence that was yet another downward spiral of a life without hope.

The school did all that it could to serve the community in their need. Visiting the sick and distributing maternity baskets and were among the priorities. Night refuges were opened which proved very popular. The school enjoyed the support of many well-known people and became one of the most famous of the ragged schools in London.

Eventually the school merged with other similar schools in London to become the Ragged School Union. In time, this became the Shaftesbury Society and when they merged with John Grooms in 2007, they changed their name to Livability.

Field Lane Ragged School, 1871.

Against the tide, the initiative of Andrew Provan moved forwards. Field Lane night refuge was established in West Street in 1851 for men and boys. A similar refuge was opened in 1857 for women and girls in Hatton Yard. Washing facilities were installed as a gift from Miss Burdett Coutts.

In 1866, the school moved to new and larger premises on the corner of Saffron Hill and Hatton Wall. However, this was to be short-lived for, in 1872, plans were announced to construct the new Clerkenwell Road. The school then moved to Vine Hill in 1878.

The work of those who made great personal sacrifices is summed up in the words of a child who came to Field Lane and went on to give years of faithful voluntary service: 'How grateful we are that we were led to Field Lane, for God was truly in that place.'

Field Lane Charity continues today, helping the vulnerable and the disabled with the same commitment as their Christian founder.

THE FOUNDLING HOSPITAL

When Captain Coram retired from the sea in 1720, he was shocked to see children abandoned and dying on the streets of London. The only option for women who had children born out of wedlock, and no means of support, was to be placed in a parish poorhouse with its high mortality rate. Thomas Coram began a campaign to create a home for these babies, overcoming widespread prejudice about children born outside of marriage.

His campaign began by enlisting the support of leading members of the aristocracy, the City, the arts and the sciences through a series of petitions. Early supporters of his endeavours included the composer Handel, the artist William Hogarth and later, the author Charles Dickens.

Hogarth gave the hospital a full-length portrait of its founder. He also donated a £120 initial subscription and painted a shield to hang over the door of the Hatton Garden building in time for the arrival of the first children. Furthermore, he gave fundraising concerts and his most famous work, 'The Messiah', indirectly benefitted hundreds of children.

Plaque at Ashlyn's School Chapel, Berkhamsted.

In October 1740, a notice appeared on the door of a house in Hatton Garden stating that twenty children under the age of two months would be received there, and that no question would be asked of any person so bringing an infant.

The hospital was London's first home for babies whose mothers were unable to care for them. The very first premises, at 73 and 74 Hatton Garden, were leased from Sir Fisher Dent, at £48 per annum for a period of six years. The first children were admitted to the Foundling Hospital on 25th March 1741.

The announcement that the hospital was 'open for business' captures the plight of those in need of support and the charitable nature of Thomas Coram's vision:

> On Wednesday 25th of this instant March at eight at night and from that time until the house is full, their house over against the Charity School in Hatton Garden will be open for children under the following regulations: that no child exceed in age two months nor shall have the French Pox or disease of like nature; [French Pox was syphilis and so called as there was a serious outbreak in the French Army] all children to be inspected and the person who brings it to come in at the outer door and not go away until the child is returned or notice given of its reception. No question asked whatsoever of any person who brings a child, nor shall any servant of the Hospital presume to enquire on pain of being dismissed ... The narrow circumstances of the Hospital confining Governors to a limited number shall be completed, a notice shall be posted that the house is full. If any particular marks are left with the child great care will be taken for their preservation. Each child will be baptised Church of England by a minister of the Church unless such a child has already been baptised.

Preparations were made for 25th March. Concerns in the Parish of St Andrew that children who were rejected might be left by their mothers and become a charge of the parish led to the involvement of two watchmen and two constables. Inside the house ten governors, including Thomas Coram, waited for the first children. The minutes from the daily committee describe in detail what happened:

> The committee met at 7pm in the evening. They found a great number of people crowding about the door, many with children and others for Curiosity. The committee were informed that several persons had offered children but had been refused admittance. The order of the general committee being that the house sho'd not be opened til 8 pm at night. And this committee was resolved to give no preference to any person whatever ... At eight o'clock the lights in the entry were extinguished, the outward door was opened by the porter, who was forced to attend at that Door all night to keep out the crowd. Immediately the bell rung and a woman brought in a child. The messenger let her into the Room on the right hand, and carried the child into the Steward's room, where the proper officers together with Dr. Nesbitt and some other Governors were constantly attending to inspect the child according to the directions of the plan. The child being inspected was received, numbered and the billet of its description entered by three different persons for greater certainty. The woman who brought the child was dismissed without being seen by any of the Governors or asked

> any questions whatsoever. Immediately another child was brought and so continually until 30 children were admitted 18 of whom were boys and 2 girls being the number the house is capable of containing. Two children were refused, one being too old and the other appearing to have the Itch.
>
> About 12 o'clock the house being full the Porter was ordered to give notice of it to the crowd who were without, who thereupon being a little troublesome, One of the Governors went out, and told them that as many children were already taken in as could be made room for in the house and that notice should be given by Public Advertisement as soon as any more could possibly be admitted. And the governors observing seven or eight women with Children at the door and more amongst the crowd desired them that they wouldn't drop any of their children in the streets where they most probably must perish but take care of them until they could have an opportunity of putting them into hospital which was hoped would be very soon and that everybody would immediately leave the hospital without making any disturbance which was immediately complied with great decency, so that in two minutes there was not a person to be seen in the street except the watch. On this occasion the expressions of grief of the women whose children could not be admitted were scarcely more observable than those of some of the women who parted with their children, so that a more moving scene can't well be imagined.
>
> All the children who were received (except three) were dressed very clean from whence and other circumstances they appeared not to have been under the care of the Parish officers, nevertheless many of them appeared as if stupefied with opiate, and some other of them also starved, or as in the agonies of death though want of food, too weak to suck, or to receive nourishment, and notwithstanding the greatest care appeared to be dying when the Governors left the hospital which was not till they had given proper orders and seen all necessary care taken of the children.

Unfortunately, not all of those who had arrived could have their babies admitted and many had to be turned away through lack of space. As the minutes noted, the cries of the distraught mothers who had left their children was equal to those of the mothers who were unable to leave theirs.

The premises in Hatton Garden was only seen as a stepping stone to something more suitable for the needs of its children. Thomas Coram's nineteen-year campaign was brought to the attention of King George II, who signed a royal charter on 17 October 1739 for the creation of the Foundling Hospital in Bloomsbury, London, which was then surrounded by fields. The Hatton Garden houses were vacated in September 1745 but were still known as Foundling House. The original lease served its purpose while purpose-built accommodation was being constructed.

Mothers brought their babies to the Foundling Hospital to be cared for, with many hopeful that their circumstances would change so they could one day reclaim them. The hospital arranged for foster families to care for the babies and children until the age of 5. They were then brought to live and be educated in the Foundling Hospital until the age of 15. Many were trained for domestic or military service.

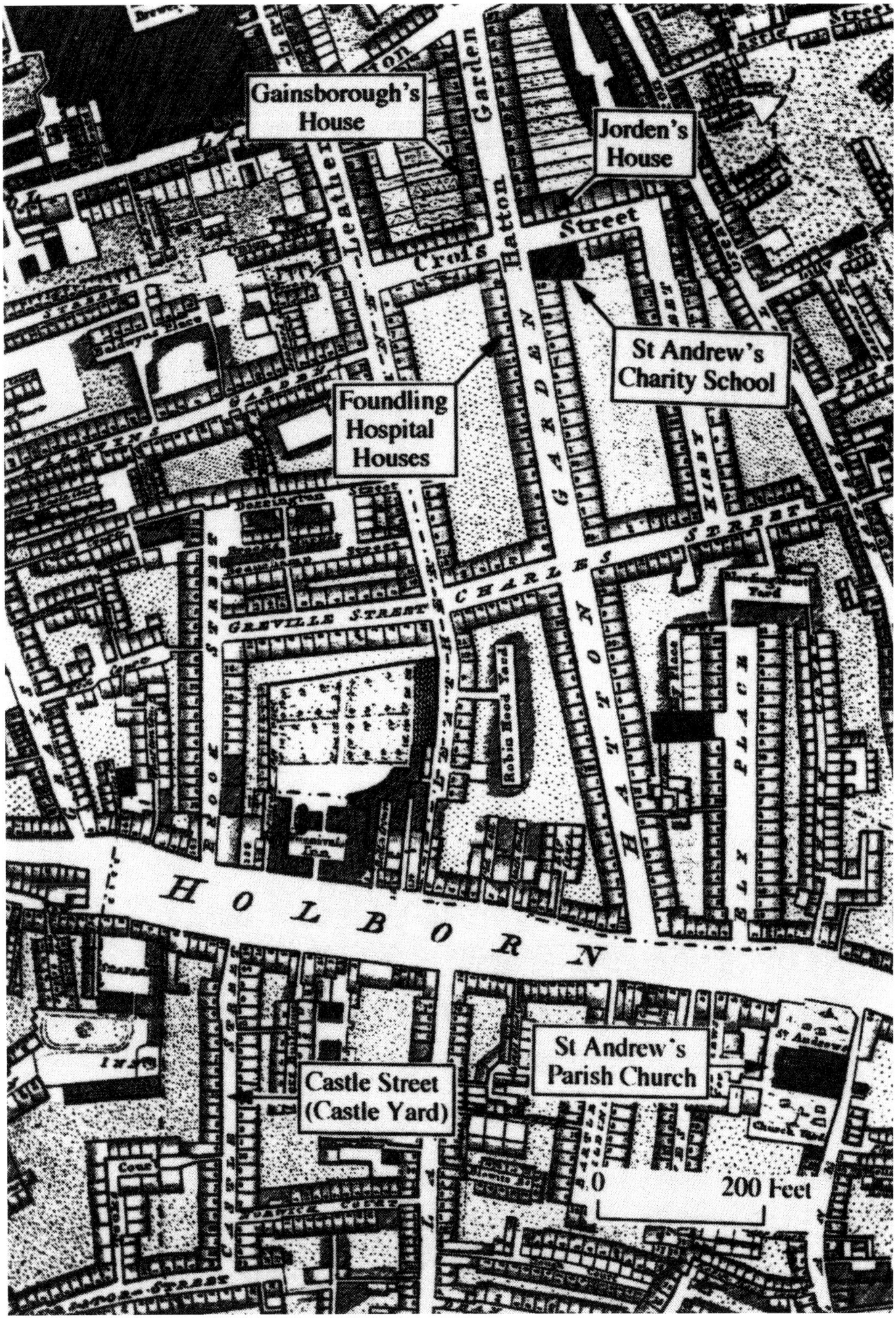

Map showing the original location of Thomas Coram's Foundling Hospital, taken from John Horwood's map of 1799.

Every child admitted to the Foundling Hospital was baptised and given a new name. Records show that the first two children baptised were named 'Thomas Coram' and 'Eunice Coram'. Mothers also left a token that could be used to identify their infant if one day they returned to reclaim their child.

Over the centuries, more than 25,000 children's lives have been saved by this amazing work. Thomas Coram's legacy continues today as the children's charity Coram.

The coming of the railways and pollution prompted the Foundling Hospital to relocate to Redhill, Surrey, in 1926, while a new, purpose-built school, closely modelled on the original Foundling Hospital, was built in the countryside at Berkhamsted, Hertfordshire, opening in 1935.

Although the London site was sold, and many buildings demolished, the hospital later bought back 2½ acres of land. Coram Fields is still a major part of Bloomsbury.

Following the Children's Act of 1948, children were taken back by birth mothers or found homes with foster parents and the residential home in Berkhamsted closed. It is now Ashlyns School and still contains stained glass windows, a staircase and monuments from the original London Hospital.

Coram was also immortalised by Dickens in *Little Dorrit*: 'the originator of the Institution for these poor foundlings having been a blessed creature of the name of Coram, we gave that name to Pet's little maid. At one time she was Tatty, and at one time she was Coram ... and now she is always Tattycoram'.

FARRINGDON

The district known as Farringdon is often related to the railway station of that name and its immediate vicinity, but in fact it covers a much wider area. Originally, it was one large area owned by the Farringdon(e) family. Part of it fell within the city walls and part of it without. It was divided into these two separate wards in 1394. There is a total of twenty-five wards making up the City of London. In medieval government, each ward was allowed a certain autonomy. Today they are largely ceremonial. Each of the wards is headed by an Alderman. It is from these Aldermen that the Lord Mayor of London is elected.

William de Faringdon(e) lived in the area and was an Alderman in 1281, when he purchased the ward. He served as Lord Mayor from 1281 to 1282. He was also a Warden of the Worshipful Company of Goldsmiths and had been implicated in the arrest of some English Jewry for treason, including some fellow goldsmiths.

The ward was previously known as the ward of Anketill de Auvergne. The name was changed in honour of William's son, Sir Nicholas de Faringdon, who was appointed as Lord Mayor ('as long as it shall please him') by King Edward II.

The area near the Fleet Ditch was populated by various trades including goldsmiths, tanners and leather curers. As the city grew, they had to move further out to avoid the overcrowding and the loss of the Fleet, which was covered over in the 18th century.

The Fleet Market was established on the reclaimed land when the southern part of the Fleet River was built over, south of Holborn Bridge. It opened its 'doors' to trade on 30th September 1737 and consisted of two rows of single-storey shops and a covered walkway. Towards the north end of the market, you would have found vegetables sold in the open air and from 4a.m. fresh watercress was available. The market also offered meat and fresh fish. A clock tower stood at the centre of the market. Within a hundred years the market had dilapidated and was then thought of as a hindrance to the increasing flow of traffic anticipated with the widening of Farringdon Street.

Charles Dickens described the market in his novel, *Barnaby Rudge*, set in 1780:

> Fleet Market, at that time, was a long irregular row of wooden sheds and penthouses, occupying the centre of what is now called Farringdon Street. They were jumbled together in a most unsightly fashion, in the middle of the road; to the great obstruction of the thoroughfare and the annoyance of passengers, who were fain to make their way, as they best could, among carts, baskets, barrows, trucks, casks, bulks, and benches, and to jostle with porters, hucksters, waggoners, and a motley crowd of buyers, sellers, pick–pockets, vagrants, and idlers. The air was perfumed with the stench of rotten leaves and faded fruit; the refuse of the butchers' stalls, and offal and garbage of a hundred kinds. It was indispensable to most public conveniences in those days, that they should be public nuisances likewise; and Fleet Market maintained the principle to admiration.

Farringdon Road, as we know it today, was laid out in 1845, following the course of the old Fleet River. Until this time, it had only been buried from Holborn Bridge southwards. Its construction led to wholesale slum clearance along its route. The east side of Field Lane was completely demolished. It has been estimated that 4,000 parishioners were displaced.

Some of the old streets and alleys were lost forever and included such descriptive names as Slaughterhouse Lane, Thieves Alley, Savage Row and 'Cutthroat Lane'. Grand buildings were put up and a magnificent viaduct was constructed carrying travellers from Holborn over the road towards the city.

A few of the original Victorian 'warehouse' structures remain today, although they are now converted to flats or offices.

A major review of the boundaries of the wards was held in 2003 and as a result some land was released to the London Boroughs of Islington and Camden among others.

FARRINGDON STATION

For many who work in Hatton Garden today, their day begins at Farringdon Station. Thousands of people, every day, get off their train here, exit via the ticket barriers and make their way to work. Very few appreciate the long history that is part of the station's pedigree and the fact that it is now becoming one of the most important stations in London.

It was built as the eastern terminus of the new Metropolitan Railway, the world's first underground railway. The original route ran from Paddington Station, just 4 miles away but, at the time, on the other side of London. It was ceremoniously opened on 10th January 1863 and known as Farringdon Street. It became a huge success. In the first six months over 26,000 people used it daily, paying the 3d fare willingly for an eighteen-minute journey that would beat the old horse-drawn bus service hands down. Three years later the railway was extended to the east and the station resited. Commuters and travellers today would find it hard to imagine what it would be like to be behind a noisy,

Farringdon Road, railway warehouses.

Farringdon and High Holborn Station.

Farringdon Station.

Steam trains at Farringdon Station.

smelly and very dirty steam locomotive travelling through a smoke-filled tunnel, before going into their place of work.

The railway continued to thrive and on 26 January 1922 a new building was opened and renamed Farringdon & High Holborn. The name was changed again on 21st April 1936 to Farringdon. Soon after that, the goods yard to the west of the station was closed, although the buildings remained for many years to come.

In its early days, the railway also carried livestock to and from Smithfield Market, only a short distance from the station. After the market stopped selling live animals in the 19th century and became a wholesale meat market, the freight section of the station fell into decline.

The large pipe that carries what remains of the Fleet River is visible just north of the station.

In recent times there has been a lot of change at the station with a new ticket hall and entrance across the road from the earlier building. It now hosts five lines: the Metropolitan, the Hammersmith & Circle for London Underground and the Elizabeth Line (Crossrail) and Thames Link for National Rail. It is estimated that in 2023 it will carry 200 train departures per hour!

It is good to see that the 1920s building remains reasonably well preserved and is Grade II listed. Evidence of its history can be seen in its architecture. Its earlier name and the inscription 'Parcel Office' are visible over the façade and on the side.

It has also had its fair share of disasters, notably:

On 5 January 1867, sixteen people were injured at Farringdon Street Station in a rear-end collision caused by a signaller's error.

On 5 January 1892, a defective axle box resulted in the derailment of part of a train shortly after it had departed Farringdon Street. Five passengers were injured.

On 26 November 1907, a train in the process of departing Farringdon Street was rear-ended by a second train entering the station.

Farringdon Station.

Farringdon Station.

Farringdon Station.

Aerial view of Farringdon Station, 1950.

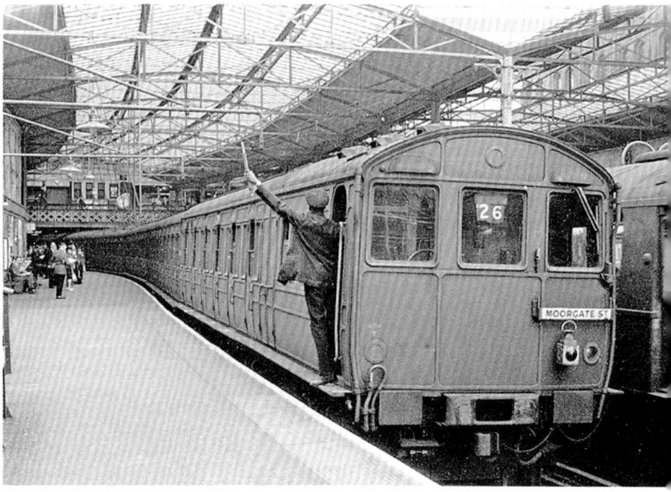

Farringdon Station.

On 1 May 1939, a total of thirty-one people were injured when a Circle Line train was involved in a minor collision with a railway engine. Seventeen passengers reported they had suffered shock and injury while a further nine subsequently complained that they had incurred minor injuries. Five crew members were also injured.

On 22 May 1954, three people in a lorry were killed when it fell from a bridge on to the tracks near Farringdon. A goods train collided with the lorry shortly after departing Farringdon.

FARRINGDON ROAD BOOK MARKET

For over a hundred years Farringdon Road was home to a market selling antiquarian books. Just south of its junction with Clerkenwell Road you would have seen a long line of wooden market barrows containing every imaginable book. People came from far and wide to search for something that would appeal to their specialist interest or maybe something that could turn them a profit elsewhere. Saturday morning would see crowds of bibliophiles sparring with each other as they fought to find a first edition or some other rare volume.

It is believed that the stalls first appeared around 1869, following the slum clearance and the laying down of Farringdon Road. It is possible that the book dealers had lost their premises as a result of this major upheaval.

One of the early dealers was James Dabs, who offered several thousand books laid out on several barrows. His starting price was two books for a penny. He is reported as saying that he made the greatest profit from theological books.

The magnetism of such stalls and the dealers' wares is most probably the inspiration of Dickens in *Oliver Twist*. The Artful Dodger and Oliver steal the pocket handkerchief from Mr Brownlow, who is totally absorbed in reading one of the books:

> He had taken up a book from the stall, and there he stood, reading away, as hard as if he were in his elbow-chair, in his own study . . . for it was plain, from his abstraction, that he saw not the bookstall, nor the street, nor the boys, nor, in short, anything but the book itself: which he was reading straight through.

The stalls always had an air of transience. In a book of 1926 called *Wonderful London*, they are described as having an 'appearance of extreme impermanence'. Despite its appearance, the market thrived up until the Second World War, when the rot started to set in.

In her book of 1939, *The Street Markets of London*, Mary Benedetta describes the scene:

> the same little group stands there, side by side for hours, searching, reading, their eyes appraising all the different qualities of each volume. The rain drips on their shoulders off the canvas roof, soaking them to the skin, but they never notice. Time means nothing to them. It is forgotten. They are all under the same spell – the romance and glamour of old books.

Farringdon Road book stalls.

Farringdon Road book stalls.

No one will ever know the extent as to what finds were made and what fortunes were achieved among the books, maps, old newspapers, original drawings and magazines. However, a New Zealand book dealer is on record as having found some original letters by Byron. The lucky searcher might even find 16th-century books, which would be highly valued. The market also attracted certain celebrities and among those known to frequent the stalls were Spike Milligan, John Betjeman and Mary Evans, who built up a collection of images for her picture library.

The advent of the internet and the opportunity to search online changed the marketplace forever. In 1995 companies like Amazon and eBay made their debut. As they grew rapidly, so the old marketplaces, like Farringdon Road, diminished. In a short time, there were no more than a few stalls left.

The last of the stalls were operated by the Jeffrey family. Theirs was a third-generation family business who had traded since 1880. In their heyday they would sell 2,500 books a week, which involved a lot of time sourcing and buying. They kept a warehouse in Clerkenwell, which was off limits to customers. One of George Jeffrey's sources was major auction houses who were responsible for country-house clearances. They selected anything that would achieve a good price at auction, and Jeffrey would take the remainder. In addition to books, there were manuscripts, engravings, maps, documents and letters.

Jeffrey was a master of his trade and was remembered for the way in which he would tantalise customers as he peeled back the tarpaulin when he was ready for business. He was admired by his customers for his straightforward honesty and sense of fair play. The death of Jeffrey at the age of 69 heralded the closure of the market, and although his son might have carried on the trade, the final blow was dealt when the council wanted to increase the price of a pitch.

Farringdon Road.

FARRINGDON MARKET & FLEET MARKET

The Fleet Market, which traded on Farringdon Road, was closed to allow the development of the street as a major thoroughfare. Farringdon Market was opened in its place on 20th November 1826, alongside the road and adjacent to the viaduct. Its location as a vegetable and fruit market was conveniently opposite Smithfield meat market. It was famous for its watercress, with about twenty vendors selling their wares from 3a.m. At its peak over 20 tons were sold a week.

It was a victim of the Blitz when, only a few weeks before the end of the war, on 8th March 1945, a German V2 rocket made a direct hit on the railway tunnels below. The massive explosion, which was heard all over London, caused the buildings to collapse into the crater. The incident occurred at a busy time of day and 110 people – workers and customers, men, women and children – were killed and many more seriously injured.

Contemporary accounts describe how among the 'fallen girders, masonry, glass and debris came the screams and shouts of the injured and the trapped. Rescue squads released those who could be got at, but for many hours afterwards the search for victims went on, and bloodhounds were brought in to help.'

Farringdon Road Market V2 bomb damage in 1945 in which 110 were killed.

THE ILLUSTRATED LONDON NEWS, Sept. 17, 1892.—357

COSTERMONGERS IN FARRINGDON ROAD—THREATENED WITH REMOVAL BY THE HOLBORN BOARD OF WORKS.

Farringdon Road, 1892.

Holborn Viaduct.

Top two images: Farringdon Road Market.
Below: Fleet Market from Holborn Bridge.

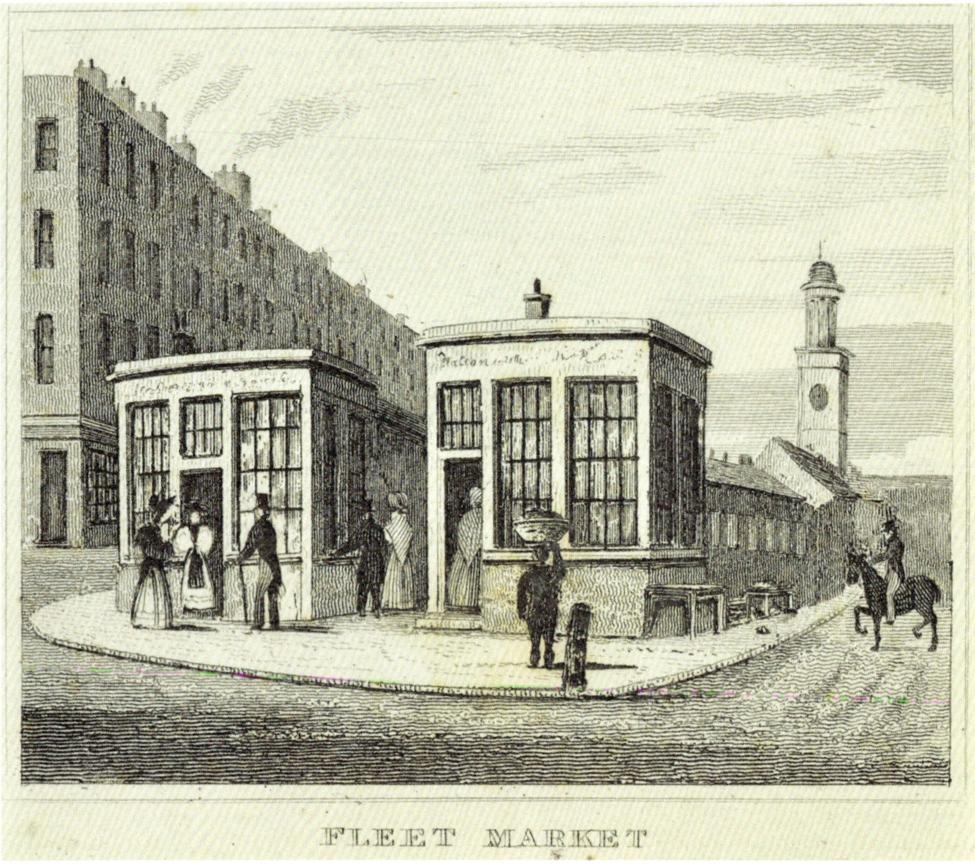

Fleet Market, Farringdon Road.

FLEET MARKET. *(From a Drawing in Mr. Gardiner's Collection.)*

Fleet Market, Farringdon Road.

HOLBORN

The thoroughfare we know today as Holborn stands on the old Roman road from London to the west. About 2,000 years ago it would be a common site to see legions of Roman soldiers marching to and from Londinium and merchants bringing fuel, wool, hides, corn and cheeses in or out. The Romans knew the street as the Praetorian Way and Watling Street; a long-distance road that began at London Bridge and was the Roman road to the north-west.

Holborn begins as an extension of Newgate Street. Originally, starting at Holebourne Bridge where the road crossed the River Fleet, it ran up Holborn Hill. Today the road runs along Holborn Viaduct, which replaced Holborn Hill, crosses Holborn Circus and continues towards the west, where it becomes High Holborn. The road is designated as the A40, which can be used all the way to reach Fishguard on the Welsh coast.

The name Holborn is derived from two words: hol, which means a hollow, and burne, which means a stream. So, it was the stream in the hollow. In former times the river ran through a steep-sided wooded valley down towards the Thames.

The *Domesday Book* of 1086 makes mention of 'two cottages by a bridge with a vineyard nearby'. In 1180, Fitzstephen wrote:

> On all sides without the houses, are the citizen's gardens and orchards, planted with trees ... On the north side are also pastures, and plain meadows, with brooks running through them turning water mills ... not far off is a great forest.

By Norman times the city, established by the Romans, was full to overflowing. Houses were built outside the city walls but within the ward of Farringdon. In 1222, the boundary of the city was redefined. The Holborn Bars were established to serve as a gateway and were like a toll gate. They kept out undesirables and were there to charge for access or to levy any duties on goods being shipped into the city.

Holborn Hill, looking east across the valley.

Holborn Circus

Holborn Circus showing Thomas Wallis in its heyday.

The Old Bell.

The route along Holborn also had a more sinister side to it. It was the route by which convicted criminals from Newgate Prison were taken to the gallows at Tyburn. Some were taken by cart and others were dragged along tied to a frame. Holborn Hill became known as 'Heavy Hill' in the 16th and 17th centuries, when such executions were a common thing. The expression 'going up Heavy Hill' was a euphemism for 'on the way to the gallows'. The locals all turned out in force to watch the procession of forgers, murderers and thieves. The street was lined with spectators, as were the windows above.

Evelyn wrote in his diary for 22nd May 1685:

> Oates, who had but two days before, been pilloried at several places and whipped at the cart's tail from Newgate to Aldgate, was this day placed on a sledge, being not able to go by reasons of so late scourging, and dragged from Prison to Tyburn, and whipped again all the way, which some thought to be severe and extraordinary ... I chanced to pass just as execution was doing to him.

One of the landmarks along the route was the Old Bell Inn, which once stood just west of where Hatton Garden joins Holborn today. The Old Bell was first mentioned in 1538. It served as a coaching inn and was the terminus for a regular service to then distant towns such as Amersham, Wendover and Uxbridge. When the inn was demolished in 1897, it was the last remaining inn north of the Thames with a galleried yard. Next door to the Old Bell was another inn known as the Black Bull. That was demolished in 1901. It was referred to in Dickens's novel *Martin Chuzzlewit*.

The same stretch along the north side of Holborn also housed the Ridler's Hotel. The site was subsequently developed and became the home of the world-famous Gamages department store.

Albert Walter Gamage had begun his business at the age of 21, in 1878, in a very modest way. He was a farmer's son from Herefordshire who had come to London at the age of 17 and was working as an assistant at a drapery store in the city. His story begins on the day he took his watch for repair to Lindsey & Co. at 127 Holborn. The watchmaker told Gamage that there was a real need for a good hosiery store in that part of London. The shop next door was vacant and with assistance from a good friend he made his debut with a 5-foot frontage on the corner of Leather Lane and Holborn. Above the door his motto stated, 'Tall oaks from Little Acorns grow'.

This was certainly his experience. The success of his business was remarkable. In his first year the profit was £1,632. From his original £40 investment, his fortunes mushroomed. By the time of the 1911 census he was living in a large house in Finchley, with his wife and four children plus nine servants.

Holborn.

Holborn.

Holborn.

From the original location he expanded by the acquisition of further properties between Leather Lane and Hatton Garden and by the 1900s he owned the whole block. His policy was to keep depth of stock and to sell below the price of his competitors. People flocked to the store. The incremental growth of his business and the additional and ever-increasing floor space made the store something of a rabbit warren with its passages, ramps, steps and different levels. Communication between the shop floor and the accounts department was by the old-fashioned tube. Cash and paperwork were put into cannisters, which were 'whooshed' upstairs.

A visit to Gamages was always an adventure. It was possible to buy almost anything from AW Gamage. Beyond the original haberdashery, he sold furniture, sporting goods, camping equipment, garden supplies and clothing, but probably the best-remembered was the toy department, particularly the model railway section. One of his successes was to become the official supplier of uniforms to the Boy Scout movement. There was also a motor department, a pet shop and he ran a successful mail order department. Tony Robson, who started as an apprentice just after his 15th birthday in 1961 and is now a retired craftsman, recalls how he went there to purchase a 'tank aerial' for his Lambretta scooter. This was a must-have accessory for all young mods back in the day.

When the business closed in 1972 for the redevelopment of the site, there were many sad people, particularly in Hatton Garden. The whole Gamages site is about 2.25 acres and was sold in 1997 for £97 million.

Needles from Gamages music department.

Another landmark stands to the west of Leather Lane facing on to Holborn. It is known to many as the 'Prudential Building', although its name is now Waterhouse Square. Its Gothic style and terracotta brick facades make it unmistakable. It was opened in 1906 as the new home of the Prudential Assurance Co. (the Pru). The building was largely the work of Sir Alfred Waterhouse, the eminent Victorian architect. It was constructed on the site of what was once Furnival's Inn, Wood's Hotel and Ridler's Hotel. Furnival's Inn was founded in 1383.

The Prudential Assurance Co. had started its life on 30th May 1848 at 12 Hatton Garden as the Prudential Mutual Assurance Investment and Loan Association. Their original business was in providing loans to individuals. Captain Charles Hanslip, attorney, solicitor and parliamentary agent, worked with William Manning and Job Conworth to form the company. Hanslip lived next door at 13 Hatton Garden with his wife and three small children but he was well connected through his work and was solicitor to two railway companies at a time when the railways were enjoying a period of rapid growth. The first minutes were dated 21st April 1847 and dealt with the election of officers and procedures. Meetings were held in the evening at 12 Hatton Garden.

Gamages.

Gamages.

AW Gamage.

Gamages, 1907.

Furnival's Inn.

Holborn Hill.

It was in 1854 that they developed their insurance services, particularly for the working classes with low-cost policies. Agents would visit homes as door-to-door salesmen and were popularly known as the 'Men from the Pru'.

On the other side of the road from Waterhouse Square and slightly further along stands Staple Inn. This was originally built in 1545 and was fully restored in 1886 when it was purchased at auction by the Prudential Assurance Co. It was destroyed by a flying bomb on 24th August 1944 but was rebuilt in 1955 using as far as possible the original materials.

It has a Grade I-listed frontage and is said to be one of only four surviving Tudor houses in London.

Plate with a view of Staple Inn on the right.

Staple Inn, Holborn.

Staple Inn, 1866.

Staple Inn, 1914.

HOLBORN BRIDGE

Since Roman times there has been a bridge across the Fleet River connecting Holborn to the city. Although the river was built over in the 18th century, the remains of the old bridge are still visible from the London sewer system. The bridge was something of a bottleneck for road traffic. There is a story of the Spanish Ambassador in the mid-17th century, who would be residing at Ely Palace, having his hat stolen while crossing the bridge. Don Pedro de Zunga wore an expensive jewel in his hat, as was the custom at that time for all who were part of a royal court. The crowd encouraged the thief, which was a measure of Anglo–Spanish relations at that time.

HOLBORN VIADUCT

During the latter part of the 19th century, this part of London saw a number of road improvement schemes collectively known as 'The Holborn Valley Improvement Scheme'. Many of the old slums that were once situated along the route of what is now Farringdon Road were cleared and a new road constructed. The demolition process revealed many of the hideouts and escape routes used by the criminal gangs. This also involved the building of a viaduct to carry the road through Holborn above the valley to avoid the difficulties of Snow Hill and Holborn Hill. Many road vehicles, particularly buses and coaches, used to struggle as they ascended Holborn Hill.

The new viaduct was opened by Queen Victoria on 6th November 1869 with a great pageant of military bands, speeches and dining. It was hailed as a triumph of engineering and a great feat for the Victorian construction industry, and was made of cast iron, in three spans supported on grey, red and black granite piers. The whole is decorated in Victorian style with scrolls, crests and shields and four bronze statues. On the north side they represent science and fine art. On the south side they represent commerce and agriculture. The total length of the viaduct is about 1,400 feet with a width of 80 feet. It was way ahead of its time, providing ease of transport even today.

The cost then was £2.5 million. It was reported that on the opening day cracks appeared in the new structure but thankfully they never got worse.

St Andrew's church had to concede a large part of its graveyard. The perspective of the church changed forever from a position where it was 11 feet above the road to a new position lower than the road. Some 11,000–12,000 human remains had to be removed from the cemetery to the City Cemetery at Ilford.

Charterhouse Street, which opened in 1868, required the demolition of buildings in Hatton Garden and Saffron Hill. Compensation had to be paid to a number of people. The two largest sums were to C Meeking for £52,870 and to Negretti & Zambra for £13,044.

A report in the *Illustrated Times* of 17th February 1866 reads:

Our readers are already aware that extensive improvements are about to be effected in Holborn Valley; that a viaduct is to be constructed stretching from the crests of Holborn Hill and of Snow Hill; that several new streets, or portions of streets, are to be made: and that the whole aspect of the place is to be changed. This is one of the great works undertaken by The Metropolitan Board of Works, and which, when completed will help to perpetuate the names of Sir John Thwaites and his colleagues and make their fame in some degree rival that of the great re-constructor of Paris, Baron Haussmann. Of course, in such operations on such a site, demolition must necessarily precede construction; and as will be seen from our engraving the work of the destruction goes bravely on. At the South west corner of Snow Hill and Farringdon Street several houses have been pulled down, and on the opposite side of Farringdon Street, at the foot of Holborn Hill, greater havoc has been made. Tenement after tenement has fallen before the vigorous attacks of the navies engaged on the work, till now there is but one house left standing between Farringdon Street and Shoe Lane. St Andrew's Church is now fully exposed to view from the foot of the hill, together with the backs of large workshops – those of Messrs. Pontifex,

Left: a ticket for the first bus over the new viaduct, 6th November 1869.

Below: Farringdon Road, 1869.

the engineers, we suppose – of the existence of which no one standing in Farringdon street could previously had any notion. Light and air have been let into the confined region of Plumtree Court, and we hope a portion of the scheme of improvements will be the total removal of that noisome slum. The present aspect of the works is not by any means pretty, though it is not devoid of the elements of the picturesque; but patience! The rubbish and dust will by and by disappear, and elegant structures take the place of the fabrics doomed to destruction.

Construction of Holborn Viaduct.

Farringdon Street.

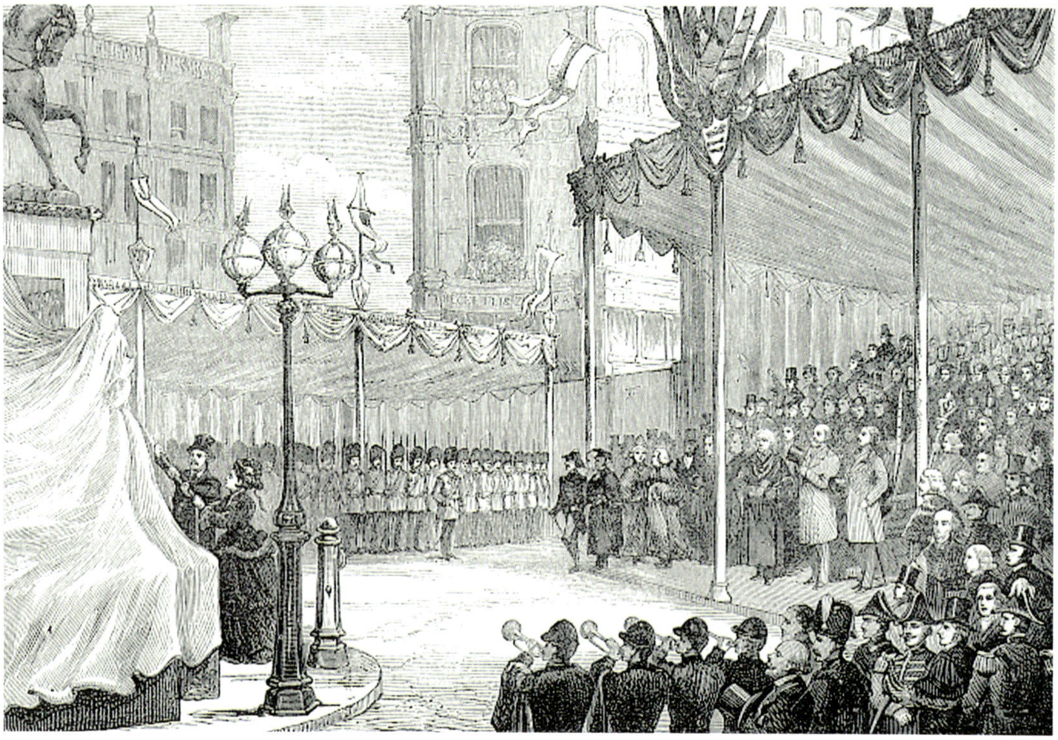

Unveiling of the statue at Holborn Circus.

Construction of Holborn Viaduct.

Demolition of slums to make way for the new viaduct, 1866.

Holborn Viaduct.

HOLBORN CIRCUS

From 1867, when it was opened, until 2014, when it was redesigned, Holborn Circus was a busy road junction in the form of a roundabout with six roads feeding into it. The original design by William Haywood established a circular plan to the buildings that surrounded the junction. It was described by Dickens in his *Dictionary of London* as 'perhaps, the sweetest piece of fine architecture in the city'. Sadly, much of the circus was lost in the Blitz and never rebuilt.

On the south side of Holborn stood a large drapers and department store called Thomas Wallis. It was bombed out on the night of 16–17 April 1941. The site was later developed as the home of *Mirror* newspapers and is now the headquarters of the Sainsbury's supermarket chain. It has been estimated that a seventh of the buildings in Holborn were destroyed by German bombs.

The circus features a large bronze statue of Prince Albert facing the viaduct and the city beyond. This was an anonymous gift to the Corporation of London in 1874. The statue was the work of Charles Bacon and shows Prince Albert in a field marshal's uniform. He is breaking protocol by doffing his cap. There is also some debate as to the position of the horse's legs. It is considered that a statue where one foot is off the ground means that the rider died of wounds sustained in battle. The statue originally stood at the centre of the circus but was relocated to the west as part of the traffic improvement scheme. Holborn Circus had a poor reputation for road traffic accidents and was known as a blackspot. The improvements cost nearly twice as much as the construction of the viaduct itself 145 years earlier.

The name Holborn related to one of the old London telephone exchanges. Originally subscribers would have to dial the letters, HOL but that became 405 at the introduction of all-number dialling as these were the numbers on the dial alongside the HOL.

Panorama of Holborn Circus around 1900.

Aerial view of Holborn Circus.

Holborn Circus.

Holborn Circus.

Hatton Garden.

Holborn Circus.

Statue of the Prince Consort, Prince Albert, at Holborn Circus.

Holborn Circus from the tower of St Andrew's Church, 2019.

Clockwise from top left: demolition work in Holborn; Holborn Circus looking north; Holborn Circus looking west.

GARDEN PATHS

BLEEDING HEART YARD

Once upon a time Bleeding Heart Yard was a rather insalubrious backwater reached from Greville Street. There would be little reason to go there, without good cause. Today, however, thanks to the entrepreneurial efforts of Robert and Robyn Wilson, this little quarter of Hatton Garden has become a destination for all lovers of good food and fine wine. Their wonderful variety of dining opportunities, spread over three different sites, offers everything from simple 'tavern' food to fine French cuisine. Their restaurant was voted by *The Times* as the most romantic restaurant in London. The décor captures something of a Dickensian feel and their service is second to none. The yard itself still retains something of its old world character with its cobbles and warehouse windows.

Visitors to Bleeding Heart Yard will often enquire as to the origin of its name. There are at least two, possibly three stories, each with its own appeal. The first relates to a sign that once used to hang outside a pre-Reformation tavern. At that time, England was very much under the Church of Rome. In the Roman Catholic tradition, the Immaculate heart of the Virgin Mary was associated with her sorrows and many artists portrayed her with a bleeding heart. The original pub stood where the tavern stands today on the corner of Bleeding Heart Yard and Greville Street. The other two stories were endorsed by Charles Dickens in *Little Dorrit*:

> As if the aspiring city had become puffed up in the very ground on which it stood, the ground had so risen about Bleeding Heart Yard that you got into it down a flight of steps which formed no part of the original approach, and got out of it by a low gateway into a maze of shabby streets, which went about and about, tortuously ascending to the level again. At this end of the Yard and over the gateway, was the factory of Daniel Doyce, often heavily beating like a bleeding heart of iron, with the clink of metal upon metal.

> The opinion of the yard was divided respecting the derivation of its name. The more practical of its inmates abided by the tradition of a murder; the gentler and more imaginative inhabitants, including the whole of the tender sex, were loyal to the legend of a young lady of former times closely imprisoned in her chamber by a cruel father for remaining true to her own true love, and refusing to marry the suitor he chose for her. The legend related how that the young lady used to be seen up at her window behind the bars, murmuring a lovelorn song, of which the burden was 'Bleeding Heart, Bleeding Heart, bleeding away…' until she died.

The popular view is the bloodier one, which refers to the murder of Lady Elizabeth Hatton, the widowed daughter-in-law of Sir Christopher Hatton, one-time consort of Queen Elizabeth I. Lady Hatton was a well-known socialite of her day and regularly hosted balls in the hall at Ely Place. In January 1662, she danced with a stranger, of whom it is suggested was the incarnation of the devil himself. Another theory is that it was a European Ambassador. Ely Place had been the home to various foreigners throughout its history. The stranger took her outside and she was not seen again, alive. The next

Above: Bleeding Heart Yard street sign.

Left: Sketch of the Windsor Grill at the entrance to Bleeding Heart Yard by GS Fletcher.

Opposite: Bleeding Heart Yard.

morning her mutilated body was discovered in the snow in the yard at the back of the house. Legend has it that her heart was still beating. It is said that her ghost has been seen in the yard washing the blood from the cobble stones.

The story is recorded in some detail in Richard Barham's *Ingoldsby Legends*, which can be found elsewhere in this book. The pump referred to in this work can be seen in older pictures of the yard. It has since been removed but a metal grille in the pavement gives a landmark as to its earlier location. Dickens also writes:

> Bleeding Heart Yard was a place much changed in feature and fortune, yet with some relish of ancient greatness about it. Two or three mighty stacks of chimneys, and a few large dark rooms, which had escaped being walled and subdivided out of the recognition of their old proportions, gave the yard a character. It was inhabited by poor people, who set up their rest among its faded glories as Arabs of the desert pitch their tents among the fallen stones of the Pyramids; but there was a family sentimental feeling prevalent in the yard, that it had a character.

Bleeding Heart Yard, 1910.

Bleeding Heart Yard today.

ELY PLACE

Of all the thoroughfares that traverse Hatton's Garden, Ely Place is by far the richest in history. Running north from Charterhouse Street, it is a cul-de-sac and a peaceful backwater. On rare occasions pedestrian access is possible from Bleeding Heart Yard via a small doorway. Otherwise the only other access for pedestrians is via Ely Court, a small passageway connecting to Hatton Garden. The street was built about 1773–1776 by a developer, named Charles Cole, over the site of the original palace of the Bishops of Ely. This involved the demolition of the ancient hall and cloisters, which had fallen into disrepair. Thankfully, the church that we know as St Etheldreda's was spared, as Cole believed it would be an asset to his new development. This had been the chapel serving Ely House. For over 500 years this location had been the home to a succession of bishops and later to Sir Christopher Hatton.

Today, it maintains its 18th-century charm, although modified in part. Walking into Ely Place has been described as stepping through a portal into a different age. Apart from the cars that enjoy the private parking, little appears to have changed on the surface, although many of the properties have been improved internally. Numbers 21 and 25 remain Grade II listed.

View of the corner of Ely Place and Charterhouse Street.

The damaged premises of Negretti & Zambra.

Initially, the street enjoyed the benefits of being under the auspices of the Cambridge See. The first occupants claimed independence from the neighbouring liberty of Saffron Hill because they believed their land belonged to the Bishops of Ely and to the Crown. The medieval liberty of Ely Place was not subject to the jurisdiction of the City of London. It even provided a refuge and sanctuary for those escaping the law, much as a foreign embassy would today. Right up until the 20th century this was still the practice. Police would have had to ask permission from the commissioners to enter.

The street is guarded by impressive gates and the beadle's lodge. The gates would be closed to strangers and the beadles would police who would be allowed entry.

By an Act of Parliament dated 18th June 1842 Ely Place remained a private road. Six commissioners meet twice a year for business and annual elections are held, if needed, to replace anyone retiring. The commissioners are chosen from the rate payers, which means representatives of the firms occupying the offices, as the street is now mostly commercial property. Their powers were reduced in 1901 when Holborn Council took over most of the responsibility, and their mandate now is focused on 'paving, watching, lighting, cleaning and improvement of Ely Place'. They employed two full-time beadles and some part-time, as and when required. Until 1948 the gates were locked at 11 p.m. and the beadle would call the hours of the night, from 10 p.m. to 6 a.m., to the residents in their beds. It has been suggested that few people wanted to know but the beadle had

John Taylor & Co., Ely Place.

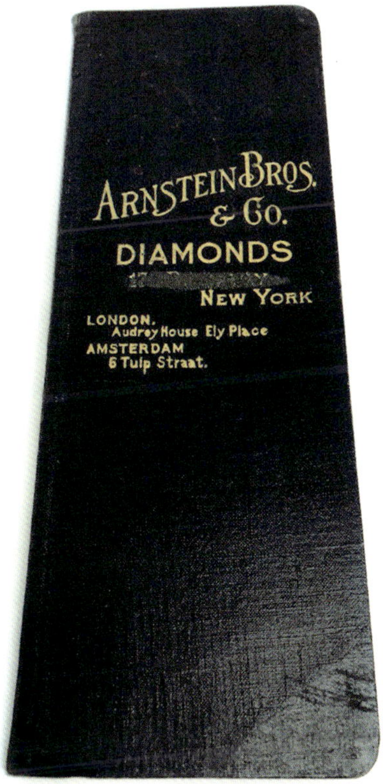

Arnstein Bros & Co., Audrey House.

Clockwise from above: Audrey House, Ely Place; St Etheldreda's and Audrey House; Ely Place.

to reassure them he was awake even if they were trying to sleep. In earlier times they also announced the weather. The beadles once dressed in fine gold-braided uniform and wore top hats. In 1947 their pay was £4 a week. The commissioners have maintained their Minute Book from 15th November 1877.

There is an account that on Saturday, 3rd December 1910 two men entered the One Tun Pub in Saffron Hill. They were described as shabbily dressed and soaking wet. The landlord remembered them well for the fact that they barely spoke any English. They stayed for about an hour. That same evening, two men were seen trying to break into a nearby jeweller's shop in Hatton Garden. The police were called and pursued the men to Ely Court and into Ye Olde Mitre tavern. As the tavern came under the jurisdiction of the Diocese of Ely, the police returned to their station and called for the Cambridgeshire Police. Needless to say, by the time they arrived, the villains were nowhere to be seen.

Income, today, is derived from the issue of parking permits and the gates are no longer locked.

Ely Place.

Ely Place.

Ely Place.

Ye Old Mitre.

Ely Place, 1950s.

The Mitre, Hatton Garden.

Reproduction from an etching by Fred Baragwanath.

The Mitre, shown on a Wills cigarette card.

The Mitre.

Clockwise from top left: Ye Olde Mitre interior, 2020; a beadle of Ely Place; the view from the Tower of St Andrew's, 2019.

Letters to Ely Place.

Visitors to Ely Place may notice the peculiar frame outside No. 8. This was the holder of an oil lamp from an age when attempts were made to light the streets, prior to having electricity. More successful lighting was obtained in the 18th century by the introduction of fanlights above the front doors, where each owner was responsible for lighting their own approach. Also of interest to the historian is the iron frame set into the entrance to Ely Court. This was positioned to prevent riders of horses using the alley as a shortcut.

Among many well-known occupants was the poet William Cowper (1731–1800) and the architect Charles Barry (1795–1860), who built the Palace of Westminster and worked on the improvement of many country houses, including Highclere Castle and Cliveden.

Ely Court, or Mitre Court, as it is sometimes known, connects Ely Place with Hatton Garden. It contains one of London's 'best-kept secrets' – Ye Olde Mitre Tavern. Approaching from Hatton Garden, the entrance to Ely Court is located between 8 and 9 Hatton Garden and is marked by an old lamp post with a Bishop's mitre.

This pub was originally built by Bishop Thomas Goodrich in 1546/7 for the palace servants. Although demolished in 1772, along with the palace, as part of the development, it was soon rebuilt. A stone mitre from the original place gatehouse is built into the wall. The preserved trunk of a cherry tree, which marked the boundary of the diocese and Sir Christopher Hatton's garden, is to be found in the corner of the front bar. It is said Elizabeth I danced the Maypole round it.

The licensing and opening hours of the Mitre tavern long remained under the control of the Cambridgeshire justices and the claimed exemption of the Ely Place residents from the payment of the liberty poor rate was ended only in 1835.

GREVILLE STREET

Greville Street crosses Hatton Garden in an east–west direction and today runs from Farringdon Road to Leather Lane. It is a mixture of architectural styles, ancient and modern, with numbers 10 and 11 being Grade II listed. It was originally called Cross Street (not to be confused with St Cross Street) and then Charles Street in honour of Charles II, King of England and a close associate of Christopher Hatton. Older maps show the west end of the street as Cross Street while the eastern side was already Charles Street.

The street is named after Fulke Greville, 1st Baron Brooke. He lived from 1554 to 1628, when he was murdered at his home in Brooke House on 1st September. He was an Elizabethan poet and dramatist and also a statesman who sat in the House of Commons before joining the House of Lords. His tomb describes him as, 'a servant to Queen Elizabeth, counsellor to King James, and friend to Sir Philip Sidney'.

His introduction to the royal court was via his uncle Robert Greville. He would have been a close contemporary of Sir Christopher Hatton and it is therefore not inappropriate that the street that crosses Hatton Garden should be named after him when it was renamed in 1937.

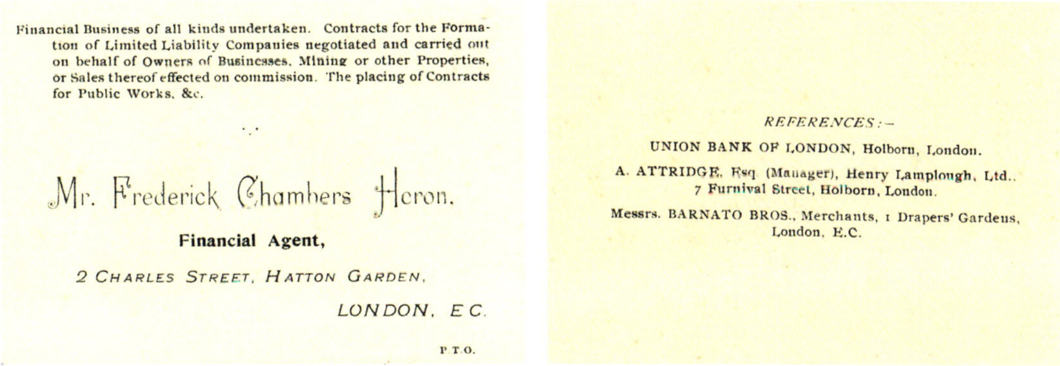

2 Charles Street: a business card for Mr F.C. Heron.

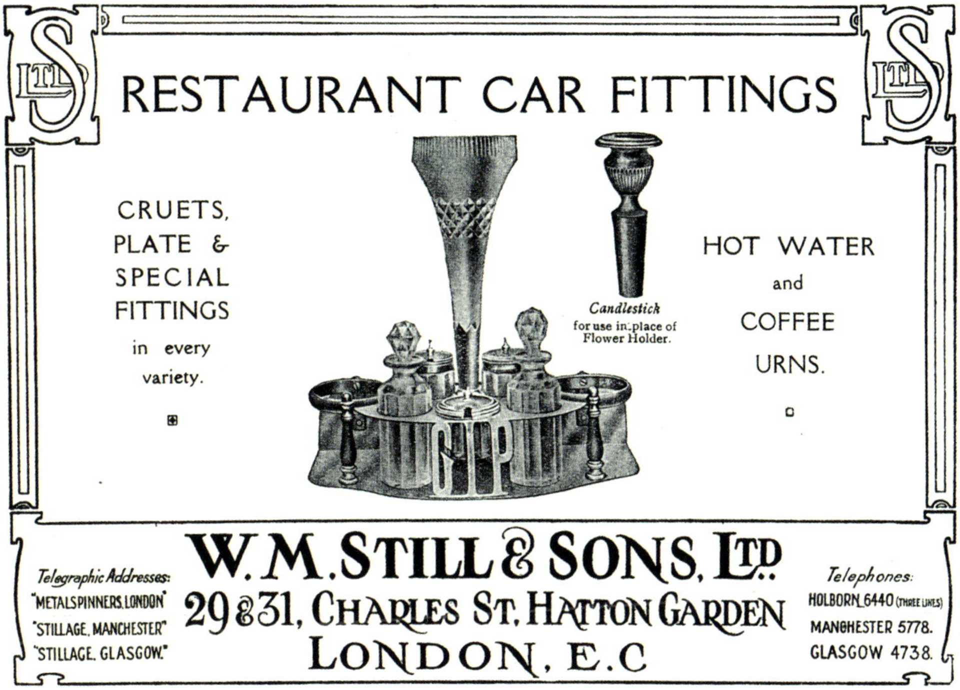

29 & 31 Charles Street, WM Still & Sons Ltd.

Brooke was killed by Ralph Haywood, who had been a faithful servant for many years. There had been a huge misunderstanding over Brooke's will, which excluded Haywood. Haywood and Brooke had a violent argument, as a result of which Brooke was stabbed. Haywood, then either out of despair or remorse, stabbed himself with the same blade.

For those who have known Greville Street personally, well-loved establishments come to mind, like the Nosherie, famed for its salt beef on rye sandwiches; the Florence, for wonderful handcrafted sandwiches freshly made while you wait; and, maybe, the Lema Buttery on the corner of Hatton Garden.

4 Charles Street, Greengross, 1935.

Other places of refreshment were the Vienna Restaurant at No. 2, known as the flea pit. The Old Leather Bottle was on the corner of Charles Street and Leather Lane and the Pewter Platter was on the opposite corner. There were dining rooms at 40 Charles Street.

Greville Street has had many notable occupants. At 4 Greville Street in 1951, was Indusmond (Diamond Tools) Ltd, manufacturers of all types of industrial diamond tools. At 5 Greville Street, from 1841–1848, Giuseppe Mazzini set up a school for Italian children on the first floor. In 1862, there was a 'Mission Room' in the basement of No. 7. At 10 Greville Street, in 1843, was William Lane, a tailor. At No. 16, in 1828, there was a small dispensary that was to become the home of the original Royal Free Hospital set up by William Marsden in 1840. At 17 Greville Street in 1848 was Davy & Sons London, publishers of *Robinson Crusoe.*

At 20–23 Charles Street in 1914 was John M Newton and Sons, a company established in 1879 as Plate and Sheet Glass Merchants and Manufacturers, employing 100 people, offering services such as glass silverers, bevellers, brilliant cutters and shop front glaziers. At 26, in 1807, was Leonard Bennett, a mathematical instrument maker. At 29 and 31 Charles Street was WM Still & Sons Ltd – manufacturer of 'Restaurant Car fittings'.

No. 35 Charles Street in 1825 was home to Daniel Straight. In 1851 he exhibited at the Great Exhibition. His business was ivory cutting, which at the time had many applications. Apart from piano keys and teeth, there were all sorts of decorative uses. It was also during a time before wildlife conservation had become an issue.

Greville Street sign.

Greville Street.

No. 35 Charles Street in 1922 was the Surgical and Optical Mfg Co., manufacturers of optical machinery and tools, optical and scientific instruments and apparatus. They were patentees of the 'Somco' Auto Optical Surface Machine. Also at 35 Charles Street in 1922 was Henry F Purser and Brother, manufacturers of cinematograph projection lenses, binoculars and field glasses.

At 36 Greville Street, in 1947 was Hathaway and Muddiman, manufacturers of hand-made fine gem-set jewellery, brooches, clips, bracelets and rings in precious metals as well as wedding rings and signet rings.

N. J. HILL & CO.

BOOKBINDERS'
PRESS AND TOOL MAKERS

AMATEUR PLANTS A SPECIALTY

LEATHER ART CLOTH AND PAPERS

BRASS TYPE, HANDLE LETTERS
AND TOOLS

Catalogues on application

6 CHARLES STREET
HATTON GARDEN

FACTORY: BALDWIN PLACE

350

Clockwise from top left: Greville Street; Fulke Greville; 6 Charles Street, Advertisement for NJ Hill & Co.

Right: A 1910 post card showing Hatton Garden looking south from St Cross Street.

HATTON GARDEN

The street, classified as the B521, that runs roughly north–south through the centre of what was once a beautiful garden has many stories and many secrets. Some have been shared in the public domain and many remain hidden. A walk from Holborn Circus along the east side and back down the west side will pass many of the doors where history was made.

The imposing building on the east corner of Hatton Garden, until recently a branch of NatWest Bank, gives us an impression of the grand scheme of Victorian building that was part of Holborn Viaduct and the Holborn Circus development project. When this building was constructed, most of the corners on Holborn Circus looked like this. Unfortunately, the London Blitz of 1940 destroyed the other buildings. However, what is called No.1 is not in the original location. Originally, the houses of Hatton Garden came further south, but the Victorian development demolished the beginning of the street, making way for Charterhouse Street.

Hatton Garden, 1960s.

Hatton Garden street sign.

Hatton Garden, 1960s.

A 1942 view of Hatton Garden.

Giuseppe Mazzini's school, 1841.

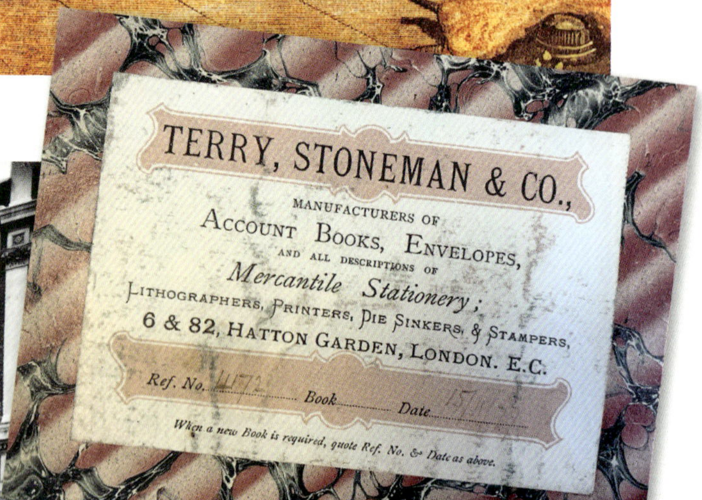

No. 6 Hatton Garden. Commissioners minute book from Terry & Stoneman Co.

No. 6 Hatton Garden.

7 Hatton Garden

This was at one time the site of the Post Office.

o. 7 Hatton Garden post office.

No. 7 Hatton Garden. A paperweight from Talis Watch Co.

Architectural detail of No. 7 Hatton Garden.

12–13 Hatton Garden (Premier House)

The Prudential Assurance Company began its life at No. 12 before moving to larger premises in Holborn. Mr Hanslip, in partnership with William Manning and Job Conworth, practised at 12 Hatton Garden because of its proximity to the legal district of the Inns of Court in Chancery Lane and Grays Inn. Through his extensive network of contacts, including two of the then expanding railway companies, their business thrived. In 1848 he was 36 years old, living with his wife and three small children at 13 Hatton Garden. The date of the first minuted meeting, at which officers were elected and procedures decided upon, was 21st April 1847. A week later, meetings were held in the evenings at 12 Hatton Garden.

12–13 Hatton Garden. Yard-O-Led Pencil Co. Ltd catalogue.

15 Hatton Garden, 1944.

13 Hatton Garden

Towards the end of the 18th century, this was the home of Perdita (aka Mrs Mary Robinson).

15 Hatton Garden

The original building was demolished in 1971.

16 Hatton Garden

Shown in images on the next page. Location of Eton Jewellery Co.

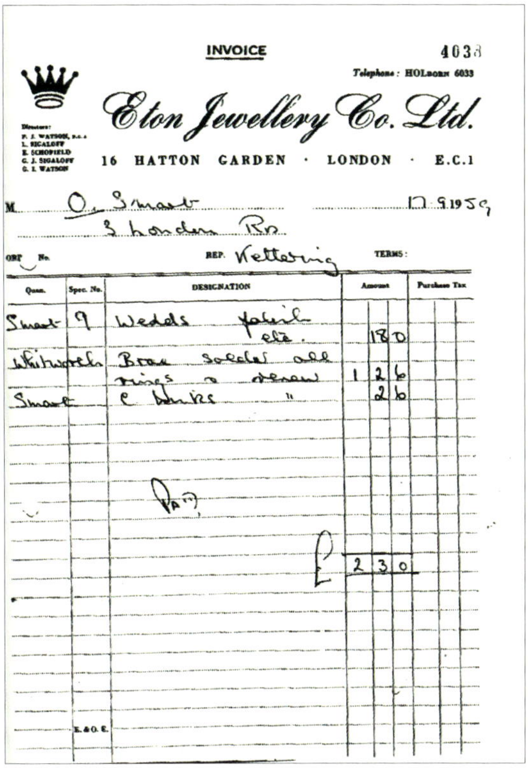
INVOICE 4038

Telephone: HOLBORN 6033

Eton Jewellery Co. Ltd.

16 HATTON GARDEN · LONDON · E.C.1

M. O. Smart 17.9.1959
3 London Rd.

REP. Kettering TERMS:

Quan.	Spec. No.	Designation	Amount	Purchase Tax
Smart	9	Wedds polish etc.	18 0	
Whitworth		Brace solder all rings & clean	1 2 6	
Smart		C links "	2 6	

Paid

£ 2 3 0

E.&O.E.

16 Hatton Garden. Eton Jewellery Co., 1959.

17–18 Hatton Garden.

17 Hatton Garden

The first office premises of TH March & Co.

19–21 Hatton Garden

Commissioned by David Stewart Dawson as the global head office for his jewellery and watch business, it was opened in 1907. Known as 'The Treasure House', its neoclassical architectural style was typical of the period, including its art nouveau wooden interior doors. The building was a showroom for his customers and even had a whole floor dedicated to a client lounge. This building has wonderful carved stone detail and is worth a closer look. The six separate features represent various aspects of a goldsmith's craft. On the left is a portrayal of the goldsmith holding a hammer in his right hand. Then there is an image of a woman sitting with her jewellery box and admiring her gems. The third image is of a foundryman depicting a furnace and a crucible of molten metal, which he is grasping with tongs. In fourth position is a miner using a prybar and also showing a miner's lamp in the background. Fifth is a man who is admiring a large trophy and lastly is a woman admiring herself in a mirror.

19 Hatton Garden Stewart Dawson playing cards.

Architectural Detail from 19 – 21 Hatton Garden:

19–21 Hatton Garden Architectural detail depicting a foundryman with crucible, tongs, and kiln.

19–21 Hatton Garden Architectural detail depicting the satisfaction of a trophy.

19–21 Hatton Garden. Architectural detail depicting a miner with lamp and bar.

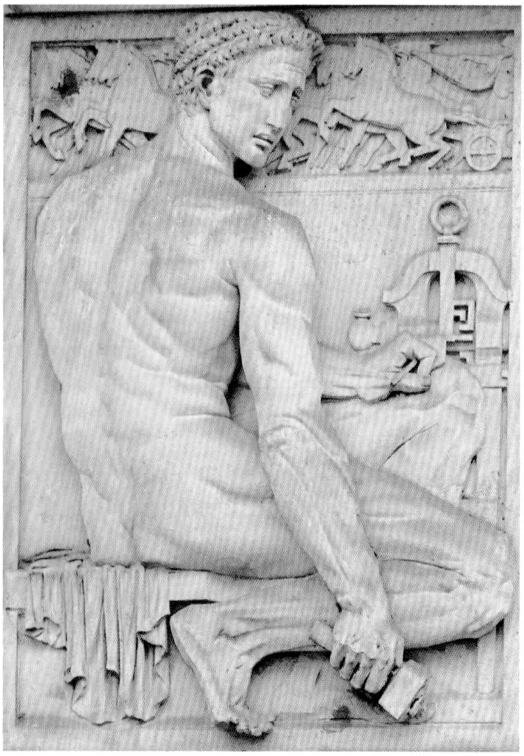

19–21 Hatton Garden. Architectural detail depicting a goldsmith with hammer and mills.

19–21 Hatton Garden. Architectural detail depicting a woman with jewellery box and jewels.

19–21 Hatton Garden. Architectural detail depicting a woman and a mirror without jewels.

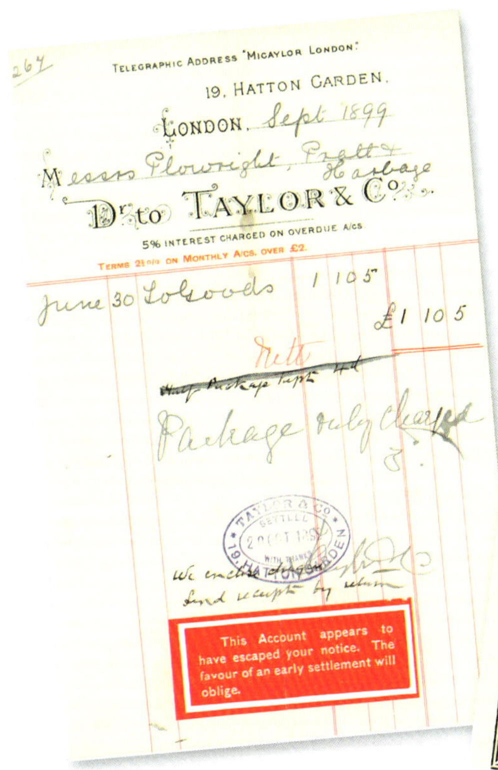

Telegraphic Address "Micaylor London."

19, Hatton Garden,

London, Sept 1899

Messrs Plowright, Pratt & Harbage

Dr. to Taylor & Co.

5% interest charged on overdue A/cs

Terms 2½% on Monthly A/cs. over £2.

June 30 Lo goods 1 10 5

£1 10 5

Nett

Package only charged

This Account appears to have escaped your notice. The favour of an early settlement will oblige.

19–21 Hatton Garden. An overdue account statement, 1899.

19–21 Hatton Garden. M Warner Bros advert.

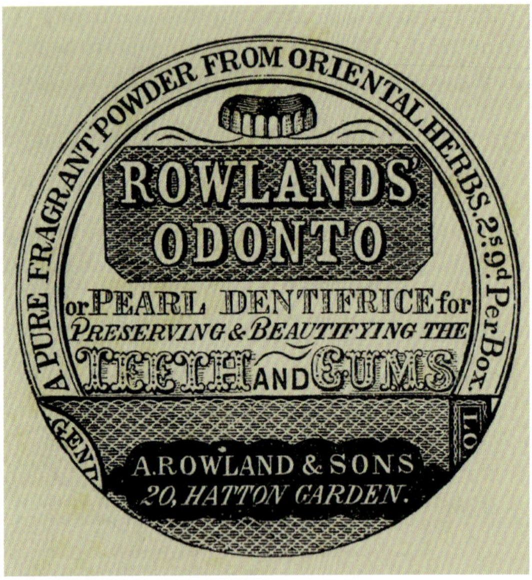

Advertisement for Rowlands at 20 Hatton Garden.

23 Hatton Garden.

24 Hatton Garden

This is one of the older buildings remaining in the street. David Halperin of Val d'Or bought the freehold in 1994 as no one else would touch it. The building was constructed without proper foundations and was at risk of collapse. It is now secured to the adjacent buildings. David came to Hatton Garden in 1954 for a job with Marryat & Place. However, when the workers went on strike he decided to look elsewhere. After a period in manufacturing he bought King's Lapidary of Clerkenwell. He was known to the Kornitzer family, who have left us with a legacy of literature providing wonderful insights to the trade of a previous generation.

25a Hatton Garden

This corner site was known to many as the Lema Buttery, a café pre-dating the modern brands and chain shop franchises. When the café closed, the site was taken over by Carlo Jewellers. Mr Carlo was previously an Italian tailor with a business in Greville Street. Local clients provided stock for him to trade and eventually his success allowed him to give up the tailoring.

Clockwise from above: 25 Hatton Garden. Finger sizing gauge from Drewell & Bradshaw Ltd; 24–25 Hatton Garden; 24–25 Hatton Garden.

26 Hatton Garden

This was the original location of the 'panelled rooms', which were removed in 1907. The panelled rooms were presented to the V&A Museum in 1912 by the National Art Collections Fund, assisted by a body of subscribers composed of Lord Leverhulme, Lord Riddell and the proprietors of *Country Life* newspaper, among others. They were on display in the museum in 1920 but later removed to their storage archives at Blythe House, in Olympia, London. In 1851 this building was home to the City Orthopaedic Hospital. An insight into the importance of this facility can be seen in an extract from the *London Evening Standard* of Thursday, 30 April 1896:

32 Hatton Garden

Before bathrooms in private houses were considered, people would have to make use of public baths. Mr Rogers built over his garden at No. 32 a facility for all to use. One of his tenants was, appropriately, a certain coal merchant named Samuel Plimsoll. Plimsoll became MP for Derby and is best known as the creator of the Plimsoll Line used when loading a ship.

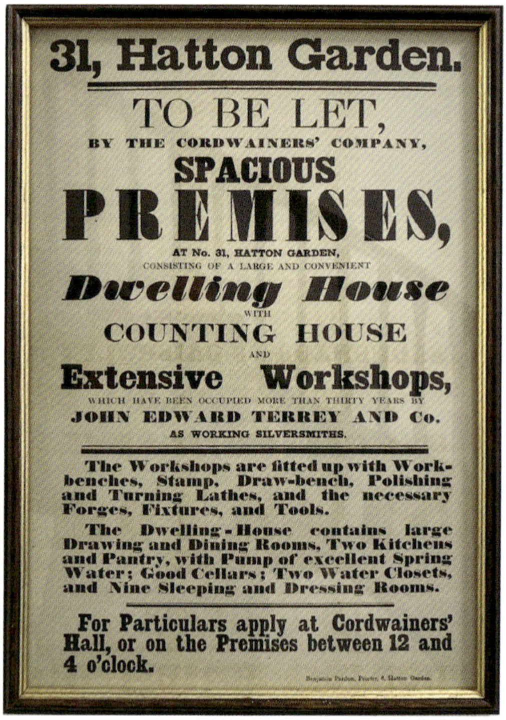

Clockwise from top left: No. 31 Hatton Garden, staircase in 2019; poster showing proposed sale of freehold; Diamond House, 37 Hatton Garden, Tidy & Blanshard glass paperweight.

Showroom of Bausch & Lomb at 37–38 Hatton Garden.

37–38 Hatton Garden Unity Watch Co. blotter.

39 Hatton Garden

The architect Charles Barry, who designed St Peter's Church, Saffron Hill, and went on to design the Houses of Parliament lived here at the start of his career. His son described it as 'a position of no great pretension, but one recommended by its quietness, centrality and cheapness'.

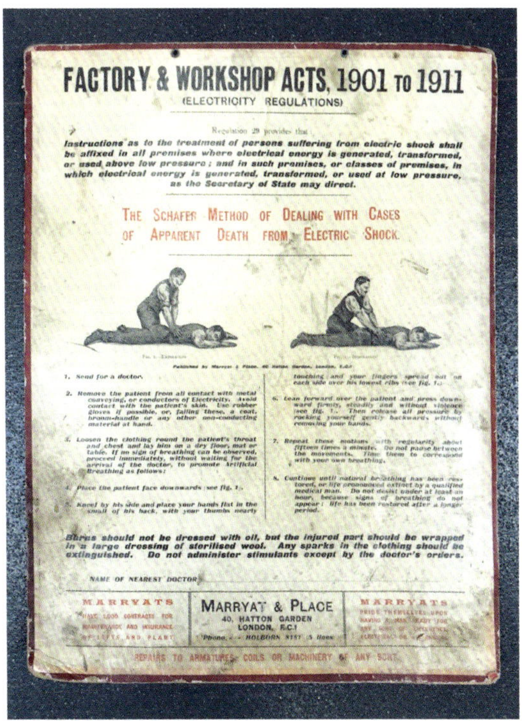

40 Hatton Garden. Marryat & Place safety notice.

Telegraphic Address: "PHONOPLEX, LONDON."

NEW CENTURY
TRADE MARK.

40, HATTON GARDEN,
HOLBORN CIRCUS,
London, ... 190
E.C.

A21052

Bought of
WATERFIELD, & CLIFFORD & Co.,
LIMITED.

GOLD MEDAL.
BIRMINGHAM.

NEW CENTURY PHONOGRAPHS.

Mr. ....

REFERRING TO THIS PLEASE MENTION ~~ORDER~~ ABOVE NUMBER.

Clockwise from top left: 40 Hatton Garden; 41 Hatton Garden. CS Harris & Sons Silversmiths; 40 Hatton Garden. A letterhead from 1905.

42 Hatton Garden

Abraham Arlidge, who produced the 1694 survey and map, lived here.

43 Hatton Garden (Wren House)

Famous for the statues of children in their blue coats, this architectural gem owes its design to Sir Christopher Wren. It was built as a church around 1670 but soon became used as a school. Today it contains a modern building within its original shell.

44 Hatton Garden

Once the home of Robert Paul, a scientific instrument maker who diversified into the production of cine projectors at the end of the 19th century.

44 Hatton Garden. Safety Products Ltd goggles.

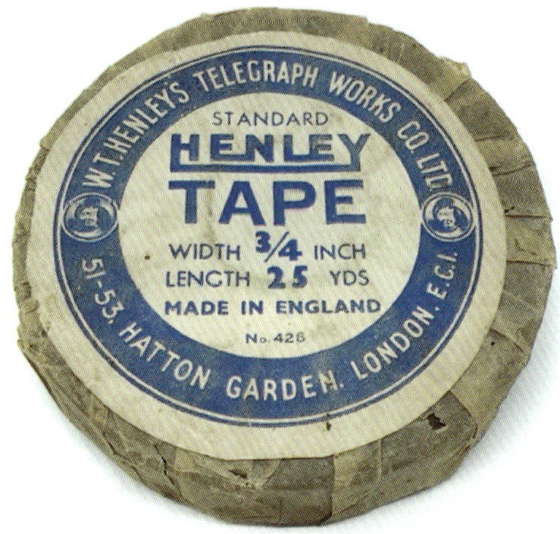

51–53 Hatton Garden. Henley's Tape.

51 Hatton Garden

This was the last of the original houses in the street to have a garden. In 1930 it was described as being 'ivy walled and brilliant with flowers'. Its survival was due to the terms of an old lease.

52 Hatton Garden

A poster in the author's collection (page 216) shows: 'This lithograph is a half sheet from Adolf Friedlander, Hamburg, Germany of Le Roy-Talma-Bosco and is of the great magicians climbing a mountain to the pentacle to reach a crate that is suspended from a chain and hook'. The crate reads 'Servais Le Roy Co, 52 Hatton Garden London New illusions Original secrets'. Servais Le Roy was the premier illusionist and conjuror of his time. Born in Belgium in 1865, he was said to have run away to England aged 12 and made his first professional appearance aged 14. The names at the bottom of the poster are those of the act he put together shortly after the turn of the century. Talma was his assistant and later his wife, who soloed in a show along with another noted magician, Bosco. He began the business of supplying illusions in 1910 with the idea of retiring, but continued to perform for another three decades. The poster is an original, not a reproduction, dating to somewhere in the trio's heyday – most likely from the late 1910s to the mid-1920s.

This was also the Hatton Garden home of H Landsberg.

54 Hatton Garden

In Charles Dickens's time this was a Police Court and, between 1836 and 1838, was run by a formidable Mr Alan Stewart Laing. Dickens used this in *Oliver Twist* but changed the name of the magistrate to Mr Fang. However, Dickens's exposure of Laing's severe ruling led to his resignation. Oliver was brought before the magistrate accused of stealing a handkerchief belonging to Mr Brownlow. The back entrance led into Hatton Yard

52 Hatton Garden Le Roy Magician.

and the guilty would be taken out this way to serve their prison sentence. The court relocated in 1842 but, within living memory, there was still evidence of its former use in the form of chains on the wall in the cellar. The court also features in *Bleak House*.

Until recently, 54 was the premises of one of the oldest surviving silversmiths, Padgett & Braham. They occupied the building from 1919 until 2000. John Padgett recounts how, some years ago, he received a letter from one of his banks advising him of proposed new charges for keeping documents in their safe. He had given no such documents to the bank and asked for sight of them. An envelope was delivered that contained papers appertaining to No. 54 Hatton Garden from 1654 to 1798. Written in old English, they were not easy to read but gave a wonderful insight into the property of that time. A Padgett & Braham catalogue includes a reference to their premises:

> In 1977, the freehold of the old Barnard factory at 54 Hatton Garden was taken over and the building was completely renovated and modernised. A showroom and offices were included in the new design and the building again became worthy of the output of its products.

The company has kept its entire ledgers, cashbooks, etc. for many years and they are now deposited with the V & A Museum on loan. They include stories of how their rep. travelled to Manchester by stagecoach. (The original Hatton Garden finished at Hatton Wall and the extension, which veers slightly to the west, was Christopher Street. When Hatton Garden was extended the numbering had to include letters as 58 was on the opposite side of the road.)

55 Hatton Garden

54 Hatton Garden.

55 Hatton Garden.

57d Hatton Garden

At No. 57d, in 1884, Hiram Maxim (1840–1896) made his first automatic gun, forging his own tools and even blowing a necessary glass instrument himself, to the amazement of his workmen. The gun fired over 600 rounds a minute. Mr Matthey, of Johnson Matthey & Co., was among the first to come and see it in action and brought the Duke of Cambridge with him. The Prince of Wales, afterwards King Edward VII, also came to inspect the new weapon, which was much commented on in the press at the time. The last machine gun made in the Hatton Garden establishment was sent to Henry Morton Stanley, then engaged upon his expedition for the relief of Livingstone.

Across the road to the west side is the earlier location of a Griffin brewery. Their buildings, which covered upwards of 4 acres, extended from Grays Inn Road, across Leather Lane, to Hatton Garden. The business was established in the 17th century and was always noted for its black beer or porter. Among many famous visitors to the brewery was the Emperor Napoleon III, who showed his appreciation of the firm's famous stout by emptying a tankard.

Clockwise from top left: 57a Hatton Garden; 57 Hatton Garden. Sike's hydrometer from TO Blake; 59 Hatton Garden. Watch movement from John Hawley & Son; 58 Hatton Garden. The Rose.

58 Hatton Garden

Once the home of the Rose Public House with its infamous first-floor strip club. The name can be seen on the front of the building up on the eaves.

59–61 (Colonial Buildings)

Although not an original building, this site still has iron railings with an aspect to the basement.

63-66 Hatton Garden

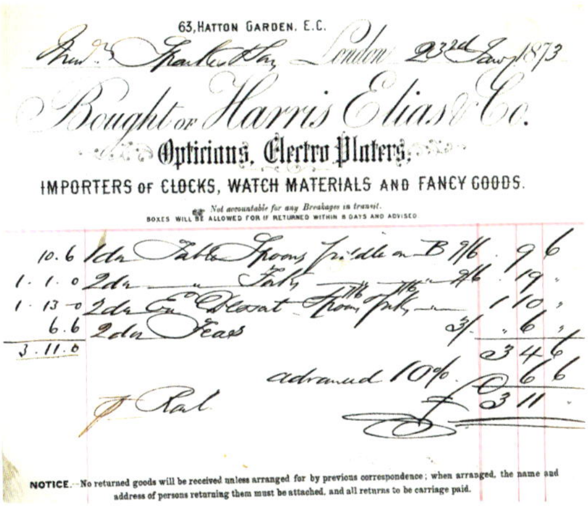

Clockwise from top left: 63 Hatton Garden. Invoice dated 1873; 62 Hatton Garden in 1888; 64 Hatton Garden; 66 Hatton Garden. Irish Whisky label; 63–66 Hatton Garden. Original doorplate for The Diamond Trust.

Clockwise from top: 66 Hatton Garden. True-Thread Screw Co., 1926; New House, 68 Hatton Garden; 66 Hatton Garden Old Irish Whisky bottle.

67–68 Hatton Garden (New House)

No. 67 was once the home of Thomas Gainsborough (1727–1788), the famous painter. On 15th July 1746, aged 19, he married Margaret Burr. His first work on public display was a view of Charterhouse. Behind 67 was a yard. This was at one time the home of Felton's coachworks. At the turn of the 19th century, Leather Lane was well known for its coachworks. Richard Trevithick's London Steam Carriage was fitted out at Felton's.

72 Hatton Garden

Another old-established business, still trading in 1930, was Langdale's. Originally located near Leather Lane, their premises were burnt down in 1780 by the Gordon rioters. The scene is described in *Barnaby Rudge* and cost many lives and £100,000 to the owner.

73 Hatton Garden

Original home of the Foundling Hospital in 1741.

69 Hatton Garden. Steven Strauss & Co Ltd.

69 Hatton Garden. Whitaker & Co. pot lid.

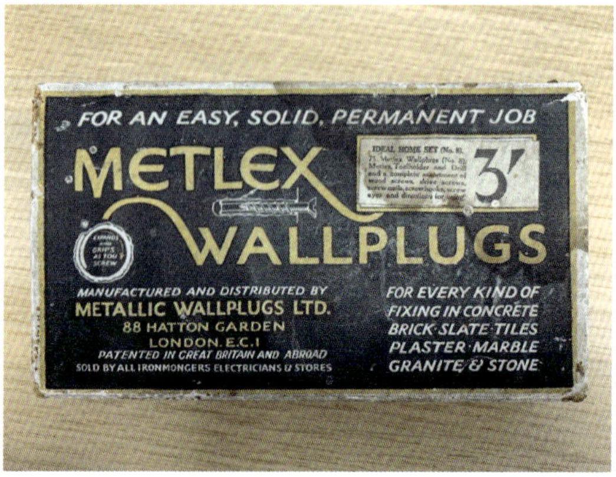

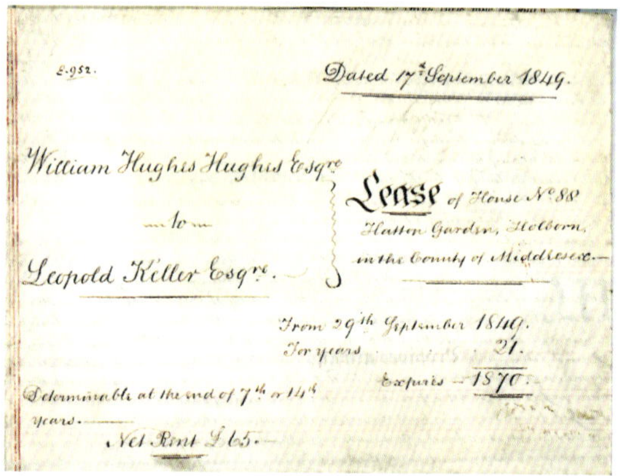

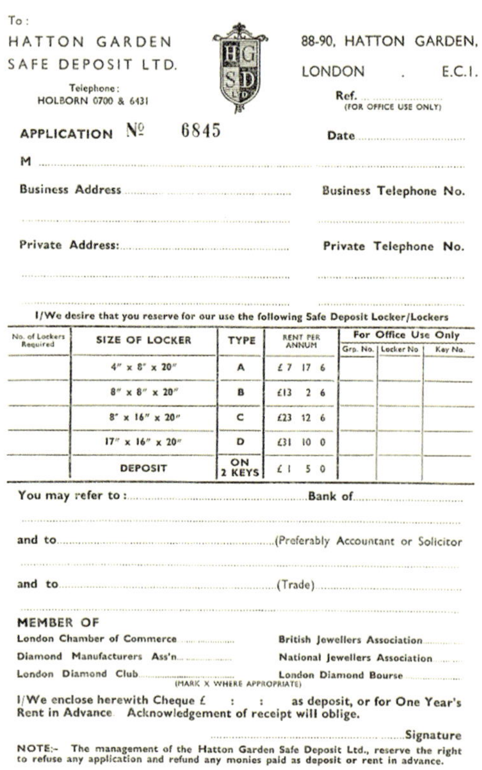

To:
HATTON GARDEN
SAFE DEPOSIT LTD.

Telephone:
HOLBORN 0700 & 6431

88-90, HATTON GARDEN,
LONDON . E.C.1.

Ref. ....
(FOR OFFICE USE ONLY)

APPLICATION No 6845

Date ....

M ....

Business Address .... Business Telephone No. ....

Private Address: .... Private Telephone No. ....

I/We desire that you reserve for our use the following Safe Deposit Locker/Lockers

No. of Lockers Required	SIZE OF LOCKER	TYPE	RENT PER ANNUM	For Office Use Only: Grp. No.	Locker No	Key No.
	4" x 8" x 20"	A	£7 17 6			
	8" x 8" x 20"	B	£13 2 6			
	8" x 16" x 20"	C	£23 12 6			
	17" x 16" x 20"	D	£31 10 0			
	DEPOSIT	ON 2 KEYS	£1 5 0			

You may refer to .... Bank of ....

and to .... (Preferably Accountant or Solicitor)

and to .... (Trade) ....

MEMBER OF
London Chamber of Commerce .... British Jewellers Association ....
Diamond Manufacturers Ass'n .... National Jewellers Association ....
London Diamond Club .... London Diamond Bourse ....
(MARK X WHERE APPROPRIATE)

I/We enclose herewith Cheque £ : : as deposit, or for One Year's Rent in Advance. Acknowledgement of receipt will oblige.

.... Signature

NOTE:- The management of the Hatton Garden Safe Deposit Ltd., reserve the right to refuse any application and refund any monies paid as deposit or rent in advance.

Clockwise from top left: Interior of the old London Diamond Club building; 87 Hatton Garden. Simmon Box eternity ring gauge; 88 Hatton Garden. Twenty-one-year lease for the house at £65 per annum dated 1849; View inside safe deposit; 86 Hatton Garden. Box of quills from Morrell's; 88–90 Hatton Garden. Application form; 88 Hatton Garden. Metlex wallplugs box.

reached its peak in the 20th century. It was once the home of Sir Moses Montefiore, who died there in 1885. He was partner and brother-in-law to Baron MN Rothschild, founder of the Allied Insurance Company. For many years the building was the home of the London Diamond Club. It was also home to Mr Taunton's Theatre of Anatomy.

88–90 Hatton Garden

The corner site was developed first and then the rear section. This landmark building has found infamy in being the scene of the Hatton Garden Safe Deposit Burglary.

91 Hatton Garden

Site of the Globe pub. It was recorded as being the meeting place of the 'Oddfellows', who used to meet here in 1748. The infamous highwayman John Everett hid at the Globe while escaping capture for robbing a coach. Legend has it that he calmly ordered wine before disappearing into the night. It is also reported to have been a favourite watering hole of well-known sci-fi writers including Arthur C Clarke and John Wyndham.

97 Hatton Garden

This was once a Moravian Monastery.

The Globe pub, Hatton Garden.

96–97 Hatton Garden.

Hatton Garden post marks.

120 Hatton Garden

This is the last address in the street.

HATTON WALL

The last crossroads at the north end of Hatton Garden is the intersection with Hatton Wall. This road marks the original boundary of the 'Garden'. The short section of today's Hatton Garden that leads into Clerkenwell Road was originally known as Christopher Street but was renamed when Clerkenwell Road was built in the late 19th century. Consequently, today there are street numbers such as 57d, where property has been included in the Hatton Garden address.

Hatton Wall street sign.

29 Hatton Wall.

Clockwise from top left: Hatton Yard, the rear of Mr Fang's Court; Hatton Place showing damage from an incendiary bomb, 1941; Hatton Yard.

KIRBY STREET

Prior to the development of Hatton Garden, the area through which Kirby Street runs was believed to have been the cemetery of Ely Palace. A report in the *London Evening Standard* of 25th May 1905 describes how workmen discovered human remains below No. 15, only a couple of feet below ground. Previously skeletons had been discovered a few doors away.

Kirby Street was originally known as Great Kirby Street and runs parallel to Hatton Garden from Greville Street to St Cross Street. It is named in memory of the last owner of Hatton House, Christopher Hatton, whom Charles I created Baron Hatton of Kirby in 1643. Kirby is a small village in Northamptonshire where the Hatton family came from. There was also a Little Kirby Street, which later became Cross Street and subsequently St Cross Street.

30 Kirby Street. Joseph Richmond & Co., makers of printing machines.

43 Kirby Street. Advert for Hirschfelds, 1937.

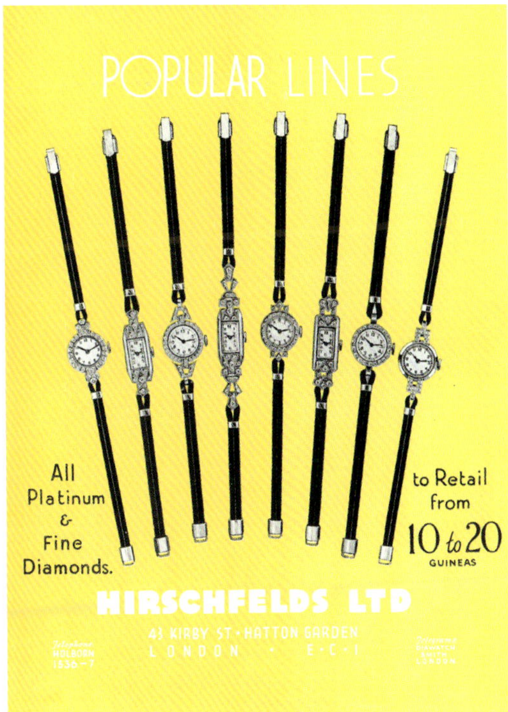

43 Kirby Street. Advert for Hirschfelds, 1937.

LEATHER LANE

67 Leather Lane. The music shop where office workers bought their music at lunch time.

Running to the west of Hatton Garden in an approximately north–south direction is the intriguing world of Leather Lane. This old right of way, which was just outside the boundary of Hatton's garden, has become a community in its own right.

It is perhaps best known as one of London's oldest street markets, being about 350 years old. Operating during the week around lunchtime, it now serves office workers, those engaged in the jewellery trade and local residents. Historically, its main activities were clothing, footwear, flowers, fruit and vegetables and household goods. One of the best-known stall holders was a man who only sold leathers such as you might use to clean your car or polish a piece of jewellery. Another was the man who sold crockery and dinner services. He would attract an audience by balancing a whole set on his arms while giving his spiel.

Today, however, it appears that nearly every stall is selling 'street food', but the market is as busy as ever. In the 1960s nearly every stall was operated by a man but that changed as more women joined the working community. Today the area is as diverse as can be imagined with the increase of all manner of ethnic groups.

Contrary to what many might imagine, the name of the street has nothing whatsoever to do with leather. The name is derived from *Le Vrunelane*. This was first recorded in a document dating from 1241.

Le Vrunelane is a Flemish word meaning Soke Lane. Leather Lane was a small farm track that led to the Soke of Portpoole. In 1240, Samson Enganet, from Flanders, owned part of the soke. As time went by, the name was corrupted to Lyverune Lane, Lovreland, Lyver lane, Liver Lane, Lither Lane and ultimately Leather Lane.

The Bishops of Ely acquired the land to the east of Leather Lane in 1290 and built a long wall of mud on their boundary. The land to the west was for the most part undeveloped.

The origins of the market are not entirely clear, but the popular view is that it owes its existence to the gambling habits of Charles II. The King had returned from exile after the death of Cromwell and had got into debt over two horses, to the tune of £500, a serious sum in its day, with a local trader known as Le Vrunelane. The story goes that the merchant got the King to agree to give him a royal charter to hold a market whereby a levy of 1d would pay off the debt.

Another explanation suggests that the name comes from the old French word for greyhound, which may have been a local tavern – and may be that of the merchant, perhaps even in the soke.

The lane was eventually built up with houses. Stow described it as 'a turning to the fields, lately replenished with houses'. By 1720, the east side was all brick built. At the back of these houses were yards for stables and coach houses belonging to the wealthy residents of Hatton Garden.

Hatton Chapel in Leather Lane was under the patronage of the Countess of Huntingdon (1707–1791) who was an ardent Methodist. Thomas Smith was one of her preachers and became pastor here in 1807.

Leather Lane.

Leather Lane, *c.*1954.

Leather Lane, 1960s.

In Victorian times it became quite down at heel and attracted immigrant workers. It was described as 'a very poor neighbourhood ... much invested with thieves, beggars, and Italian organ-grinders'.

Prior to the Second World War there was a very strong Italian community at the Clerkenwell end of the lane. The disruptions of the war meant that this was lost and never really recovered, although some establishments lingered on. Life was hard. Most dwellings had no kitchen or bathroom and only the use of a communal toilet. Water also was supplied via a sink on the landing and had to be carried up the stairs to fill the tin bath.

In the post-war period and throughout the second half of the 20th century the market thrived. There was an increase in the number of office workers in the Hatton Garden area, many of whom were commuters. So, the market was no longer serving locals but reaching a far wider audience.

It has been suggested that there was no better place in London to see the vibrancy of post-war Britain than in the theatre of human life that was Leather Lane. At this time, it had in the region of 150 stalls.

One of the many characters was a certain Tommy Cooper, who was destined to be one of the top comedians of his generation. His gift of the gab would have been an asset, as would his height, which might have enabled him to spot a policeman approaching. There

17–19 Leather Lane. Sidney Levy photographic.

is nothing to suggest that his activity was anything other than above board but there were many who were less honest. At that time policemen had to be close to 6 feet tall and wore a helmet to make them stand out in the crowd.

Those trying to sell stolen goods could quickly pack their goods into a suitcase and withdraw to the shelter of a café until the coast was clear.

Apart from the market stalls there were many shops, some catering for specialist needs and others for daily needs such as Brett's Dairy. Sidney Levy was an excellent photographic shop selling cameras for 35mm and 8mm cine.

Leather Lane, 1960s.

Leather Lane, 1960s.

At the end of the lane on the corner of Clerkenwell Road is the Magic Shop. This unprepossessing shop front is the way into an amazing world of conjuring, magic tricks and practical jokes.

One of the landmark buildings of Leather Lane is the Clock House public house on the corner of St Cross Street. It is a Grade II listed building and has an amazing interior.

Leather Lane Magic Shop.

THE HEARTH OF THE HOMELESS: EVICTED TENANTS OF CONDEMNED HOUSES IN LEATHER LANE, HOLBORN. (See page 5.)

1153

'The Hearth of the Homeless' – evicted tenants from condemned houses.

Top row: two different views of Leather Lane. Bottom: Leather Lane, 1930s.

Clockwise from top left: Leather Lane, 1840; Leather Lane; Leather Lane. Sunday Morning workman's home.

The 1960s comic double act Flanders and Swann immortalised Leather Lane in their song 'Down Below' about a sewerage worker.

> Hatton Garden is the spot, down below
> Where we like to go a lot, down below,
> Since a bloke from Leather Lane,
> Dropped a diamond down the drain,
> We'll be going there again, down below.

Painting by TH Shepherd.

LEATHER LANE.

Leather Lane.

Leather Lane road sign on the Prudential building.

Leather Lane at the corner with Holborn in 1899.

130 Irish residents evicted during slum clearance, 1891.

EVICTION OF POOR IRISH FAMILIES IN LEATHER LANE, HOLBORN.

Leather Lane. The Clock House pub.

Leather Lane. The Clock House interior.

SAFFRON HILL

Running parallel to Hatton Garden, and located between Kirby Street and Farringdon Road, is Saffron Hill. This is one of a number of streets in the area whose names refer to the former existence of a beautiful garden. The garden of Ely Palace was renowned, among many things, for its vines and saffron.

In the early 13th century the land that subsequently became Ely Palace and its garden was partly owned by a man named Richard Gold. It has been suggested that he built the road to give access to the adjoining land, then owned by the Abbotts of Missenden. The road was originally called 'Golde Lane' and was known as Gold Lane for many years.

It is referred to in documents of 29th October 1291 when Robert de Dorset granted land at the corner of Golde Lane and Holborn to William de Herlawe. Again, on 7th May 1346, Robert le Maresschal, citizen and goldsmith, occupied six cottages and courtyards in Golde Lane. This may be the earliest record of a goldsmith in Hatton Garden. Another goldsmith lived there according to a record of 14th November 1407.

John Stow wrote in 1598 of Saffron Hill 'sometime a filthy passage into the fields, now both sides built with small tenements'.

Later it became Field Lane as it gave access to the fields north of Holborn. Saffron Hill was originally the northern section with Field Lane in the south. Later Field Lane was dropped and the whole street became Saffron Hill.

Strype, in 1720, describes the locality as 'of small account both as to buildings and inhabitants, and pestered with small and ordinary alleys and courts taken up by the meaner sort of people; others are,' he says, 'nasty and inconsiderable'.

Field Lane and Saffron Hill were built upon the banks of the Fleet River, which was described in 1772 as 'a nauseous and abominable sink of nastiness, into which the tripe dressers, sausage makers and cat gut spinners, who shared the lane with professional thieves, flung their offal'.

In Hughson's *History of London, Volume IV*, written between 1806 and 1809, we read about Field Lane:

> In Stow's time, was distinguished as a filthy passage into the fields. It has undergone no improvement since his time; but is still one of the most dirty, narrow avenues in the metropolis; though constantly crowded with passengers to the various petty streets and alleys of Saffron Hill liberty, and St Sepulchres Without. It abounds with shops for the sale of clothes, tripe, old iron and too often with receptacle for the receipt of stolen property.

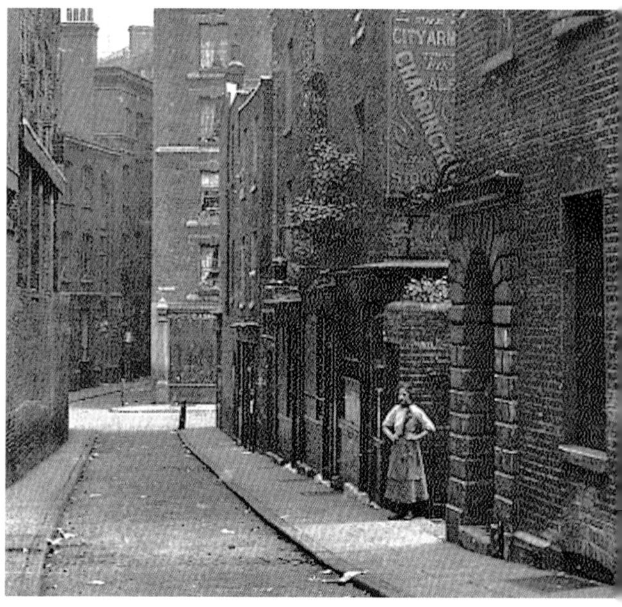

Saffron Hill.

Dickens called Field Lane an 'Emporium of Petty Larceny' and sketching it in *Oliver Twist* in 1837, wrote:

> Near to the spot, on which Snow Hill and Holborn meet, there opens, upon the right hand as you come out of the City, a narrow and dismal alley, leading to Saffron Hill. In its filthy shops are exposed for sale huge bunches of pocket-handkerchiefs of all sizes and patterns, for here reside the traders who purchase them from pickpockets. Hundreds of these handkerchiefs hang dangling from pegs outside the windows or flaunting from the doorposts, and the shelves within are piled with them. Confined as the limits of Field Lane are, it has its barber, its coffee-shop, its beer-shop, and its fried fish warehouse. It is a commercial colony of itself—the emporium of petty larceny, visited at early morning and setting-in of dusk by silent merchants, who traffic in dark back parlours and go as strangely as they come. Here the clothes-man, the shoe-vamper, and the rag-merchant, display their goods as signboards to the petty thief, and stores of old iron and bones, and heaps of mildewy fragments of woollen-stuff and linen, rust and rot in the grimy cellars.

Saffron Hill.

In Dickens's novel, Jack Dawkins, the Artful Dodger, leads Oliver Twist to Fagin's den, which was in Field Lane. He writes:

> ... a dirty and more wretched place he [Oliver] had never seen. The street was very narrow and muddy, and the air was impregnated with filthy odours. There were a good many small shops; but the only stock in trade appeared to be heaps of children, who, even at that time of night, were crawling in and out at the doors, or screaming from the inside. The sole places that seemed to prosper amid the general blight of the place, were the public-houses; and in them, the lowest orders of Irish were wrangling with might and main. Covered ways and yards, which here and there diverged from the main street, disclosed little knots of houses, where drunken men and women were positively wallowing in filth; and from several of the door-ways, great ill-looking fellows were cautiously emerging, bound, to all appearance, on no very well-disposed or harmless errands.

Saffron Hill is also mentioned by Arthur Conan Doyle in his Sherlock Holmes story *The Adventure of the Six Napoleons* as the Italian Quarter where the Venucci family can be found.

Cunningham (1849) mentions that so dangerous was this neighbourhood in his day that when the clergy of St Andrew's, Holborn, visited it, they had to be accompanied by policemen in plain clothes.

Field Lane from Farringdon Road.

Opposite: Old houses, c. 1884.

Saffron Hill.

Saffron Hill street sign.

When the Clerkenwell Road was built it divided the road into two and the roads were called Great and Little Saffron Hill. Subsequently, the northern part became Herbal Hill.

According to an article in *The Builder* of 24th April 1869 describing the demolition of the old streets, nothing of interest was discovered but the plethora of secret passageways for escaping the law and the various nooks for stashing stolen goods.

During the 18th and 19th centuries, Saffron Hill became renowned for its brothels and vagabonds.

The One Tun Pub located on Saffron Hill was often frequented by Charles Dickens and is mentioned in *Oliver Twist* by the name of The Three Cripples. The One Tun pub started trading in 1759 and is one of two taverns still trading under that name.

The name refers to the size of the largest of the casks used to store the beer and wine, its capacity being four hogsheads or 252 gallons.

On a more positive note, the Saffron Hill Mission established a church dedicated to St Peter and St Paul in 1842.

The area suffered badly in the Blitz, including the church in Saffron Hill. The bomb sites became adventure playgrounds for children with a sense of discovery. Patricia Clarke writes in her *Memories of Holborn* under 'Toys and Games':

> For older children an adventurous activity was to go over bomb sites, walking along the tops of walls, both the outer walls built to guard the public and along the ruined walls within the site itself. There were holes to explore and cellars and old cupboards, all of which smelt musty and sooty. Buildings were usually boarded up and inaccessible ... I well remember St Peters Church in Saffron Hill. There was dark rubbish filled passages, and then the enormous ruined body of the church with its gaping windows, tumbled masonry and iron strewn floor.

Another link with literature can be found in a building displaying a plaque depicting a swan, a sailing ship and the letters L&Co with a date of 1726. Thomas Longman had used his inheritance to purchase a successful publishing business operating out of a shop called the Ship in Paternoster Row. He published Daniel Defoe's *Robinson Crusoe* and on the success of this work was able to buy the neighbouring premises called the Black Swan. Hence, the ship and swan became the company's logo.

The Saffron Hill works were established in 1887 as part of the Longman Publishing Company. The company's shop in Paternoster Row could not manage the increased demand for quality, leather-bound books. Longman became a world-class business, but its premises was destroyed in the Blitz.

Family control of the company ended in 1968, when the business was sold. The *Longman Dictionary* is available online, still using their ship logo.

Saffron Hill is now principally a residential area. Luxury flats dominate the landscape and will probably increase in value as the new Elizabeth Line improves transport to and from the area.

FIELD-LANE.

Field Lane, 1841.

Old house in Saffron Hill.

Saffron Hill 1903. Thousands of applicants responding to an advertisement for a few hands.

ST CROSS STREET

Originally known as Little Kirby Street, this road runs across Hatton Garden from Farringdon Road in the east to Leather Lane in the west. However, there was also a Cross Street, which can be seen on old maps where Greville Street now runs.

Former occupiers of premises in St Cross Street include Pastorelli & Co., manufacturers of barometers, thermometers and a variety of instruments from 1851 to 1865. In 1839 James Strugnell was a cabinetmaker at No. 14. In 1862, J Stickley was a beater of gold leaf and other metals.

In an age before state education became the norm, children from poor families had little or no hope of receiving an education without the philanthropic help of a benefactor. A good example of such a school was set up at 16 St Cross Street by members of the Highland Society in London. Having formed a charity in 1815, it wasn't until December 1819 that a suitable premises could be found. Six boys were selected and were looked after by six women, who were paid a shilling (5p) a week.

It was known as the Caledonian Asylum and provided lessons and accommodation for orphans of the Napoleonic Wars. It later moved to Islington, giving its name to Caledonian Road, and in 1852 succeeded in having Queen Victoria as its patron.

The Caledonian Church attracted people from all over London. The Reverend Edward Irving (1792–1834) ran the chapel from 1822 and was known as the 'Scottish divine and mystic'.

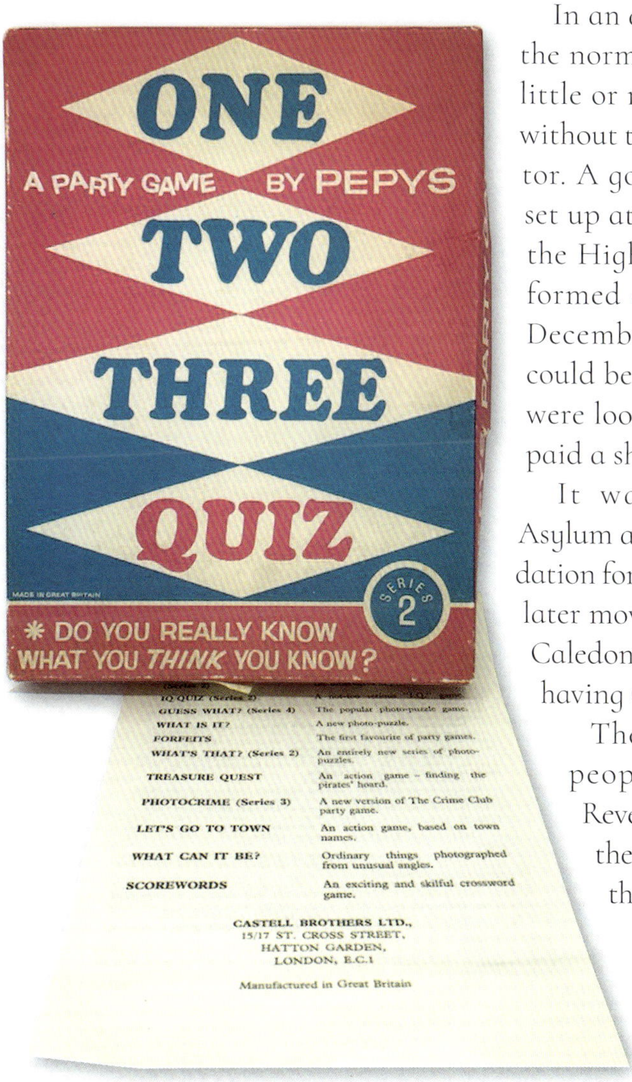

A selection of games from Castell Brothers, St Cross Street.

UNION COURT

In the south-east corner of the Hatton Garden estate was a small yard known as Union Court. It had previously been known as Scroope's Court after the Scroope family from Bolton, who had a townhouse here. Most of the court was demolished to make way for the new Holborn Viaduct.

At one time Union Court was home to William Henry Toms (1700–1750), a well-known engraver of his day.

GROWN IN THE GARDEN

Although Hatton Garden is thought of as being the home of the diamond industry, it has been and continues to be the home of other industries. There are many, but among the best known are the small selection that follows. Long before the houses in the garden became associated with industry, they were also home to a number of people who would have been in the news headlines of their day.

JOHN GERARD (1545–1612)

John Gerard spent a large part of his life living in the Holborn area. Although there is some debate as to the exact location of his home, it would be agreed that it was a very short walk from Hatton Garden, either in Fetter Lane or adjacent to Holborn Hill.

His place in history is due, in the main, to the publication of his works on plants – the first of their kind and leaders for over a generation.

Born in Nantwich, Cheshire, in 1545 he moved to London and was apprenticed to Alexander Mason of the Barber Surgeons Company at the age of 17. On 9th December 1569, he was admitted to the Freedom of the Company and permitted to open his own practice. It has been suggested that at some

John Gerard`.

stage he may have served as a ship's surgeon and developed his knowledge of plants from northern Europe.

His interest lay very much in matters botanical. He published a twenty-four-page catalogue in 1596 of the plants in his garden, which he called *The Catalogue*, and in 1597 he published *The Great Herball* or *General Historie of Plants*. The only surviving copy of his first work is in the British Library. At that time, his home would have been well outside the city, as Holborn was still not much more than a village. Gerard tells us in his writings that:

> in Gray's Inn Lane he gathered mallow, shepherd's purse, sweet woodruff, bugle and Paul's betony, and in the meadows near red-flowered clary, white saxifrage, the sad-coloured rocket, yarrow, lesser hawkweed and the curious strawberry-headed trefoil. Wallflower and golden stonecrop grew on the houses.

He died in February 1612 and was buried at St Andrew's Church, Holborn on 18th February.

RICHARD LOWER (1631–1691)

Richard Lower was an English physician who heavily influenced the development of medical science. He is best remembered for his works on transfusion and the function of the cardiopulmonary system.

Lower came from an old, affluent family with an interesting history. He was admitted from Westminster School to Christ Church, Oxford, in 1649. He took his BA in February 1653 and his MA in June 1655.

In 1666, Lower moved from Oxford to London, principally to establish a medical practice. He settled at first in Hatton Garden, but during the next decade moved several times, in each case to a more fashionable location.

He was admitted as a candidate of the Royal College of Physicians on 22 December 1671 and became a fellow on 29 July 1675.

Lower, having strong Protestant and anti-Popish sentiments, was closely identified with the Whig Party, and his later career followed its fortunes. In the 1680s, with the discreditation under Charles II of the Whigs and the ascendance and accession of James II, Lower fell into some disrepute. He lost his court appointment and steadily lost much of his practice.

Nevertheless, he carried on for several years, probably spending much of his time in Cornwall, until his death in 1691. In his will, he left money to St Bartholomew's Hospital in London and to the French and Irish Protestant refugees.

JOHN MOORE (1646–1714)

John Moore spent time in Hatton Garden while Bishop of Ely, a position that he held from 1707 until his death in 1714. Before taking up this post he had been Bishop of Norwich, where he had served since 1691.

He had been educated at Clare Hall, Cambridge, and later became a Fellow in 1667. His career in the Church started at Blaby in Leicestershire and took him, among other places, to be Rector of St Andrew's Church, Holborn. He caught a cold in Ely Palace while going about his business, died on 31st July 1714 and was buried in Ely Cathedral.

John Moore.

He was a passionate collector of books on all subjects and accumulated a library of almost 30,000 volumes, plus nearly 2,000 manuscripts. His large collection now forms part of the Royal Library within the Cambridge University Library. When George I came to the throne in 1714, he purchased the collection from Moore's estate for 6,000 guineas and presented it to Cambridge University by way of recognition of their loyalty and support of the House of Hanover. At the time it almost trebled the size of the library.

SAMUEL WILSON (SAMUEL WILSON'S LOAN TRUST)

Samuel Wilson lived in Hatton Garden in the 18th century. He was a Quaker who made a fortune as a wine merchant. He died a widower with no children. In his will, he left the sum of £20,000, which formed the basis of the Samuel Wilson Trust, set up in 1771. His will specified that the trustees should include the Lord Mayor, the First and Second Aldermen, the Recorder and Chamberlain of the City.

The trust continues today as a registered charity (No. 206964) and is operated by the City of London Corporation. It will consider grants to young people for establishing new businesses. The main requirements are:

Applicants must be under 40 years of age.

Loans may be up to £50,000 over five–ten years, at the discretion of the trustees.

Operate in the Greater London area or in the counties of Buckinghamshire, Essex, Hertfordshire, Kent, Surrey, East Sussex or West Sussex.

Not be a publican, a distiller or a vendor of alcohol.

JOHN STANLEY (1712–1786), MUSICIAN

John Stanley suffered a tragic accident when he was about 2½ years old. He fell on a marble hearth while carrying a china basin, which left him almost blind.

At the age of 14 he was appointed as organist at St Andrew's Church, Holborn, 'in preference to a great number of other candidates'.

He moved into Hatton Garden in 1751, opposite the home of the musical historian John Hawkins. Stanley and Hawkins became good friends and Hawkins later supplied many of the texts for Stanley's solo cantatas.

Stanley's last work was probably an ode written for the King's birthday (4th June 1786). Stanley never heard its performance – he died at his home in Hatton Garden on 19th May 1786, aged 74.

THOMAS GAINSBOROUGH (1727–1788)

Thomas Gainsborough arrived in London from Sudbury in about 1740.

After a period with other artists in St Martins Lane, he decided to rent his own rooms and found lodgings in Hatton Garden in about 1743, when he was just 16 years old. He began painting landscapes and portraits in a small size. By 1748 he was recognised as one of the country's leading artists. It is believed he left London in 1749 to return to Suffolk.

Thomas Gainsborough.

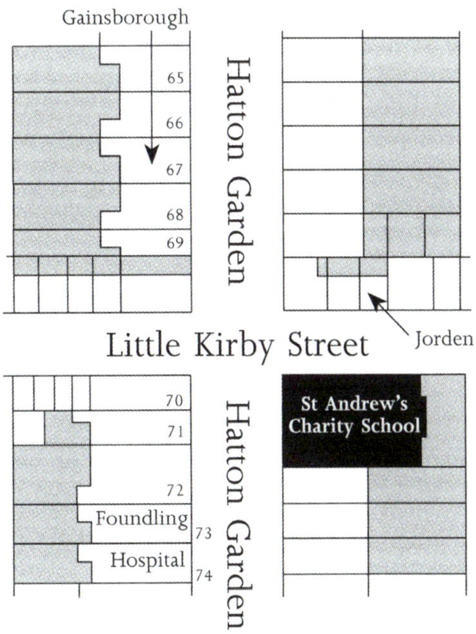

MRS MARY ROBINSON (OR PERDITA) 1758–1800

Mary Derby was the daughter of a Bristol whaling captain and was born on 27th November 1758 at College Green. She was sent to school in Chelsea. At the age of 16 she married a man named Robinson, with whom she led a fashionable life at 13 Hatton Garden until their lavish lifestyle caught up with them and she accompanied him to prison for a debt.

On her release in 1776 she went on the stage through the good offices of Garrick, and while playing the part of Perdita in his version of William Shakespeare's *A Winter's Tale*, attracted the notice of the Prince of Wales. In the letters she subsequently wrote, she signed herself as Perdita and the name stuck. It was rumoured that she and the Prince had a brief affair and when he ended their liaison she resorted to blackmail. She became one of the best-known actresses of her day and made a name for herself in writing.

She was also one of the most painted subjects of her day, particularly in her role as Perdita. Perhaps the best-known portrait was commissioned by the Prince of Wales (later George IV) in 1781 from Thomas Gainsborough. It is considered to be one of his best works, although he withdrew it from the Royal Academy exhibition in 1782 after criticism. The original work is now in the Wallace Collection.

MARY PRINCE (*C.* 1788–1833)

Mary Prince was born into slavery in Bermuda. When she was 12, she was sold for £38 to Captain John Ingham, but never took easily to the indignities of her enslavement and was often flogged by her cruel owners.

She was sold again in 1818 to John Wood, who sent her to Antigua to be a domestic slave. She joined the Moravian Church and, in 1826, married Daniel James, a former slave who had bought his freedom and worked as a carpenter and cooper. For this impudence, she was severely beaten by her master. In 1828, Wood took her as a servant to London. She remained with Wood until he threw her out.

She took shelter the same year with the Moravian Church in Hatton Garden. Within a few weeks, she had taken employment with Thomas Pringle, an abolitionist writer, and Secretary to the Anti-Slavery Society. Prince arranged for her narrative to be copied down and it was published in 1831 as *The History of Mary Prince*, the first account of the life of a black woman to be published in England.

An example is Prince's description of being sold away from her mother at a young age:

> It was night when I reached my new home. The house was large and built at the bottom of a very high hill; but I could not see much of it that night. I saw too much of it afterwards. The stones and the timber were the best things in it; they were not so hard as the hearts of the owners.

ROWLAND & SON

Alexander Rowland (1747–1823) was a London barber whose success was in part due to his invention in 1783 of Macassar Oil. His product for styling hair was made from a blend of coconut or palm oil and other secret ingredients that added to its fragrance. It was a huge success and a must have for any well-groomed man in Victorian times and beyond. Rowland registered 'Macassar Oil' as a trademark in 1888. The name is said to be derived from the Dutch East Indies location of Makassar, from where some of the ingredients were sourced.

Rowland's Macassar Oil has been immortalised by the invention of the antimacassar, a small cloth that covers and protects the head rest of a chair. The downside of the grooming product was that it left an oily stain wherever the user had sat and rested his head. In Edwardian times, an antimacassar was often a stylish piece of crochet work but later a simple piece of linen was used. Today, antimacassars can still be found on aeroplane seats and on first-class train seats in the UK and elsewhere, although they are now mostly made of paper.

A Rowland & Son, 20 Hatton Garden.

ROWLAND'S MACASSAR OIL AND KALYDOR WAREHOUSE,
20, HATTON GARDEN, LONDON.

JACQUES

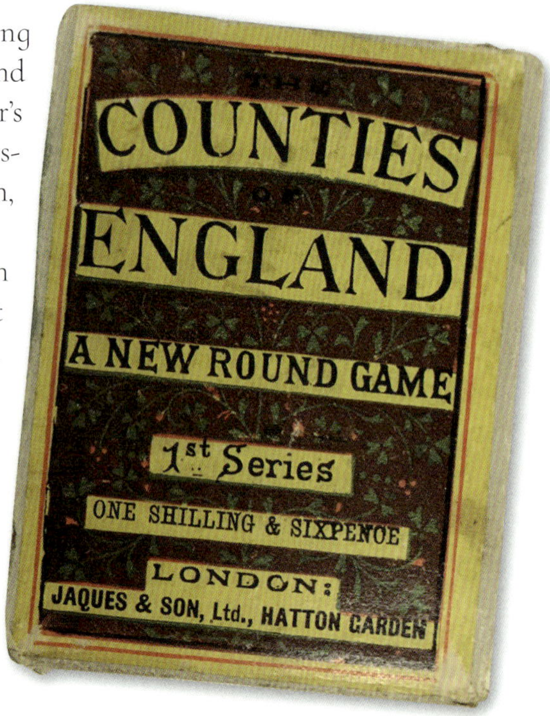

Jacques & Son Ltd. County card game 1st Edition.

Hatton Garden has a tradition of establishing family businesses, but not all are in the diamond trade. Thomas Jacques, born in 1765, was a farmer's son from Wiltshire with a French Huguenot ancestry. In 1780, at the age of 15, he travelled to London, on the back of a wagon, to seek his fortune.

He was able to use his creative skills as an apprentice to Mr Ivy, a bone and ivory turner, at 65 Leather Lane. At 21, he married Mr Ivy's niece. Then at the age of 30, his employer died. His skill and experience enabled him to take over the business and he established Thomas Jacques (Manufacturer of Ivory, Hardwoods, Bone, and Tunbridge Ware) in 1795. He traded as a one-man business and worked in wood, bone and ivory producing snuff boxes, brushes, paper knives, among other things.

His third child, John, was born in 1795 and at the age of 15 joined his father in the business. They subsequently became T & J Jacques – wholesale ivory turners. This was a period of history that could not foresee the damage caused by the killing of elephants for their tusks.

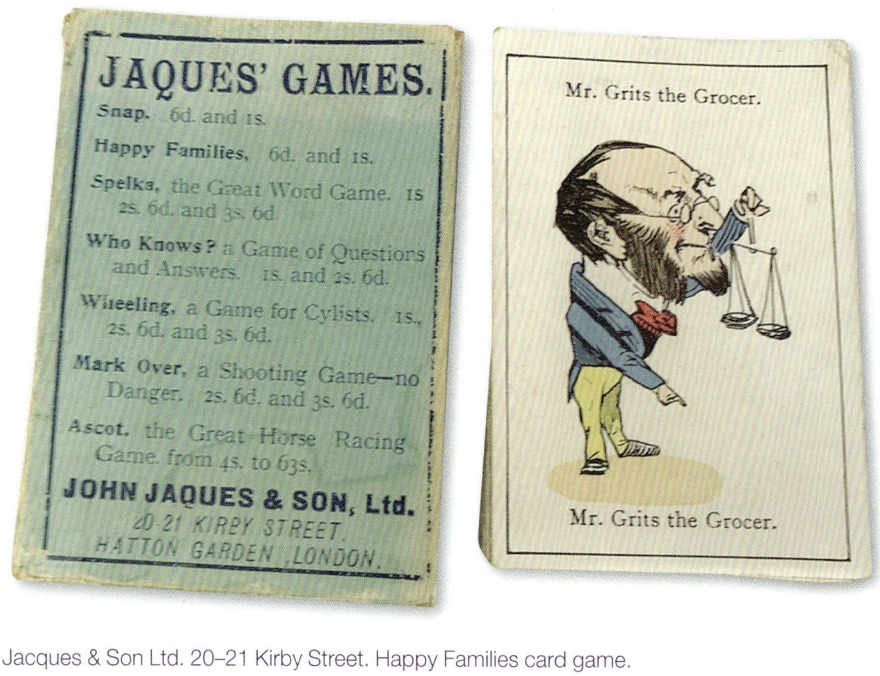

John Jacques & Son Ltd. 20–21 Kirby Street. Happy Families card game.

A selection of games from John Jacques & Son.

However, as their business grew, they expanded into other materials and their world-famous croquet sets were made from Turkey Boxwood. Eventually, they progressed from ivory into wood for most of their products.

The third generation of the Jacques family was established when John Jacques II joined the firm. They now also had premises at 102 Hatton Garden as well as the Leather Lane workshop. Here they continued to develop their games and it has been said that 'they taught the world to play'.

John Jacques II is credited with the invention of such games as Happy Families, Tiddlywinks, Ludo and Snakes and Ladders. His father-in-law, Nathaniel Cooke, created a totally new look to the game of chess that is still with us today. The design, based on the Elgin marbles, so impressed the chess expert Howard Staunton that he allowed his name to be used to describe the design.

At the Great Exhibition of 1851, Jacques won a gold medal for the introduction of croquet to Great Britain and in 1864 he wrote the 'Laws and Regulations of the Game'. He was awarded the Freedom of the City of London in 1869.

When John Jacques II joined the business in 1884, they further developed their range of sports equipment into tennis, football, hockey, badminton, cricket and archery. They now needed larger premises and moved to Kirby Street.

In 1902, John Jacques III invented a new game called Gossima. It was an immediate success and became better known as ping-pong and later table tennis.

The factory in Kirby Street was a victim of the Blitz and received a direct hit in 1941. All that remained was the burnt safe that contained their original pattern book of designs from 1795 to 1870.

The business was by no means lost and new premises were found in Thornton Heath, South London, where they remained until a larger more suitable location was found in Edenbridge, Kent.

The company continues to thrive and appropriately for the inventor of Happy Families is now in its seventh generation.

HAZELL'S

Printers and publishers also found the type of premises in Hatton Garden well suited to their needs. One such company was Messer's Watson & Hazel.

They had premises at 5 Kirby Street from 1841 and a head office in Charles Street from 1869. Their work was well known in Victorian England, but they reached the headlines in 1869 when a serious fire broke out and destroyed their warehouse. It was called 'The Great Fire of Hatton Garden'.

About 10 a.m. on Tuesday, 14th December, the fire started at the back of the ground-floor room in which piles of printed papers were stored. It was estimated that there would have been 600 or 700 reams, including issues of the *British Workman* and *Band of Hope Review*. Those that weren't destroyed by the fire were ruined by the water and smoke. The fire spread through the three-storey building, but all the workforce, numbering about ninety, managed to escape without harm. The fire was extinguished by noon before it could spread to neighbouring buildings.

ROBERT W PAUL (1869–1943)

The story of Robert Paul illustrates how just one incident can change the course of someone's life and of history. Paul set up a precision instrument-making company in 1891 with a workshop at 44 Hatton Garden, London.

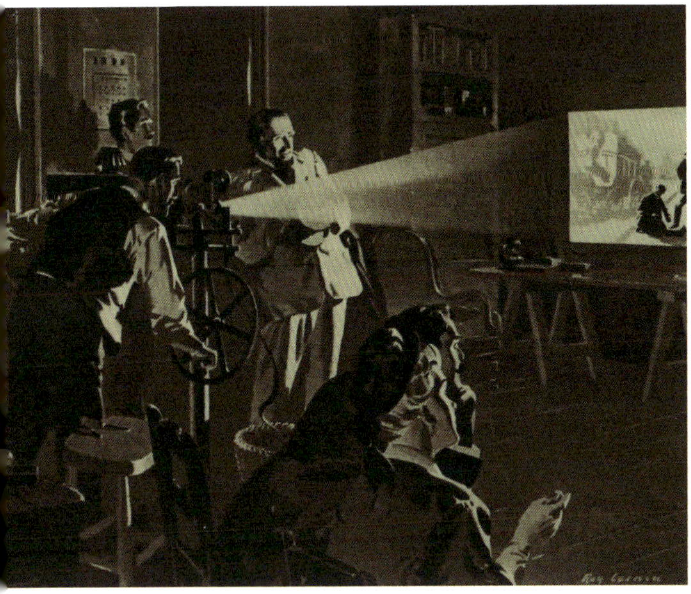

Robert Paul.

In 1894, aged 25, he was approached by two Greek entrepreneurs who wanted him to manufacture six duplicates of the Edison Kinetoscopes they had purchased in New York and were already operating in London. To his surprise, the machines were not patented in England and he was free to do so. He actually made sixty, which he also sold to other showmen. (Edison had some years earlier waived aside his attorney's suggestion of foreign patents.)

These machines he placed on exhibition in Earl's Court, London, to a large and immediate profit. The fame of Paul and the Kinetoscope spread, and a large demand arose in Great Britain and extended over to the Continent. Orders for the machines came from all directions. (Edison had not only overlooked foreign patents, but the whole foreign market as well.) When Paul and his assistants appeared at his shop in the mornings, they found the stairway lined with waiting customers, some asleep on the steps after a night-long vigil there in Hatton Garden holding their places to book orders for Kinetoscopes.

However, not being licensed Edison operators, Paul's customers were unable to obtain films to show on their machines. Paul applied his mind to the development of a camera and within a month the first film to be produced in Great Britain was shown. He used the roof of the Alhambra Music Hall. One of his first films was entitled *The Soldier's Courtship* and he ended up marrying the heroine.

Tradition has it that when he first projected his own film at the Hatton Garden studio a cheer so loud went up from the audience that it caused the police to be called.

In 1894 Paul collaborated with a certain HG Wells to produce a film called *The Time Machine*. Wells had been a science teacher who abandoned his career in the classroom for a more fulfilling role as a writer/film producer. This no doubt also helped him with his career as an author.

In June 1896, Paul filmed the finish of the Derby at Epsom, processed the film overnight and screened it the next day, thus creating one of the first news films.

Demand for his machines increased and he expanded his operations, including the training of other projectionists. He was very much a pioneer in the movie industry, a forerunner of what was to grow into a vast multi-million-pound business. However, it is reported that one day he took his entire stock of films and set fire to it in the yard, He gave no explanation at the time or afterwards but then went back to instrument making.

SIR HIRAM MAXIM

Hiram Maxim was born on 5th February 1840 in Maine, USA. From an early age, he showed a keen interest in things mechanical. One of his many inventions was the automatic resetting mouse trap.

He came to London in 1881 as an employee of the United States Electric Lighting Company. It was about this time that he began to work on what was to become his most famous invention, the automatic machine gun.

Housed in a small factory in London's Hatton Garden, Maxim invented and perfected a single-barrelled gun that could fire 666 rounds per minute. Many eminent people, including the Prince of Wales, went to view this extraordinary new weapon. The gun was adopted by the British Army in 1891 and was first used by the colonial forces in the First Matabele War in Rhodesia (1893–94).

Sir Hiram Maxim blue plaque.

It played a major part in the colonisation of southern Africa in the late 19th century, both by its firepower and its reputation.

The effectiveness of the Maxim gun was such that it inspired the poet Hilaire Belloc to pen the lines:

> Whatever happens, we have got
> The Maxim gun, and they have not

The popularity of the gun was so great that Maxim had to relocate and in 1884 moved to Crayford. He became a naturalised British subject in 1900 and was knighted in 1901. He died on 24th November 1916, aged 76, and today there is a blue plaque on the building in Hatton Garden where he created his infamous weapon.

RENTOKIL

Hatton Garden was also the launch pad for a company whose name would become a household word: Rentokil.

In a small laboratory in Hatton Garden, Mr Harold Maxwell Lefroy started to produce bottles of a woodworm treatment. He was a professor of Entomology at Imperial College, London. In the 1920s he had been asked by Sir Frank Baines, Principal Architect of the Office of Works for the Houses of Parliament, whether he could help deal with the epidemic of deathwatch beetles in Westminster Hall.

Word of his work spread and in a relatively short time he was receiving orders for all manner of concoctions to eradicate pests. These he produced in Hatton Garden with the assistance of Miss Elizabeth Eades. They called their products 'Ento-Kill' fluids – *ento* being the Greek for insect.

Their success led to the formation of the company in 1925. They were unable to register Entokill as a name, so chose Rentokil Ltd. This also reflected the changing demand of their customers, whereby they would be hired for their services rather than just selling poisons.

Disaster struck when Lefroy was accidentally poisoned in his own laboratory while carrying out an experiment. This might well have been the end of the business but under the capable hand of Miss Eades it continued to grow and eventually left Hatton Garden.

SIR MALCOLM CAMPBELL MBE (11TH MARCH 1885–31ST DECEMBER 1948)

Major Malcolm Campbell is best remembered for his achievements in setting land speed records in his famous car Bluebird and for his equally famous speedboat of the same name.

Malcolm Campbell.

Malcolm was the only son of a successful Hatton Garden diamond merchant, William Campbell. He first became involved with racing while in Europe studying the diamond business, as his father had done before him. His son Donald (1921–1967) was equally celebrated for his land speed records.

Sir Malcom competed in Grand Prix motor racing, winning the 1927 and 1928 Grand Prix de Boulogne in France driving a Bugatti T37A.

Bluebird.

He broke the land speed record for the first time in 1924 achieving 146.16 mph (235.22 km/h) at Pendine Sands near Carmarthen Bay in a 350HP V12 Sunbeam, now on display at the National Motor Museum, Beaulieu. Campbell broke nine land speed records between 1924 and 1935, with three at Pendine Sands and five at Daytona Beach. His first two records were achieved in racing cars built by Sunbeam.

On 4 February 1927, Malcolm Campbell set the land speed record at Pendine Sands, covering the Flying Kilometre (in an average of two runs) at 174.883 mph (281.447 km/h) and the Flying Mile at 174.224 mph (280.386 km/h), in the Napier-Campbell Bluebird.

He set his final land speed record at the Bonneville Salt Flats in Utah on 3 September 1935, and was the first person to drive an automobile over 300 mph, averaging 301.337 mph (484.955 km/h) in two passes.

He developed and flotation-tested Bluebird on Tilgate Lake, in Tilgate Park, Crawley. He set the water speed record four times, his highest speed being 141.740 mph (228.108 km/h) in the Bluebird K4. He set the record on 19 August 1939 on Coniston Water, Cumbria, England.

He died after a series of strokes in 1948 in Reigate, Surrey, aged 63 years. He was one of the few land speed record holders of his era to die of natural causes, as so many had died in crashes.

TH MARCH

It is inevitable that insurance has played an important part in the jewellery trade, but the jewellery trade and Hatton Garden have also played a part in the development of insurance.

By the mid-nineteenth century, by which time Hatton Garden was becoming the home of increasing numbers of jewellers, insurance was still largely concerned with fire, life assurance, and its original base of marine insurance, which included goods in transit. Lloyd's almost exclusively dealt with marine insurance until Cuthbert Heath, known as the 'father of modern insurance', started underwriting there in 1880 and introduced new forms of insurance, including burglary insurance in 1889, loss of profits cover and All Risks insurance for personal valuables. Heath was subsequently responsible for much of the international reputation of Lloyd's after the efficient way he dealt with claims from the 1906 San Francisco earthquake.

Around the same period, Thomas Harold March, known as Tommy March, or THM as his business became known, was working as a salesman and bookkeeper for his father, who was a diamond dealer in Hatton Garden. Some of Tommy March's travelling was on the Continent, some in America, where he travelled as an optician with diamonds hidden under his lens tray. Early insurance records are lacking, but it appears that by 1887 he or his father were also acting as insurance agents for several insurance companies, probably providing cover for jewellery and diamonds in transit. By 1905 he was working as an insurance broker, valuer and loss assessor from 17 Hatton Garden with an extensive book of business for some 243 clients, mainly for members of the London Wholesale Jewellers and Allied Trades Association and the Birmingham and District Commercial Travellers Association. However, with London then being the business centre of the world he also had fourteen overseas clients in six different countries.

Also, in 1905, TH March took on a 15-year-old office boy, Frederick A Ferraro (FAF). As the son of Italian immigrants from Piedmont, Italy, he was naturally trilingual, and was responsible for a substantial expansion of March's overseas business. The thirty Paris jewellers TH March placed insurance for by 1907 may also have been an excuse for FAF's later trips to France, culminating in his marriage to a Parisienne girl in 1914.

Through this period, natural pearls were a major part of fashion-conscious society jewellery. Just how important is emphasised by their values: one Paris pearl dealer was insured in 1913 for £700,000 of stock, equivalent to £81.3 million in 2020. The effect of the First World War on imports forced prices even higher; a single strand of pearls was insured in 1916 for £16,000, £1.4 million today.

T . H . M

1869 – 1920

Thomas (Tommy) Harold March, founder of TH March.

One of the problems of commercial insurance for jewellers in the late nineteenth century was the Average Clause. It was normal practice in fire and burglary insurances, and still is in many forms of commercial property insurance today, to reduce an insurance claim in proportion to the degree of under-insurance, so if one insures 80% of the value at risk, the insurer will pay 80% of the loss. That may be practical in many trades, but for jewellers and diamond dealers values at risk fluctuate unpredictably. It was also a problem that even combining fire, burglary and goods in transit covers left many risks for the jeweller uncovered. TH March negotiated a solution to these problems with the innovative Cuthbert Heath: the Lloyd's Jewellers' Block Policy, which had no Average Clause and, instead of listing the risks covered, covered all forms of loss or damage except those specifically excluded. This form of cover still provides the majority of insurances for jewellers around the world today.

It was a retail version of this policy, with even fewer restrictions, that Tommy March negotiated for the National Association of Goldsmiths (NAG) in 1906. In 1907, by which time the business had moved to Audrey House, Ely Place, Tommy March introduced Carey L Burnett to the NAG. Burnett went on to become the NAG's secretary. Thus began a very close relationship between THM and the NAG, which expanded THM's business nationwide and benefitted the NAG via new members who joined, in part, for the NAG's special insurance.

TH March became a limited company in 1911, with Frederick A Ferraro, who became a director in 1916, increasingly becoming responsible for running the business apart from a period spent with the Royal Flying Corps acting as a balloon observer. The relationship with jewellery trade associations was strengthened during the First World War when FAF offered the British Jewellers' Association (BJA) free accommodation in Audrey House.

In the years after Tommy March's death in 1920, FAF maintained a close friendship with Carey Burnett who became a mentor and a director and shareholder of THM. THM became Lloyd's broker in 1924 and remained so until it voluntarily resigned in the mid-1990s. After the Second World War, FAF acquired the rest of THM's shareholding and was succeeded by his son, Roger, and grandson, Michael, who still serves as a non-executive director today.

The company stayed in Audrey House until 1947. The building was bombed during the Second World War, but insurance records had been moved to the country. Temporary accommodation elsewhere led in 1955 to it once again sharing a building with the NAG and the BJA, St Dunstan's House, next to Goldsmith's Hall and owned by them, until 1997 when the building was redeveloped. More temporary accommodation followed until the company returned to Ely Place in 2001.

THM were formally appointed as brokers to the BJA in the late 1960s. That appointment, and the appointment to the NAG, continue today under the National Association of Jewellers.

THE 'CAROLE PARKER' TAPES

Over a period of about ten years, starting in 1997, Carole Parker interviewed about forty-five people associated with Hatton Garden. Most were elderly at the time and had retired from business. Many have since died. Each of the interviews lasted roughly between an hour and an hour and a half.

Carole was secretary to the Institute of Professional Goldsmiths and was working towards a PhD in the 'Oral history of the trade in Hatton Garden'. Unfortunately, the work was never finished as Carole passed away before it could be completed. For some years, the recordings remained on the original magnetic reel-to-reel tapes.

In due course, Carole's daughter, Sarah Parker, who is an architectural historian, had the recordings converted to digital format. They are now in the safe custody of the Victoria & Albert Museum, where they will be available to anyone doing research or with a specific interest in this fascinating area of history. Contact V&A's Archive of Art and Design for more information.

In this publication, the author has produced a synopsis of some of the interviews and where appropriate added more information to the stories from his own relationship with the interviewee.

Demand for coloured stones is on the increase as consumers are better educated and appreciate the variety available. Unlike diamonds, which have been hugely promoted by De Beers and others, coloured stones only get into the limelight when a celebrity or royal chooses one for an engagement ring.

ALEC FARN

There are, among the many names who made Hatton Garden what it was in the 20th century, a few who contributed to the greater good of the community. One such was Alec Farn, who with his three colleagues ran the 'Laboratory', or to give it its full name – the London Chamber of Commerce, Diamond, Pearl & Precious Stone Laboratory.

Alec was born in Barking in Essex in 1916, halfway through the First World War. Life was difficult. He recalls how they had an outside loo – fairly common at the time – with newspaper for toilet paper, and played street cricket – there were very few cars, and there were gas lamps in the street. In 1924 the family moved to Woolwich, and they lived over a pawnbroker's shop, where his father was the manager. On a Monday morning there was usually a queue of women bringing in their pledges to enable them to pay the rent. He found it somewhat embarrassing as he ran the gauntlet to get to school. On the positive side, his father was able to give him advice about which girls to date or not to date based on his inside knowledge.

Alec enjoyed his education, particularly physics. He had some idea that he might become a research chemist, but the reality was that he became a warehouse boy for his father. He was very much back of house and handled the storage of all the pledges, including musical instruments, cutlery, sheets and blankets. However, he didn't get on with his father and at the age of 17 left home to go to another pawnbroker in Ealing Broadway. He recalls how he had to share a bedroom with two other 'boys'; one was from the workhouse and the other was totally malnourished. This was only a stepping stone and he searched the *Pawnbroker's Gazette* for something better. So it was that in 1938 at the age of 22, he was given a position with WW Scott, an upmarket pawnbroker in London's Oxford Street, close to Tottenham Court Road. For the first time he had his own room and took an interest in gems. Alec recalls how all the male staff went upstairs to the dining room for their lunch and were given half a pint of Indian pale ale. He also remembers how he helped to apprehend a thief who had brought in a sapphire and diamond brooch for sale. An alert had previously been received that this piece had been stolen and when the crook brought it in, they were able to delay him until the police arrived.

One of his superiors was a qualified gemmologist using the coveted FGA initials after his name, so Alec signed up at Chelsea to study for the award. His tutor was Basil Anderson, who worked at the laboratory in Hatton Garden. He began to see more jewellery but in June 1940 he was called up and spent the next six years in the army.

After the war his job had gone to someone else, and he wrote to Mr Anderson asking if he knew of any vacancies. He was invited to come to Hatton Garden and duly arrived in his corporal's uniform. He was delighted and so amazed to be offered a job in the laboratory that he completely forgot to ask about the salary. That was May 1946, as London was recovering from the war. The laboratory was located on the second floor of 55 Hatton Garden. Alec was part of a team with Robert Webster, who had been given the Military Medal in the 1914–18 war and served in the Home Guard in the 1939–45 war, and Mr Payne. This group of four were considered by many to be the fathers of modern gemmology. They all produced definitive textbooks on the science of gemmology. Alec was 30, Robert Webster 44 and Basil Anderson 47. Alec speaks well of Webster's kindness and generosity.

Pearl testing was much in demand. The large auction houses such as Christie's and Sotheby's would send in rows for testing. In order to test each stone, the string had to be cut, and the necklace restrung afterwards. New methods of testing were invented. In 1925, Basil Anderson flew by Imperial Airways from London's Croydon Airport to Paris to purchase an endoscope. In one year alone, they tested 138,000 pearls or cultured pearls. With an average of sixty-three pearls to a necklace, this equated to well over 2,000 necklaces. In the early days they were the only laboratory in the world to offer such a service.

In the post-war period, a large number of synthetic rubies started to appear among calibre parcels that had come from Burma, via Bombay where they had been cut. There was a small wave of panic among dealers and jewellers and hundreds of stones were sent into the laboratory for verification. In one year alone, Webster and Farn tested 104,849 such stones.

Alec tells of one particular case of a particularly fine necklace that belonged to Philip Antrobus. He allowed it to go out on approval to a dealer who said he had a client for it. However, the dealer committed the cardinal sin of giving it out to a third party, thus losing control and responsibility. This came to light when the third party offered the necklace to Mr Antrobus. He immediately recognised his own necklace. However, two of the real pearls had been substituted with cultured pearls. It took months to establish the culprits who were, of course, immediately blackballed from the trade.

However, imitations and synthetics weren't limited to would-be crooks. A brooch was sent in by a court jeweller for testing. It had been a gift from Queen Mary and so everyone was surprised when the stones were discovered to be not genuine. Although the laboratory reported the facts to the jeweller, there was some reluctance on the part of the jeweller to tell the owner. When Queen Mary was staying at Sandringham, she would take time to visit the nearby town of King's Lynn and wander around the shops. Her favourite expression when she saw something she liked was apparently, 'Send it to the House'. At first the local retailers were delighted and honoured but when it took months to get paid, they decided that they couldn't afford to do business this way. So, when they learned that Queen Mary was in town, they removed from their displays all their better pieces.

Before becoming a director of the laboratory, Alec Farn would do the occasional dealing on the side to supplement his income and use his own skills. He used to scan the pawnbrokers' windows and find the odd bargain. There used to be a stall in Leather Lane market that sold costume jewellery. On one occasion he found an alexandrite, which was worth a lot of money.

COLIN TREBLE

Colin Treble.

Colin Treble came to Hatton Garden at the age of 17, in 1958, as an apprentice to Maurice Barnett. Mr Barnett was a governor at the Gravesend College of Art and Design. It was his practice to offer the best student each year a position in his company in Hatton Garden.

His early recollection of Hatton Garden was that of a street of dark doorways all adorned with nameplates of hundreds of companies involved with diamonds in one way or another. Many traded on the street and others used the cafés and bars to avoid the English weather. Mrs Cohen's Café, which became the London Diamond Bourse, was one of them. There was only one shop in Hatton Garden at that time.

The workshop had a seven-place bench and Mr Barnett sat in the corner. They only had one electric drill that hung from a curtain rail and was passed around as needed. The smell of wintergreen, used for brightening up setting edges, pervaded the atmosphere. Part of their trade at that time was to reassemble jewellery imported for Van Cleef & Arpels. Finished jewellery attracted high import duty but the component parts didn't. It was one of Colin's duties to go to Johnson Matthey to buy the metal. The trade counter at that time was yards long. It had various serving bays and it was normal to queue. Originally, all the work was done by hand but in the late 1950s and early '60s casting came in and prefabricated findings were also available. They made for many top-end retail county jewellers, such as Boodle & Dunthorne, who at the time had just their original shop in Liverpool. Barnett's had a French designer who visited them three times a year. The selection they made was then offered to their clients. Manufacturing in Hatton Garden was more price sensitive than that being done in London's West End. Speed was of the essence. The working week was forty-eight hours, for which Colin started on £2 2s. Out of this he had to pay £1 in train fares and 10s in housekeeping, leaving only 12s (60p) for himself.

Later, Colin accepted a position with a firm called Davis & Chadwick, where he specialised in higher-value items. Business was good and they would often work until 8 p.m. and feast on chip butties from Dena's Café in St Cross Street.

His third position was in 1966 when he was taken on by Peter Watson to run the workshop for PJ Watson Ltd from their premises in New House, 67 Hatton Garden. After a good innings there, he then set up on his own but continued to rent a bench in the PJ Watson workshop.

CYRIL BENJAMIN

Cyril was the eleventh of a family of twelve children and was born in 1923 in London's East End. His father was a jeweller. Times were hard. Their existence would have been much like those seen in *Call the Midwife*. The family later moved to Stoke Newington. Cyril found a job with a firm of lapidaries called Kings, whose business was based in Albemarle Street, a short distance from Hatton Garden. This didn't last long, and he then found himself working for a well-known firm of jewellers called J Richard Attenborough in Oxford Street. As an apprentice jeweller, it was his job to scrape the benches, make the pickle and carry out more of the menial tasks that form part of the workshop routine.

The jewellery workshop of the first half of the 20th century was not far removed from its Victorian predecessor. Gas was still used for lighting in many places. Carboys filled with copper sulphate solution were used to diffuse the light. A blowpipe was used for soldering and several pipes would run off one source. Archimedes drills were commonplace before electricity began to transform the workplace.

Although he enlisted for the RAF in 1941, Cyril's poor eyesight wouldn't allow him to fly. Cyril joined the Bourse in 1948 and remembers the vibrancy of trade. European refugees were everywhere. Many had come over from Dunkirk.

DAVID HARRIS

David Harris was one of those who had the dubious privilege of seeing Hatton Garden both before and after the Second World War. Born in Stepney, East London, in 1919, just after the First World War, he grew up in London's East End. He left school at the age of 13 and started work in the fur trade. He worked a six-day, forty-nine-hour week but it only lasted six months. His mother had found an opportunity through her brother to become an apprentice jeweller/goldsmith in Hatton Garden for eight shillings a week (40p).

The firm, called MP Greengross, was well respected but they wanted a lot from their craftsmen. There was no paid leave and the pay was based on meeting production targets. They produced a variety of jewellery. On one hand were the inexpensive engagement rings, illusion set, which they sold to Bravingtons. On the other hand, they made platinum watch cases, which were sold to the West End jewellers such as Bensons. Everything was made by hand as the casting of components wasn't yet introduced. There were no punitive taxes and although there were cycles of feast and famine, they did well.

The workshop conditions were somewhat Dickensian. Dark doorways and poorly lit stairs led to a warren of rooms each containing either a small workshop, a diamond or a coloured-stone office. It was part of David's job as an apprentice to be the 'rat-catcher'. There was a craftsman in the workshop who had a wooden leg. His favourite prank on the new boys was to pretend he was annoyed about something and shove a scorper into his leg. It was also part of David's routine to lift the racks on the workshop floor and sweep up anything that may have fallen through. He also emptied the filter on the wash-hand basin to recover any metal that had been washed away.

David was away during the war and on National Service for six and a half years, returning to Hatton Garden in 1946.

On his return, he saw the bomb damage of the Blitz, which had destroyed many of the buildings. He also observed the large increase in Jewish refugees working as brokers or merchants. Many worked from the cafés and pubs in the vicinity. J Lyon's tea shop provided tables with chess or dominoes for when things were quiet and you could buy a cup of tea for 2d. Eighteen-carat gold had been banned during the war and even work for Cartier was done in 9ct, all of which was rationed. Purchase Tax had been introduced and a large black market underpinned the economy. As there was no tax on second-hand items, dealing in antiques and pre-owned flourished. Manufacturing started to decline as pay was better outside the industry. There was also a lucrative market in the USA.

In February 1952, David set out on his own, dealing and manufacturing. He had a small office in Diamond House for which he paid £3 a week. He remembers his first trip to the USA, which was organised by the Board of Trade, who provided significant subsidies to encourage export. The Pan Am flight was occupied by about twenty other similar would-be exporting jewellery dealers and manufacturers. To his horror, a public announcement was made to the whole plane welcoming the delegation of British jewellers. Security is paramount when travelling with goods and his cover was blown before he even left the ground.

DENNIS STELLMAN

Dennis Stellman joined the family firm at the invitation of his Uncle Solomon, who was then 68 and looking for continuity of their jewellery manufacturing business. The offer was presented in a very much 'take it or leave it' style. Dennis was already making a career in the film industry. He was told he had to start immediately but managed to negotiate a week's notice to his employers. The business had been started in 1933 and Dennis joined in 1958, at the age of 22, perhaps when Hatton Garden was at its peak. Solomon (Salo) Stellman also had a son, David, who was deaf and worked at the bench as a setter. Dennis learned the trade from his uncle and from the 'university of life'. His uncle had left Vienna along with many others at that time to avoid the approaching difficulties they foresaw in Europe in the 1930s. Having all the skills of a first-class manufacturing jeweller and diamond mounter, he was able to establish himself in Hatton Garden's 'Diamond House' well before the Second World War with several other fellow Viennese. By the 1950s they had fifteen men in the workshop.

In the 1950s there were far more county jewellers who were loyal to their suppliers. It was difficult to open a new account, but when you did, the relationship would be one that would last. Among their clients were Gowland Bros in Cornhill, in the City of London and in the West End, Garrard & Co. Dennis felt that trade used to be friendlier in the earlier days than towards the end of his career.

Diamond House was something of a landmark because of the large clock hanging over the pavement. Vertex owned the clock and maintained it throughout. Dennis remembers the Hatton Garden Safe Deposit Burglary, which took place long before the big one of 2015. He feels that Hatton Garden has changed out of recognition. A street that was once the home of several large workshops has evolved into a retail-focused shopping street.

Stellman's was a highly regarded business. In 1947, they were chosen to make a brooch for the wedding of Princess of Elizabeth and Prince Philip. Sponsored by the Goldsmiths Company, the competition attracted seventy-six entries. The final selection of six designs was presented to the Princess herself, and she selected Stellman's design. Stan Denham was the workshop foreman and he had the privilege of making it. All the work was done in-house apart from polishing, which was done by Oliver & Bennett in Greville Street. They also worked with De Beers' Diamond Promotion Service several times in the 1970s and 1980s.

Letter from Buckingham Palace expressing gratitude for a wedding present made by S Stellman, 1947.

BUCKINGHAM PALACE

19th November 1947.

Dear Major Bailey,

The Jewellers and the Silversmiths of Great Britain have given me a most generous Wedding Present for which I should like to send them my most grateful thanks. The Canteen of Silver from the Silversmiths is something which Lieutenant Mountbatten and I will always have occasion to use and we are delighted that it should be such a fine example of the craftsmanship of British Silversmiths. I should like all sections of the industry, the manufacturers, the designers, the craftsmen and the operatives, to know what great pleasure their present has given us both and how glad we are that they have chosen to show us their goodwill in this most acceptable manner.

BUCKINGHAM PALACE

2.

I am no less delighted with the beautiful brooch which the Jewellers have given me. This is something which I shall always be glad to wear and I know that all who see this magnificent example of the jewellers art, set with diamonds and rubies, will share my admiration for the skill with which it has been made.

Yours sincerely,

Elizabeth

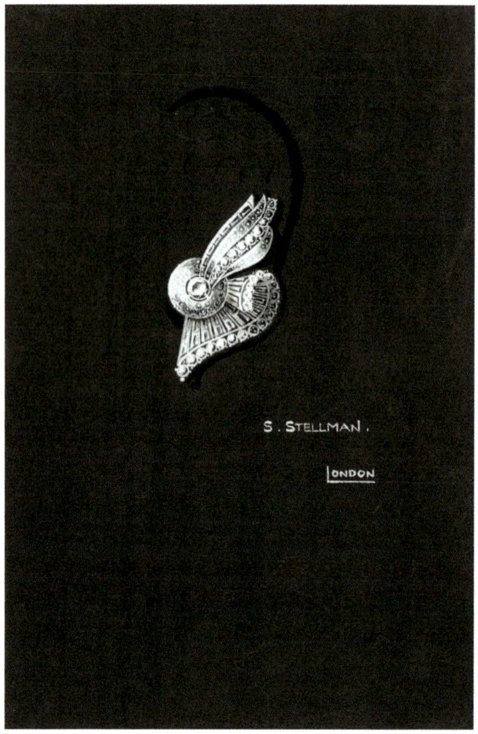

S Stellman, 38 Hatton Garden. Original hand-painted jewellery designs.

Dennis was given the job of being a sales representative for the firm but, unlike other manufacturer's reps, his uncle wouldn't provide a car until he could prove himself. Security on the road was always of great concern. He recalls how a passing vehicle might indicate that there was something wrong with the car and when you pulled over to check, you were a target for a gang of robbers. Even in a shop there was a risk, particularly if you were having to do a presentation over the counter.

In the late 1970s they appointed an agent to look after the customers in the north. He arrived early for an appointment with a shop in Bradford, on a hot summer's day. At that time, it was still possible to park near the shop. However, it was strictly forbidden to leave any samples in the car. Although he had twenty years' experience, something caused him to forget the basic rules of security. The retailer invited the agent to join him for lunch but when he returned, the car had been broken into and the bag was gone. The agent's negligence made him responsible and the range had been worth at least £50,000. He managed to repay about £4,000 and would have had to sell his house to pay the rest. Dennis was more compassionate than his uncle and wrote off the debt.

Family relationships were often a cause of anguish. Solomon's daughter had a car and a salary from the business, even though she lived in Leeds. Dennis managed to buy her out in 1991 and also bought his cousin David out about the same time.

One of his customers was Garrard & Co. and he recalls with high regard the buyer Mr Higginson Snr, who was a role model to him and many others.

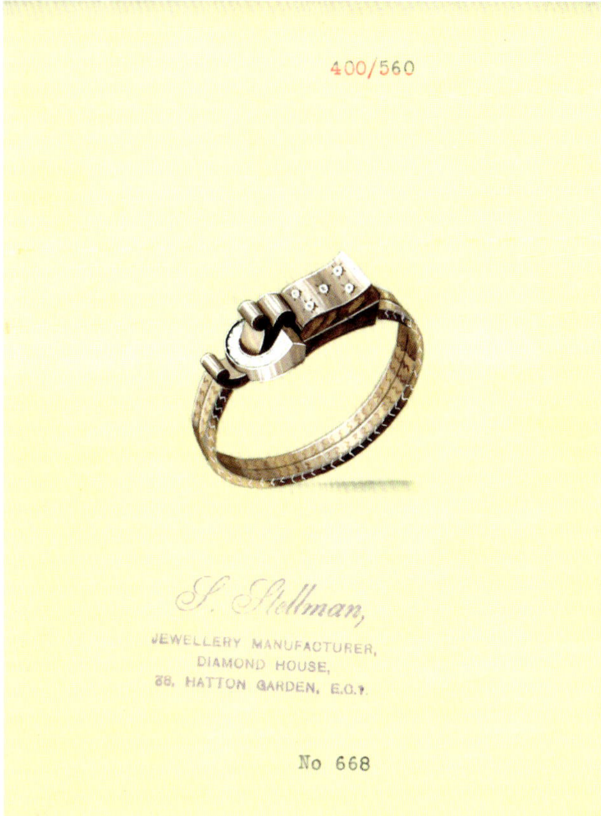

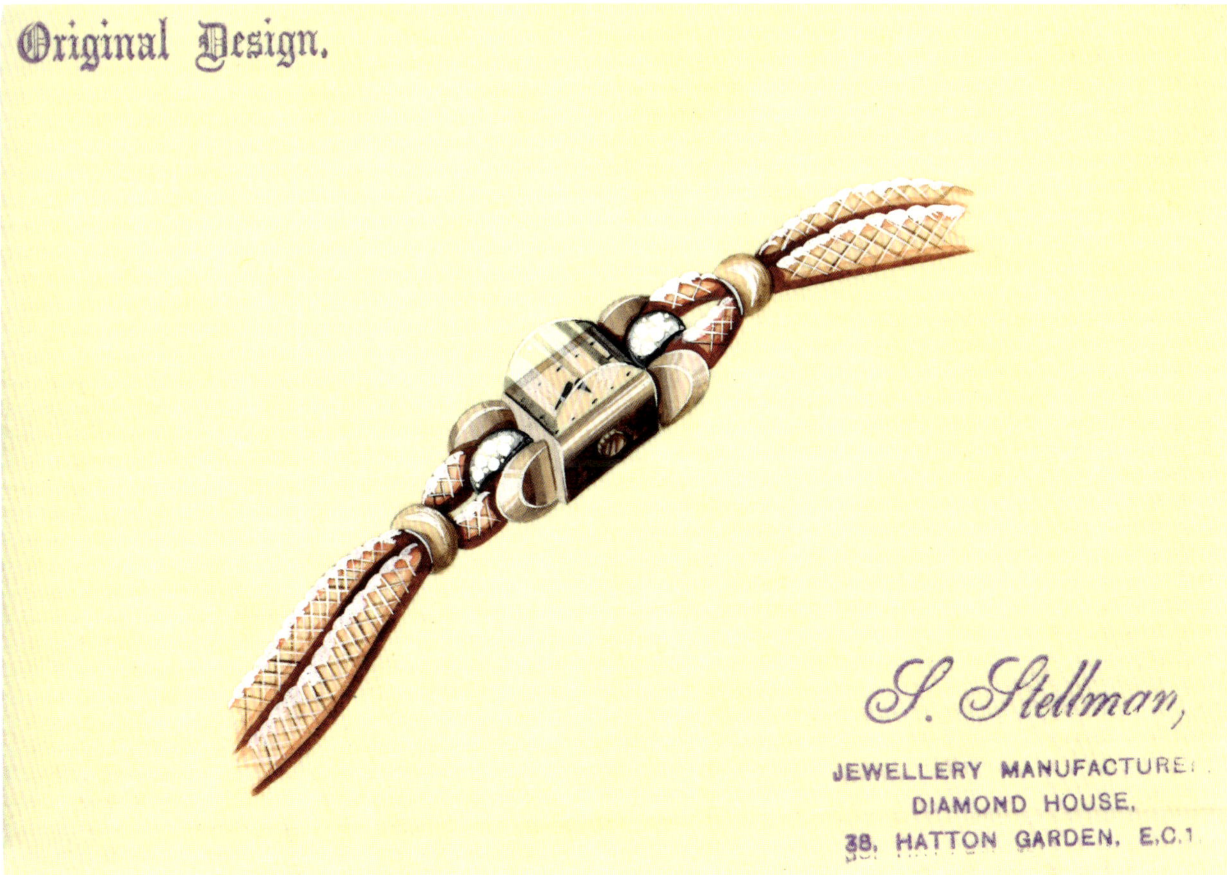

S Stellman, 38 Hatton Garden. Original hand-painted jewellery designs.

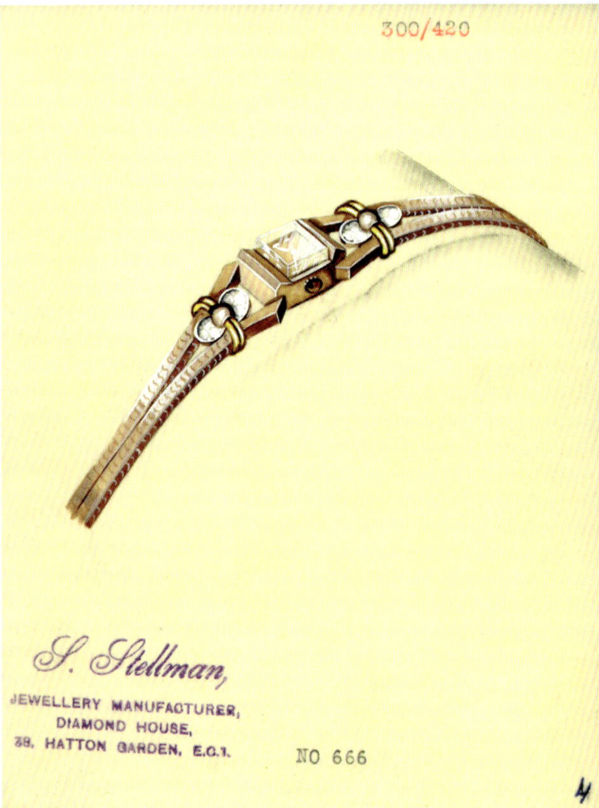

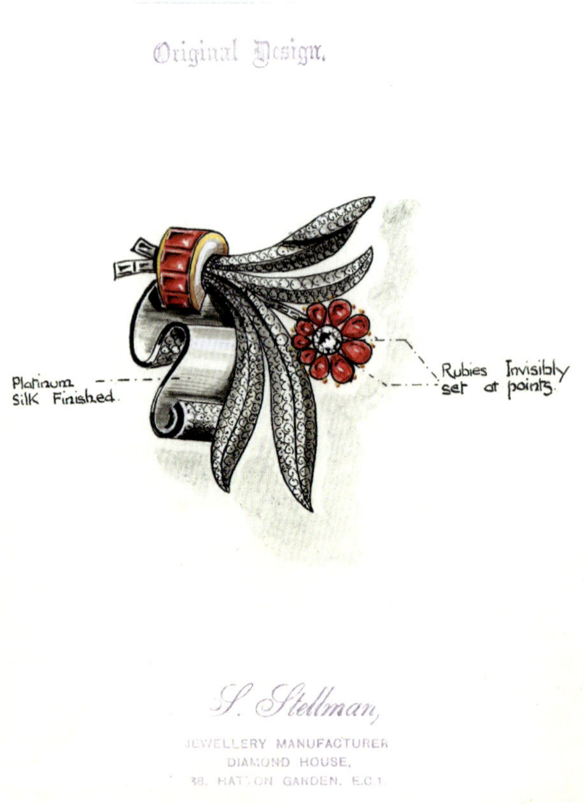

S Stellman, 38 Hatton Garden. Original hand-painted jewellery designs.

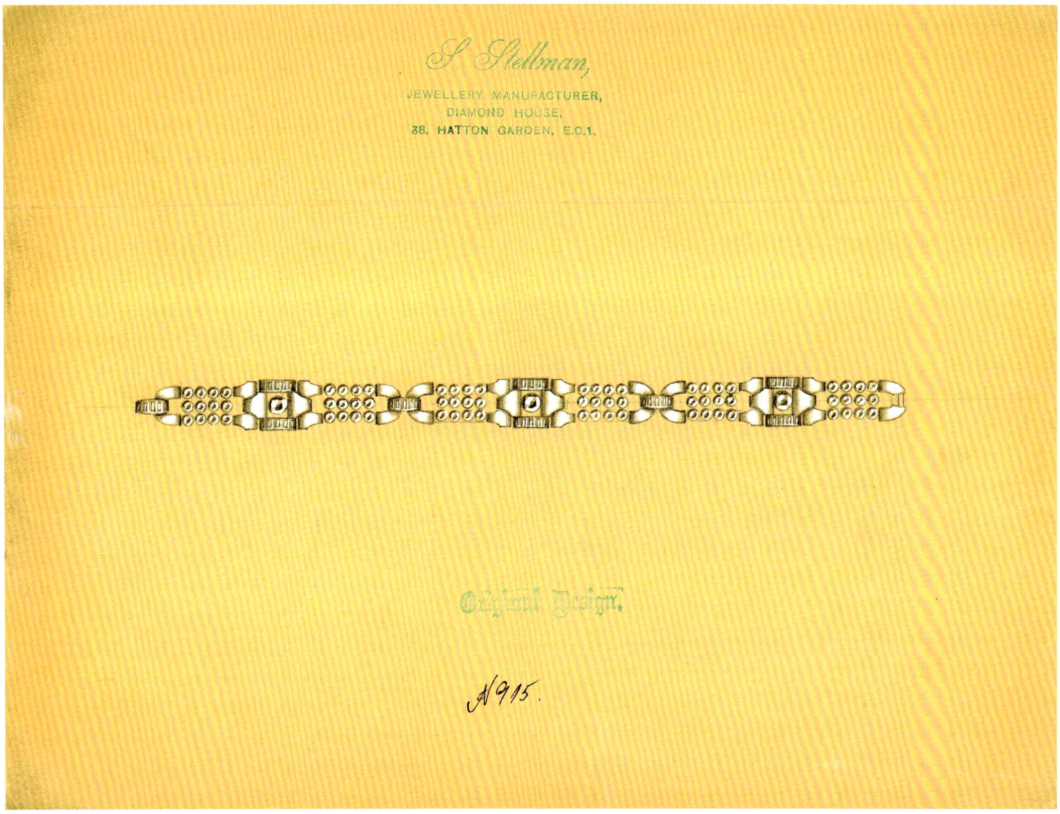

S Stellman, 38 Hatton Garden. Original hand-painted jewellery designs.

Over a period of time they stopped taking on apprentices and the older craftsmen retired. Consequently, the workshop faded away to nothing. Work was then done by self-employed craftsmen. Dennis negotiated a new lease at Diamond House, but now it was for just the office without the workshop.

His uncle died in 1980, aged 90, and Dennis retired in 2002, when the business closed. At the time of his interview, he sold twenty of his original hand-painted designs to the author for his private collection.

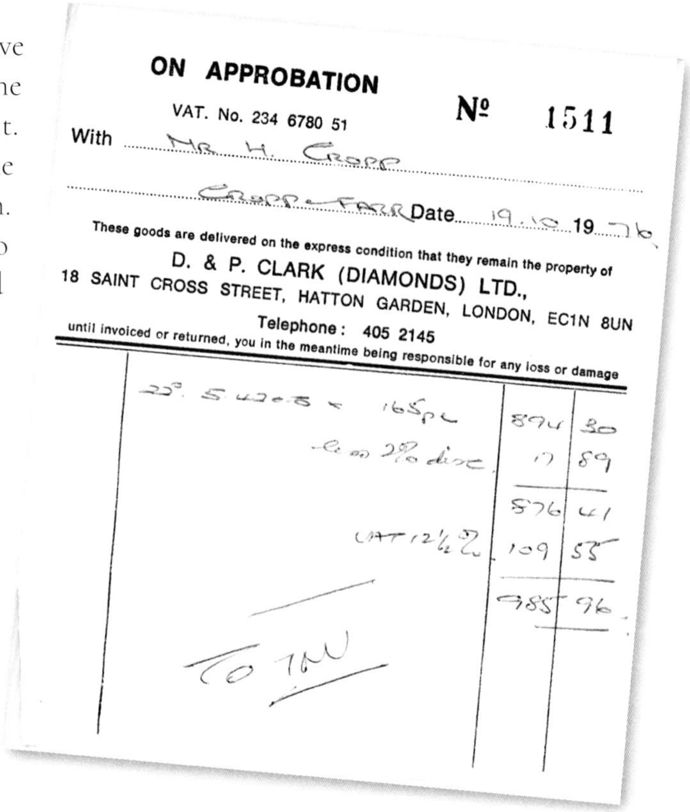

ON APPROBATION

VAT. No. 234 6780 51 № 1511

With Mr H. Cropp

Date 19.10.1976

These goods are delivered on the express condition that they remain the property of
D. & P. CLARK (DIAMONDS) LTD.,
18 SAINT CROSS STREET, HATTON GARDEN, LONDON, EC1N 8UN
Telephone: 405 2145
until invoiced or returned, you in the meantime being responsible for any loss or damage

A 1976 'appro' note from D&P Clarke, 18 St Cross Street.

Don continued to study and improve his knowledge of the business; by the age of 19 he was virtually running it. All was going well until war broke out in his second year with the firm. In the political uncertainty prior to the start of the war there was good business to be done in selling stones for investment or security. Over and above regular sales, Don was able to persuade customers to lay up stock. Supplies could be interrupted, and the skills would be dissipated. A 1ct stone could be purchased for £30 a carat before the war and after the war the same stone would cost £300 a carat. Refugees came to London from the Low Countries, many from Antwerp and Amsterdam, which were then significant centres for cutting diamonds. Don proved valuable as a translator for Joe. In turn Don learned the basics of cutting diamonds. When he received his call-up papers in 1941, he was in a position to state his professional occupation as a diamond cutter, which was deemed to be an essential skill or reserved occupation. He could have avoided serving, but Joe insisted that he 'should do his bit for his country'.

So, Don enlisted aged 20. He now had an opportunity to use the skills he had developed through his amateur dramatics by joining ENSA, the Entertainments National Service Association. He was privileged to work alongside some of the great names in show business. He played the piano and compered reviews to keep up the spirits of troops in remote situations.

When he returned to JC Ginder after the war, he discovered that his old job had been taken. The business had relocated to Stafford to avoid the Blitz. However, there was a binding legal obligation on the firm to take back employees who had served their country. Prior to the war he had been earning £4 10s a week; now he was on £7 a week. This would appear to have been a large increase, but cutters were now earning £25 a week and the foreman, a Mr Meakin, was on £75 a week. Mr Meakin also had a place for his son to work at £50 a week. Furthermore, Mrs Meakin was employed for £25 a week to run a canteen. Don was, therefore, justifiably disenchanted by his old firm – maybe this was intended. Don was now expected to be the one who got in early to light the boiler. He also found himself as the go-between when the employees wanted a better deal. Joe Ginder threatened to sack the whole staff, but they were too valuable to him as the business had a large export business to Canada and with the demise of the European cutting industry, they were major export earners. They had a sight from the Diamond Trading Company and were one of the few in the UK at that time.

Joe Ginder had a son called Cyril, but they couldn't get on with each other. As a consequence, Cyril set up his own diamond business, CJ Ginder, in Hatton Garden.

Another firm that became well known was that of Louis Kornitzer. He published a number of books, from which it has been said he made more money than he ever did trading in stones. His books were all based on facts and actual events, but he was able to develop them to make them more readable.

Don continued to thrive alongside Jack but sadly Jack contracted leukaemia and died young. So, at the age of 27, Don found himself as joint managing director with Jack's brother, Sam. Aardewerk Diamonds had offices in Ely Place.

Their bankers were Hambros, who also had an office in Ely Place. They were generous in providing the necessary funds to enable the diamond companies to purchase supplies. They used to hold a cocktail party in the Mitre Tavern, where Don would meet with members of the Syndicate and De Beers brokers. Don knew Harry Oppenheimer and had a great respect for him. He describes him as a modest man, which considering his vast wealth must have been difficult.

Then in the 1950s, D&P Clarke was formed. Peter was Don's younger brother and ran the Birmingham office. One of their suppliers was an international company called Diamond Distributors of Halton House, Holborn. They had interests in mines and in cutting but needed a better channel of distribution. They bought into D&P Clarke, allowing Donald to achieve greater things.

There was a serious threat to De Beers when John Williamson wanted to market the production of his mine in Tanganyika outside the cartel. There were fears that prices would crash, but ultimately he agreed to channel his production through the Diamond Trading Company.

Don retired from business in 1982. Diamond Distributors had also decided to close, and they made redundancy payments to all the firm's employees. Don was happy to take the cash but not before ensuring a good future for all his staff by setting them up in a new business under the name of his protégé, David Gann.

Don looks back with affection to the days of his time in Hatton Garden. He believes that the trade has shrunk by 50% since then and it will never get back to where it was in its heyday. The demand for fine jewellery was greater in former times. The nature of trade has changed too. In his day you would need to decide where you wanted to be in the supply chain. A diamond merchant didn't sell coloured stones and vice versa. You could either supply a wholesaler or manufacturer but not a retailer. If you were to do that your other customers would blacklist you, making it commercial suicide. He only supplied retailers with workshops such as Garrard, Asprey and Cartier.

EVELYN STERN

Evelyn was born in Berlin in 1924 and came to England as part of the Kindertransport in 1939. Her parents were also able to escape from Europe soon after. Evelyn joined them in Worthing, where she was able to finish her education. The family then moved up to London, where Evelyn found her first job with a firm in Chancery Lane. Acting for a firm of chemical research laboratories, she assisted in the translation of German into English. Then one day a woman she knew told her that there was a job going with De Beers. Her application was successful, and she remained with the company until the 1980s, when she stepped down to pursue other interests in the trade. She was an examiner for the Gemmological Association's Diamond course (DGA), which she had helped Eric Bruton to create.

Evelyn's first role with De Beers was in research, which was mostly paperwork. The small team of seven people operated out of St Andrew's House, which stood on the corner of Holborn Circus in front of St Andrew's Church. During her time here, about four or five years, she met her husband. Her work on 'Industrial Diamonds' appeared in the *Gemmologist*. Among fond memories of her time here was how kind the butler to the directors was to her. She had been ill and was advised to eat bananas, which weren't available in the shops at that time. The butler, who had a pantry at the back of her office, was able to procure some for her.

Another fond memory was that of the royal visit from Queen Mary during the war. The Queen had remarked upon the beauty of a large diamond. This would normally be interpreted to mean 'I want it'. However, legend has it that it was supposed to be already sold to an American buyer. During her time with the company she met most of the Oppenheimer family and had great admiration for Sir Ernest, who died in 1957.

After the war the system of 'sights' was revived but the Germans were excluded to appease the Belgians. However, De Beers needed foreign currency and eventually the Germans were included again. Evelyn's husband had become a broker for De Beers and as he came from Idar he looked after the German sight holder. Evelyn was able to join him as an assistant in 1971. Originally, a broker received 2% commission from De Beers and 2% from their client. However, De Beers put an end to this practice and thereafter the broker only received commission from the client. In some cases, this was reduced to 1% or had to be shared with a third party.

The role of the broker was to look after both the interests of the client and of De Beers. There were ten sights a year and the broker had a five-week cycle. In week one an application had to be put into De Beers on behalf of the client. This was normally for more goods than required as De Beers rarely gave what was being requested. In the second week the broker was advised of the sight by De Beers. In the third week the sight took place. In some instances, the broker would act for his client. The Germans were known for wanting repeat business and this was somewhat predictable, whereas the Belgians were more specific in their requests. In week four the funds had to be chased before the box could be released. Week five was used to tie up any loose ends, usually by visiting the client and discussing future needs.

When Evelyn's husband passed away, she applied for his position. There was objection from only one of the other brokers who had hoped for the clients himself. So, Evelyn became the first female broker accredited by De Beers.

She remembers the delight in seeing the Williamson Pink being cut in London. This beautiful natural pink diamond of 23.6ct was discovered by John Williamson at his mine in Tanzania in 1947. It was presented, as an uncut stone of 54.5ct, to Princess Elizabeth and Prince Philip on their wedding day in November that year.

It is with a sense of sadness that she says the atmosphere in the trade has gone completely and trust has been lost. There was a diamond broker who was blind and took goods to show clients. Never once did anyone take advantage of him.

It was a dubious pleasure to have to look after some of the clients, who would want to take advantage of their privilege. Entertainment, lunches and chauffeuring were all part of her role. De Beers was something of an autocratic set-up at the time, but they always took care of their staff. They also ensured stability in the market by creating demand through their marketing department to match the increasing supply of rough.

Most of the research work was moved to Johannesburg. About that time the arrival of synthetic diamonds for industrial use was announced. Evelyn remembers being invited to the opening ceremony of the Shannon factory. There were many speeches interspersed with Irish coffees. This was followed by a drinks reception and dinner. Another guest had a special diet and only wanted one egg with his breakfast instead of the two normally served. Everyone else was served and getting on with their breakfast and he still hadn't been served. When he complained to the server, he was told that his was a special order and would take longer.

GEOFFREY COOPER

Most craftsmen who are part of the Hatton Garden story would be familiar with the name Charles Cooper. For three generations they were the major supplier of tools and equipment to the workshops that form the backbone of the street.

Charles returned to the UK from South Africa in 1862. The family speculate as to whether he had made a small fortune in the early diamond days, but little is known. His voyage was not without incident as he was intercepted by the US Navy during the American Civil War. He had to serve under General Lee as a muleteer for a short time but managed to get back to England later that year.

He opened his business in tools with just a small supply of files and piercing saws. Little did he know that over the next two generations the company he established would grow to be the most highly regarded in the market and they would remain at the same address, 93 Hatton Garden, for the next 100 years. He commuted to Hatton Garden from Hendon in North London by pony and trap. It was a condition of his lease from Gamages that he was responsible for clearing up any mess that the animal might make in the street. Mr Gamage was quite particular about the environment around his store.

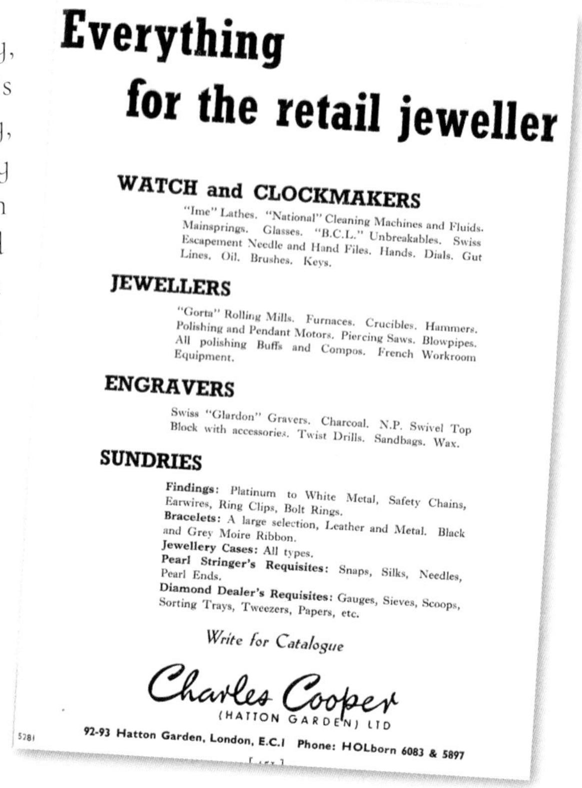

Advertisement for Charles Cooper.

Charles was followed by his son, Sidney, who developed the business further until his death in 1937. Charles's grandson, Geoffrey, then took over the reins aged 25. Sidney was a very strict archetypal Victorian father and when Geoffrey challenged him about his decisions it didn't go down well. Consequently, Geoffrey was sent to Birmingham to open a branch there. Until then he would travel with his father by train and visit various workshops to secure orders.

Geoffrey remembers how business changed during the Second World War. There were more watch manufacturers in the UK. On one occasion a refugee turned up at their premises from Europe and could only speak Yiddish. He had with him a scrap of paper that simply said 'Charles Cooper, Hatton Garden'. Geoffrey went outside and asked one of the newly arrived diamond dealers to translate for him. It transpired that the man was a specialist in radium and producing the powder to make luminous dials for watches and clocks. Geoffrey helped him set up a workshop in Kilburn and he became a supplier to Charles Cooper. There was little or no concern over health and safety at that time and Geoffrey recalls how the man would lick the small paintbrush while applying this hazardous substance.

His business was classified as a reserved occupation as tools were essential to the various workshops, many of which had been given over to the production of instruments. Profit margins were restricted to 10% on all such work. There was also 120% Purchase Tax on new jewellery. This led to a huge black market and Geoffrey took time out to explain to the government that they would collect more by way of tax if they were to lower the percentage. It took a while, but they eventually saw the light.

As he was not called up, Geoffrey joined the Home Guard and spent many nights with others on fire watch duty on the roof of his building, acting as lookout for incendiary bombs. One night during the Blitz there was a particularly devastating raid. The department store Wallis's, which stood across the road from Gamages, was destroyed. In a somewhat matter-of-fact way Geoffrey recounts how that same night the thirty of them put out no fewer than forty-three fires on the roof of Gamages. The next day 'Old man' Gamage, who had been a friend of Sidney Cooper, presented each of them with a cheque for £30 by way of thanking them for saving his store.

The site was eventually acquired by Prudential Assurance, whose flagship office was next door, just to the west of this significant Holborn location. The store closed in March 1972, and the whole site was redeveloped. All traces of the old Gamages store and of Charles Cooper were lost.

GEORGE BULL-DIAMOND

Another story of someone coming into the trade without a family connection is that of George Bull-Diamond. George left school in 1922 at the age of 14, which was the normal school leaving age at that time. He searched the jobs section in a newspaper and found a position as apprentice to a lapidary in Hatton Garden called Charles Matthews. He had always wanted to work with his hands rather than in an office, so he said to his mother, 'I am going up for that.' Charles Matthews had set up his business in 1894 when he was 21 years old.

When he arrived in Hatton Garden, he was somewhat taken aback to see a queue of boys waiting outside, stretching from No. 14 up to Treasure House, three or four doors along. A policeman was deployed keeping the queue in good order, when finally, the manager, a Mr Mountjoy, came out. He said, 'I can't interview all these,' and made a random selection of about half a dozen to take inside. The remainder were dismissed. George was one of the few. A week or two went by after the interview and he hadn't heard so he was preparing to look elsewhere. Then, out of the blue, he received a letter offering an apprenticeship.

Charles Matthews also had an interest in another operation a few doors up the road, at Treasure House, called the British Gem Cutting Company. This was a government-sponsored business for disabled servicemen. The government paid the rent and provided all the equipment. The workers received both a salary and a war pension. Cropp & Farr, a well-known manufacturer in their day, also had a stake in the operation.

14 Hatton Garden. Home of Charles Matthews.

George started work on 10s a week plus a further 6d he received by way of running an errand for a Professor Gordon of Kings College. Hatton Garden was then the 'world centre' of the trade. There were other lapidaries at that time, all importing and exporting valuable gems. Pavement traders were everywhere. There were fewer cars then so the road was used too. It wasn't uncommon to see dealers, who had dropped the contents of a parcel, using a dustpan and brush to recover their goods.

In 1923, Charles Matthews chaired the Jewellery and Gem section of the London Chamber of Commerce. It was his acquaintance, Professor Gordon, who introduced a young Basil Anderson, who founded the Gem Testing Laboratory.

George remembers how when Premier House was built to replace Nos 12 and 13, his building at No. 14 was left exposed, so that when he used the stairs he could look straight out. On the plus side he also had a once in a lifetime view of the famous window of St Etheldreda's Church in Ely Place. The window was removed during the war and replaced later. The Second World War also saw the coal cellars at No. 14 adapted into air-raid shelters. During the earlier raids all the staff diligently made their way downstairs but later on the sirens were ignored.

War work included polishing knife-edge agates for balances and other instruments. Lapidary work was considered to be a reserved occupation and as such George was not allowed to enlist despite his wish to serve. Agate had originally been imported from Germany but now the Ministry of Supply sourced it from Brazil. A lot of the work was for Baird & Tatlock, scientific instrument makers. There were no specific instructions on how the stones should be cut so it was a little bit trial and error.

Charles Matthews died in December 1941 and donated his large collection of gemstones to the London Museum of Natural History, where it can be seen today. His son, Charles Reginald, Reg, took over.

In 1942, George cut a piece of rock crystal as the pommel on a sword, which became known as the Stalingrad Sword. The sword itself was made by Wilkinson's. It was presented by Sir Winston Churchill to Stalin. Other noteworthy work was a crystal dog rose for Princess Alexandra. George was also responsible for refinishing the emeralds in one of Mrs Simpson's pieces purchased by a London business from the famous Sotheby's sale in 1987. Although there was less work after the war, the services were much in demand from top manufacturers and retailers.

George recalls how in his early days, he was tasked with polishing a large ruby of considerable value. Many years later he had a call from 'Jack' Cartier asking him to make a visit. He was astounded to see the very same gemstone, now in need of some TLC.

Reg Matthews made George a partner and he continued to run the business when Reg stepped down. They were officially incorporated on 4th January 1947. During George's time they trained a number of apprentices. One is remembered by virtue of the fact that he carved his initials, PA, neatly over the bench.

PA was Patrick Aldridge, who went on to build a very successful international business. When George received a gold watch as he retired, at the age of 70, he had clocked up fifty-six years with the same company. However, he continued to work part-time for another five years. Throughout his long career, he showed great skill and patience, a steady nerve and an even steadier hand.

GERALD STONLEY

A well-known character in the Hatton Garden heyday was Gerald Stonley. He came from a family displaced by the Second World War and found refuge in London. Born in Idar on 28th August 1917, he was the son of a stone dealer. At the age of 16, he left his native Germany to join his brother at boarding school in Sussex, where he learned English.

His father was attacked and beaten up as part of the Nazi persecution of Jews. So, he sold his house and put his money into goods and travelled to London. The family lived in a boarding house in Hampstead and moved to Wembley in 1936. Unfortunately, he couldn't get a work permit on leaving school, but found a job in 1938 for a shipping company. The following year he moved to a company selling fancy goods. Then in 1940 he was called up and joined the Signal Training Regiment at Dover Castle. He was involved with the D-Day landings, this time with the Horse Artillery.

After the war he joined his older brother, who had already set up a business in Hatton Garden, trading as Steinfels Ltd After three years he decided to branch out on his own. Initially he concentrated on second-hand jewellery as there was no Purchase Tax but as time went by, he developed a manufacturing jewellery business. He qualified as a gemmologist in 1948 becoming an FGA. His first office was in 88–90 Hatton Garden, still referred to by some as the Safe Deposit building. The same year he formed a partnership with Ben Revan of 11 Hatton Garden and moved into new offices at 34–35 Hatton Garden trading as Stonley & Revan.

They sold beads, strung in the 1930s in Idar to customers in Hatton Garden and Birmingham. They also made their own classic style of gem–set rings, earrings and pendants, specialising in unusual and rare stones. On-street trading was commonplace as many of the dealers particularly the refugees didn't have the luxury or the expense of an office. On a busy day you couldn't walk a straight line down the pavement. Some traders worked out of the Express Dairy and Lyons' cafés. Street trading died out in the 1960s as police efforts to improve security came into effect.

The 1960s brought an influx of overseas stone dealers selling their goods to the manufacturers and stone merchants in Hatton Garden. In order to trade they needed a partner or alliance with a local company. Stonley & Revan acted for two Brazilian companies. Payments could not be sent abroad without permission from the Bank of England in the form of a stamped purchase invoice. In due course Gerald Stonley travelled to Brazil to source his own material.

In 1977 Gerald left to go part-time and Ben Revan, with his son Robert, continued their core business. Ben died in 1982 and the company closed in 1999. The Hatton Garden manufacturing industry had thrived for over 100 years but towards the close of the century the arrival of products made in Asia with cheap labour costs gradually squeezed the domestic manufacturing market. Some moved into retail and some formed alliances with overseas factories. Gerald remembers a time when companies like T O'Donoghue would take on two new apprentices a year. Cropp & Farr had eighteen of their own craftsmen in their workshop at its peak with outworkers hiring a bench space. Whitehorns had eighty craftsmen working in-house at their peak.

Towards the close of the century rents rose to new heights and many were squeezed out, having to relocate closer to home. London and Paris were the global centres of the pearl trade, but, after the war, import restrictions prevented the British from dominating this market and the UK lost out to France.

Among Gerald's many memories of the 1950s was a dealer known locally as 'Blue-white Giles'. At that time blue-white was the most desirable colour in a diamond, the equivalent of a D colour today. His trick was to paint the back facets of a diamond to improve their colour. Another of his tricks was to send a lady into a West End shop with a pearl earring claiming that she had lost the matching one. The jeweller had a brief to locate a match. Later Giles would come in with the original and sell it to this delighted jeweller at an inflated price. Needless to say, the lady never came back.

In the 1950s coal was the main source of heating and many of the buildings had coal cellars. Deliveries were made by emptying sacks down the chute. On one occasion, a street dealer dropped an important diamond into the coal cellar by accident. The owner of the cellar refused access unless the trader was willing to buy the coal at a hugely inflated price. Reluctantly, the trader agreed and was able to recover his stone. That wasn't the end of the story, however. The owner of the property told the trader that he couldn't store his newly acquired coal there without paying an extortionate rent.

HARRY SAPER

There are more stories of hardship and persecution of the Jews that can be told here but one that stands out is that of Harry Saper. His grandfather owned a silver mine in Russia but at the beginning of the 20th century the pogroms that displaced the Jewish communities from their homes had begun. Very much like the story told in the musical, *Fiddler on the Roof*, the family had to leave their homeland and settle elsewhere. As Harry's father had started to learn the art of diamond cutting, it seemed like a

Harry Saper.

good idea to head for the Low Countries. It was certainly safer than Russia and eastern Poland. So, it was in Amsterdam that Harry was born in 1920. His father continued to work with diamonds, becoming a dealer in polished goods.

Then in 1940 the Germans invaded Belgium and Holland and started to round up the Jews. As a young man, Harry had the foresight to know that they needed to get away before it was too late. He persuaded his parents, some other members of the family and a few friends to leave. They quickly packed a few things and a group of forty of them caught the last train to leave for Bayonne in France before the border was closed. They travelled for three days without any fresh food or water. There were no toilet facilities and they had to sleep in the woods. There were also 5,000 Polish troops making their way to England and there were three boats to evacuate them. They sailed at dawn and two of the three boats were torpedoed by an Italian submarine. They escaped. Three days later they landed at Liverpool, where they were transferred to a detention centre in London for interrogation. No doubt some German spies had tried to gain access to the UK in such a way. Harry finally got his passport stamped 'Landed in England'. Many of his family had chosen to remain in Europe. Perhaps the older ones were too set in their ways or they trusted the Germans.

German High Command issued a degree that the diamond industry would not be harassed as the stones were needed for the economy. For two years they were allowed to trade but one fateful night the Nazis raided all the offices, confiscating the goods and shipping the Jews off to extermination camps.

Harry had a cousin in Hampstead and as a diamond cutter he was able to walk into a well-paid job straight away. Diamonds were an important foreign currency earner and the demand from the USA was only met by the supply from London, which for a while was the only cutting centre in the world. Harry recalls working on a 100ct diamond for export. He worked for a company called the Paramount Diamond Polishing Company in Hatton Garden and by the age of 22 was their head cutter.

He saw many refugees come to Hatton Garden during the war to sell the diamonds that they had managed to bring with them. On one occasion he was offered a painting by Monet for £40, such was the desperation of these immigrants.

HARRY STANFIELD

Harry followed his father into the diamond manufacturing business and built for himself an enviable reputation as one of De Beers' elite diamond brokers. The journey was not without its problems. He started work in Greville Street with a firm called Roselare. It was very Dickensian in so far as they used equipment that had been around since at least Victorian times. Each wheel was driven by a central motor and belts that ran along under the bench. You had to be careful your overalls didn't get snagged. Stones were set in lead dops rather than mechanical clamps. Innovation didn't come in until well after the war.

In the pre-war period, life was less frantic. Hatton Garden was very different. There were no shops apart from SH (Sammy) Harris. Security was less of a consideration. Some offices didn't even operate behind locked doors. Most people were honest. There was a large number of small workshops and a small number of large ones, such as G Music & Son.

One of Harry's first visits to Hatton Garden was, as for so many, as a boy visiting his father. On one occasion in 1937, his father's firm had to recut a huge Golconda stone for a maharajah. The stone was to be worn in a turban for the coronation of King George VI. The facets were applied by eye. Thankfully, Harry's father was well experienced with larger stones.

During the war, work was limited to repairs or recutting old cuts unless you had a licence. So, work was taken on from others. One morning Harry's father had gone to the offices of Briefel & Lemur to collect some work while Harry had gone to the factory in Greville Street to open up. There were fire engines and hoses across the road at the corner of Hatton Garden and Greville Street. When he turned the corner, he was confronted by a load of rubble. Their building had received a direct hit from a German bomb. He could see their benches and equipment among the debris and climbed over the wreckage to retrieve as much as possible. He then went to meet his father and greeted him with the words, 'I won't be making tea for you this morning!' His father assumed that the water supply had been interrupted again. Harry told him that there was water but no factory. True to the wartime spirit, some friends at 84 Hatton Garden provided bench space for them to continue their work.

Harry joined the London Diamond Club and business continued to grow. His father retired in 1965 and Harry spent less time at the bench in order to concentrate on diamond dealing. When he gave up the factory, Harry needed an office and was kindly given a room by a Mr Goldie. H Goldie & Co. were De Beers brokers and in due course Harry was invited to become a partner. They had ten clients that they looked after very well. Today, brokers are no longer essential in the supply chain. However, names like Goldie, Henig, Bonas, Nagel, Rothschild and Morgan will always be part of Hatton Garden's history. There are no sight holders in the UK today.

Harry knew the Oppenheimers, who owned De Beers, well and has nothing but kind words towards both Harry and Nicky. Although much criticised elsewhere by others, he believes their interests have always been the greater good of others. For example, when when the Indians started to develop their diamond-cutting industry in the late 20th century, De Beers insisted that working conditions must be appropriate. Air conditioning, proper toilets, canteens and more were required before a 'sight' could be considered.

ISRAEL DIAMENT

There were many stories of those who escaped the Nazis when they marched into Antwerp on 10th May 1940. They, however, represent the minority, as a far greater number of Jews were rounded up and shipped out to camps, never to be heard of again. One who managed to get away was Israel Diament. He was born into a family of diamond merchants and cutters in Antwerp in 1929. On that fateful day, he simply packed his bags and left. One of his brothers was not so lucky. Israel and some of his family fled to the south of France, where they worked on a farm and endured great hardships for over four years.

After the war Israel married and settled in London. His wife was originally from Manchester and London was a compromise between Manchester and Antwerp. He found Hatton Garden much more like a village compared to Antwerp and very friendly. However, the style of business was very similar, and he fitted in very quickly. He joined the Bourse and the club and had an office at 1 Hatton Garden for twenty years, which at the time was fully occupied by similar businesses.

Gradually he became more of a dealer than a hands-on cleaver but still practised his traditional skill throughout. He claims to have been the last cleaver in Hatton Garden.

JOHN TAYLOR

John's route into the trade was rather unusual. He knew that he didn't want to work in a big factory but didn't know where he should go. In the school library he picked up a book on gemstones. He wrote to a number of people in the trade and was rewarded by the offer of an apprenticeship with Charles Matthews Lapidaries, one of the most highly regarded names in Hatton Garden. He came under the watchful eye of Mr Bull-Diamond, the owner of the company, and Mr Woodcock, his number two. There were three other apprentices at the time, with varying experience, as well as four trained lapidaries.

Initial work was done on quartz and synthetics until a level of competence was achieved. A variety of gem materials were used, and each had its own requirements. All work was carried out in the traditional way of using one's eyes to make judgements.

There were no shops in Hatton Garden in the early 1960s. It was still a street of manufacturing jewellers. Regular crates of rough were shipped in and when polished produced beautiful sapphires, rubies and other gems. Some of these were sold by Charles Matthews to dealers and merchants; some were exported.

John's loyalty to the company was rewarded when Mr Bull-Diamond retired and he and his partner, Peter Rome, took over.

Today there are no new apprenticeships in his skill area, and we will soon lose his expertise altogether.

KURT EICHNER

Kurt Eichner.

Kurt Eichner was born 23rd January 1927 in Vienna. He was the son of a kosher butcher, who originally had a shop at the railway station in Auschwitz.

On 12th March 1938, when Kurt was 11 years old, the Nazis invaded Austria and started to round up the Jews. Anti-Semitism had preceded the invasion, but from now on there were tangible changes. Initially all Jewish children were made to sit at the back of the class in school. Later, they were expelled.

The 9th November 1938 was Kristallnacht. Jewish people and their businesses were the target of violence. Shop windows were smashed, synagogues burned, and the German authorities stood back and refused to intervene. Homes were ransacked and valuables and cash were stolen. The Jews were moved into ghettos and were not allowed to leave.

However, in spring 1939, 10,000 children were permitted to go to Great Britain. This mass evacuation of children became known as the Kindertransport. When Kurt was sent off in July that year, he didn't know that he wouldn't see his mother again. She was taken to an extermination camp. So, on 23rd July 1939, Kurt arrived at Liverpool Street Station along with hundreds of other children. The Jewish Refugee Children's Committee oversaw the adoption and welfare of the new arrivals until they were 14 years old and could go out to work. Kurt was taken in by a Jewish family from Hackney. Some of his possessions had been shipped to London, including a collection of books, but tragically they were lost when the warehouse fell victim to the Blitz. His sister had also been able to escape, just before, but they remained separated.

On 3rd July, he was evacuated to Old Welwyn, Hertfordshire. The Blitz lasted from September 1940 to May 1941. Over 20,000 civilians in London were killed and over one million homes were damaged. He was grateful for his education but disappointed that where he had come from in Vienna, the students were somewhat more advanced than in rural Hertfordshire. However, he was on a steep learning curve as he got to grips with the English language and culture.

In the autumn of 1941, at the age of 14, he was summoned to the committee in London to choose a trade. He had hoped for a further education but that wasn't on the cards. There were plenty of traditional apprenticeships on offer but the one that appealed to him was that of diamond polisher and so he made his way to Henley-on-Thames, where a small factory operated on Remenham Hill. Known as Sapin Works, it was run by a former Hatton Garden watch importer called Max Reber. Mr Reber had a strong social conscience and took on twelve boys to give them employment.

However, proper training was not available, and neither were rough diamonds. They had to practise on steel ball bearings. Initial pay was 15s a week. That business closed in 1942 and Kurt now found lodgings at a hostel in Ladbroke Grove, West London, along with forty other refugees. Here, he made new friends with other Jewish boys who had come through similar experiences, including one he had known in Vienna. Among them were Fred Durst and Johnny Neijman, who also had careers in Hatton Garden.

He had to go back to the labour exchange to seek further employment. He wanted to pursue his apprenticeship but was told in no uncertain terms that he should do what he was told and be grateful. He was sent to a firm in Windmill Street that manufactured military buttons. He was also engaged by Lyons' Corner House to peel potatoes. With a desire to do better, he took the telephone directory and contacted all the diamond polishers that he could find. One of them agreed to take him on. So, his apprenticeship continued with a company called Diapol, who had a small factory in Greek Street in the Soho area of London. There were two apprentices and twenty-five polishers. He worked from 8 a.m.–5 p.m. for £2 a week but was trained by experienced Dutch and Belgian diamond polishers. When he completed his apprenticeship in 1945, he now earned £20 a week.

In the spring of 1947, he had an emotional reunion with his father in Paris. His father had escaped Austria on foot over the mountains and joined the French army. However, when the German army captured him, he was deported to Auschwitz. He was one of the few who survived the horrors and after the war he opened a butcher's shop in Lyon.

After seven years with Diapol, Kurt was able to set up on his own. The Holborn Diamond Polishing Company was registered on 23rd February 1948 and operated out of very dingy premises in a cellar in Leather Lane. The winter of 1947–8 was one of the coldest on record. There was also a period of post-war depression and government restrictions dictated that he could only do repair work or improving old cuts. A licence was required, and an inspector would call to make sure he wasn't polishing rough. This was the prerogative of companies employing injured servicemen.

Despite difficult economic times, trade grew. 'There was much more street trade at the time.' It was almost impossible to walk along the section of Greville Street near Leather Lane between 11 a.m. and 2 p.m. 'There was a different atmosphere.' There was a whole variety of different nations represented on the street, in a very international business. London could have become the diamond capital of the world.

In 1950, aged 23, he moved to the third floor of 57 Hatton Garden, on the corner of Hatton Wall. The new premises were previously owned by Alec Fishberg, who had run a larger diamond polishing factory. It was agreed that Kurt could take it on for the same rent as he had been paying in Leather Lane.

About 500 cutters had arrived from the Low Countries during the war, mostly Jewish. The Diamond Club was formed for those who dealt in rough and the London Diamond Bourse for those who dealt in polished or in jewellery. The club was predominantly Jewish, having its own kosher restaurant and a synagogue under the same roof. After the war most of the refugees returned to their homelands or moved on to Israel.

Later in the decade, the business relocated to the third floor of 24 St Cross Street and later expanded to the ground floor. Influenced by many of his customers, he started dealing in second-hand jewellery. Initially, he was loaned stock by friends to trade, but later built up his own collection.

Kurt pays tribute to the many who helped him on his journey, particularly Manfred Seymour, Andrew Ullmann, Adler, AT Watkinson, Byworth Antiques, G Music, Landsberg, M Abram, Monty Stanton, Paul Fisher, SH Harris, TJW Diamonds, Tom O'Donoghue and W Truman.

He is succeeded today by his daughter Sally, who has learned the trade from not only her father but also some of the best-respected dealers in Geneva and in New York. Their ethos remains the same: of selling only good, honest value for money items, and they attract an international clientele.

MOISE FREI

The 1993 movie *Schindler's List* tells the true story of how Oskar Schindler managed to save the lives of around 1,200 Jewish people from the extermination camps by employing them in his factories. One of those who owe their lives to him was Moise Frei, no. 190 on the list.

Moise was born in Korczyna, Poland, in 1929, the youngest of five children. He was victimised at school for being Jewish and hated every day of the seven years he spent there. One day in 1942, the Germans came to his village and rounded up all the Jews. Moise was not at home and didn't see his parents again. As a young teenager, he was alone in Krakow. Jewish families were not allowed to work and lived on charity. He was chosen by Mr Schindler and met him several times while in his employ and remembers him as a kind man.

His eldest brother had escaped to Britain from Antwerp via France. He had learned the skills of diamond cutting when he arrived in Belgium in 1929.

On 8th May 1945, the Russians liberated the prisoners from the labour camps in Poland and Moise made his way back to his village but to no avail. All had gone. After two years, he managed to contact his brother in London and made his way by boat and train to start a new life. He recalls the emotional reunion at the station as if it were yesterday.

His brother taught him the trade and they joined the Bourse. His membership number was 111, one of the earliest members. He well remembers Mrs Cohen's Café, as it was in its infancy. There were two floors and all the dealers and brokers met for coffee. They also paid a membership fee but that didn't go to Mrs Cohen. Moise reckons that more business was done there than in any of the subsequent purpose-built locations. He also maintains that you could have written a book about the characters who made up this community. They all had their own seats, much as today in the current Bourse. The partnership with his brother lasted for thirty-five years and never was there a cross word spoken between them. Moise also observes that the original Bourse was located where today he has access to the car park that serves the current Bourse. His car was well known to his colleagues as the number plate was more valuable than the car itself: FRE1.

PETER ROME

Peter says that he entered the trade by accident. When he left school at 16, he wanted to become a police cadet. He also applied for a job at the Royal Mint. However, he eventually stumbled across a job as an apprentice diamond polisher for a company called Diapol in Greek Street, London. The company employed about twenty-five men as London still had a significant role in polishing diamonds. All was going well until the firm went bust in 1965 and he found himself looking for a job along with all the other diamond polishers. He had been studying gemmology at evening class and had a textbook in which a number of trade companies advertised. Charles Matthews took him on as an apprentice and he set about relearning his skills at the bench. He ended up running the business with his partner, John Taylor.

The business has changed out of recognition. Prior to the introduction of the payment of VAT at the point of importation in 1975, they would receive large consignments of unpolished stones from overseas. When the work had been done, some was sent back, and some sold in the UK. Peter feels that Hatton Garden will fade away. There are already many other trades and professions established there, perhaps making more money than he can.

The nature of the work has changed too. At the start of his career little cutting was done in the Far East. Sometimes he would get a native-cut stone for improvement. Much of his work does come from abroad but it is mainly repairs now. After a battle with Customs & Excise, a concession was given that VAT on the total value would not be assessed. Peter regrets that the expertise that was once available is all but lost.

He has cut tanzanite but says that it has its challenges, as do all stones ending in 'ite'. Originally tanzanite was cut to reveal the blue in order to make it look like sapphire. Now it is more popular to cut it in the other direction to reveal the purple. This also produces a heavier stone.

SAUL WEISSBART

Those who knew Saul Weissbart might have described him as a modest man, but under the façade was someone who achieved many great things. Born in Berlin in 1925, he witnessed the aggression of the rising Nazi Party and the persecution of the Jewish people. His father was beaten by the Nazis in 1933. In August that year he fled to England with his brother to live with his grandmother, who had settled in the East End of London in 1905. He never saw his parents again.

Antwerp, prior to the war, was a major cutting centre for diamonds. However, with the demise of the industry, which had been predominantly Jewish, many cutters moved to London. De Beers supplied the rough and the diamond trade became the UK's biggest export earner as a ratio of manpower to output. Most were based in the Hatton Garden area. In the 1930s there were about half a dozen diamond polishing companies; by the mid-1940s there were around 500.

So it was that in 1939, at the age of 14, Saul left school and started work. His grandmother was able to find him an apprenticeship with a firm of diamond cutters at 44 Hatton Garden. The business relocated to Richmond during the war but returned to Clerkenwell Green. In 1943 the firm took on several ex-servicemen who had been injured in the Western Desert Campaign and Tobruk. They integrated well despite not being Jewish. Many other diamond-cutting factories relocated from Hatton Garden during the war. Such places as Luton, Bedford and Brighton had businesses.

Saul Weissbart in his younger days at the wheel.

Mr Weissbart in his office with his two sons, Jonathan and David.

They had around fifty workers and Saul became the shop steward for the union. During the war years, it was a requirement to have a licence to cut diamonds. These were only available to British citizens, so partnerships were formed. The London Diamond Club was formed in 1940 and the Bourse soon after. When the war was over, many of the refugees returned to Antwerp and his firm ceased to trade in 1948, due to government money control regulations. Saul was then unemployed for about three months. He spent a short time running his grandmother's grocery business but missed the diamond trade.

However, his skills and reputation were well known, and he was sponsored by Time Products to start dealing. He joined the London Diamond Bourse in 1959. Gradually building up by buying and selling on short credit, he turned over his stock frequently and became a major player. In due course, he was elected as treasurer to the Bourse, a post that he held for over thirteen years. Other dealers would come to him to have their 'old cut' stones repolished. He set up a small workshop at 35 Greville Street. However, he always maintained that he was not good at polishing and preferred the trading of goods. So, from 11 a.m. to 3 p.m. you would have found him in the Bourse.

The main market at that time was the USA. De Beers had promoted the theme of 'A Diamond is Forever' and the strength of the dollar enabled buyers to take advantage of the many old jewels being sold in Europe. Dealers now started quoting prices in US dollars instead of the old Dutch guilders. Some of the Antwerp cutters chose to settle in New York after the war to maximise the opportunity.

Until the 1950s the description of a diamond's colour or clarity was a matter of opinion and debate between the buyer and the seller. Until the GIA introduced their now world-renowned system of grading there were fierce arguments about the stone and, therefore, its value. The old-school traders didn't welcome the new grading as they lived by a combination of their experience and their wits.

The new grading system paved the way for the price lists introduced by Martin Rapaport in the early 1980s. Again, older dealers believed that this commoditisation of diamonds would be the end of 'romancing the stone' as they had done since time immemorial. They threatened to have Rapaport expelled from their community.

It was in 1973 that Saul finally started trading without a backer. The introduction of VAT payable at the point of importation changed the way business was done as large sums of money had to be paid upfront. The way of trading changed too. Whereas previously, goods were sold as a parcel for an agreed price, dealers were now willing to allow clients to pick from a parcel at a premium price.

The role of the broker as a go-between disappeared about that time. Customers would now come directly to Saul.

One of the most memorable diamonds he saw was the Williamson Pink. The stone was polished in London by an old-school Belgian cutter at his previous employers and presented to Princess Elizabeth. Weissbart's was one of the first to introduce the 'Princess Cut' to the UK market, although originally it was known by another name.

Saul's two sons joined him in the business and learned the trade by shadowing their father.

TOM O'DONOGHUE

Tom O'Donoghue.

Unlike so many of Hatton Garden's well-known people who came from far and wide, Tom was a Londoner through and through. He was born in Clerkenwell in 1920, the twelfth of thirteen children, and was proud of his working-class family background. He loved metalwork at school and thought that he might go into the print. Living conditions were bordering on slum environments. Communities were divided by nationality or religion and also by occupation. There was a very strong Italian ghetto in Clerkenwell and the north end of Hatton Garden in the 1930s. Clock and watch manufacturers based themselves in Clerkenwell. Johnson

Matthey began the redevelopment of their site before 1939 but the work was interrupted by the war.

Tom served as head prefect and soon after leaving school received a call from his headmaster saying that there was a Birmingham jeweller who wanted to open a business in Clerkenwell, London. The firm was called Nightingale & Pritchard and they specialised in low-priced rings for companies like Bravingtons. They received £1 for making twelve illusion-set rings. The working conditions would have made anything Dickensian look like luxury. On a particularly cold winter's day, Tom was asked by a superior to put some more coal on the fire while the boss was out. This was strictly forbidden, but Tom decided to do it anyway. Just as he had the shovel in his hands the boss returned to the workshop and caught him red-handed. This resulted in instant dismissal. To be fair, his superior, Albert Morley, who had put him up to it, owned up and he was dismissed too.

Tom remembers going into Johnson Matthey to buy gold and seeing the huge pile of sovereigns, which were loaded on to the weighing scales with a shovel.

There was little opportunity to find work as the country was recovering slowly from the Great Depression. However, he was taken on by a firm called TN Balson, who made quality jewellery for the West End. They had seven craftsmen, including mounters and setters, on the fourth floor at 89 Hatton Garden. He received an apprenticeship and worked from 8 a.m. to 6 p.m., Monday to Friday and 8 am to 1 pm on Saturdays. In addition to the day work at the bench, he opted for night school at Sir John Cass College, five nights a week from 7 p.m. to 9 p.m.; three nights were diamond mounting, one was on design and one was on engraving. Tom's hard work paid off as he started winning prizes.

In 1935, they were commissioned to make coronets for the Silver Jubilee celebrations. However, in 1938, conscription came along and before long he found himself in the RAF. From 1943 to 1946, he served in North Africa, and the company gave its production capability over to small arms manufacture. He returned to a somewhat reduced Balson after the war. However, they continued to make fine jewellery, often sourcing designs from Paris.

Tom describes Hatton Garden as being like a market street at that time, such were the large number of dealers and brokers, all earning a living on the street.

These were difficult trading times in that only 9ct gold could be used. At the same time, there was demand from the US servicemen, who wanted to take back presents to their loved ones at home.

Then, in 1951, Tom started on his own. Initially renting a bench space in another workshop at 96 Hatton Garden for £4 a week, he received repair work from dealers and his reputation for quality work soon spread. The 1950s were boom years and he was soon taking on help to meet demand. Two of his new staff were previously his mentors at college and during his apprenticeship. He soon needed more space and moved into 84 Hatton Garden, where his business occupied two floors. He now had three setters and his own polishing shop.

The business continued to thrive and in the mid-1960s another move was needed to larger premises. This time it was to Kirby Street that the business relocated. As time went by Tom spent less time at the bench and more time with customers or travelling to the Far East to source coloured stones. At their peak they had over fifty people in the workshop. He also followed most of the jewellery auctions. Tom was joined by his son, John, in 1974. John studied gemmology and business studies, and helped transition the business into a new age.

T O'Donoghue exhibited its collections internationally but found that the annual Swiss fair in Basel attracted the best customers. About 50% of its sales were in export and 50% of the products sold were second-hand or antiques. The Americans appreciated our relatively inexpensive labour costs, and the Germans had an insatiable appetite because much of their jewellery, particularly antiques, had 'disappeared' during the war.

Tom recalled with great pride how he had to deliver an item to Buckingham Palace for Princess Margaret. He hailed a taxi and when he told the driver the destination, the driver was over the moon. He pulled out from his glove box a pair of gloves and a peaked cap, entirely appropriate for such a journey. The driver had been waiting for years to receive such a ride.

Tom continued to work past retirement right up to the age of 86. He passed away in 2010. The business continues today assisted by the capable hands of the third generation: Tom's grandson, Luke, who joined the business in 2000.

CRIMES

Whereas most people work for a living, with varying degrees of success, some look for shortcuts to acquiring wealth. In most cases, it is greed that makes a man or woman steal from another. Sadly, those without compunction may not only steal but will sometimes injure or even kill anyone who gets in their way. The entertainment industry uses historical events and the misfortunes of others for their stories for our enjoyment. We should never forget that in all crimes, there are victims. Some may lose their hard-earned stocks and their livelihoods. Others may lose more. Hatton Garden has attracted all sorts of criminals who, like moths to the flame, can't resist the allure of riches. It was estimated in the 1960s that over half of the cars parked in the Garden were known to the police.

88/90 Hatton Garden. Safe deposit robbery.

One of the earliest crimes on record took place well before the jewellery trade had become established. What was described at the time as 'The Great Robbery of Hatton Garden' took place on Sunday, 29th December 1778. A gang, consisting of twenty thieves, targeted 'a gentleman of considerable fortune and quality'.

They deceived the owners of the house into believing they had a search warrant, then forced them into an inner room at pistol point. The owners were locked inside while the gang ransacked the house. One of the victims managed to escape and raise the alarm.

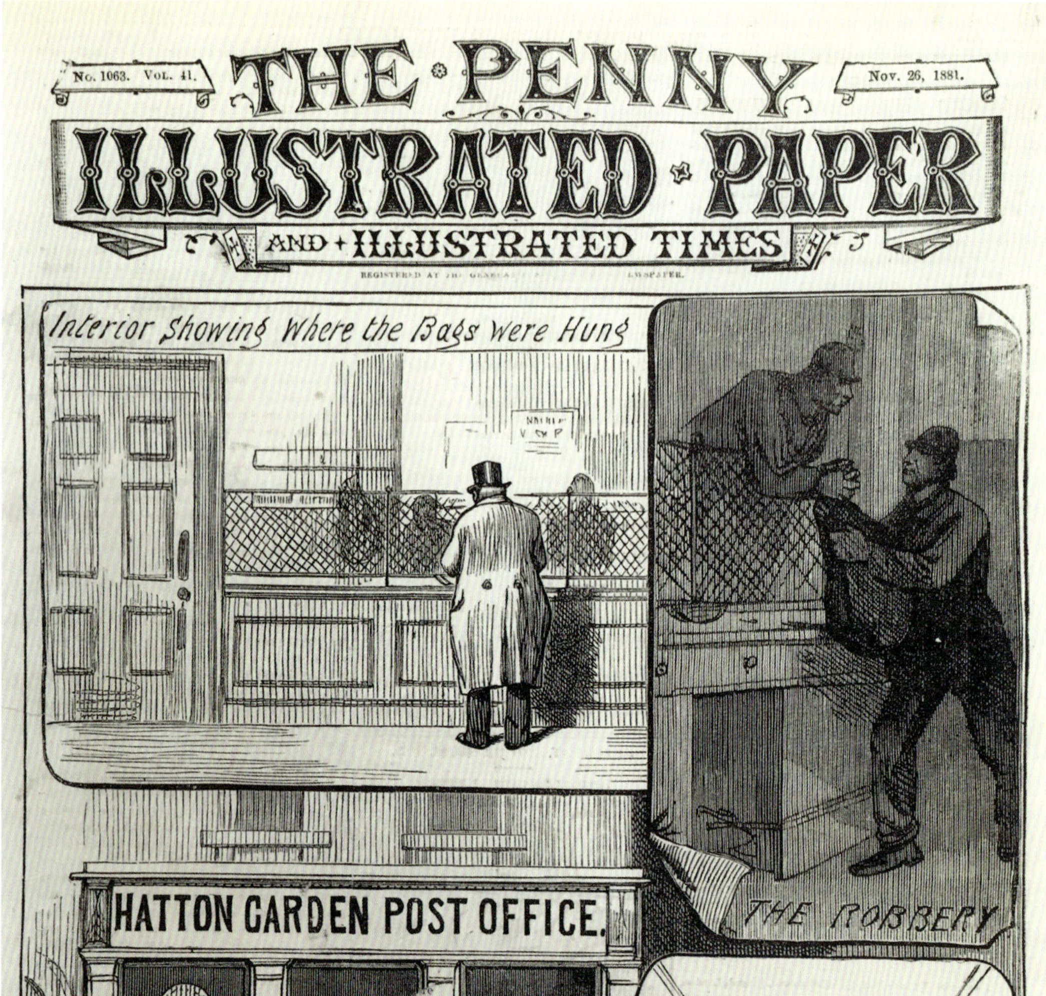

The Post Office robbery at 110 Hatton Garden.

The Hunchback of Hatton Garden, A 1925 novel featuring Sexton Blake.

The robbers panicked and fled with what they could. However, two days later they were apprehended as they tried to dispose of their loot.

Another incident took place in Hatton Garden a short time later. Laurence Jones was a Londoner who had the good fortune to receive a large sum of money from a deceased relative. For a time, he lived comfortably in St James with his servants, but eventually he felt the need to top up his bank balance. He became a swindler and persuaded his servants to become his accomplices.

Jones rented a house in Hatton Garden to stage the crime that would become his downfall. He set up an appointment for Mr Campbell, a banker, to visit him at home. Mr Campbell, unwittingly, walked into a trap. He was kidnapped, robbed and chained up in the basement while the crooks escaped.

It wasn't long before Jones was apprehended and committed to Newgate Prison. He was tried and found guilty at the Police Court in Hatton Garden, only a few doors away from the scene of the crime. He was sentenced on Wednesday, 8th December 1793. However, he committed suicide three days before he was due to be hanged.

These crimes were not unique to Hatton Garden and could equally well have occurred elsewhere. However, when the diamond and gem dealers came to the area, so did the criminals. Despite elaborate security systems and strong safes, a few determined crooks found a way to get what they wanted.

Max Mayer Pearl necklace robbery reward poster.

The Great Pearl Robbery of 1913 was one of the earliest crimes of significance. One of the leading pearl merchants in Hatton Garden was Mr Max Mayer. His integrity was second to none and, like bona-fide dealers today, he would have considered his reputation to be his greatest asset.

He was born in 1859, and from a young age and humble beginnings began trading in costume jewellery, all the while using his skills to build enough capital to invest in semi-precious stones. From semi-precious he graduated into dealing in diamonds. His business acumen and good fortune enabled him to rise through the ranks and achieve an international reputation. In each generation there are those whose success is enviable. Max Mayer was one of them, but this made him a target for any would-be criminal.

As time went by, he branched out into pearls. At that time, cultured pearls had not been invented and oriental pearls were extremely valuable. Edwardian society had put great emphasis on pearls to display their wealth. By 1913, Mayer had become as well known as a pearl dealer as he had previously been a diamond merchant. His safes must have held some of the most valuable merchandise in the whole of Hatton Garden.

The theft was discovered on 16th July 1913. Mayer lost a pearl necklace that was reported to be worth more than the Hope Diamond. Known as the 'Mona Lisa of Pearls', the necklace consisted of sixty-one flawless, blush-pink pearls.

The necklace had been offered to a Paris jeweller, but the sale fell through and it was returned by registered post to Hatton Garden. However, when Mayer opened the three monogrammed seals on the package, he was shocked to find not the necklace but eleven lumps of sugar. Scotland Yard and Lloyds worked together to trace the stolen necklace. Lloyds, who had insured the necklace for £135,000, offered a £10,000 reward for its recovery.

The mastermind behind the theft was Joseph Grizzard. He had managed to have the parcel intercepted en route and arranged the substitution, which made the parcel the same weight. Posing as potential buyers, the police were able to lure the gang to a meeting near Chancery Lane Underground Station. The gang members were arrested, however, the pearl necklace was still not recovered. It would be almost impossible to sell the pearls legitimately as they were unique.

Two weeks after Grizzard's arrest, Mr Augustus Horne, a piano maker from Highbury, was on his way to work when he witnessed an unusual sight. Someone dropped a small package rather deliberately in the gutter and rushed away. Curiosity caused him to investigate and he found a broken row of pearls. He hadn't realised what he had found and assumed that they were fakes. He gave one to a street urchin to use as a marble and handed the rest in to the police, who informed him of what he had found.

16 HATTON GARDEN

On Monday, 25th May 1885, the *London Evening Standard*, under the headline of 'Mysterious Affair in Hatton Garden', reported that at 7 p.m. on Friday evening, a strange occurrence had taken place. The incident happened at the premises of Alexander Brothers, diamond merchants, of 16 Hatton Garden:

> The ground floor was rented by Alexander Brothers, diamond merchants, the front parlour being cut off by a semi-circular partition, and the windows looking directly onto the main thoroughfare. Mr. J. F. Alexander, the senior partner, had been engaged during the day collecting accounts, and returned to the office at about twenty minutes past six. According to his statement his usual practice was to leave business at five o'clock, but in view of the approaching holidays he deemed it necessary to finish some correspondence on Friday and was thus detained a few hours later. At the time mentioned, while writing at a desk in the left-hand corner of the room, he was suddenly startled by seeing a hand seize his pocketbook, which he had previously placed on the desk by his side. It contained ten £10 Bank of England notes and precious stones – diamonds, emeralds, rubies, garnets, pearls, coming to the value of nearly £3000. Mr. Alexander turned partly round, and before he could seize the man, he received a large quantity of snuff in the eyes, which for the second blinded him. On making a second dash at his assailant be caught the muzzle of a revolver, which he for the moment believed to be his pocketbook. The next instant a report was heard, and the thief dashed out of the room with his booty. The cries of the injured man and the report of firearm brought Mrs. Duval, wife of the care-taker, and other persons on the scene. They found Mr. Alexander in the centre of the room, blood running from his hand, and he himself in a semi-conscious state. Mrs. Duval sent for her husband, a servant in the City police, stationed at the fixed point at the corner of Hatton Garden. After applying restoratives Mr. Alexander was conveyed in a cab to St. Bartholomew's Hospital, where it was found that he had been shot through the right hand, and that he was suffering from a nervous shock. The wound having been dressed by the house-surgeon Mr. Alexander returned to his office, and there saw Chief Inspector Hunt and Inspector Flood of the G Division, information of the affair having in the meantime been transmitted to King's-Cross Police-station. The Inspectors having taken down Mr. Alexander's statement, proceeded to examine the office, and found a bullet embedded in the wall opposite the desk, about seven feet from the ground. There was also a quantity of snuff on the merchant's clothing as well as on the floor, and near a chair, which had been overturned, was a Colt's five-chamber revolver. This weapon was loaded, with the exception of one chamber, and was comparatively new. On being further examined, previous to going home. Mr. Alexander was able to give only a vague description of the robber, his statement being that he was a dark man, about 5ft. 10 in height. Mr. Superintendent Hume and Inspector Peel have since been making inquiry into the matter. The police fancy that more than one person was engaged in the transaction, and that they must have been acquainted with the habit of the heads of the firm. The chance of detection appears at present to be slight.

locked cases, containing nothing. The carpet is exceedingly thick, no doubt for the purpose of deadening the sounds of any scuffle. The room was only taken on Wednesday. The landlord asked for references, and these were given, but what may have tended to remove any doubt was the payment of a quarter's rent in advance. Mr. Spyzer has been in the habit of travelling between Amsterdam and London once a week, and during the last twelve years has, whilst in town, resided at a private hotel in Great Prescot Street, Aldgate. He is regarded as an intimate friend by Mr. Joseph Bonn, the proprietor of the hotel, who, becoming alarmed at his absence on Thursday evening, made inquiries at Leman Street Police station. In consequence of information there obtained from the police, Mr. Bonn and his son proceeded to Kings-Cross-Road Police-station, where they found Mr. Spyzer, who had been awaiting their arrival. He was much cut about the hands and arms, which were still slightly bleeding, and a bruise under the left eye had swollen to a painful degree. Mr. Spyzer had, however, sufficiently recovered to walk to a cab, and he was at once driven to Great Prescot-Street, where he arrived at half-past nine p.m., in a greatly excited condition. Yesterday he made the following statement: – 'I am annoyed at the mis-statements of certain papers, which assert that I produced my parcel and laid the gems upon the office table at No. 70, Hatton Garden. Nothing of the kind occurred. The moment I entered the room with Morris, the door was securely locked and bolted behind us. Three men dashed from behind a screen, one thrusting his hand, which contained some black suffocating object, across my mouth. I struggled madly to escape, but my strength seemed to desert me, and I sank exhausted and senseless to the floor. That chloroform was used I am confident, as, upon recovering, I experienced that terrible sensation of deathly sickness which is one of the characteristic indications of that anaesthetic. I must have been unconscious some time, and it was with great pain and difficulty that I eventually managed to get upon my feet. When I was able to stand, I smashed the glass panel of the door, and shouted with all my strength for help. In smashing the glass my hand was cut, as you see. As nearly as I can estimate, without reference to books which are kept in Amsterdam, the diamonds in my possession at the time amounted to £2800 cost price, their actual trade value being, perhaps, nearly £3000. I had in addition bonds and other deeds worth certainly not less than £3000, although these documents have now been rendered useless. My purse, watch, and chain, and every other valuable about me were likewise stolen. It is almost impossible to give any accurate or authentic description of the three masked men who attacked me. Everything happened with such overwhelming rapidity. I can, however, safely assert that two were of short stature and one was rather tall'. Mr. Spyzer spoke in broken English, and his statement was, for the most part, interpreted by Mr. Bonn. He added that the stolen gems were his own property, and that the loss is in no way covered by insurance.

THE HATTON GARDEN SAFE DEPOSIT BURGLARY

The Hatton Garden Safe Deposit was officially opened on 24th October 1949 in the basement at 88–90 Hatton Garden. For over sixty years it provided a service to the trade and others wishing to store their valuables or cash in a secure vault. It was a matter of routine for dealers, manufacturers and merchants to store goods overnight or over a weekend. There were a variety of different-sized boxes from floor to ceiling, but most dealers only required a basic facility. Each member had a unique metal box inside their own safe. The safes could only be opened when the owner and the official both used their keys simultaneously.

Over the Easter weekend of 2015, which coincided with the Passover, a team of burglars entered the building and broke into the vault. They arrived on Thursday night and were given assistance by an accomplice, who had a key to the front door and knew how to disable the alarm system and CCTV. The accomplice was known as Basil and wasn't part of the gang, most of whom had met inside prison or previously been involved in other jobs. Basil also removed the hard drive of the security system. (It has been suggested that the name Basil is simply an acronym for Best Alarm Specialist In London.)

However, all did not go as planned. An alarm signal went out to the monitoring company who, in turn, alerted the police. The alarm company attended the premises and found no trace of intruders. The police didn't attend and later apologised for a breakdown in their communications. The protagonists laid low until the all clear was given for them to continue work. One of the team, John 'Kenny' Collins, had the task of surveillance from an upstairs window across the road at 25 Hatton Garden.

Basil then opened the rear access and they were able to move in with their equipment. Once inside the building they had to enter the vault in the basement. This involved descending a lift shaft, drilling through a reinforced concrete wall that was half a metre thick and forcing over a rack of deposit boxes with a hydraulic ram. The police assumed that anyone who could do this would be young and fit, but most of the gang were in their 70s. Once again, the gang's efforts were thwarted when the lever on the hydraulic ram broke. They hadn't realised that the cabinets were all bolted to the walls and couldn't easily be pushed over. Brian Reader, who was the mastermind, said that they should abandon the job and they all went home feeling frustrated. Over the next forty-eight hours, however, some of the gang decided that they should go back and acquired a replacement ram. So, on Saturday night they were back again and this time the ram did its job.

It was initially estimated that they took between £10 and £200 million worth of goods, making it the largest ever burglary in British history. The perpetrators were keen that it should be a burglary and not a robbery as the maximum sentence was only ten years for that offence.

It was eventually decided that £14 million was probably a better estimate of the value of the items taken. In all, seventy-three boxes of a possible 999 were forced open, and the true value of the goods taken will never be known. Many dealers had no record of what they had put away and may have overstated their claims, while some less than honest box holders were not able to declare their cash or other ill-gotten gains. There was a period of tension after the burglary was discovered as it took some time to advise owners which boxes had been opened.

The Flying Squad were called in and were able to make quick work of their enquiries and surveillance. On 19th May, over 100 officers were involved in simultaneous swoops at twelve different addresses across London and nine men were arrested. Brian Reader, who had previously been involved with the Brinks Matt Robbery in 1983, was arrested at his home and the others were caught red-handed as they were about to divide up ('slaughter') the remainder of the haul.

Five of the gang pleaded guilty and received between six- and seven-year prison sentences. Terrence Perkins, who had been part of the Security Express Robbery in 1983, died in prison in 2018. It has been suggested that one reason the gang were caught so quickly is that they were analogue men living in a digital age.

Only about one-third of the haul was recovered, suggesting that there is the best part of £10 million still to be found.

Basil (aka Michael Seed) had kept himself apart from the gang and was not there for the carve up. However, he was arrested in 2018 with £150,000 of unexplained loot, and in 2019 was sent down for ten years.

The safe deposit company went into liquidation in 2015. Many honest dealers lost their stock and were forced to leave the trade. Some lost their 'pension funds' and have been forced to work longer than planned.

Several books have been written, and a number of films and TV programmes were made, all telling the story with either a dramatic or a factual slant.

22 HATTON GARDEN

The Gershon brothers, Samuel and Edward, diamond merchants of 22 Hatton Garden, suffered a burglary at their premises in 1936. On current values their claim was equivalent to £250,000. The police, in their wisdom, however, said that as there were no signs of breaking and entering it may well be an inside job and a bogus claim. This view was further supported by the fact that the business was on the brink of bankruptcy. There was also previous form, where claims had been made in times of financial difficulty. Without a police crime reference, the insurers dismissed the claim. As a result, Samuel committed suicide because he couldn't face the shame on his family and the wrath of his creditors. Sometime later, the insurers settled the claim. Samuel Gershon was the great-grandfather of Daniel Radcliffe of *Harry Potter* fame.

There are, of course, many other stories and they could fill a book themselves. Security systems have improved over the years and lessons have been learned. So has the cunning of the criminal and sadly, there will be more stories in the future.

HANDS UP!

Crimes of all sorts are never far away when items of high value are to hand. One Friday afternoon, Vaughan Segal was finishing his work for the week and looking forward to a hot summer's weekend. His 'boys' or apprentices had already left, and he was alone when he got a call from a friend in the Garden asking what was going on in his building. When he looked out of the window, he saw dozens of police officers, some with guns pointing up at the building. Greville Street had been shut and a police helicopter was deployed. Clearly something significant was going on.

It transpired that the police had been called by an elderly lady who lived in a flat across the road. She had seen a number of gunmen on the roof of the building opposite and feared the worst. The police were to be congratulated on the speed of their response and the resources used to catch the gunmen before anybody was hurt.

What was not known was that Segal's boys had been down Leather Lane at lunch time and equipped themselves with water pistols. It was their way of having fun. A chase across the rooftops was exciting and a soaking with cold water on a hot day was welcome.

Once it had become apparent that this was a false alarm and the police were stood down, there was much embarrassment. The commanding officer visited the workshop the following Monday and gave the boys an appropriate telling off.

THE GARDEN'S MARKET

ALBERT JOLLIS

Albert Joris, in his book *A Destiny in Diamonds*, gives a wonderful insight to the world of diamond dealing in Hatton Garden in the 1950s:

> Through a mutual friend, I made contact with a man called Marcel Mendelson. His family originally came from Antwerp, but he settled in London and became well known in the diamond trade. At one time Marcel did a fair amount of business in cut diamonds with Indian diamond merchants. In India, bargaining is an accepted part of business life, and an Indian buyer likes nothing better than the prospect of being able to get a parcel of diamonds or even a single stone at below the asking price. One had to expect, therefore, that negotiations would be fairly spirited. But Marcel used to be known in Bombay as, 'One Price Mendelson'. When he put a price on his diamonds, he wouldn't budge from it, for even one cent. In London, Marcel had an office in Hatton Garden, in a building full of diamond people. It had a strongroom in the basement where the goods could be locked up for the night.
>
> The diamonds I took to London were surplus to our requirements and were somewhat of a mixed bag, varying considerably in size and quality. Marcel contacted only those buyers he knew would be interested in industrial diamonds of that sort and arranged a series of appointments for them. On each occasion he sat behind his desk with the prospective buyer in front of him while I took a position directly to one side and slightly behind the buyer's chair. I always kept a copy of the Times held at eye level, feigning a total lack of interest in the proceedings while Marcel, in Yiddish, conducted the business side of things, discussing the quality of the stones and so on with his client. Invariably I would be introduced as a friend from Australia, no name mentioned, and my presence would soon be forgotten as the bargaining got underway. The buyers did not know, and Marcel certainly did not let on to

them, that I could understand every second word of Yiddish. With my Belgian background and fluency in both Flemish and German, I was able to get the general drift of the conversation and monitor the progress of negotiations.

As they bargained, I sat there mutely, and occasionally Marcel would glance over to me to see my reaction. If I shook my head very slightly, it meant I wasn't satisfied with the price, and they would haggle some more. When eventually they had reached a price that was acceptable, a slight nod of my head would indicate to Marcel that he could close the deal, whereupon they would say 'Mazlam Broka'. After the deal was completed the purchaser would pay in £5 notes. Five-pound notes in those days were sheets of white paper of enormous size, known everywhere as 'blankets'. So bulky were they, I had to go out and buy a small briefcase, somewhat like a flat music case, in order to get the money safely to the bank. With anything from three to ten thousand pounds worth of blankets in my little case, I would make my way, either by tube or by bus to the Bank of New South Wales in Threadneedle Street, London. There the unfortunate teller would laboriously count it all out and double-check it, before issuing his receipt. With two hundred five-pound notes in a thousand pounds, it became quite an ordeal for the teller to have to stand there and count out several thousand pounds worth. On about the third occasion, the teller spotted me on my way into the bank and I was greeted none too enthusiastically with a ##### not you again!

THE ULLMANN FAMILY: ANDREW R ULLMANN LTD

Within a modest shop in Greville Street, close to its junction with Hatton Garden, you will find an Aladdin's cave. Antique jewellery, old silver and other treasures fill the cabinets and counters. Every few minutes someone comes in either to sell an old unwanted item or to purchase a gift from the extensive collection on display.

The atmosphere of a family business is all too evident as Joe discusses a recent purchase with his son, Max, while his daughter, Lucy, serves a customer.

Joseph Ullmann, the patriarch of today's business, has six children, three of whom work with him in the business. He is also assisted by his granddaughter, Amelia, who is the fifth generation of the family. Joe's grandfather ran a similar jewellery business in Budapest in pre-war Hungary, which he had established in 1902. His son, Andrew, joined the business in the 1920s. The increasingly difficult political situation forced Andrew to flee Hungary in 1938. Joseph joined his family in 1944, when the Nazis invaded Hungary and started sending Jewish people to Auschwitz. Their shop was raided, looted and destroyed. It has been estimated that about half a million Hungarian Jews were killed in the extermination camps

In pride of place, inside the shop today, hang two large portraits of Joseph's grandparents. His grandfather was from Transylvania and his grandmother from Germany. They came to England in the 1930s, escaping the Holocaust.

It is not easy to appreciate today how dangerous it was to bomb occupied Europe and even more to bomb Germany. But stark figures speak for themselves. On one mission to Leipzig seventy-nine aircraft were lost due to the weather forecast not advising of adverse winds.

'The flak was so thick over the Ruhr, you could walk on it,' Pagliero remembered. 'It was bedlam up there with night fighters shooting past, intense anti-aircraft fire and other bombers hurtling about all over the sky. On one occasion, over Berlin, one of our own aircraft accidently bombed us. He was about 500 feet above our plane, and we were showered with incendiaries. Then his big bomb passed between the cockpit and our starboard wing. A couple of feet either way and ... How did we survive? We were lucky I suppose, but we were also a good team, a good crew with a special unbelievable bond that was forged in the fire.'

Their tour of duty ended with a mission to Nuremburg, after which they said good-bye to *V-Victory*. The aircraft crashed soon after. The only survivor was Roy Bradley, who managed to salvage the oil can from the wreckage and later presented it to Harry Hudson and Bill Seymour. It remained a treasured possession for many years.

When the war was over, they decided to stay together. Under the name of their pilot, Cyril Ginder, they formed a Hatton Garden diamond company, went into business and stuck together for another forty years until old age and retirement thinned the ranks.

Cyril Ginder was incorporated 9th October 1954 and closed on 13th July 1988. Ginder, who won the DFC for his exploits, was chairman and was quickly joined by navigator Don Pagliero, another DFC, who became managing director of the Antwerp-end of the business. Bomb aimer Bill Seymour, who won the crew's third DFC, became managing director in the UK, and flight engineer Harry Hudson became managing director of the export company, while Wally Fox, the wireless operator, became the firm's accountant.

Harry Hudson.

CJ Ginder crew. L to R: Bill Seymour, Don Paglero, Cyril Ginder, Harry Hudson and Wally Fox.

Pagliero eventually became Honorary Consul General for Belgium and was awarded a CBE to go with his DFC. But he traces everything back to the tarmac at Metheringham. The old 'crew' remained in touch for years after retirement.

DONALD MCDONALD AND JOHNSON MATTHEY

Donald McDonald worked for Johnson Matthey and lived on the top floor above their premises at 78–80 Hatton Garden. He started with the company in 1910 and retired in 1954, having completed forty-four years of service. He began as a junior assistant through a connection of his father's. Then, at the age of 21, he was moved to the platinum lab, which he subsequently ran when his superior went off to war.

His story is told by his daughter, Alison. She and her sisters were christened at St Andrew's Parish Church. As young girls their parents believed they were in Sunday School, when in fact they had gone to the sweet shop.

In 1912 Donald had to go to British Columbia, Canada, as a potential platinum mine needed a metallurgist/assayer to sample its production. The mine belonged to Lord Osborne, later Duke of St Albans. Apparently, he was due to sail on RMS *Titanic* but because a board meeting had overrun, he missed the ship. The time to visit was June to October and Donald stayed out until the autumn.

In August 1914 he signed up to 'Kitchener's Army'. After training he saw active service in France, where he was severely wounded by a piece of shrapnel. The skill of the field surgeon saved his life.

He insisted that each of his five daughters were properly trained in a skill that would enable them to become self-sufficient if needs be.

The family left Hatton Garden in 1937, when they moved to Beckenham. Alison remembers the Rolls-Royce delivery vans that moved the bullion. The arched entrances to Johnson Matthey featured in the 1951 Ealing Studios movie *The Lavender Hill Mob*.

Alison's sister, Joan Amy, was born on 15th August 1924 and wrote in the family archives:

> Hatton Garden was a lovely house, looking over a street that was busy but not noisy, during the week, quiet at the weekends. A 4-storey building, the ground floor was part of Johnson Matthey's, with offices behind. An inner front door led up a straight flight of some 18 stairs then branched right and left to two entrances. To the left the stairs went on upwards through two more floors, to end at the front door of Mr and Mrs Fuller's dwelling (2 floor apartment) where George Fuller (Johnson Matthey's works dept) and his wife, and their little girl about my age, and Mr Fuller Snr., all lived.
>
> On the right-hand side of the stairs was the McDonald's own front door – a large, solid door with a knocker that nobody ever knocked on and a letter box that nothing was put into as we had our own letter box and doorbell in the ground floor entrance hall. And there was always a big pram parked in the entrance for there always seemed to be a baby in the family. Inside the upper front door there were four more stairs, and immediately on the

right, a huge walk-in larder with shelves around the sides. The larger entrance hall had two staircases leading off it. One straight flight up to a door that led to the second floor of Johnson Matthey's premises (our own entrance hall being already at first floor level); this was known as the works door and Daddy went that way to work each day or to make his Sunday morning routine inspection, for which Margo and I would sometimes join him. The other staircase was a hansom polished wood, carpeted affair to our second floor, with steep banisters and carved wooden posts. When we eventually moved out of 80 Hatton Garden this staircase was said to have been moved to a museum in Barking, as an example of Georgian/Victorian elegance, but I never went to see it there.

The drawing room occupied the whole of the front of the house, with three full length sash windows, and an elaborately carved marble fireplace, yellow painted panelled walls and a decorated plaster cornice around the ceiling. A big coal fire would burn in the fireplace all through the winter evenings, the coal being delivered by a big man called Jimmy who carried huge buckets of it through Johnson Matthey's premises and down through the Works Door to deposit it in the hall where newspaper was laid out ready to receive the buckets on. He took back all the rubbish, the fire ashes and I suppose anything else that was to be disposed of, for no dustbin was ever lugged down the stone stairs – Johnson Matthey's was the back door! If a plumber, carpenter or electrician, a repair man of any sort was needed, the Johnson Matthey's equivalent would come in and deal with the crisis. Hot water came automatically from taps in the kitchen and bathroom Monday to Friday, and for Sundays and baths there was a huge copper geyser over the bath which Daddy had to light with a long match and it was apt to make explosive noises, though the water was very hot indeed and filled the bathroom with steam.

In the drawing room stood my grandmother's Chappell boudoir grand piano, which had been her wedding present from her husband. Here, she gave me my first piano lesson at the age of 5 or 6. There was a big sofa and several armchairs, and over the wide mantlepiece, a round convex mirror with the eagle on top and glass clusters each side – a perfect place to show off this fantastic piece. On the other side of the hall was the dining room, with two big windows looking over the glass roofs of the Johnson Matthey works. A huge mirror hung over the fireplace (with a gas fire) with a green marble clock – if I wasn't at the breakfast table by 5 minutes to 8, I lost that day's pocket money (which was 7 pence a week, so it was easy to calculate). I often lost my penny; one day I produced a brilliant excuse – I had so far to come! My bedroom was on the top floor, a whole two flights away. I don't think Margo ever lost her pocket money pennies – she was far more organised than I, and anyway, she only had one flight of stairs to come down.

A kitchen had been added, leading off a corner of the dining room, with a white china sink, big gas cooker (the top all fretted, which had to be soaked and scrubbed once a week) and the walls covered with shelves and a great dresser. No fridge, but an ice box just inside the dining room door for which the fishmonger in Farringdon Market delivered a huge block of ice (wrapped in sacking and carried up the stone stairs on his shoulder). This would melt slowly in the lead lined icebox, which had a drain hole in the bottom and a container underneath to catch the water. Several years later, and not long before the move to Beckenham, an electric refrigerator was installed in its place, and this was water cooled which meant it dripped water into the pan all the time. Mum got so enthusiastic about ice on the premise that she bought an ice-cream maker – a wooden bucket with a handle attached to a paddle. You put a custard mixture into the inner metal container, broken ice cubes between that and the wooden bucket and stirred the handle round and round. You stirred until your arms ached, but the custard only got colder and colder – it never turned into 'proper ice cream' as it was supposed to. Still it was quite nice, and I'm sure we ate it all.

Up the fine staircase, with many gloomy pictures on its walls, plus a swordfish sword and the old barometer, and a deep blue and red patterned stair carpet, was the big landing (second floor – first floor to us). Mum and Daddy's bedroom was on the left, the size of the dining room below it, with the bathroom above the kitchen. A huge bath – Margot and I were usually bathed together and there was plenty of room but a constant argument over who should have the tap end and sit on the plug! The wash basin had three taps, the middle one was 'Works' water and sometimes the top came off and a jet of hot water shot up into the air. No problem – phone through to Johnson Matthey's and their plumber would immediately appear. Off the landing was the loo – about big enough to make a small bedroom – and in the front of the house was a big, two-windowed bedroom that, when my grandparents were alive, was their bedroom. Beside it, with one window looking into Hatton Garden, was my father's long, narrow study with his desk at the far end near the window, and his glass fronted bookshelves all along one side. Now I cannot remember the sleeping arrangements very clearly, but I slept in a single bed in the study, at the end away from the window, for quite a while and presumably Margot was still in Mum and Daddy's bedroom with them. Fa-Fa died in 1931 when I was 7 and Margot 5. He often suffered from gout and had one foot bandaged up, and this made him more bad tempered than usual, but I don't know what he died of. Mum must have found his death a relief as he shouted at her a lot. My grandmother (who I, in my infancy had christened Ga-Ga, nobody knowing at the time that this word had another, most uncomplimentary meaning) died the following year, in 1932 just before Dean was born. Mum told the story that Ga-Ga died because she knew the house wasn't big enough for all of us plus a new baby. I'm sure there was more to it than that, as I do not remember her being ill. She was quite a spritely lady and only 73 when she died. [Editor's note: she died of bronchitis.]

On the top floor was a big playroom, the Den, at the back, with a sloping ceiling under the roof where Margo and I spent most of our pre-school lives. We had a radio on the shelf on the wall, high up so we couldn't reach it, which consisted of a tuning cabinet with dials, a battery box, an accumulator in another box, and a speaker in another box with a fretted front. Every now and again the accumulator (which fed the batteries – I think) had to be recharged and would be put in the hall beside the rubbish bins for Jimmy to replace / recharge / return as necessary. All along one side of the Den hung a flowery cotton curtain behind which trunks and suitcases were stored, but we had a 'garage' at one end for pedal car and a doll's pram, and a 'house' at the other end. Over the bathroom, the flat roof was the garden with big boxes of soil in which Mum grew plants – always daffodils and tulips in Spring and always pink geraniums, purple petunia and yellow calceolarias in Summer.

Margo and I were not allowed to touch these, except in between one season and the next when they were empty when we could dig and make mud pies. Imagine our delight when we found a worm in one of them! Every year thereafter we would dig around until we found him again, and he actually got bigger and fatter over the years, so the poor thing must have found something to live on. A high trellis was put up over the parapet walls round the roof and we were strictly forbidden to climb on to the parapet. Daddy had a tiny little office that looked up towards our roof and if we so much as leaned on the parapet he would be on the phone to alert Mum and she would dash up the stairs to rescue us. On the higher roof of the next-door building was a flagpole, and on the King's birthday a huge Union Jack would fly up there, which was very exciting.

At the back were the various roof tops of Johnson Matthey buildings, a higgledy piggledy mixture of glass, brick and slate, at all levels from ground floor fanlights to the 4 or 5 storey block to our right (from the roof) of the new 'ER' block (Electro refinery). Over in the Leather Lane direction was one of the original Johnson Matthey buildings and on its back wall was a large bell. This was rung at 5.25 p.m. to warn that closing time was approaching and again at 5.30 p.m. when everyone went home. I think it was also rung at 12.30 p.m. for the lunch break. In later years there was a night shift and Daddy would sometimes be called in for an evening discussion, but not often.

It was an idyllic existence, though we had no friends in the neighbourhood in our pre-school years, but there was always a maid to chat to – there were several, but I best remember Millie, a placid girl who would let us shell peas, or help with whatever she was doing. She had a twin sister Norah who worked in a pub around the corner and sometimes we would meet her out shopping – the first time I had come across twins and it amazed me that two people could look so alike.

Shopping.

I often tried, many years later when we shared Sunday lunch at Scotts Lane, to take Mum's thoughts back to her early days in Hatton Garden. How did she manage as a new wife, managing a cook/house-maid, learning a new household routine with more elaborate meals than she had met before and served with wine? The main grocery shopping was done at the Army and Navy stores, where Ga-Ga would do the ordering with Mum in tow, wines ordered by the case (these presumably under Daddy's instructions) and these goods would be delivered by van. Nothing was ever carried from the stores.

When we were big enough Margo and I would join these shopping trips, and we would all end up in the restaurant for tea with toast and little pots of jam, and cakes chosen from a two-layer cake stand. Or in Summer a visit to the Soda Fountain for ice cream – Margo liked strawberry ice, so strawberry it had to be when it was her turn to choose. How I disliked it – and I still do! A big round pink blob with a wafer stuck in it – I would eat her wafer and she would eat my ice cream. Ordinary daily groceries came from Hudson Brothers in Farringdon Road – Mum would do this shopping each week. Meat came from Hart's in Smithfield and there was also a fish shop in Farringdon Market. Often shopping was done in Leather Lane – Coulson's the bakers on the corner of Greville Street, Charley's vegetable stall (who would deliver the potatoes), and there was an ironmonger who sold firewood and paraffin and methylated spirits, and all the smelly things associated with old-fashioned ironmongers. A paper shop delivered the Times, the Daily Herald and the Daily Sketch every day. There was Clara who had a flower shop and stall. Miss Delaney's cake shop in Brook Street was just around the corner from Lewis & Burrows the chemist and was always stuffed with gorgeous homemade sponge and fruit cakes, and she also sold chocolates and jam. She taught Mum to make jam and I think the 'family recipe' for marmalade came from her. She has a little chocolate making business in Cross Street and Mum and I visited once, saw the girls in white overalls and caps dipping chocolates by hand. I was told I could choose one to eat – but what a choice. Unfortunately, I chose a ginger one and had to eat it out of politeness.

Hatton Garden was a quiet street. Goods were delivered by horse and cart or by van, or by daring boys on bicycles with baskets, weaving in and out of the traffic, or on tricycles. There were few cars, a taxi or two, an occasional parked van unloading or Johnson Matthey's big chocolate brown, immaculately polished, Rolls-Royce vans backing in and out of the yard a little further along Hatton Garden. At weekends there was nothing, and Margo and I were allowed to play along the pavement with our skipping ropes. A few older children would emerge – Bett and Peggy Smith lived in the caretaker's flat at the corner of Charles Street, Joan Vigus and her brother Douglas in the mansions at the back of Leather Lane by St Albans Church. But in our pre-school days we had no local friends and played together. Mum told me that daddy's reaction to the move to Hatton Garden was 'thank goodness there will be no neighbours'.

Before we started school, Margo spent our days playing in the 'Den' or on the roof or going for afternoon walks. Mum would take us to Lincoln's Inn Fields, to Staples Inn to see the fountain playing, to Postman's Park, a tiny slip of garden off St Martin le Grands' main Post Office where there were often postmen relaxing between one delivery and the next. We would go to Gamages or Selfridge's around Christmas time, to Hamleys to look at toys, to the Medici Society shop to choose Christmas cards and tree presents. Daddy would wrap up lots of mystery presents for Mum, and Margo and I were allowed to write comical labels for some of them – I remember a pair of oil and vinegar bottles – Oily Obadiah and Vinegary Victoria. He made Christmas an exciting time for her and always helped to decorate the ceiling-high (8 feet) Christmas tree that stood in the corner of the drawing room. This would be after the annual visit to Mead & Field's cracker factory, behind Leather Lane, where dozens of boxes of crackers would be on show. They would choose 10 or 12 boxes for use on different occasions over Christmas or for parties round the year.

Amy Sullivan writes about Christmas: I remember Ga-Ga at Hatton Garden for Christmas. We used to go by tram on Christmas morning and have a slice of bread and dripping and a glass of juice to keep us going till dinner time. I remember once – utter luxury – seeing Auntie Amy squeezing tangerines for us! One year I remember being on a landing. Uncle Donald lit one of those bombs at the bottom of the staircase and all the gifts flew up for us to scramble for (possibly from the cracker factory). We also used to get 'new' money at Christmas too. I still have my silver crown – 1935 I think the date is. We used to stay for the night and go for a walk on Boxing Day before lunch. We saw Tower Bridge open up at one time and the bells with the men with hammers hitting them. Amy and Donald were very kind to us all year but especially at Christmas.

One Sunday each year there would be a street procession from a nearby Roman Catholic church. This would come down Cross Street past the old school. By hanging out of the drawing room window we could watch it go by – long lines of men in white carrying crosses and candles, then crowds of children all walking in line. I used to wonder who they were and where they were going. Margo thinks that this must have been the festival of Corpus Christi, as there was a considerable Italian community living in Clerkenwell, at the Northern end of Hatton Garden.

E WOLFE & CO.

E Wolfe & Co. only came to Hatton Garden thirty years ago, having been in the West End since they were founded in 1850 by Ernst Wolfe. They were famed as makers of tiaras, of which they have made over 1,000. Their unique expertise and experience have earned them a reputation as true masters of their craft. In 1902 they were commissioned by Carrington & Co. to make the royal crown for the coronation of Queen Alexandra and in 1911, Garrard & Co. commissioned them to make the Imperial Crown of India. Their archives are full of wonderful old drawings and designs that portray the very best in fine jewellery design. Perhaps one of their most remarkable pieces is the 'Cambridge Lover's Knot Tiara', which was made in 1913 and was a favourite of the Princess of Wales. Richard Cornelius recalls that his great-grandfather used to deliver the finished tiaras to their Bond Street and Regent Street retail customers by wearing them under his top hat.

At its peak, the workshop employed eighty mounters. In the 19th and early 20th centuries all work was done by hand as casting wasn't introduced until later. Each piece was painstakingly created by skilled hands.

During the Great War, Mr Wolfe converted his Rolls-Royce into an ambulance and drove it to pick up casualties after Zeppelin raids. Most of the men in the workshop enlisted in the army and served their country. The war did not prevent Garrard ordering the 'Russian Fringe Tiara', which was worn by Queen Elizabeth, the Queen Mother, and the Princess Royal at their respective weddings.

In the Second World War, the workshop was requisitioned to manufacture items for the military, including instruments for aircraft such as Spitfires. They worked three shifts a day with pre-paid orders to keep them going right through to VE Day, when all outstanding orders were cancelled. They were further helped by the government in the form of a £100,000 overdraft to purchase equipment. Some of the more able men served in the army and the workshop designer Mr Winchcombe was among those evacuated from Dunkirk. While waiting for transport and standing in the sea, he realised that he was next to one of Wolfe's London customers, Collingwoods, who were also royal jewellers.

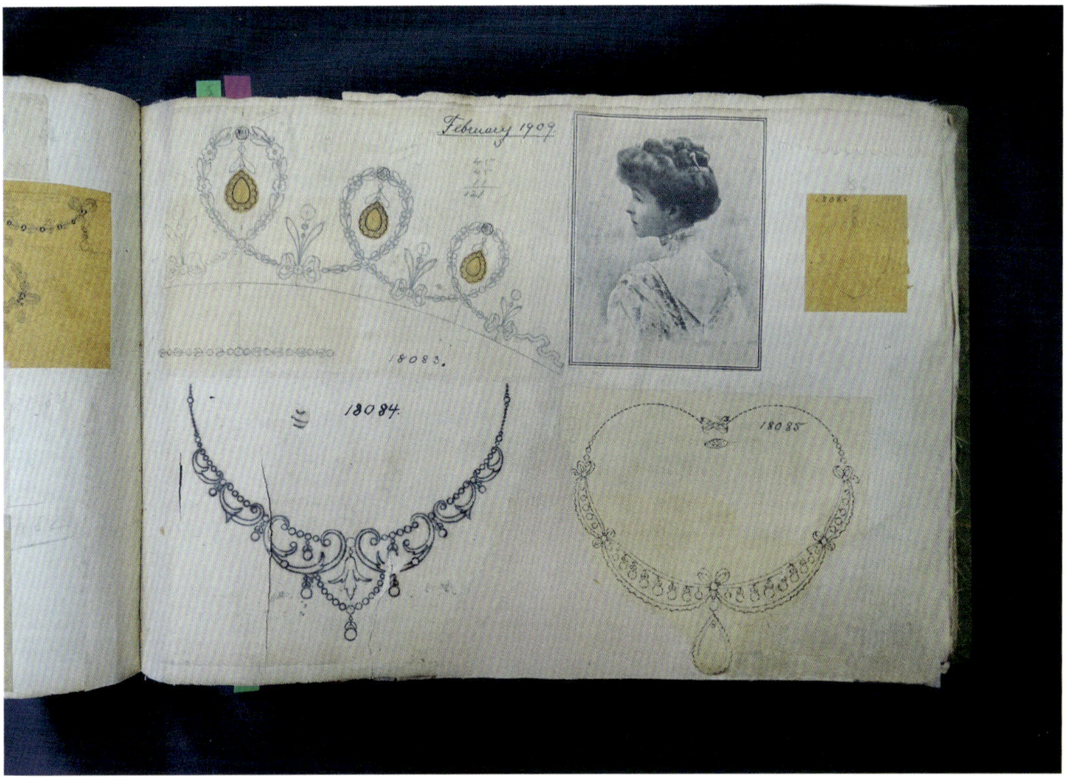

Pages from one of E Wolfe's design books, February 1909.

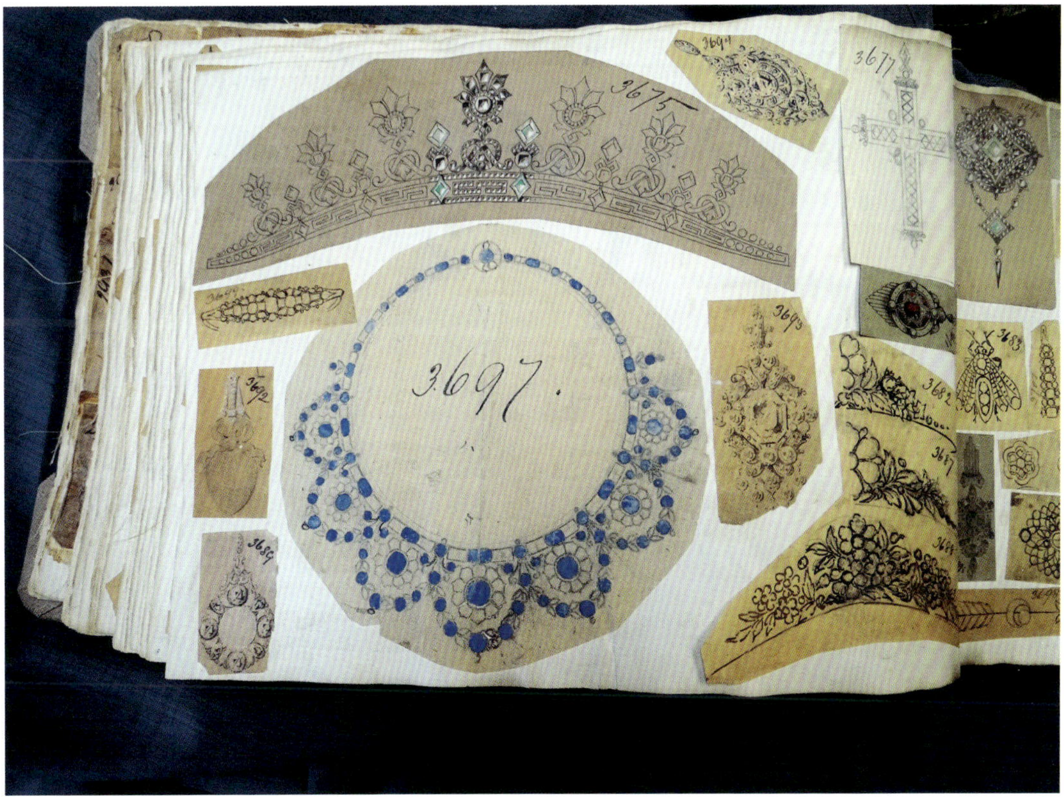

Like all businesses, they had good times and poorer times, largely dictated by government policy and the economy. The demand for tiaras and crowns has somewhat diminished but their well-equipped workshop still produces some of the finest jewellery and objects made in the UK. Their signature collection focuses on wildlife, particularly birds. In a modern world of 3D printing and CAD design they continue to successfully handmake engagement rings, bridal jewellery and an array of cocktail rings along with the occasional tiara order.

The business is run today by Richard Cornelius and his daughter, Victoria, who oversee orders as they travel through the various stages of production in their Hatton Garden workshop. The workshop continues to be one of the largest in London, employing many skilled craftspeople. Richard's grandfather, William Cornelius, was part of the jewellery design team employed by the Wolfe family and he was able to buy shares in the business in 1932 when the last of the Wolfe family left the trade. Richard and Victoria continue to be in touch with descendants of the founder.

GEORGES

One of the two 'original' shops in Hatton Garden was Georges. It was actually located just around the corner in Greville Street, although it had a Hatton Garden address at 88–90. The other was SH Harris & Son at 5 Hatton Garden, who sold second-hand and antique jewellery.

The business was initially run by Mr Gordon, who also built the Hatton Garden Safe Deposit. When he died in 1960, his wife and their daughter, Dorit (Fox), took over. Dorit recalls how her mother had no commercial training. 'She couldn't even write out a cheque.' However, she had a wonderful gift of being able to sell. Her charm would win many customers over the years and she created a loyalty that brought people back time and time again. Dorit had been allowed to help out in the shop while still at school by putting in the windows in the morning and talking to customers.

One of their sales techniques was to use a countertop mirror to show prospective clients how beautiful a ring looked on their finger when seen from a different perspective. At the time this technique wasn't widely used but now most shops would use it.

The shop floor was very small and could only accommodate half a dozen people, who would have to stand at the counter or wait patiently in the doorway. At Christmas time customers used to queue outside in the cold weather but were guaranteed a warm welcome once inside. Mrs Gordon would arrange for the commissionaire, Mr Lovet, to go out with a notepad to gather a list of what people would be looking for in order to save their time once they had got through the door. On more than one occasion the commissionaire was sent across the road to the Globe pub to buy a tray of drinks for those queuing.

Hatton Garden Safe Deposit.

They enjoyed what they did and worked six days a week, allowing themselves just one week off for a holiday, when they would go down to the Chewton Glen Hotel in the New Forest for a much-needed break. They didn't go out for lunch, but two ladies from the Greville Buttery would carry a couple of plates up the road and leave them on the cluttered desk in the small back office, on the off chance that there might be a lull in activity with customers in the shop.

Mrs Gordon was quite a formidable character to the trade. She had a commanding voice and an Austrian accent and was able to make it quite clear as to whether a supplier had a chance of selling her anything or not. It was not uncommon to be allowed into the back office and then to be left alone for a long time while she carried on serving. Suppliers included Hortons, Tidy & Blanchard, Cropp & Farr, T O'Donoghue, Lionel Wiffen, M Jays and PJ Watson. Although some of the stock in the window was on approval, most of it had been bought and paid for.

Despite the business façade, Mrs Gordon had a heart of gold. When one of their staff came into work looking sad because they had lost their budgie, Mrs Gordon went straight to Gamages and bought another. You could buy almost anything there.

Security was a concern for two women running a shop on their own. They experienced a number of incidents over the years. Dorit recalls receiving a kiss of thanks from a policeman for foiling one attempted robbery. Other robberies included an armed attack via their inside door that led to the safe deposit. On another occasion, there was a snatch of a sapphire and diamond ring pad, which was immediately recovered in the street.

HARRY LEVY: LEVY GEMS

Harry Levy started work in Hatton Garden in the 1960s, having been introduced to the trade by his father, 'H Levy – diamond and gem dealer'. Their family roots go back to Iran, where they were part of a small Jewish community. Persecution forced them to leave the land of their birth and seek refuge elsewhere. They were given the option of either converting to the Muslim faith and remaining or leaving.

H Levy Snr was one of the founder members of the London Diamond Bourse. Harry Levy Jnr remembers being smuggled into the Bourse as a child. He recalls how the room was full of smoke, but that was not uncommon for many offices at that time.

Harry Levy.

Many Jewish people left Amsterdam in the early 20th century and moved to Antwerp, where trade flourished for some years. Threats of German invasion caused some to move to France and for a time they lived in Cognac. However, this was short-lived, and they found their way to London. In all about 10,000 Jews made it to the UK in 1939–1945.

Those who were in the diamond trade arrived with little other than their stocks. Originally, they traded on the streets and in doorways. Eventually they congregated at Mrs Cohen's Café. An upstairs room was used, and a sergeant hired for security with the cost shared between members. Legends like Max Rabstein, Eddie Fischer, Moise Frei, Norman Rokach, Israel Jacober and Eddie Goldstein were the backbone of this community. Yiddish was the common language for many of the Bourse members at that time. A new vocabulary was adopted by the trade. A *strop* was used to describe a stone you shouldn't have bought and would probably lose money trying to sell. A *metsiye*, on the other hand, was a bargain. The specially folded papers in which loose stones were presented were and are known as *brivkes*. A deal was sealed with a handshake and the Yiddish '*Mazal*' and '*Bracha*', meaning 'luck and blessing'. 'How is the *gesheft*' means 'how's business'. Strict payment terms have always been part of the way of doing business. If a purchaser should pay late, he was said to *shlep* his supplier. Worse still, a thief was known as a *ganif*. A 'swimmer' is the name given to a diamond put into a parcel where it wouldn't naturally belong – a bigger stone adds value and makes the parcel more attractive.

The Bourse found its way to a bigger home fairly rapidly as membership grew. The next move was to No. 57d and then to 35, where they had the whole of the first floor. While there, they were given an option on the purchase of the freehold but there was insufficient support. What could have been purchased for thousands in the 1960s is worth millions today.

The London Diamond Club (LDC) met at No. 87 in an old Georgian building. The freehold was acquired with support from De Beers and Bonas & Co. There was an opportunity for the London Diamond Bourse to move into the top floor, but the building was in a sorry state of repair. When the Bourse merged with the Diamond Club there was a committee of about twenty members and two joint presidents! The Bourse has about 320 members today, but there are very few rough diamond and polishing companies.

The trade in polished goods was changed forever when Martin Rapaport introduced his price list. It has been referred to as the commoditisation of the product. Feelings were very strongly against what the list represented, and you could have been expelled from the Bourse if seen using it. When he published a fall in prices, he was nearly lynched!

The Bourse, through its committee, flexed its muscle on more than one occasion. An application for membership was declined to a young man who they didn't like because of his East End wide-boy style and they believed would amount to nothing. He later went on to be an international success.

Today, the global nature of business and international trade shows have removed the barriers that once separated the different parts of the supply chain. Retailers explore sourcing upstream, while manufacturers move into downstream retailing.

THE HOLT FAMILY

Those who have visited Holts in Hatton Garden can't fail to have been impressed by the wonderful collection of gemstones on show. What is not generally known or appreciated is the fascinating history that brought the present-day business into existence. Robert Ackerhalt was a refugee from Vienna who came to England, aged 15, with his parents, to escape the threatening situation in Europe. After he retired at the age of 90, he wrote his life story for the benefit of his family and friends. He completed the work on the very day that he died.

Robert's early years were difficult, like so many Jewish people of his generation who had been based in Europe. He was born near Vienna in 1923 and grew up in a rural community. His parents had previously moved to England, where they were living at the outbreak of the First World War. As 'enemy aliens' they were rounded up and interned on the Isle of Man, prior to repatriation in Austria. When the Germans came in 1938, the family were moved to a ghetto in Vienna as part of a 'purification' process. Robert remembers being called out in front of the school of 400 pupils and humiliated by the headmaster, who threatened trouble to anyone who spoke to him. Robert remembers how they relied on handouts, and in particular the Society of Friends gave them much-needed support. He made a living by becoming a professional queuer. Robert would

R Holt & Co. Ltd. The Early Days.

stand in line, sometimes overnight, on behalf of more wealthy people so that they could obtain their rations. He tried unsuccessfully to escape across the border into Switzerland with some friends. Finally, he obtained legal entry to the UK and was processed through various camps.

Robert wrote: 'In my early 20s, I was living back in the East End. I didn't know what to learn or what to do. But I knew I wanted to do something that would establish me in business or as a professional.'

Still without a plan or any idea of his future, he enrolled in an apprenticeship scheme run by the government for ex-servicemen. This was with a company called Star Diamond in Hatton Garden. He progressed with his training in the art of diamond cutting until he fell out with the management. A royal visit from Princess Elizabeth had been arranged; the premises were spruced up and new uniforms were issued. Robert had been campaigning for such improvements for years and by way of a protest wore his old factory coat on the big day. This led to his dismissal the following week.

He then decided to make a trip to India. Bombay was experiencing difficult times and he made his way to Goa, then a Portuguese colony. In a previous century, Lisbon had been a major hub within Europe for the Indian diamond trade. While still travelling he became seriously ill and had to be repatriated.

Now back in the UK and still without a plan, he went to visit his brother in Jersey. While there he was introduced to a jeweller by the name of Monsieur Le Neindre, who noticed the gold ring that Robert was wearing. Le Neindre said that there was a real shortage of good jewellery in the Channel Islands as very few reps were visiting since the war. Jersey was becoming a holiday destination as it was the sunniest place in the UK. Package holidays as we now know them were not yet generally available and Jersey was set to benefit from this new opportunity.

Looking for an opening, Robert approached a Hatton Garden company called Ideal Jewellery, who had sized his ring for him when he received it as a gift from his father. Mr Schutzman of Ideal Jewellery gave Robert a collection of gold jewellery to sell. He promptly went back to the Channel Islands, where he did amazingly well; so much so that he was able to buy his first car. Le Neindre became a major account and R Holt & Co. was born. Robert spread his wings and started visiting other jewellers around the UK.

The scars of the Second World War were still very fresh, and survivors of the Holocaust and concentration camps found their way to London. Robert was very proactive in providing support and shared his London flat with a number of victims. He writes: 'They all had such painful memories and didn't speak much about what they experienced. Food that I'd just bought would disappear. They would hide it under their mattresses. If I gave them a bottle of milk, they would take it with them when they went out so nobody else would take it.'

Business continued to grow, and an office was established in two rooms on the first floor of 35 Greville Street. Then in 1948, Holt was approached by a businessman who had imported a large consignment of gems and mineral specimens from Brazil. The businessman had not managed to sell the goods himself and had to return home. He therefore proposed to leave the whole consignment with Holt on the basis of whatever might be sold could be paid for in due course. This turned out to be an overnight success, so Holt looked at setting up his own cutting factory where imported rough could be transformed into fine gemstones. It took a great deal of time and money to get the business to where he wanted it to be. Buying rough gemstones at source and cutting them into beautiful gems meant travelling to many exotic locations.

As a young man, Jason Holt was enthralled by his father's stories of his international travels and felt an attraction to the world of gems. However, before committing to gemstones as a career he studied to become a lawyer and went into practice in the legal profession. Although enjoying a successful time in his chosen vocation, he still felt a calling to his father's business. In May 1998, when Robert turned 75, Jason called his father to explore whether he might accept the baton as Holts progressed to the next generation.

Jason brought a fresh approach to the business and was particularly interested in the skills of older craftsmen in Hatton Garden. He immediately recognised that there was a need to train the next generation before some of those skills were lost. This came at the time when some of the jewellery manufacturers and gem cutters, for which Hatton Garden had become known, were starting to lose out to competition from the Far East. The demise of the Hatton Garden industry was something Jason was not willing to stand by and watch.

With some significant support from European grants, which had to be matched like for like, he set about creating what was to become Holts Academy in the basement of 98 Hatton Garden. Critics at the time thought that he was taking a huge risk to his reputation and his finances but were quickly proved wrong when the school became an overnight success. Within a short period of time some of the original students qualified as trainers and introduced more people to the various crafts and skills. Starting with the art of cutting gems and lapidary skills, they progressed into jewellery design and other areas, filling all the available space in the basement. Then an opportunity came along for a cooperation with Holborn to take a subsidised lease on new premises in St Cross Street. They began with six benches and rapidly expanded to forty. In a period of fifteen years over 10,000 people benefitted from Jason's vision to teach and maintain the skills of British craftsmen and women in the jewellery industry. The first jewellery apprenticeship school had been established.

Jason stepped down from his commitment to the school to pursue his other interests in the trade. The school has now become the British Academy for Jewellery and has premises on Holborn Viaduct.

Jason's passion for education went beyond jewellery and in 2017 he was awarded a CBE for his contribution to the government's apprenticeship scheme. In 2011, approximately 50,000 people were engaged in apprenticeship schemes. Eight years later that number had increased to 1,000,000.

The core business of Holts continues to thrive at different levels. At street level for the consumer, Holts Gems is one of the flagship stores in Hatton Garden where the lover of gems can find a bespoke service specialising in 'one of a kind' pieces from design to creation.

The trade can have access to a separate showroom where all manner of coloured stones can be seen and access to their award-winning lapidary services is available.

Jason is a Liveryman of the Worshipful Company of Goldsmiths and a member of the Council of Management of the Gemmological Association of Great Britain, and he has several other directorships.

JOHN KESSLER

John's roots were in Brazil. His father, IM Kessler, was a diamond cutter and polisher. At the weekends John, at the age of 8, was taught how to make eight cuts. His mother was English and when John was 16, he came to the UK and stayed with his grandparents. He found employment as an apprentice diamond mounter in the workshop of Sannit & Stein. They employed thirty people at the time and produced jewellery exclusively for Kutchinsky. After a while he returned to Brazil, where he studied economics.

It was in 1968 that he arrived in Hatton Garden with a collection of Brazilian emeralds. He studied gemmology at the Sir John Cass College in London. He joined the London Diamond Bourse and without any previous connections, he knocked on doors up and down the street offering his goods. With only a very limited amount of English language, it was a struggle to build a new business but fifty years later he was able to retire from the one and only occupation that he had always enjoyed. Whether he was sitting on the floor of a mud hut in a remote part of Brazil or dining with VIPs in London, he considers that he has been very privileged.

His father had also come to the UK, where he continued to work with diamonds. They worked from a small office in 88–90 Hatton Garden. Mr IM Kessler always looked down on the coloured-stone trade until one day John showed him an emerald that was far more valuable than any diamond his father had ever sold. He also worked with African emeralds, which were then being cut in Israel. With the first consignment he was able to sell the whole lot to an old friend from Brazil. Over the years he has supplied most of the famous jewellery houses in London and beyond. Some of those names used to lunch in the Nosherie and some in the Bourse.

One famous West End customer had been tasked by a client with finding a pair of 3ct, D colour, internally flawless, Asscher cut diamonds with GIA certificates. The buyer had tried all his usual contacts without success. Although John was a specialist in coloured stones, he had a valuable network of contacts in other areas of the trade. The buyer explained that he had searched the New York market and the Antwerp market and failed to come up with anything to offer his client. His frustration was clear. He risked losing, not only an important sale but also a loyal client. The client had originally purchased a pair of 1-caraters and upgraded regularly, increasing the size each time. John accepted the challenge to source something to satisfy the client. It soon became clear that there was nothing out there to match the brief. However, a contact in Geneva had a pair of 5-caraters and duly 'faxed' the certificates through. In order to import the stones into the UK it was necessary to pay 20% VAT upfront. Considering the value of the stones, this would have had impossible ramifications on John's cash flow. It was agreed that the client would handle the importation directly. All went well, until John took a call from the supplier saying that De Beers had just announced a 10% price increase on goods. The retailer was not happy to accept an increase, so John requested the diamonds to be returned. After a few days of negotiating, the stones were sold at the new price and everyone was happy. It was the largest sale that John made during his career and he never even saw the goods.

LANDSBERG

Landsberg & Son (Antiques) Ltd was formed in 1955 to continue the long-established family business of H Landsberg. For generations the business has been one of the most celebrated in Hatton Garden, occupying a prestigious ground-floor office and showroom at 27 Hatton Garden, until relocating to London's West End in 2019.

The firm of H Landsberg & Son was founded in 1835, during the reign of King William IV. It is still controlled by a member of the original family, James Dallas, the nephew of Mr Anthony Landsberg, who retired in 2019.

Mr H Landsberg.

The founder, Hirschfield Landsberg, was born in 1815, which is perhaps better known as being the date of the Battle of Waterloo. So, it was at the age of 20 that he established himself as a dealer in silver, gold and precious jewels. His licence, dated 1843 and still in the possession of the firm, shows that he was then based at 20 St Mary Axe in the City of London. St Mary Axe is best known today as the site of the Gherkin. Hirschfield travelled the country with his goods visiting county jewellers. As many of his customers did not have bank accounts, he accepted payment in gold. After a promising start he continued to prosper but had a major setback in 1883 when his entire stock was stolen. Commercial Insurance was not then widely available, and he had to start again.

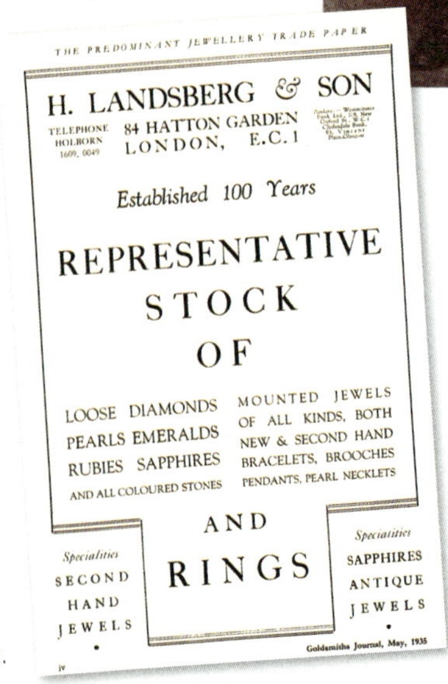

THE PREDOMINANT JEWELLERY TRADE PAPER

H. LANDSBERG & SON

TELEPHONE HOLBORN 1609, 0049

84 HATTON GARDEN LONDON, E.C.1

Established 100 Years

REPRESENTATIVE STOCK OF

LOOSE DIAMONDS PEARLS EMERALDS RUBIES SAPPHIRES AND ALL COLOURED STONES

MOUNTED JEWELS OF ALL KINDS, BOTH NEW & SECOND HAND BRACELETS, BROOCHES PENDANTS, PEARL NECKLETS

AND RINGS

Specialities SECOND HAND JEWELS

Specialities SAPPHIRES ANTIQUE JEWELS

Goldsmiths Journal, May, 1935

H Landsberg & Son, 1935 advert.

Hirschfield was joined by Louis, his eldest son, in 1870, but continued to travel throughout the country until he was over 70. Travelling at that time was very different to that of today. Cars were not yet an option, railways were still being built and a certain level of discomfort was unavoidable. Hirschfield died in 1889, aged 74.

Louis also carved out a great reputation in the trade and was known for his 'voluminous' pockets and 'black bag', which contained a king's ransom. Louis had three sons: Frank, George and Harold. Frank ran an office in Amsterdam. George was only able to serve the firm for a few years before being killed at Ypres in 1915. The business had relocated from their original address to Tavistock Square before coming to Hatton Garden in the 1920s. Harold took the business further but also fell victim to robbers in 1933 while driving his car in St James. It was Harold who maintained a presence in Hatton Garden throughout the Second World War, allowing the rest of the family to move to Bude, in Cornwall.

It was in 1945, as the war ended, that Harold's eldest son, Michael, joined the firm and is remembered for his classic English dress of a bowler hat, a three-piece suit and furled umbrella. As well as visiting established customers in the UK, he travelled to the USA and Canada opening new accounts, some of which still work with the company today. In 1958, Anthony Landsberg joined the company and Michael retired in 1990.

LEONARD SANITT

In 1990 Leonard Sanitt wrote an interesting book entitled *On Parade: Memoirs of a Jewish Sergeant-Major*. Although the larger part of his writings describes his war years, there is a valuable insight into life as an apprentice in a jewellery workshop in Hatton Garden in the 1930s. For five years (1934 to 1939) from the age of 14 Leonard learned the skills of a diamond mounter; a career to which he returned after the war. His 'Master' was Ralph Glick of 40 Hatton Garden.

Leonard writes ...

> In order to become a jewellery apprentice I went along to the Jewish Board of Guardians, which had a local Boys Industrial Department run by a gentleman called Mr. Gee. I told him that I wanted to be a jeweller and, after a long examination of the reasons and my background, he said that as soon as I left school, I should visit him again and he would see what he could do.
>
> It was very difficult to get an apprenticeship in one of the large, important jewellery firms like Cartier, Boucheron or Garrards, not because they would not take on Jewish boys – although it certainly played a part in limiting the number of jobs that we could expect – but because there were only a limited number of apprentices required. It was the nature of the trade that there were always relatives or friends of the people already working in these firms who were on the waiting list for the few vacancies that became available. Despite all the efforts of the Board, Jewish boys mostly went to jobs in very

small firms where the quality of work was usually of a lower order than the large West End firms.

Thus, when I left school, I saw Mr. Gee as promised and he sent me to a small firm in Hatton Garden. I went along merrily for a month's trial to a tiny room, in a back street off the Garden, which contained only a single workbench since it was a one-man business. The owner was the only craftsman although there was another apprentice who had already been there for two years.

I started work immediately and at lunchtime, just before one o'clock, the governor told me to go out and buy him a sandwich for his lunch. I was perfectly happy to do so as cleaning and errands were part of my duties. He told me to fetch a ham sandwich from one of the local cafes in Hatton Garden. I got him his sandwich, and in the afternoon, I told him that I was very sorry but I was not going to be able to return the following day.

The next day I returned to Mr. Gee, who was somewhat surprised to see me; I told him that I couldn't stay at that firm and requested that he should please send me to another. Naturally he asked me for an explanation. I told him that the firm was okay, but as they had sent me out to buy a ham sandwich, I didn't feel as though I could remain there. Mr. Gee looked at me and explained that the purchase of a ham sandwich did not mean that I, myself, had to eat non-kosher food; life was not as simple as that. I must expect, in the new world into which I was going, to adjust and adapt the ideas that I had been taught as a child. While he was lecturing me, a telephone call came through from another Hatton Garden firm with a vacancy for an apprentice and the next day I returned to the Garden to a firm called 'Ralph Glick'.

Ralph Glick was a larger organisation consisting of about eighteen men and boys of various ages – I was the only Jewish person among them. I started to work, cleaning and so on and, at twelve o'clock I was instructed to go around with a list for the lunchtime orders. By the time I had completed the list, instead of one ham sandwich from one cafe, I had a variety of ham sandwiches plus other non-kosher foods to obtain from a variety of cafes in the area. However, by this time I had learnt one of the first lessons of life and cheerfully accepted it, fetching everybody's orders.

I settled at Glick's very quickly, making many friends, some of whom became lifelong friends of mine. It was a completely new world to me because this was the first time I had lived as a Jew in a non-Jewish environment.

The system in this company was that each year (an apprenticeship lasted five years from the age of fourteen to nineteen) a new apprentice would be employed as the senior one finished his time and became an improver. It took five years to become a mounter. Then one was an improver until the age of twenty-one. I took to the work immediately, having no difficulty whatsoever and I thoroughly enjoyed my five years there.

The senior apprentice, an eighteen-year-old named Horace Craddock, sat next to me and was responsible for teaching me in my early years. The mounters were on two benches not more than five yards from each other and each bench had seven places. Most of the time everybody was talking to everybody else and we could all hear each other's conversations whilst we were working, since the nature of the work was that it was fairly quiet. It was very cosy and under these circumstances we got to know everything about each other.

Bill MacDougall came from West Ham, Eddie Sayer from Plaistow and Sid Harvey came from the Alexandra Palace area. Sid left before his apprenticeship finished to join the Merchant Navy. During the early part of the war he achieved some fame because he was on an armed merchantman that engaged a pocket battleship, and I was very pleased when I read about him in the newspapers.

Other apprentices at Glick's included Mick Schlain (who afterwards became Mick Slade of Slade & Woolf, one of the leading manufacturing companies) and Archie Cooper, who had two older brothers, Alf and Frank. I was very close to Alf because we had the hobby of weightlifting in common. Frank Cooper was a composer in his spare time and was one of the first men in the jewellery trade to recognise the importance of the 'lost wax casting system'. This was a modernised system for economic jewellery production, which I was able to develop many years later for producing very complicated jewellery of international quality. Just before the war, Frank left Glick's and went to one of the large firms in the Garden to set up a casting workshop for them.

The foreman was Bill Whittlesey who, a few months before the war broke out, got some form of food poisoning and, to our great astonishment, died. His funeral was the first non-Jewish religious ceremony that I had attended, and it impressed me greatly. It was so simple for he belonged to a Protestant sect that did not believe in anything ornate, using a very sparse bare church.

I often went to the houses of my co-workers, joined them socially and never found any difficulty because of the fact that I was brought up in a completely Jewish environment. During my apprenticeship, I led two separate lives: one revolving around the Jewish family and Jewish boys' club life and the other a normal English working life.

At first, I was paid 5s 0d (25p) a week which increased by 2s 6d, then by 5s 0d each six-month period until during the final six-month period of my apprenticeship, at the age of 18 and a half, I was paid £1 10s 0d (£1.50) a week. The cost of being apprenticed was £15, which my mother had to pay half on the day that I signed the documents; 5th November 1934. The Board of Guardians loaned my mother £7 10s 0d at the start of my apprenticeship and, two and a half years later, the second instalment of £7 10s Od. I had to buy a kit of tools, costing £2 5s 0d, and both the money for the apprenticeship and the money for the tools were loaned to my mother by the Board of Guardians. I remember the ritual of going along to the Board of Guardians' offices in Middlesex Street each Sunday morning where I would repay them 6d (2½p) for the premium and 3d for the kit of tools.

My 5s a week was used as follows; the fare money from St Mary's Station to Farringdon Street was 10d (5p) for a weekly season ticket, the national insurance stamp was 2d and then there was the 9d repayment money. I was left with the princely sum of 3s 3d. My mother allowed me to keep 6d for myself and the rest I duly gave across to her each week to contribute to my support and clothing.

My working day started at 8.30 a.m. and finished at 6 p.m. including a one-hour lunch-break and a short tea-break. On Saturdays we worked from 8.30 a.m. to 1 p.m. but most of the time I tried to work overtime. Overtime was optional for most of the year and, after a few months in the firm, I had made myself useful enough to be included in the overtime rota. At first, I was paid one penny an hour but, towards the end of my apprenticeship, this had risen to 6d an hour. Two or three hours' overtime a week supplemented my personal income, for my mother would not take any of this extra money from me. Thus, with my 6d allowance plus 3d for three hours' overtime, 1 had increased my spending money by 50%.

Most of my leisure time was spent at the boys' club but, often on a Saturday night, I would go to the Paragon Cinema at Mile End. Here, in a former music hall, there were stalls, a dress circle, an upper circle and a gallery. The gallery was not considered very suitable for watching films so a ticket here only cost 4d, for which one could see a programme consisting of two major films and a stage show. After the cinema, my friends and I would go over to Johnny Isaacs to buy a penny portion of chips, a halfpenny bagel and a halfpenny pickled cucumber. This sixpenny night out was thoroughly enjoyable yet still left me with a further 3d for the rest of the week.

Most of the work that I was being trained to do was with platinum since very little gold was used for jewellery at that time; platinum was the modern metal. As a junior, my chief tasks were to keep the workshop clean, to make the tea at lunchtime and tea-break and to wax and clean the benches each morning before the senior men started work at 9 a.m. During the day, I would be given some simpler tasks to do with jewellery-making such as milling out metal or drawing out wire, doing the pickling and bending round circles of metal wire for collets. Gradually, as I became more experienced, so I would be given more complicated work.

I also had to do all the necessary errands such as going to the Bullion Merchants Johnson Matthey or Baker Platinum and ferrying work to the outdoor workers such as polishers, setters, engravers and any of the other splinter trades that were part and parcel of the industry in the days before such craftsmen would be incorporated into the main firm.

Occasionally I would deliver to customers in Bond Street or other parts of the West End, thoroughly enjoying these expeditions and feeling very proud when I recognised articles in their windows which had been made in our workshop. Later on, as I was more senior, I would be thrilled to note items in shop windows which I had made myself.

Twice a week I attended evening classes at the Central School of Arts and Crafts. In the mounters' class some of the people were not jewellery apprentices but were people like schoolteachers who wanted to make jewellery as a hobby and many of them were very amateurish. I stopped going after about six months simply because I was far ahead in my knowledge gleaned from my daily work. The first few months did help, however.

After a while I became very familiar with the whole of Hatton Garden and the area around it, getting to know the character of areas such as Leather Lane, Cross Street and Clerkenwell. I became acquainted with other apprentices from firms in the Garden that were similar to ours, the suppliers of gemstones or lapidaries or the host of small firms that went at that time to make up the jewellery industry. Most of them have disappeared now.

At Christmas, we were able to supplement our income with Christmas boxes from the polishers, setters and customers with whom we dealt. The custom was that the two junior apprentices, who had shared the work during the year, shared the bonuses. We used to get a small notebook, take it round to the various firms, hand it in and say, 'Happy Christmas'. The polisher or setter would look at the previous names in the book to see how much had been given, write in their own names and put down the amount that they were going to donate; 6d or 1s 0d. Every apprentice in the Garden discussed this book, trying to estimate what the take was going to be. There were many systems to try to increase the amount of money that would be given, the most common being to write a number of names of different firms and put by the side a larger sum of money than was reasonably expected. It may have appeared to us that we were fooling the people we went to but, as the custom had probably gone on for the last hundred years, they were all well aware that the books were being padded out to try to entice them to give a higher Christmas box. This was all taken in good clean fun, as were the various other things to do with apprentices.

Every apprentice, at some time or another, would be sent to a local firm that sold tools to buy a diamond magnet. A diamond magnet in the jewellery trade is the equivalent to the left-handed hammer in engineering. A diamond is a mineral that has no magnetic properties. Apprentices would often have to spend hours every time a diamond dropped to the floor searching for the valuable missing stone. It was not unusual to spend two or three hours hunting since ultimately the gem had to be found. Therefore, the diamond magnet would have been a wonderful tool. All the shops in the area knew of the diamond magnet ruse so it was common practice when a green apprentice went in to buy one that Coopers, for instance, would say that they were sorry but they were out of stock, but they would suggest going to Salvo's. Salvo's would send the boy to Pike's and so on until finally the boy would make the rounds of all the tool shops in the area before returning to the workshop and discovering that no such thing existed.

Underlying this fun was a determination to spend as much time as possible at the bench, for all apprentices realised that it was only by sitting at the bench that the trade could be learnt. All the errands had to be done but the sooner one got these out of the way the more time one could spend learning one's craft so that when the five years were finished one could be a good enough craftsman to obtain a job.

Our workshop, like all the others, was tiny relative to the number of men in them but was kept scrupulously clean and tidy. Every tool that was for general use had a place of its own and woe betide any apprentice if any of these tools were either missing or absent from their proper places, hanging upon their correct nail. We all wore leather skins, tied with strings round our necks, to catch and conserve scraps of metal that might fall as we worked. The rules of conserving losses of metal were so strict that nobody, not even the foreman, would dream of ignoring them for fear of being dismissed. Metal conservation was of paramount importance. Nobody left their seat until they had vigorously brushed their hands and the front of their working coats to ensure that any metal was captured in the skin.

We had to wear these brown working coats, which we had to supply ourselves at the cost of about two weeks of a new apprentice's salary. Most junior apprentices made do with any that were no longer considered as suitable by previous owners who may have discarded coats because they were too tattered or left them behind as they were not worth taking.

Such coats were usually far too large and invariably patched, so boy apprentices were easy to recognise as they walked around in what looked like tattered brown rags which went right down to the ankles.

When Baker Platinum opened in a smart new building in High Holborn, the word soon went around that it was possible to go to their cloakroom where, apart from hot water and washing facilities, there was a boot polishing machine and a free dispenser of Brylcreem hair cream or something similar. All these were available to anybody who had a reason to go to the building. This was a sensation among the apprentices, and for a few short weeks, all the boys could be seen still in their ankle-length raggedy coats but with highly polished boots and hair liberally plastered down! Needless to say, the powers that be soon put a stop to that nonsense.

There was also a continual battle of wits between apprentices and some of the caretakers of the various buildings. Most of the caretakers also acted as lift operators and considered that they had so much work to do that unimportant people, like apprentices, could jolly well walk up and down the stairs. The apprentices tried to outwit them in every way they could, usually by trying such subterfuges as having a large parcel in one's hands which then required the use of the lift. We used to collect together empty boxes so as to pretend that a heavy parcel had to be taken up to various offices.

I remember on one occasion someone dared me to use the lift at No 1 Hatton Garden, right on the comer. Here we used to visit an office on the sixth floor, and I took a very dim view of walking up and down six floors when there was a lift on the premises. I pretended to have a limp and told the carefully questioning caretaker that I had hurt my foot playing football. I informed him that the doctor had told me to take it easy, so I really needed to use the lift. He only half believed me, grudgingly took me up to the sixth floor, watched me hobble along the corridor, took me back down to the ground floor, continued to watch me as I limped to the front door and then, like a shot, saw me run down the road laughing my head off.

There was a disadvantage to this because for a period of time, on the occasions I was sent to this particular office, I had to reconnoitre the ground, go to the front of the building, wait until the caretaker was busily occupied in the lift, so that I could nip in and run up the stairs making sure he couldn't spot me.

Leather Lane was a fascinating place containing a market. My early apprenticeship ran concurrently with the gold break-up, coming off the gold standard. Enormous amounts of gold articles were sold and broken up and a lot of them found their way to one or two stalls in Leather Lane. I became friendly with one of these stallholders and was able to oblige him by doing small jobs for him. As a result, whenever he got a pocket-watch to break up for the gold content, he would allow me to strip the watch and keep the parts. These movements were pretty useless because there were thousands and thousands of broken movements around, but I got very interested in the dials of some of these watches. Some were Victorian or Edwardian, some perhaps were even Georgian, and the dials were absolute works of art. They were mostly enamel with flowers, motifs, decorations of all kinds and usually they were in perfect condition, so I used to collect them as a hobby. By the time war broke out I had about 200 of these beautiful dials, which could never be obtained again because the watches had been destroyed and it was the end of an era. Nobody thought they would have any value, but I simply kept them because I enjoyed the look of them. When I went into the army, I left the box of dials in the cellar, which was later converted into an air-raid shelter.

Some months after I was demobbed I remembered the dials, searched for them but never found them. Nobody at home knew what had happened to them, although my mother remembered my collection. That should have been the end of that story but, oddly enough, about ten years later during the mid-fifties, I read that there was going to be an auction of a collection of dials at Sotheby's. I went along, looked at the dials and, although it was many years since I had seen them, I was pretty sure that they were my property but could do nothing about it. They fetched £1,500, at the time an enormous sum of money.

In the workshop, as I have explained, we were always having problems with dropping stones. When one is handling tiny objects, it is obvious that at times a stone will flick out from the tongs and land either in the leather skin in which filings etc were collected or on the floor. The apprentice would have to get on his hands and knees to look for it every time a man dropped a stone. This was disruptive to us all.

On one occasion, I remember I was sizing a single stone ring. I had cut out a piece at the back of the shank, had the ring in a pair of pliers in my left hand and another pair of pliers in my right hand. As I was closing the two ends of the shank together ready to solder it, the governor came by, saw me doing this and said, 'Give it to me and I'll show you how to do it.' I handed him the pliers and the single stone ring. After I had passed it to him, he looked and said, 'Where's the ring?' I stood up thinking that the ring would have gone into the skin, but it wasn't there, and he said that it must have fallen on the floor. We searched and searched but the ring had disappeared. The governor had put the pliers back in place where they sat with the rest of my pliers, about ten of them in row by my skin, all hanging on a piece of wire.

Everybody began anxiously to search for the single stone ring which, containing a one carat diamond, was nowhere to be seen. Suddenly someone noticed that the window near to us had been opened about three inches at the bottom as it was a hot summer's day. This was not supposed to happen for fear of things jumping out of the window and normally only the top of the window should be opened, but it had been very warm indeed. Every individual in the workshop got up and went down the street to search the pavement. After two or three minutes – in Hatton Garden everyone was interested in everybody else's business – there were people from all over the Garden. Once we said we were looking for a single stone ring, the crowd grew larger as everybody joined in the search. The governor started to become anxious in case somebody was to find the valuable ring and keep it. He kept saying, 'Thank you very much, we don't need your help!' but nobody took any notice of him and there must have been a crowd of about a hundred by the time we abandoned the quest.

Finally, we returned to the workshop, desperately looking there again. I sat at my place and, hanging on the pair of pliers that the governor had put down, was the ring. A sigh of relief all around – he just hadn't noticed the shank on the pliers as he had replaced them on the wire.

There are many incidents I could recall about the years of learning the trade. Any individual who takes a piece of raw material, turns it into an article, especially one that is admired and treasured, changes his character once he becomes a craftsman. I personally believe that every person should produce something, even if it is simply putting seeds into a garden and growing flowers. There is in each human being a need to make something out of nothing. It is my experience that craftsmen, whether they are carpenters, fitters, welders, polishers, mounters, setters etc, are a different breed to people who simply work in offices and don't produce anything. Non-producers are necessary but are a different breed.

There were so many characters in Hatton Garden that are remembered to this day. I recall one engraver that I used to visit: the first time I went into his workshop, he sat down at a similar bench to ours and merrily continued engraving a silver plate. In his hand, he held a sharp-pointed instrument (a scorper or graver) and began to talk to me as I stood by him. Suddenly the instrument slipped, he said, 'Blast!' and, with one thrust of this sharp scorper, he went smack and dug it into his leg. I nearly jumped out of my skin, but he laughed his head off and I discovered that the leg was wooden! He had lost the limb during the war. He was known throughout the Garden and it was the usual thing for every new apprentice to experience this act of his.

There were various characters who paraded the streets as one-man bands, or groups of people playing banjos and other instruments. Everyone in Hatton Garden would throw money to them out of the windows. We would often heat the halfpenny with a blowpipe, watch the man from the street pick up the coin and promptly shout out curses to whoever had sent the coin down. Any busker in our area knew full well that the coin would be hot, so the cursing was only an act, for the buskers either wore gloves or would hold something in their hands into which they could scoop up the coin.

By and large, life was very exciting, time went by quickly for we all had a terrific sense of humour considering the conditions – but then, this was the only life we knew; we were happy to be alive.

I was happy to be rapidly learning a very complicated craft which has stood me in good stead for all my life. I found that I had a natural instinct to working with metal, having always been completely at home with any metal object whether it required repairing or manufacturing. To this day, if I see anything made of metal, I understand immediately its advantages, its disadvantages and all its problems. Over the years I have worked on things as tiny as a one-pointer diamond (a stone not metal) and as huge as ten-ton lorries or six-inch guns or military tanks. Thus whether it was tiny or enormous, a hand object or a lathe, a milling machine, soldering with a small blowpipe on precious metals or welding with an oxyacetylene pipe on sheet metal, cast bronze casting or cast iron casting, it was all the same to me: all metal.

I have always looked back with joy on the years that I spent as an apprentice before the war. I think it was the finest decision I ever made in my life to become a jeweller and have never ever regretted it. Nor did I consider doing anything else in my early years.

M VAINER

Milos Vainer.

The enthusiasm of brothers Richard and Martin Vainer is something that, although inherited from their father, Milos, is very clearly a personal passion for beautiful gem diamonds. It was only by chance that Milos was in the right place at the right time, so that they were able to make a significant name for themselves in the industry.

Milos lived in Prague and was studying law when the Communist Party staged a coup in 1948. As a young student, he joined in protests with his peers but when the new regime turned their guns on the crowd, he realised that he needed to leave Czechoslovakia. He had heard that Canada offered better prospects to a young man like himself and made his plans to travel across the Atlantic. His journey took him to a refugee camp in Germany along with many of his fellow countrymen. He eventually obtained a visa for Canada and set out via London.

Milos's father had been a wealthy industrialist and through family connections he was acquainted with the Oppenheimer family who owned De Beers. An invitation to lunch and a game of bridge provided a small distraction during his journey but turned out to be the beginning of Milos Vainer's career in the trade. The lunch invitation became an invitation to join the Oppenheimer's family business.

So Milos started working with De Beers as a trainee on £2 10s a week. Within a short time, his skills were noticed by the company and in 1956 he was sent to Sierra Leone. De Beers used to buy in rough diamonds from other producers and Milos excelled in setting up contracts. He was on a fast-track course to becoming a director and significant player in this global company. However, his first love was the stones themselves and he passed up the opportunity of furthering his career with the corporation. In 1962, he left De Beers to set up his own business. His charisma and business acumen brought immediate success. He was appointed government valuer to Botswana in 1970 at a time when that country was developing its diamond mines. His role also included training nationals in sorting and looking after sales, particularly to De Beers. The work that he did for Botswana came to the attention of many other diamond-producing countries, including Angola, Namibia, Sierra Leone and Russia. He was also involved with the Argyle Mine when diamonds were found in Australia.

Over his many years in the trade, as a consultant and dealer, he built up an enviable collection of rare, rough, coloured diamonds and other oddities, which he presented posthumously to the GIA on the occasion of their 80th birthday.

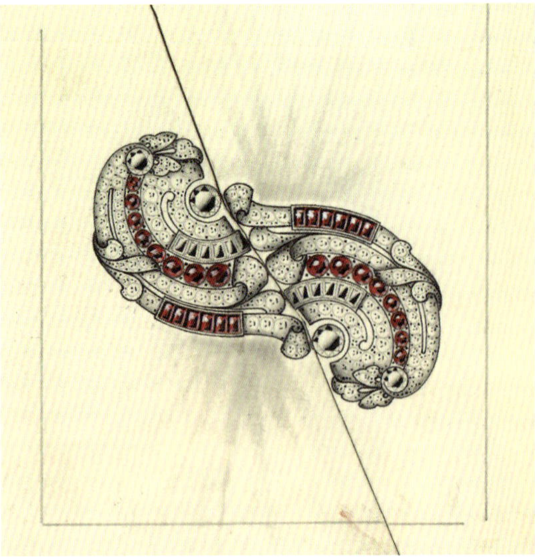

Paul Podolsky brooch.

E Podolsky, 23 Hatton Garden.

town in Germany he would be given train tickets to Antwerp, money and food. This is what he did, and the promise was made good. He spent four years in Antwerp before moving on to London with his wife and daughter in 1915. In 1920 he set up a business at 35 Greville Street. These premises were hit during the Blitz and he moved to 23 Hatton Garden. Paul told of coming to work that morning to find their building fallen into the street and of their struggle to recover furniture and move it to Hatton Garden.

During the war their manufacturing was moved over to the production of munitions (fuses, valves, etc.). He worked the nightshift to ensure maximum productivity.

Another firm that went over to producing munitions was Blankensee of Birmingham. However, when the war was over they decided to continue in light engineering rather than go back to making jewellery. They had machinery to mass produce chains, which Paul sold off to the British Machine Chain Co. Their products were sold as Albion Chain Co., but Paul changed the name to Albioncraft as he didn't want to be in mass production. To assist the process, Johnson Matthey provided a £10,000 loan. They had about 1,200 retail customers throughout the UK.

Paul told of how two 'Kinder' children, Fred Durst and John Neijman, set up in the jewellery business after being apprenticed to a manufacturer. Their company became Fred Manshaw and was one of the UK's largest in its time.

He remembered Mrs Cohen's Café in Greville Street, which served coffee to the dealers and later became the London Diamond Bourse. Levi Cohen was one of the instigators.

Paul recalled a Steve Wager of 35 Hatton Garden, who used to attend trade shows with a lump of silver and transform it into a spoon over three hours.

Barclays Bank stood on the corner of Hatton Garden and Greville Street. Dealers used to gather outside, and the English bank staff learned words of Yiddish from hearing their conversations and haggling. Sometimes the dealers were moved on by the police.

The Rosenfeld family was a dynasty of multi-millionaires, of which Josel was the father. There were three sons. Paul, the eldest, followed a legal profession. Ben, the middle son, couldn't get on with his father and set up on his own. The youngest, George, took over the family business.

From the very beginning of his career, he was passionate about the industry and loved to learn the skills of the various craftsmen in their workshop. Throughout his life he maintained the level of skills established by his father. He trained ten apprentices during his watch, thus passing the baton to future generations.

Paul is remembered now, among other things, by the Podolsky Award, which is presented annually to young people who show outstanding potential as tomorrow's craftsmen and women.

THE WATSON FAMILY

Four generations of the Watson family testify to the tradition of family businesses in the jewellery trade. PJ Watson Ltd was established in 1966 by Peter J Watson. He was introduced to the diamond trade in Hatton Garden by his mother, Constance Watson, who was already established with another jewellery company at the time.

It was when the men went away to serve in the First World War that Constance had an opportunity to join a jewellery company in London's West End. In 1919, aged 17, she came to Hatton Garden to take up a position with a company called Bennell, King and Titmus, or BKT as they are known today.

She loved every aspect of gems and jewellery but took a risk as working mothers were frowned upon by their employers. She used to walk several yards ahead of her son, Peter, when he made visits to Hatton Garden as a boy.

In 1945 she qualified as an FGA, having studied gemmology at the Chelsea Polytechnic under Robert Webster and Basil Anderson. Their studies and exams were interrupted by air raids.

Constance was able to find a job for Peter when he finished his time of National Service after the war. He started in Hatton Garden by selling loose diamonds for a Belgian company with a London office. One of his customers was a manufacturing jeweller called Segaloff & Schofield. Mr Schofield was the older of the two partners and when he retired in 1957, Peter Watson took his place and together they changed the name of the company to the Eton Jewellery Co. They were based at 16 Hatton Garden and then later on at 14 Hatton Yard.

The Watson family. L to R: James, Philip, Vivian and John.

The partnership was successful for a number of reasons, not least of which was the unusual combination of Jewish and non-Jewish management. Some customers would prefer to buy from one and other customers would prefer the other. It was a case of having the best of both worlds.

However, in 1966, Peter set up a new company and the partnership was ended. The reason for this was that both partners each had two sons whom they wanted to come into the trade. It was clear that one business couldn't support all four, so a move had to be made. Eton jewellery continued to thrive and PJ Watson Ltd started to grow. From a modest office/workshop in New House at 67 Hatton Garden, Peter quickly established a reputation for fine-quality, hand-made jewellery. The standard of the work attracted customers like Asprey, Garrards, Boodles, Mappin & Webb and many other well-known names. Customers were not limited to London but were to be found across the UK. Two sales representatives would travel the country between Aberdeen and Falmouth and from Aberystwyth to Great Yarmouth calling on the top county jewellers with their collections.

Peter was joined by his sons, Vivian, in 1967, and Philip, in 1969. Both studied gemmology and became the third generation of FGA gemmologists in the family. Their passion for rare coloured stones was and still is the hallmark of PJ Watson's jewellery.

Vivian made it his business to visit all of the company's retail customers and built up a huge network of friends throughout the country. Under his directorship, PJ Watson Ltd worked closely with the Diamond Promotion Service of De Beers and produced many diamond collections that were featured in national media. Vivian was also invited to join De Beers' exclusive Carat Club. PJ Watson Ltd was one of the few original suppliers to the buying groups that flourished at this time. Although Philip also spent some time 'on the road', his main responsibility was overseeing production and buying. PJ Watson Ltd achieved recognition in receiving numerous industry awards over many years.

PJ Watson Ltd has exhibited at trade shows in London, Birmingham, Basel and Tokyo. In addition, they have worked with customers who have hosted local events in their shops or at suitable venues nearby. Vivian became a director of the Gem Testing Laboratory in 1986 and served as Chairman of the Gemmological Association after their merger with the laboratory.

Peter Watson retired at the young age of 60 and left the business in the hands of his two sons. A year or so later Philip announced that he was planning to start a new company as he had different ideas that he wanted to pursue. It took a little while to sort out this new move. Although potentially a cause for a rift within the family, their deeper values have ensured a good relationship was maintained. Philip's new business is known as Anna James and is today being run by his son, James, from their base in Hatton Garden.

Vivian was joined by his younger son, John, in 2002. John became the fourth member of the family to become a qualified FGA gemmologist. Vivian became a Liveryman of the Worshipful Company of Goldsmiths in 1995 and enjoys the rich history associated with the Goldsmiths Hall. He was also made a life member of the Gemmological Association for his services to the organisation. The business developed new outlets in Japan in the 1990s and created the brand name JOY for diamond jewellery.

PJ Watson Ltd can claim many 'firsts'. It was the first company to introduce Canadian diamonds to the UK market. Vivian secured a contract with a cutting firm in Yellowknife who had one of the three allocations from the new Ekati mine in 2001. When manufacturing in Asia became a threat to the UK industry, Vivian visited several countries to explore the opportunities of working closely with an Asian partner.

In 2005, against a background of increased costs of maintaining a Hatton Garden presence, it was decided to relocate the business to Berkhamsted in Hertfordshire, where increased space allowed for further growth. A visit to the office clearly shows the passion that is inherent in all things PJ Watson. A library of well over 1,000 books on gems, diamonds and jewels lines one wall of their showroom. A collection of postage stamps on the theme of gemstones is part of their pride and joy, as is a collection of Hatton Garden memorabilia.

PJ Watson FGA.

Constance Watson FGA.

Peter J Watson died in 2012. Vivian officially retired in 2017 but continues to act as a consultant. The business continues to prosper under the able leadership of John Watson. John has the same passion for gems that has been evident throughout the history of the company. His enthusiasm for good design enhances the natural beauty of each stone as rings, pendants, earrings and other jewellery are created.

ROY HUDDLESTONE

There are a number of people who can claim many years of service and experience in the jewellery trade. Perhaps the longest serving was Roy Huddlestone, who retired at the age of 87 in October 2017 after seventy-four years in the trade. For many it is a passion and so much more than a professional occupation. Letting go means saying goodbye to clients and suppliers, many of whom are close friends. It is also stepping away from beautiful gems and jewellery that have fuelled the passion.

Roy started in the trade in 1944, at the age of 14, when he became an apprentice clock and watchmaker in Nottingham, his home town. Older men had been enlisted in the armed services, so his mentor was aged 60-plus. Limited materials meant cannibalising old timepieces for their parts whenever possible. Most watch parts were produced in Switzerland and the war made it almost impossible to access them.

The hours were 8 a.m. to 5 p.m. and the pay was £5 per week. Gold was $35 per ounce. Purchase Tax had risen to 125% on all new jewellery items, which increased the demand for second-hand pieces. Wartime austerity measures meant that you could only sell 9ct gold, D-shaped wedding rings with the utility mark. Even alarm clocks were not available to the public at this time without a special licence, which was only available to those involved directly in the war effort. Working men all wore suits and ties to their place of work. Roy served in the RAF and used his skills in looking after the various instruments on aircraft such as the Avro Lancaster.

After the war, Roy managed various retail jewellers around the UK but came to Hatton Garden to run the newly opened City Jewellers in 1967. This was the first modern shop to open in the Garden. They were located opposite 100 Hatton Garden, or what was then Gamages department store. He was involved with the opening of David Morris's shop in Conduit Street. Roy joined both the London Diamond Club and the London Diamond Bourse well before they merged. Roy recalls that there were well over a thousand diamond cutters and polishers working in the Garden at the time. The largest was a company called Briefel & Lemer. They were tasked with the cutting of the Williamson Pink, a 23ct round, brilliant, cut pink diamond now in an exquisite flower brooch often worn by Her Majesty the Queen. The diamond was named after the Canadian geologist who, having studied in Canada, went to East Africa and discovered a diamond mine in Tanzania that was also named after him.

In 1969, Roy opened the first diamond grading laboratory in Europe. He traded as DGL (Diamond Grading Laboratories) from the basement of 46 Hatton Garden. At the time, the other lab in Hatton Garden would only provide a service of gem identification and not the quality of the diamond. The GIA had only recently begun their own grading system and it would take several years for the different ones to merge. Initially, diamond grading was not welcomed by the trade. The older, more romantic dealers liked 'romancing the stone' as they could achieve a higher price for it. Roy also pioneered a system of recognition of a specific diamond under the name of Identiprint. It was featured by the BBC on *Tomorrow's World.*

Roy's incredible understanding of diamonds and his incomparable presentation skills mean that he has been much in demand as an expert witness and has served as a consultant and lecturer to many people through the media or on a one-to-one basis. Much respected by his contemporaries, he was called 'A giant of the diamond trade'.

SMITH & HARRIS

Walking into the basement workshops of Smith & Harris is like walking back into another century. Gareth Harris, with his partner, Dennis Smith, took over the workshop from its previous owner, Richard Hodd, who in turn had taken over the business of John Edward Terry. Terry was a renowned silversmith of his day, on a par with Paul Storr and Samuel Hennell. He entered his own mark at Goldsmiths Hall in 1816 and moved into 31 Hatton Garden on 9th May 1819. For over 200 years this unique workshop has seen an output of some of the most beautiful works of art, not just in Great Britain but throughout the world. R Hodd & Son were silversmiths to Queen Victoria and exhibited at the Great Exhibition of 1851. In its heyday the firm occupied both 31 and 30 Hatton Garden and the address was 'Minerva Works', not to be confused with Minerva House further down the street.

Every square inch of space is filled with a variety of tools and equipment that describe the history of the craft for at least 200 years: mills, anvils, draw plates, hammers, lathes, a drop press and various moulds, to name but a few. All the traditional skills which gave Hatton Garden its reputation for world-class craftsmanship can be seen represented here.

Not only is their workshop something of an insight into the history of the trade, but their building is also. Being one of the few surviving 17th-century structures originally designed for residential purposes it is now a rabbit warren of rooms, each hosting a separate business, each with its own security and entry systems. In many ways it resembles a house of multiple occupancy where individuals may come and go without seeing their neighbours. Typically, many craftsmen arrive early in the morning and once at their bench don't leave their premises until they go home.

Smith & Harris workshop.

Smith & Harris workshop.

Gareth Harris wanted to work with precious metals since he was a small boy and his grandmother lovingly showed him how to read a hallmark during a visit to her home in Devon. Although his family were farmers, he started his career in silversmithing with Padgett & Braham with an apprenticeship in box making, which is considered by many to be the most challenging way to start. It was in 1975 at Sir John Cass College that he first met Dennis Smith, who would become his business partner when they started up together in 1981. The last surviving member of the Hood workshop was still working, then in his 70s, having commenced work at the age of 14. With the style of someone from a different age, he would throw caution to the wind and place both of his arms into the electro-plating bath while working on an object. The shock was regarded as an occupational hazard and more or less ignored. Before central heating was installed most properties were heated by coal fires. However, there was a cost and a practical consideration to this, so he used a paraffin heater that doubled up as a grill for toasting his cheese sandwiches at lunch time.

Smith & Harris are the go-to people for commissioning work of significance. Not long after they had started together, they were contacted by 10 Downing Street. Margaret Thatcher was in office and rather than go to a traditional retailer, she enquired of their supplier to make something. Livery companies, the Guildhall and other institutions all use their services. In 1989, they were instructed by De Beers to make a trophy for the King George VI Diamond Stakes at Ascot. The trophy, complete with its tailor-made box, was presented by Sir Philip Oppenheimer of De Beers to Sheikh Mohammed, whose horse won the race. However, perhaps their most unusual request was to make a life-size model of Kate Moss in 18ct gold. This statue, known as the Siren, took a year to make and weighed over 50 kilos, although a further 50 kilos had to be used during its production. It is the largest single item to be hallmarked and is reported to be the largest gold object made since the days of the pharaohs.

Gareth Harris is a Liveryman of the Worshipful Company of Goldsmiths and is passionate about local history, of which he and Dennis are very much a part.

TREVOR TYLER

Trevor Tyler began work in Hatton Garden in 1952, at the age of 16, and retired in 2002 having completed fifty years in the business. His company achieved international recognition, having strong export business as well as a good domestic market. He specialised in rare and unusual gems set in 18ct gold jewellery.

He began his career with his father, HV Tyler, in Hatton Wall as an apprentice because that was what he was told to do.

He finished at No. 5 Hatton Garden, a Grade II-listed building, which he purchased from SH Harris in 1984. He also owned, from his father's estate, jointly with his sister, the St Cross Street premises of HV Tyler.

Trevor recalls how one of the craftsmen in the HV Tyler workshop used to wear chamois leather gloves. The foreman of the workshop wore a bowler hat and was paid £3 10s a week, and he could afford to buy a house on that. There were sixty-three workmen in the workshop, five of whom only did platinum. They had duck boards on the floor, which were normal at that time. HV Tyler was the first to bring casting in from the USA, which revolutionised the trade.

HV Tyler's company policy wouldn't allow the employment of 'blacks' or Jews, or any left-hander as all production was geared up to right-handed people.

The working week at HV Tyler was from 8.30 to 5.30 Monday to Friday and 8.30 to 12.30 on Saturdays with a forty-five-minute lunch break during the week. As an apprentice Trevor was paid 37s 6d for a forty-eight-hour week. (Approx. £1.87 a week or 4p an hour.)

There was a strong Italian presence in Clerkenwell pre-war with manufacturers of clocks and barometers such as Committi. The northern end of Hatton Garden was dominated by the Old Holborne tobacco factory and the smell of tobacco pervaded the atmosphere.

Trevor did his National Service in the Royal Marines between 1955 and 1957 and proudly wore his tie to many trade events. During National Service he earned 28s a week.

Pre-war, the manufacturing industry was mostly handmade work. Trevor believed that the war was responsible for the change that saw no new investment from 1938 to 1952. Purchase Tax was introduced during the war and ranged from 25% to 125%. It was the manufacturer's responsibility to levy the tax on their sales and it wasn't recoverable. Second-hand jewellery was exempt, so the trade in older items flourished at the expense of new goods. There was at that time and for some years afterwards a strong black market, with goods being manufactured as second-hand or new goods sold for cash. For this reason, record keeping was not done in the way it was before or is done now.

The Second World War saw the introduction of 9ct gold as an economy measure. Local bomb damage was extensive. It was reported that at one time you could stand in Hatton Garden and see the spires of eleven churches.

Trading on the street was common as war refugees had no money to rent their own property and all their capital was in goods. From trading out in the open, the dealers moved to the cafés and one in particular later became the London Diamond Bourse.

Gamages was the main feature of the southern end of Hatton Garden. It was an emporium where you could buy almost anything from a car battery to a haircut.

The Nosherie, now closed, was originally located on the opposite side of Holborn Circus but moved to Greville Street in the 1960s. The Bell Grill in Holborn was excellent for a cooked dinner.

Trevor worked for a time for Tidy & Blanchard as a salesman. They nearly merged with Whitehorns (Leon Exact) but couldn't agree the shareholding. Some of the leading manufacturers of their day were Bostock & Rayner, Hathaway & Muddiman, Alan Jones, and Barnetts. The rising stars were Andrew Grima, Lawrence Graff and David Morris (many of whom moved into retail).

WHITEHORN'S

Founded in 1837, by John Whitehorn, Whitehorn Brothers flourished throughout the reign of Queen Victoria, survived two world wars, and finally closed its doors in 1992. Their 155-year innings was remarkable in many ways. Well known to the trade in the post-war period for their very fine quality diamond-set jewellery, they supplied most of the county jewellers throughout the UK. One of their top accounts was Reid's in Newcastle upon Tyne, from whom they had regular special orders for brooches to commemorate the launching of a new ship. Originally at Featherstone Buildings in Holborn, they moved to Hatton Garden in the 1940s after their building had been hit by a 250kg bomb. They had previously made an informal arrangement with the Diamond Trading Company, who kept their stock in their vaults during the war for added protection. However, the DTC also took a direct hit.

Like all successful businesses, they have had to reinvent themselves many times as fashion and demand has changed. In early Victorian times more men wore jewellery, and this was

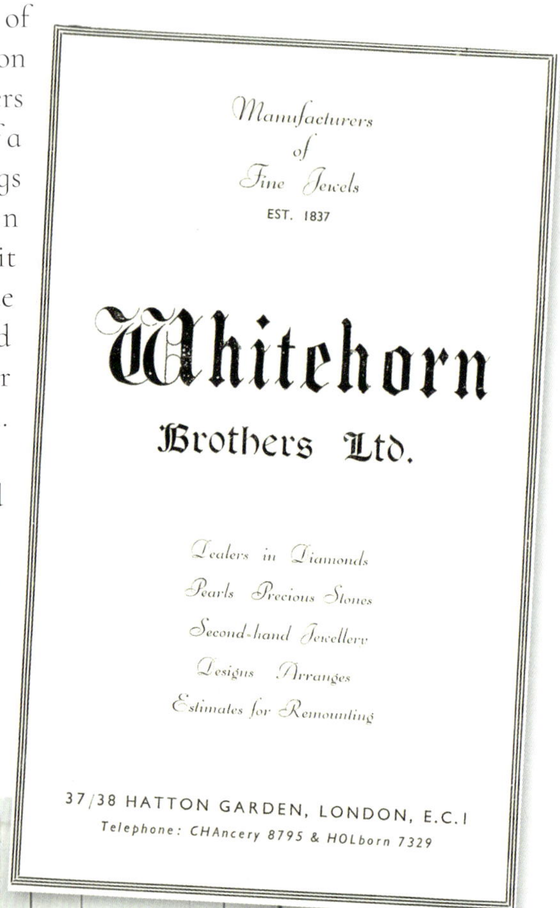

Whitehorn's advert.

Whitehorn's workshop.

an important market for them. Their earlier work was mostly in gold lockets, necklets, chains and bracelets, as the supply of diamonds from South Africa was not yet known. However, as the supply of diamonds increased in the second generation of the company, the diamond mounter became the creator of the late Victorian and Edwardian jewels that satisfied the new and growing demand for fine jewellery. Many of those older jewels eventually found their way back to Whitehorn's, where they have been remodelled or sold to lovers of antique jewellery. Under John Whitehorn junior, the firm established its reputation as makers of tiaras, riviere necklaces, bow and crescent brooches. Perhaps their speciality was the floral spray brooch, in which the cluster of diamond-set flowers was attached by a spring to the stem of the design, creating a 'trembler' or '*en Tremblant*' piece in which the flowers continuously moved and sparkled. It is not hard to imagine the candlelight at a dinner party creating a myriad of rainbows across the room.

It was in the third generation that John and Ernest renamed the firm as Whitehorn Brothers. They extended their premises, which had originally been their home, by building over the garden. John had actually been born in the house before the workshop took over. They also acquired the neighbouring properties as workshop and office space, where they employed over sixty people. Even in the second half of the 20th century they were one of the larger workshops in Hatton Garden.

They were also famous as pearl dealers, and well before the arrival of cultured pearls from Japan they had established themselves as leaders in this field.

M CHAPLIN/TURNER & LEVERIDGE (T&L)

Nobody can say for certain who Mr Turner or Mr Leveridge were, assuming that they were both men and not women. The company was founded during the First World War by Mrs Molly Chaplin, who incorporated M Chaplin & Co. and used the joint names as a trading entity. Molly used to travel with a collection of jewellery, watches and clocks, that she put together from the firm's stock on a Sunday afternoon. She was picked up on Monday morning by her chauffeur and spent three days visiting various retailers throughout London and the home counties. On a Thursday she would give her attention to her family and this time the chauffeur would take her to the bakers, grocers and butchers. On Friday she would prepare for the Sabbath and then the weekly routine would begin again. She had two sons, Douglas and Maurice, who later joined the family business. Molly worked until the 1970s.

At one time the family had their own shops: one in Short Wyre Street, Colchester, one in Bayswater, and one in Brook Street, London, known as AB Davis. Douglas's son, Stephen, joined the business later in life after his father had suffered a stroke in 2008.

The business continued to grow and in the 1960s they traded from 44 Hatton Garden, as well as being members of the London Diamond Bourse. Finally, in 2000, they relocated to 100 Hatton Garden, where they continued to operate until their closure in 2019. The business continued to use the services of the same branch of Barclays Bank throughout its 105-year history.

Dougie Chaplin was known as 'One-pound Dougie' as he would always be willing to purchase items from another dealer allowing a £1 mark-up.

According to Stephen Chaplin, Joey Turek, a fellow Diamond Bourse member, 'would welcome my father as he came into the Bourse singing: '£1 Chaplin is his name; £1 profit is his game.'

Today, the 'Turner' name is to be found in New York, where Stephen Chaplin works with his wife, Cindy, under the name of Turner & Tatler. Their international business now ships goods throughout the world, selling on various digital platforms.

The transformation of the industry in the last generation has left behind some of the old ways of doing business. The mutual trust that was once fundamental is now increasingly rare. Brands have become for many the destination shops, with consumers willing to pay more for a name. The old professional approach it would appear is now only for the discerning.

MONNICKENDAM

One of Hatton Garden's oldest and most highly regarded diamond houses is Monnickendam's. Now located in Ely Place, they operate one of the few remaining diamond-cutting workshops in London. Using state-of-the-art equipment, they ensure that the future of the industry in the area is guaranteed for another generation, as the fifth generation, Arthur Monnickendam comes on board. The founder was Louis Monnickendam, who traded in Amsterdam in 1890. Dutch interests in South Africa had created a channel of supply from the recently discovered diamond mines.

In 1914, with Europe in turmoil, Louis relocated the business to the United Kingdom with a head office in London. His son, Albert, was now part of the family business and would go on to fame through the publication of two books telling the story of the diamond trade. *The Secrets of Diamonds* was published in 1941 and *The Magic of Diamonds* in 1955.

After the Great War, the company employed injured ex-servicemen in their cutting and polishing facilities. In 1929, the good reputation of the business earned them an invitation to become sight holders at the newly formed Diamond Trading Company's sale of De Beers' rough.

During the Second World War, when London became a target for German bombers, production was moved to the country. A factory was set up in 1940 in Bangor, north Wales, which recruited, trained and employed sixty local people.

Fancy Vivid Blue.

At the end of the war, a further 120 diamond cutters were taken on for a new facility near Brighton in Sussex. Recognition was achieved in 1948, when they received a commission to produce a pair of emerald cuts from rough given to HRH Princess Elizabeth by the Government of Tanganyika as a wedding present. In 1966, they were honoured with the Queen's Award for Industry for export achievement.

The third generation was represented by Arthur and the fourth by Gary and his cousin Jeffrey.

The globalisation of business and lower costs in Asia led to the opening of factories in Thailand and Mauritius for the production of smaller stones. Their Sussex production facilities were then moved to Hatton Garden. In 2003, they withdrew from being a De Beers sight holder after more than seventy years of mutual benefit.

Perhaps one of their greatest achievements to date was in 2009, when they cut and polished the remarkable 7.03ct, Fancy Vivid Blue, internally flawless diamond. The unique gem sold for the highest price per carat ever recorded at the time.

A short extract from Albert Monnickendam's book, *The Magic of Diamond*, gives a wonderful view into the Hatton Garden of his day:

> To the British public Hatton Garden represents a street of make-believe, an Ali Baba's alley of strange customs and untold wealth, where men swap diamonds in the doorways and the gutters. Nor, in principle, is this a mistaken idea, for that is exactly what does happen. Not only small dealers and brokers, but many prosperous merchants prefer to dispense with a proper office. All day the trading goes on, with parcels changing pockets, and deals involving thousands of pounds being decided over plates of soup in a little restaurant off Hatton Garden, with bundles of stones glittering on the tablecloths.
>
> At one time two teashops in the Garden became so much the haunt of street dealers that they began to look like jewel exchanges. The tiny weighing scales were pulled out, the jeweller's glass made its scrutiny, and a harsh gabble of voices preceded the deal. Great honesty and good fellowship are shared by the Hatton Garden street traders, and parcels of diamonds are often given on approval, without signature or even an approbation note.
>
> When the stock market crashed in 1929 diamond merchants lost heavily, both on investments and bad debts, for large credits were often give(en). Some of the most prosperous dealers became paupers overnight, and it was pathetic to see them dependent on charity discreetly given by the Diamond Club's Committee specially appointed to deal with cases of distress. Some tried desperately hard to earn a little as brokers, and their reputation allowed them to be trusted with thousands of pounds worth of diamonds. Often, men walking about with fortunes in one pocket had not enough money in the other to buy a decent meal.
>
> I once saw an attack on a diamond merchant in Hatton Garden. The victim used to carry an attaché case full of valuable jewels. He was in the habit of dressing in a morning coat and high silk hat, and drove about in a large limousine, his valuable bag being with him.
>
> One fine summer morning I was about 10 or 15 yards from his office, when his car drove up and he stepped out with the attaché case in his hand. I had approached to within about two yards of him when one man suddenly stepped in front of me, and another snatched

the bag from the astonished merchant; a third knocked the chauffer down. It was all done so quickly that before one could realise what had happened two of the men were escaping down Hatton Garden. I was nearest to the man who had snatched the case and gave chase. I was then about seventeen and very fast on my feet and had almost caught up with him when he suddenly turned and threw something in my face. I was temporarily blinded, and the thieves got clean away.

BKT (RINGS) LTD AND TJW (DIAMONDS) LTD

Charles Darwin might well have been speaking of BKT, when he famously said: 'It is not the strongest of the species that survives ... It is the one that is most adaptable to change.'

An evolutionary process covering over a hundred years of history has made BKT what they are today, and is a remarkable story. They have had to adapt to keep ahead of a changing market. They have also had to deal with the pressures of two world wars, and the economic challenges of their time. Their private offices in Hatton Garden are full of wonderful memorabilia. There are, on the oak-panelled walls, old black and white photographs of Hatton Garden in days gone by and portraits of family members who are part of their pedigree. They have antique glass showcases displaying a whole variety of objects, each of which could tell its own story.

The day-to-day operation of the business is now in the hands of Stephen Wright FGA, DGA, and his son Will, who is also an FGA, DGA. It was Stephen's grandfather, Joe, who was largely responsible for making the decisions that would allow future generations to become the well-respected business known throughout the trade.

Joseph Wright was born in 1887. At the age of 18, he joined the Illinois Watch Case Co., USA, suppliers of gold and rolled-gold watch cases. They had an office at 65 Holborn Viaduct. In this position he was able to travel and further his knowledge of the industry. Watch manufacturing in the UK was on the decline and the Swiss were fast becoming the major players. It became the practice to put Swiss movements into English cases. Joseph married Ida and they moved to London in March 1913.

In 1915, at the age of 28, he was invited by one of his customers, Thos. Russell & Son, to become a director of their pocket-watch manufacturing business based in Church Street, Liverpool. They were established in the 18th century and continued production in one way or another up to the 1960s. Their London office fell victim to German bombs on 10th May 1941. The safes fell through to the basement and when they were finally recovered only contained unsaleable, damaged goods. The business then relocated to the suburbs. Thankfully, the Liverpool business, which had now evolved into retail, was spared. Joe's appointment was in part due to his entrepreneurial skills and to a certain degree the need of the owners to ensure continuity of an old-established business. Wrist watches were now in vogue and the business thrived during the Great War.

Thomas John Wright (as in TJW), usually known as John, was born in 1921 and joined his father in the family business.

Joseph Wright, 1887–1967.

In 1925, Joe set up another business, Horology Ltd. He traded in the mass market with inexpensive clocks through retailers like Marks & Spencer. He selflessly gave a lot of time to trade organisations such as the London Wholesale Jewellers Association, of which he was chairman. He became a Liveryman of the Clockmakers Company in about 1927.

He also threw himself into the work of the London Chamber of Commerce, becoming Chairman of its Horological Section for no fewer than thirty-three years. Through 'the chamber', he also sat on the International Chamber of Commerce and went to a congress in Canada on their behalf, making friends with one of the Birks family (Henry Birks & Son) – the Canadian chain of high-quality jewellers. He was also Treasurer of the National Jewellers Association.

It was the London Chamber of Commerce that was entrusted by the Board of Trade with administering the Import licensing system through its Horological Section. For this, the Horological Trade Pool Ltd was founded – and so Joe became Chairman of that also. He was the right man in the job – with a widely cast and representative Board of Directors able to control firmly the wheelers and dealers and whingers and whiners who wanted to manipulate or find ways past the Licensing System. It worked post-war until eventually freer trade in the 1950s led to its natural dissolution.

It was through his trade work that he received an introduction to a manufacturing and wholesale jeweller known as Bennell, King & Titmas.

H Bennell had been the manager of the diamond department of a large wholesale jeweller in Clerkenwell called H Williamson & Co. but after the First World War the company had started to break up. In 1923 H Bennell & Co. was formed. Not long after, he took in HA King, also ex-Williamsons, as a partner. Hence, they were known as Bennell & King. Later they also added Miss Margaret M Titmas, who had been the diamond sorter and picker at Williamsons. Her role involved regular trips to Antwerp pre-war to buy diamonds. Their business flourished through the 1930s and '40s despite the difficulties of the Second World War. They were located in Premier House, 12–13 Hatton Garden, and later at 44 Hatton Garden. Sadly, Mr Bennell died in 1941, but he had already established a successful operation with sales representatives calling on retail jewellers throughout the UK. Mr King was a staunch Baptist and no doubt responsible for

Badge of Chairman, London Wholesale Jewellers Assoc.

setting the foundations of trust and reliability on which the company grew.

By the mid-1940s Mr King and Miss Titmas recognised that there would be no succession as they were due to retire and there wasn't another generation to follow on. They had considered closure but that didn't happen.

It was their accountants who brokered the introduction to Joe Wright in 1949. For Joe and his entrepreneurial skills this was a great opportunity to venture into new waters. Although he was well established in watches and clocks, diamonds, gems and jewellery were all new to him. He was well aware that he already had good connections with many jewellers that could enhance the new business. There was increased mass production of clocks and watches in the post-war period, particularly with the Japanese entering the arena. It was agreed that Mr King and Miss Titmas remain as directors in the new business for at least three years. It was then on 1st January 1950 that BKT (Rings) was born.

Joe's older son, Billie, had joined his father and his younger son, John, also joined soon after. It was now necessary to move their business back to the Hatton Garden area and they found two premises. One was on the top floor of 7 Hatton Garden. This had been occupied by Chas. Schierwater, a wine merchant and owner of the London office of the Waltham Watch Co., USA. In due course they spread to the first, second and third floors. The Hatton Garden Post Office was located on the ground floor and their staff restroom was on the fourth floor. In due course they were able to acquire the freehold. The other premises was across the road at No. 105, which they leased from FW Elliott, clock manufacturers. Billie and John both became Liverymen of the Clockmakers Company in the late 1940s.

In 1957, another company was formed called BKT (Gemstones) Ltd. Rather than sourcing gems and diamonds from local suppliers as so many of their competitors were doing, they saw the advantage of going further afield to buy at lower prices. This also gave them the opportunity to sell to other manufacturers with a margin for themselves. Initially John and Miss Titmas travelled to Antwerp, where they had the use of an office belonging to IS Lowenthal. Various brokers were invited to come along and show their goods. Grading, as we know it, had not yet been standardised and one's wits were challenged in deciding true values. Broker after broker, wallet after wallet and parcel after parcel: it was a long and tedious process to find the stones they needed. Finally, the selection was made and consigned to Hambros Bank in Charterhouse Street, the goods paid for and then collected. There were also trips to Idar-Oberstein, which was then the hub of gem cutting in Europe.

Another string to their bow was dealing in second-hand or antique jewellery. This had enjoyed a period of being tax free during the war and in the following years. In 1965 another company was formed and dedicated to buying and selling pre-owned jewellery. The new business was called TJW (Diamonds), using John's initials. Many of the retail customers who were already known to BKT now became a source of second-hand stock for TJW.

Joe passed away in 1967, peacefully at home with his family around him. He left the legacy of a portfolio of successful businesses for his sons, grandsons and now great-grandson as Will, the fourth generation, picks up the reins. After Joe's death there was some serious rationalisation of the businesses. They discovered that they had in their watch and clock business some 40,000 units of stock. Unlike the diamond jewellery whose value usually increases, the horological items become dated and thereby worthless. So, the watch and clock businesses were run down, as were other companies that Joe had established.

John studied gemmology under the renowned Robert Webster and achieved a distinction in his FGA qualification. He married Mollie on 2nd September 1950, and they had four children. Two of the sons, David and Stephen, joined the family business. Stephen qualified as a gemmologist in 1979 and went on to achieve a distinction in his diamond exam. Stephen's cousin, Robert Hailey, also joined the business and attained his FGA in 1978.

Their emphasis today is very much on the antique jewellery market. Their reputation brings customers from across the world, and it is not unknown for a queue to be found when they exhibit at a trade fair.

BKT Ring Guide.

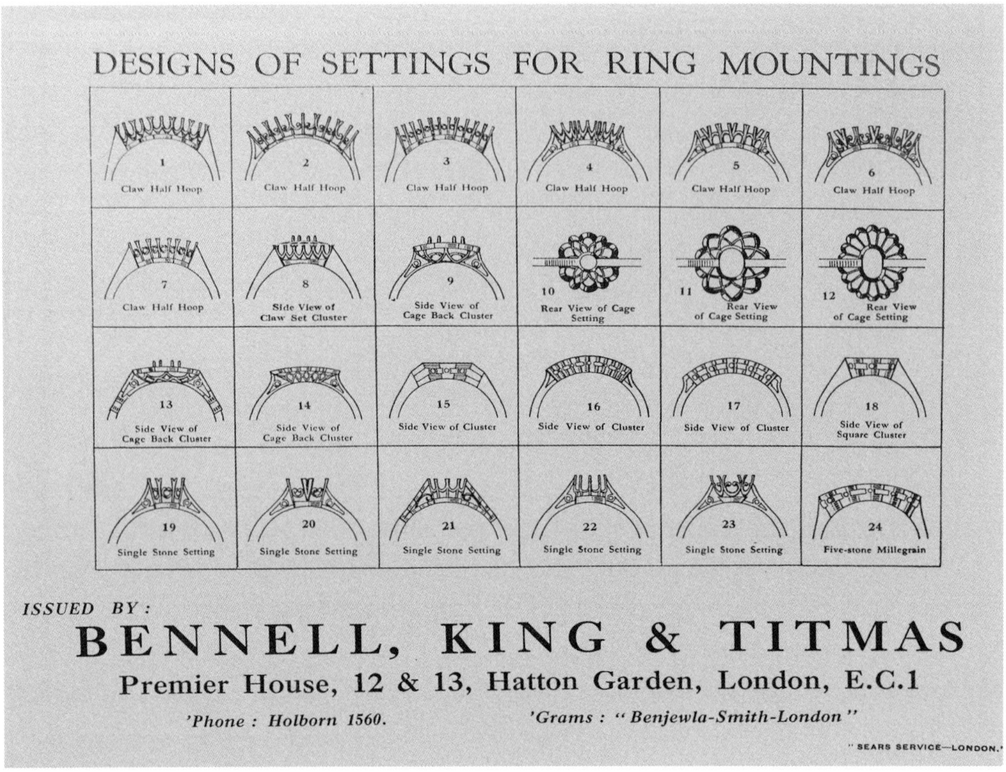

BKT Ring Guide.

RM SHAH

One of the great pioneering stories worthy of attention is that of Ramanlal Shah. Arriving in London from India in 1956, Ramanlal built a gemstone business that at one time handled 99% of rough gemstones traded in London.

He was one of the first Indians to arrive in Hatton Garden. In the early days, with very little money, he was not able to afford his own offices and like so many others traded on the street and in the cafés. A tribute to his industrious and tireless attitude to business was described in a comment of the day that said Hatton Garden opened and closed with Ramanlal Shah. In other words, he was the first to arrive for business and the last to leave. With a network of contacts in India he was able to import gemstones, which he sold on to other gemstone dealers and merchants.

His base was normally at a Formica-topped table in the Lema Buttery, a café that was located on the corner of Hatton Garden and Greville Street, diagonally opposite the Globe pub. Gemstone dealers would gather there, much like the diamond dealers who met at Mrs Cohen's Café. A simple coffee would last for hours, during which goods were shown and deals were struck for thousands of pounds.

After five years of diligent work, the business was officially incorporated in 1961. RM Shah Ltd is now run by Nilesh, who joined his father full time in 1983 and has just celebrated the company's diamond anniversary.

As well as importing precious stones, Ramanlal' s connections allowed him to access the big Indian cutting centres of Jaipur and Cambay. Slowly buyers looking at rough gemstones approached him to source emeralds and rubies, so they became the first company to export rough gemstones to India.

In the mid-1960s they started to go directly to Brazil and Colombia to buy rough. They were the first to deal in Zambian gemstones, both amethyst in the early 1970s and emerald when it was discovered there a few years later.

In the 1970s, together with a pioneer of the Indian gemstone industry, Pooranchanji Godika, they set up the first and only emerald-cutting unit in the UK at Cricklewood in London.

At that time firms such as Aldridge & Lewin were importing rough emeralds from South America and Benjamin Warwick was importing from Africa. Only the best-quality stones were cut in the UK, Germany or Switzerland. The vast majority was low grade, for which there were no buyers. The importers approached RM Shah to help them dispose of these rough gemstones. The company continued to grow, exporting rough to India, Israel and Germany as well as supplying polished gemstones to dealers, designers, jewellery manufacturers and retailers in the UK. Patrick Aldridge of Aldridge & Lewin went on to become one of the biggest and most well-known dealers in gems, diamonds and jewellery in Europe. Ian Roberts made Benjamin Warwick one of the largest gemstone merchants in London with a phenomenal inventory of emeralds from South Africa, Rhodesia and then Zambia. He was equally well known for the finest polished rubies and sapphires from around the world.

These dealers and many others sold their unwanted rough gems to the Indian buyers through RM Shah and London became the biggest trading centre for rough, precious stones in the world. Gems considered as semi-precious were traded through Idar-Oberstein in Germany.

In each generation there has been a wave of wealthy buyers. In turn we have seen Americans, Arabs, Japanese, Russians and more recently Chinese. Some of the earliest clients and friends of Ramanlal were what is often referred to as Persian Jews, who had lived in India and come to the UK after the war. Many spoke Hindi and they welcomed and befriended Ramanlal. Buyers also came from Lebanon and Iran to buy gems and jewellery with a taste for large gems, particularly emeralds.

In the 1980s the business from the Middle Eastern buyers made Bond Street the jewellery capital of the world, even usurping the major centres of Paris, Geneva and New York for a time.

Nilesh remembers how as a boy aged 5 or 6 his father would take him up to Hatton Garden on a Saturday for a visit to the Lema Buttery to meet some of his friends. If business had been good, he was treated to a hot chocolate and a digestive biscuit. If business was very good, he might get two biscuits.

Having cultivated good relationships with most of the major players, the time had come for his father to have an office of his own and a suitable location was found at 101 Hatton Garden. Not only was this building home to many other gemstone and diamond merchants, it was also more famously known as part of the celebrated Gamages

Department Store. Nilesh remembers going there regularly on a Saturday morning during the school holidays. The pretext was that he was there to help his father, but the reality was hours spent looking at toys, games and comics. In those days it was totally safe for young children to wander around alone in Hatton Garden.

Business was conducted rather formally with very little use of first names, unless one became friends on a social level. A suit was pretty much compulsory and there were very few women dealers/brokers in the 1950s and '60s. Many businesses were family owned. By and large people were honest and hard-working, and you did not have to worry about getting paid if you dealt with the right people. Ramanlal was highly regarded and respected by all who knew him, and left a tremendous personal and business legacy.

Ramanlal always remembered the way he was helped and guided by others in his early years and made it a point to help and support those who came after him. He passed away in 2001. Although deteriorating health had prevented him from being so active, he still managed a trip to Africa only months before he died. He continued to take a close interest in the business until the end.

Nilesh recalls: 'With my father's enormous expertise in rough gemstones, and his close relationship with the key players in the gemstone world, particularly amongst miners and wholesalers of rough gemstones, he became well known throughout the world. In India he was known by many customers as Ramanbhai (Raman is short for Ramanlal and bhai means brother – more respectful than just using a first name). In Africa he was known as "Shah of London", his reputation always preceded him, guaranteeing a warm and friendly welcome wherever he went.'

In the 1960s and early 1970s it was easy for gemstone buyers and sellers from around the world to bring goods to the UK market, make purchases and export them. London was a trading hub. Hatton Garden boomed and industry prospered.

In 1973 when VAT was introduced, competition from other European countries increased and business started to move abroad. Then with the introduction of VAT payable at the point of importation the huge import/export trade died. Unfortunately, the appeals to government for support for the industry fell on deaf ears. Although Hatton Garden is still the centre of the gemstone, diamond and jewellery business for the UK, the vibrant and exciting atmosphere of those international trading days has sadly waned.

RM Shah was a founding member of the ICA (The International Coloured Gemstone Association), an organisation supporting all areas of the gemstone industry, from artisanal miners to gem cutters in mining countries to dealers, local trade bodies and the industry as a whole.

Before joining his father, Nilesh had completed his Gemmologists Diploma at the GIA, and spent valuable time learning about the trade in New York, Geneva and Jaipur. Jewellers from Hatton Garden to Bond Street welcomed him with open arms at the mention of his father's name. Nilesh says: 'In fact most of what I know about the trade, I learnt from my father and the many dealers and brokers who over the years became like family to me.'

Today RM Shah is one of the oldest family-owned businesses in Hatton Garden and is also the oldest surviving gemstone or diamond merchant of Indian origin in the UK. Furthermore, it is now the only major UK and Hatton Garden player in the rough gemstone industry. It works closely with major miners such as Gemfields to source rough stones, not just for its own manufacturing requirements but also to supply to its many customers in India.

The ethos of a bygone age pervades companies that have gone down the generations both in Hatton Garden and the wider UK jewellery industry. Honesty, integrity, the provision of knowledgeable information, along with reliable customer service, will always be the hallmarks of such operations. Even today millions of pounds of business is done on the shake of the hand. For the vast majority of us 'Our Word is Still our Bond'.

G MUSIC

Carl Fabergé is known throughout the world as the jeweller to the Tsars. Apart from his renowned Imperial Easter Eggs, his exacting standards and creative design talent gave him a well-deserved place in the international jewellery hall of fame. However, success is not without its problems. It was not possible for Fabergé to meet high demand by producing everything himself in-house. Consequently, the workshop in St Petersburg used outworkers. One of their most notable was a Mr G Musikensky.

A very young George Musikensky had just completed a seven-year apprenticeship and in 1896, at the age of 16, had set up in business on his own, having learned diamond mounting, setting and polishing. He worked for Fabergé and other leading Russian jewellers, and in 1899, aged 19, he won a prestigious first prize at an exhibition, which gave him both recognition and enabled him to travel throughout Russia and beyond. The Russian Empire was already under siege from within prior to the revolution in 1917 and the pogroms were targeting Jewish people across the country. Large numbers of people left their homeland at this time to avoid persecution and financial ruin as the Bolsheviks became increasingly more powerful.

George left Russia and travelled via Germany and France, arriving in England in 1900. By 1914 he had formed a manufacturing jewellery company called Music & Goodrich Ltd. He formally changed his name to Music by deed poll on 26th April 1922 and, after it had become clear that he wouldn't be going back to Russia, he also became naturalised. He was initially assisted by his sons, Albert and Leslie. The business changed its name in 1925 to G Music & Sons Ltd and in 1931, the third son, Mr Bertram (Bertie) Music joined them. In a relatively short time, they built up an enviable reputation as one of London's leading manufacturing jewellers, designing exclusively for some of Bond Street's most prestigious names. From a jeweller to the Tsar, they became jewellers to the stars.

The association with Fabergé was not forgotten as George was often called upon to repair or help restore some of the masterpieces produced in St Petersburg. In particular, the famous 'Bay Tree Egg' needed their special skills and understanding. The work usually arrived via West End jeweller Wartski & Co., who enjoyed a valuable working relationship with Musics. Wartski had started to specialise in Fabergé when, between 1927 and 1933, Emanuel Snowman, the son-in-law of Morris Wartski, purchased work that had been smuggled out from Russia or confiscated items from the Soviet Government Department.

George was a well-known figure in Hatton Garden and would often have lunch with friends in the Mitre pub in Ely Court. The pub had peculiar licensing laws at the time as it was partly within the jurisdiction of Ely, Cambridgeshire, which had different opening hours to those in London. George was therefore able to start his 'lunch' in the front bar and when that closed, he would remove himself to the back bar, where he could continue to enjoy himself for longer.

In its heyday, G Music employed over a hundred top craftsmen in their workshop. At the outbreak of the Second World War, George retired. He then diversified into growing sunflowers at the family farm in Chipperfield, Hertfordshire, and was initially helped by his grandson, Michael. Bertie volunteered to serve in the RNVR in 1938. The business switched from jewellery production to making gauges and instruments for the government. They were then at 2 Charterhouse Street and 39 Holborn Viaduct. In May 1941 their premises fell victim to German bombs during the Blitz. They relocated to 48 Hatton Garden, where they remained until the 1960s.

George and Tamara Music, *c.*1900.

George died in September 1949 having established a dynasty that was then in the safe hands of Albert, Leslie and Bertie, each of whom had children; some of whom would join the family business. After eighteen years on the farm, Michael joined but Leslie's son and daughter didn't come into the trade. Bertie had Laurence, Bryan and Gregory. Gregory is the 'last man standing' of the original family.

Albert was very active in the industry, serving as President of the Master Goldsmiths Federation, and was instrumental in the abolition of Purchase Tax, which was replaced with VAT in 1973.

Before the last member of the original family retired, a new business was set up with a similar name to provide future employment for some of the workshop staff.

STATISTICS

A close examination of the jewellery trade in Hatton Garden and its related activities reveals a peak in the mid-1950s. Since its rapid growth throughout the 19th century following the arrival of South African diamonds and its continuing expansion into the following century, Hatton Garden attracted more and more people working with diamonds, coloured stones and jewellery. Refugees from Europe gave an unexpected boost to activity in the 1930s and 1940s. Apart from the impact of the two world wars, growth continued unchecked until halfway through the 20th century.

After the war, immigration slowed and some even moved out to new attractive locations overseas or returned to their former homes in Europe. At the same time, more manufacturers were using centrifugal casting for the first time. This meant fewer people in the workplace. Whereas many items had been made by hand, there was now the real advantage of increasing production using new equipment.

A study of the *Post Office Directory* for 1957 captures the area as it was and shows, perhaps, the heyday of the Garden. It was never exclusively a jewellery area and hosted other industries; some related and others quite different. The optical industry and the printing industry to a lesser extent also considered Hatton Garden their home. It is interesting to see that a number of the firms listed in 1957 are still operating today. Some have changed their names, with new owners, but many no longer exist.

In our own generation, businesses have relocated as the need to be in the Garden is not so vital as it was previously.

There are some interesting occupations listed in the directory. One that stands out is that of T Wigan of 39 Greville Street, listed as an oil and colour man. He appears to be the only one. His speciality was improving the look of a coloured stone. An emerald that has been damaged by heat or cleaning can be improved with a little cedar oil and maybe even, dare I say, a little colouration. He was often called out to customers in the West End to improve or cover up damaged stones. There was also a pearl skinner who could improve a damaged pearl by gently removing the surface layer like peeling an onion.

Trades in Hatton Garden Area 1838

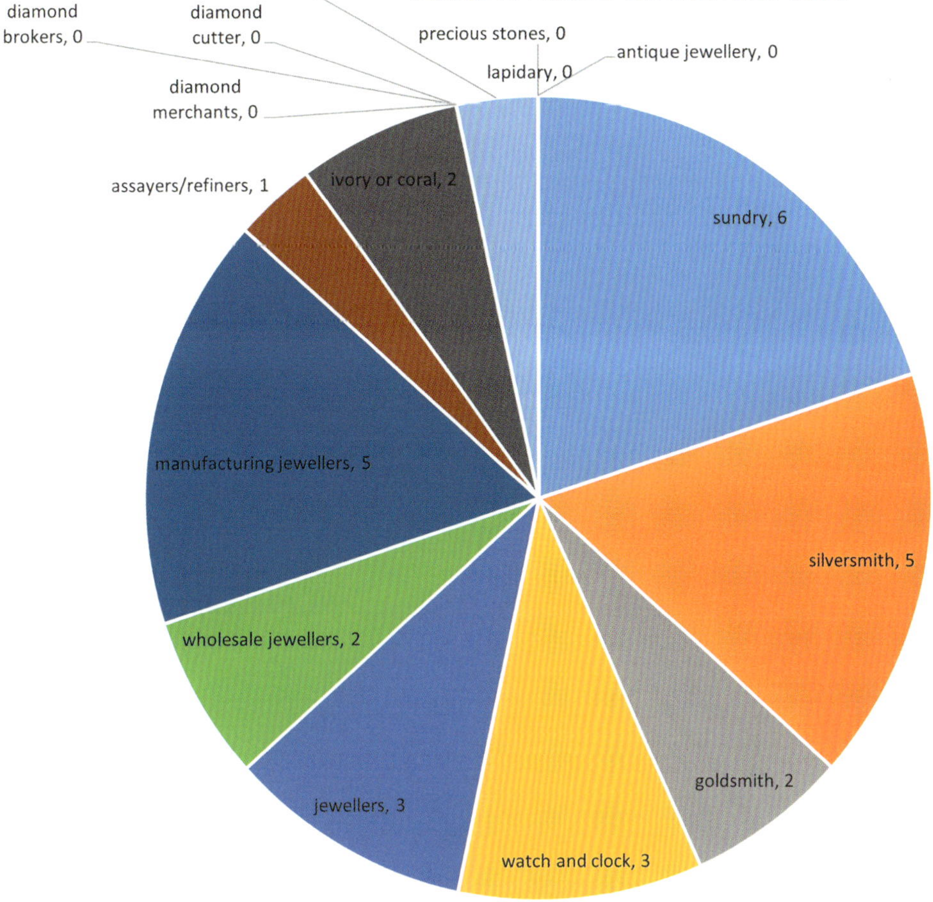

Trades in Hatton Garden Area 1897

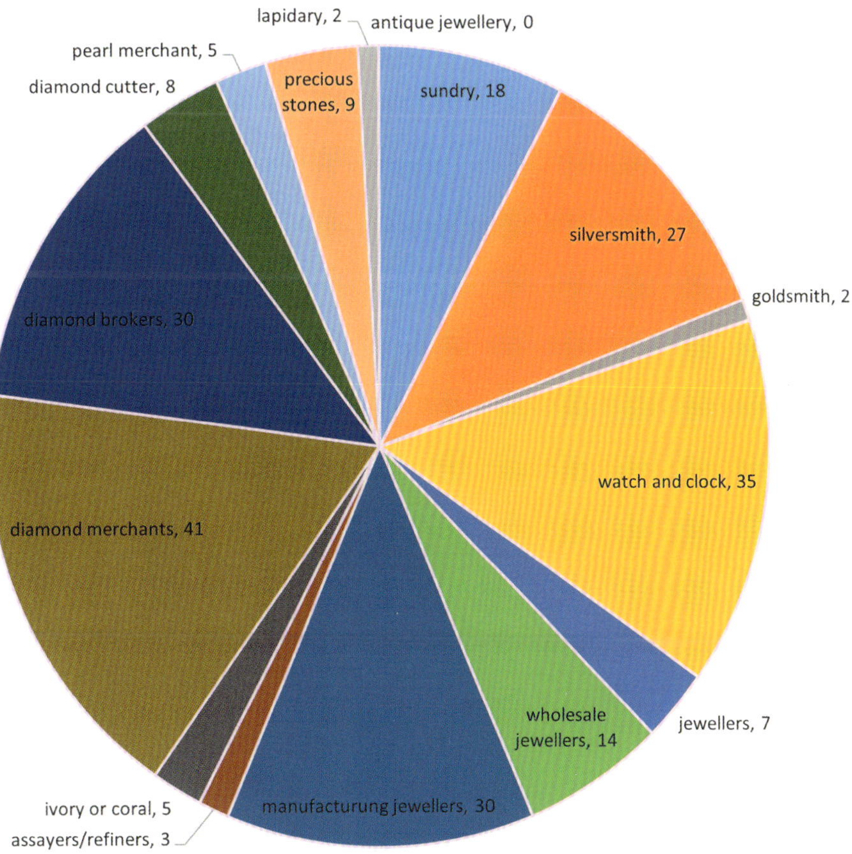

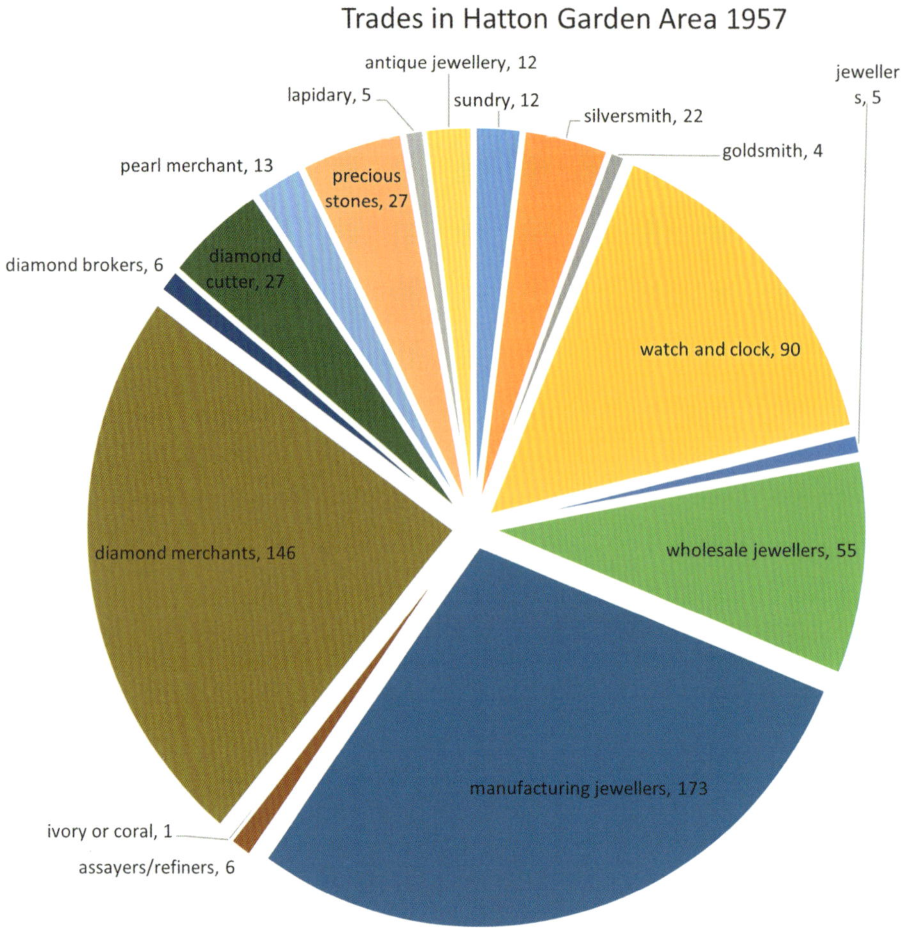
Trades in Hatton Garden Area 1957
antique jewellery, 12
lapidary, 5
sundry, 12
silversmith, 22
jeweller
s, 5
goldsmith, 4
pearl merchant, 13
precious
stones, 27
diamond brokers, 6
diamond
cutter, 27
watch and clock, 90
diamond merchants, 146
wholesale jewellers, 55
manufacturing jewellers, 173
ivory or coral, 1
assayers/refiners, 6

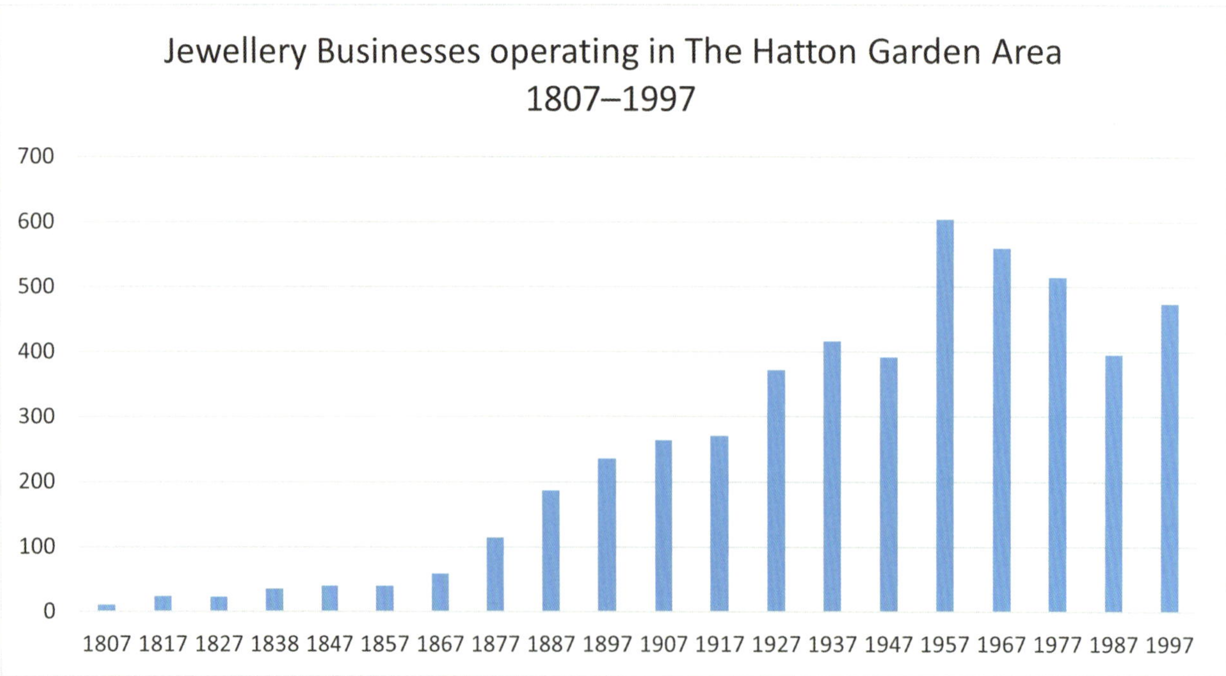
Jewellery Businesses operating in The Hatton Garden Area
1807–1997
700
600
500
400
300
200
100
0
1807 1817 1827 1838 1847 1857 1867 1877 1887 1897 1907 1917 1927 1937 1947 1957 1967 1977 1987 1997

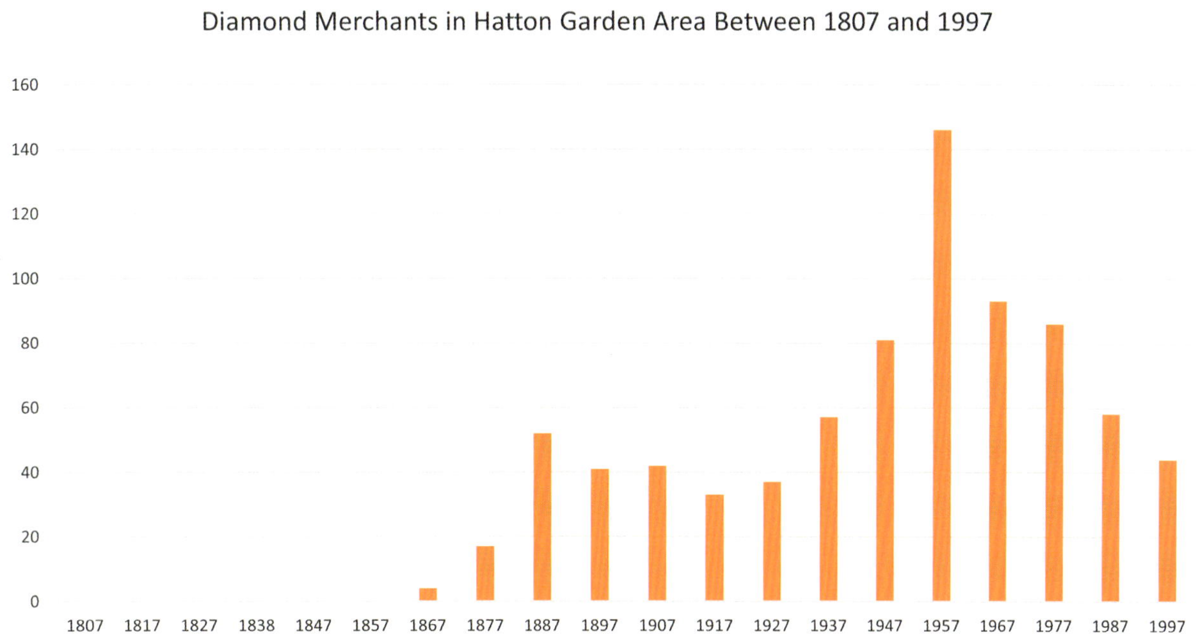

In the first part of this study, the area covered was that occupied by the original garden. Where an entry in the directory states more than one activity, the first one has been used. Only the part of Charterhouse Street west of Farringdon Road is included. Over a period of time some streets changed their names. 'Sundry' includes such entries as trade associations, laboratories, suppliers of equipment and boxes. 'Silversmith' includes all silver-related processing, such as polishers and engravers. 'Watch and clock' includes makers and importers. 'Wholesale jewellers' includes importers. 'Manufacturing jeweller' includes working jewellers, mounters, setters polishers, etc. 'Ivory and coral' includes all organic gems but NOT pearls. 'Diamond cutters' includes all processes such as cleaving and polishing. 'Precious stones' includes gem dealers. 'Pearl merchants' includes stringers. 'Antique jewellery' includes all 'Second-hand' dealers.

DIRECTORIES 1807–1997

Summary 1807 – 1997

Year	sundry	silversmith	goldsmith	watch and clock	jewellers	wholesale jewellers	manufacturing jewellers	assayers/refiners	ivory or coral	diamond merchants	diamond brokers	diamond cutter	pearl merchant	precious stones	lapidary	antique jewellery	Total Number of Entries
1807	2			6	2	1											11
1817		1	1	4	15	1		1	1								24
1827		4	4		10				5								23
1838	6	5	2	3	3	2	5	1	2	0	0	0	1	0	0	0	35
1847	5	7	3	3	5	6	4	4	1				2				40
1857	6	3	6	11	2	2	3	4	2	0	0	0	0	0	1	0	40
1867	2	3	6	16	3	9	5	2	3	4	1	1	0	3	1	0	59
1877	6	4	8	22	4	13	7	2	4	17	6	10	0	10	1	0	114
1887	1	9	6	29	8	11	12	1	8	52	30	8	1	11	0	0	187
1897	18	27	2	35	7	14	30	3	5	41	30	8	5	9	2	0	236
1907	7	35	4	32	5	23	45	4	5	42	29	7	5	19	1	1	264
1917	10	30	4	44	2	26	58	1	2	33	19	9	17	12	3	1	271
1927	9	34	3	68	3	38	95	3	7	37	13	7	33	18	4	0	372
1937	7	27	2	92	3	36	116	6	2	57	10	7	23	21	6	1	417
1947	10	18	3	80	6	37	85	5	1	81	6	13	12	29	4	2	392
1957	12	22	4	90	5	55	173	6	1	146	6	27	13	27	5	12	604
1967	8	20	1	57	10	44	216	8	0	93	8	13	16	54	3	9	560
1977	8	15	0	33	27	37	202	4	0	86	4	7	11	61	4	16	515
1987	8	9	0	15	46	40	140	12	0	58	5	3	13	39	4	4	396
1997		1	5	7	114	43	201	0	0	44	0	8	11	40	0	0	474

TIMELINE

		Year
LONDON	Romans arrive with 40,000 troops and establish Londinium	43-50
LONDON	Boudica sacks London; 70,000 killed	60
LONDON	First reference to Fleet	98
LONDON	Roman wall defines the City boundaries and square mile	200
LONDON	London Mint established	290
NATIONAL AND INTERNATIONAL	Christianity made the official religion of the Roman Empire	312
LONDON	Romans leave. Londinium abandoned and civilians move out	420
LONDON	Saxons settle and establish Lundenwic (market)	670
LONDON	Ely Cathedral founded in Cambridgeshire	673
NATIONAL AND INTERNATIONAL	Charlemagne crowned Holy Roman Emperor	800
NATIONAL AND INTERNATIONAL	Vikings attack Ludenwic	842
LONDON	Alfred the Great restores the walls and makes London capital of England	886
NATIONAL AND INTERNATIONAL	Alfred the Great – Anglo–Saxon Period	886

	YEAR	
	927	NATIONAL AND INTERNATIONAL Viking raids and settlement
NATIONAL AND INTERNATIONAL Alfred – King of all England	954	
HATTON GARDEN St Andrew's	959	NATIONAL AND INTERNATIONAL Viking raids and settlement
	1066	NATIONAL AND INTERNATIONAL Norman Conquest
HATTON GARDEN Holborn	1086	NATIONAL AND INTERNATIONAL Domesday Book
	1091	LONDON 17th October - Tornado 200 mph – about 600 houses flattened in London
NATIONAL AND INTERNATIONAL First Crusade	1096	
HATTON GARDEN Holborn	1118	LONDON Knights Templar settle in Holborn until 1184
LONDON St Bartholomew's founded	1123	
	1158	LONDON River Thames runs dry and Londoners are able to walk across
LONDON Weekly horse fair set up in Smithfield	1170	
	1180	TRADE First mention of Goldsmiths Company
LONDON First Mayor of London	1189	
	1211	LONDON Town ditch begun to be made
TRADE 15th June - Magna Carta signed	1215	
HATTON GARDEN Holborn	1221	LONDON The Black Prince settles in Holborn
HATTON GARDEN Holborn	1223	LONDON Holborn Bars established, expanding the City of London's jurisdiction

Year				
1248			TRADE	Trial of the Pyx instigated at Goldsmiths Hall
1251-1268	HATTON GARDEN	Ely Palace	LONDON	John le Francies builds an oratory on the site of what would become St Etheldreda's
1272	HATTON GARDEN	Holborn	LONDON	Land bought by John de Kirkby
1281	HATTON GARDEN	Farringdon	LONDON	Was a goldsmith and Alderman
1286	HATTON GARDEN	Holborn	LONDON	22nd September - John de Kirkeby becomes Bishop
1290	HATTON GARDEN	Holborn	LONDON	20th March - John de Kirkeby bequeaths nine cottages and a messuage in Holborn to his successors in the see
1292	HATTON GARDEN	Ely Place	LONDON	Ely Place town house of Bishops of Ely since 1292
1298	NATIONAL AND INTERNATIONAL	Marco Polo publishes his *Tales of China*		
1300			TRADE	First use of leopard's head as hallmark
1309	LONDON	Thames freezes		
1315			LONDON	Great Famine
1317	HATTON GARDEN	Fleet	LONDON	Bursts its banks causing fatalities
1327			TRADE	25th February - First charter granted to the 'Goldsmiths Company'
	HATTON GARDEN	Ely Palace	LONDON	Philippa of Hainault entertained in Ely Palace on her way to marry Edward III in York

YEAR		
HATTON GARDEN Field Lane	1329	LONDON Reference
	1347	NATIONAL AND INTERNATIONAL Black Death kills half the population in 18 months (Bubonic plague)
HATTON GARDEN St Andrew's	1348	LONDON John Thaive's bequest to St Andrew's
TRADE First mention of Goldsmiths Hall	1358	
	1371	LONDON Charterhouse Monastery established
NATIONAL AND INTERNATIONAL Peasants Revolt	1375	
HATTON GARDEN Holborn	1376	LONDON Mention of 24 shops on Holborn adjacent to the Bishop's Gatehouse
TRADE 22nd June - Act preventing importation of gold and silver into the UK	1377	
HATTON GARDEN Ely Place	1381	LONDON John of Gaunt moves into Ely Place after his Savoy Palace is sacked NATIONAL AND INTERNATIONAL Abolition of Serfdom
HATTON GARDEN Furnival's Inn	1383	LONDON Founded as an Inn of Chancery
HATTON GARDEN Farringdon	1394	LONDON Farringdon ward divided into within and without
LONDON Dick Whittington made Mayor	1397	
HATTON GARDEN Ely Palace	1399	LONDON John of Gaunt lies in state in Ely Place

	YEAR	
	1411	LONDON Guildhall completed
NATIONAL AND INTERNATIONAL 25th October - Agincourt	1415	
HATTON GARDEN Holborn	1417	LONDON Holborn paved
	1431	NATIONAL AND INTERNATIONAL 30th May - Execution of Joan of Arc
HATTON GARDEN Fleet Bridge		LONDON Fleet Bridge rebuilt
LONDON 25th November - Thames freezes	1434	
	1455	NATIONAL AND INTERNATIONAL Wars of the Roses
TRADE 17th April - First recorded diamond betrothal ring given by Archduke Maximillian of Austria to Princess Mary of Burgundy	1477	
	1478	TRADE Hallmarking becomes law, 18ct set as standard
HATTON GARDEN Ely Palace	1483-5	LONDON Shakespeare's Richard III re strawberries
NATIONAL AND INTERNATIONAL Henry VII becomes first Tudor King	1485	
	1492	NATIONAL AND INTERNATIONAL Christopher Columbus sails to America
NATIONAL AND INTERNATIONAL Plague	1498	
HATTON GARDEN Fleet	1502	LONDON Fleet Ditch made navigable by order of Henry VII
	1506	NATIONAL AND INTERNATIONAL Mona Lisa completed
HATTON GARDEN Ely Palace	1531	LONDON Henry VIII and Catherine of Aragon entertained in Ely Palace

	YEAR	
	1531	NATIONAL AND INTERNATIONAL Church of England breaks from Rome
NATIONAL AND INTERNATIONAL Reformation	1534	
HATTON GARDEN Holborn	1538	LONDON Old Bell first mentioned
HATTON GARDEN Christopher Hatton Born	1540	
	1543	NATIONAL AND INTERNATIONAL Copernicus proposes that the sun is the centre of our solar system
HATTON GARDEN Holborn	1545	LONDON Staple Inn built
HATTON GARDEN Ye Olde Mitre	1546	LONDON Pub built
LONDON Georg Hoefnagel survey and map	1550	
NATIONAL AND INTERNATIONAL 1st January - Elizabeth becomes Queen at age 25	1558	LONDON First map of London by Robert Agas
HATTON GARDEN Ely Palace	1559	LONDON Bishop Cox appointed
HATTON GARDEN Christopher Hatton	1560	LONDON 26th May - Christopher Hatton enrolled in Inner Temple
HATTON GARDEN Christopher Hatton	1562	LONDON 18th January - Christopher Hatton catches the eye of the Queen in 'Master of the Game'
NATIONAL AND INTERNATIONAL William Shakespeare born	1564	

	YEAR	
HATTON GARDEN Christopher Hatton	1564	LONDON Christopher Hatton made Gentleman Pensioner
HATTON GARDEN Christopher Hatton	1571	LONDON Christopher Hatton becomes an MP
HATTON GARDEN Christopher Hatton	1576	LONDON 20th March - Granted a lease for 21 years on the gatehouse of Ely Place
		TRADE 22ct gold replaces 18ct as the standard
NATIONAL AND INTERNATIONAL Drake circumnavigates the globe, returning with great riches plundered on the High Seas	1577-80	
	1581	NATIONAL AND INTERNATIONAL 16th January - Catholicism outlawed in Britain
LONDON Agas map	1561	
HATTON GARDEN Ely Palace	1578	LONDON July - Freehold transferred to Hatton by the Queen
		NATIONAL AND INTERNATIONAL 20th August - Drake renames Pelican as Golden Hind in honour of Sir C Hatton, who sponsored the voyage
HATTON GARDEN Christopher Hatton	1584	LONDON 1st January - Presents opal parure to Queen Elizabeth
HATTON GARDEN Christopher Hatton	1587	LONDON 29th April - PChristopher Hatton becomes Lord Chancellor
NATIONAL AND INTERNATIONAL Spanish Armada	1588	
HATTON GARDEN Fleet	1589	LONDON Works carried out to direct more tributaries into the Fleet to improve its flow
HATTON GARDEN 20th November - Christopher Hatton Dies	1591	LONDON 16th December - Christopher Hatton's Funeral at St Paul's

	YEAR	
	1597	NATIONAL AND INTERNATIONAL Shakespeare publishes Romeo and Juliet
LONDON John Stow publishes his *Survey of London*	1598	
	1603	NATIONAL AND INTERNATIONAL 24th March - Queen Elizabeth dies
LONDON Guy Fawkes' gunpowder plot	1605	
HATTON GARDEN Lady Hatton Gives evidence to the Privy Council as to her title to the estate	1616	NATIONAL AND INTERNATIONAL Death of William Shakespeare
HATTON GARDEN St Andrew's	1618	LONDON John Gerard buried in St Andrew's
HATTON GARDEN Ely Palace	1620-24	LONDON Ely Palace used as Spanish Embassy
HATTON GARDEN Ely Palace	1626	LONDON Ingoldsby Legends written by Richard Barham
	1633	LONDON 10th April - The herbalist Thomas Johnson put a bunch of bananas in his shop window in Snow Hill. This is the first time that the fruit had been displayed in the UK
HATTON GARDEN Holborn		LONDON Zenith of splendour of Holborn houses
HATTON GARDEN Hatton House is confiscated by Cromwell	1641-52	NATIONAL AND INTERNATIONAL Civil War
NATIONAL AND INTERNATIONAL 30th January - Charles I executed	1649	
HATTON GARDEN Christopher Hatton (III) makes over Hatton House to Robert Smythe	1654	LONDON Earliest surviving document of lease to Robert Smythe by Lord Hatton

	YEAR	
HATTON GARDEN Hatton Garden	1658	LONDON Faithmore's map shows layout of garden
HATTON GARDEN Hatton Garden	1659	LONDON 7th June - John Evelyn, diarist, visits Hatton Garden
NATIONAL AND INTERNATIONAL Bubonic plague 100,000 die	1665	
	1666	NATIONAL AND INTERNATIONAL 2nd September - Great Fire of London destroys 80% of the City
HATTON GARDEN Hatton Garden	1667	LONDON Trinity Chapel built LONDON The Nursery, a new playhouse
HATTON GARDEN Christopher Hatton (IV) succeeds father as Lord Hatton	1670	
HATTON GARDEN Hatton Garden	1672	LONDON 26th September - Fountain still in the garden
HATTON GARDEN Hatton Garden	1673	LONDON Houses in Hatton Garden had blue and gilt balconies
HATTON GARDEN Fleet		LONDON September - Fleet River reopened for vessels, after the Great Fire, up to Holborn Bridge
NATIONAL AND INTERNATIONAL Tavernier, at the behest of his patron Louis XIV, publishes Les Six Voyages de Jean-Baptiste Tavernier (Six Voyages, 1676)	1675	
HATTON GARDEN Hatton Garden	1677	LONDON In a list of City merchants, six resided in HG LONDON Ogilby's map

	YEAR	
HATTON GARDEN Hatton Garden	1678	LONDON 29th December - The Great Robbery of Hatton Garden
LONDON 1st December - Thames freezes	1683	
	1686	HATTON GARDEN St Andrew's rebuilt by Wren in stone
HATTON GARDEN Christopher Hatton (IV) proposes new church in HG, corner of St Cross St	1687	
HATTON GARDEN Hatton Garden	1694	LONDON Abraham Arlidge's map shows 367 properties, original survey for Lord Hatton LONDON Foundation of Bank of England
NATIONAL AND INTERNATIONAL Arrival of craftsmen (European economic, political and religious migrants)	1700s	
	1711	HATTON GARDEN Hatton Street described as 'an esteemed place for the gentry'
HATTON GARDEN Hatton Garden	1712	LONDON William Whiston, Preacher to 1715
LONDON Blome's map	1720	
	1726	TRADE Diamonds found in Brazil
HATTON GARDEN Hatton Garden	1728	LONDON Strype wrote 'Hatton Garden is a very large place now containing several streets'
HATTON GARDEN Farringdon	1732	LONDON 16th January - Act of Parliament to fill up the ditch that was the Fleet
HATTON GARDEN Fleet	1737	LONDON 30th September - Fleet Market opens

	YEAR	
	1739	LONDON 17th October - Foundling Hospital receives royal charter
HATTON GARDEN Hatton Garden	**1741**	LONDON 25th March - Captain Thomas Coram opens Foundling Hospital at 73–74 Hatton Garden (first 40 babies admitted)
LONDON Rocque's map of London	**1745**	
HATTON GARDEN Hatton Garden		LONDON Foundling Hospital moves from Hatton Garden
LONDON 15th March - The Great Storm	**1752**	
	1760	HATTON GARDEN William Hatton dies, 3rd Lord Hatton
HATTON GARDEN Hatton Garden	**1761**	LONDON Hatton Garden, a broad straight and long street
HATTON GARDEN Samuel Wilson died and left trust money for young businessmen	**1766**	LONDON City walls demolished and removal of gates begun
HATTON GARDEN Ely House	**1772**	LONDON Act passed vesting Ely House in her majesty
TRADE 29th January - Birth of Friedrich Mohs	**1773**	
	1776	NATIONAL AND INTERNATIONAL 4th July - American Independence
HATTON GARDEN Ely Place		LONDON Charles Cole buys Ely Place for £7,600
HATTON GARDEN Hatton Garden	**1778**	LONDON The Great Robbery in Hatton Garden
HATTON GARDEN Hatton Garden	**1784**	LONDON Mirabeau, French revolutionary, lived in HG

	YEAR	
	1785	NATIONAL AND INTERNATIONAL Times newspaper published
HATTON GARDEN Hatton Garden		LONDON Whole estate now sold house by house
HATTON GARDEN Hatton Garden	1786	LONDON Leaseholds converted to freeholds
	1789	LONDON 18th March - Last person to be burned at the stake in Newgate
NATIONAL AND INTERNATIONAL 26th February - First £1 note issued due to gold shortage	1797	
	1798	TRADE 18ct reintroduced alongside 22ct
HATTON GARDEN St Andrew's	1799	LONDON Marc Brunel married in St Andrew's (father of Isambard Kingdom Brunel)
NATIONAL AND INTERNATIONAL United Kingdom formed by union of the kingdoms of Great Britain and Ireland	1801	NATIONAL AND INTERNATIONAL London Stock Exchange founded NATIONAL AND INTERNATIONAL First official census
NATIONAL AND INTERNATIONAL Trafalgar. Britain now rules the waves	1805	
	1806	NATIONAL AND INTERNATIONAL Cape Colony becomes part of Empire
LONDON Building of Regent Street begins	1811	
	1813	TRADE 1st June - Ranjit Singh acquires Koh-i-noor
LONDON 1st Febraury - Frost Fair on the Thames	1814	
	1815	NATIONAL AND INTERNATIONAL Waterloo
HATTON GARDEN Hatton Garden	1817	LONDON Percival Johnson is refining platinum behind No. 79
HATTON GARDEN St Andrew's		LONDON Benjamin Disraeli christened in St Andrew's

	YEAR	
HATTON GARDEN Holborn	1818	LONDON Furnival's Inn rebuilt
NATIONAL AND INTERNATIONAL Discovery of Antarctica	1820	NATIONAL AND INTERNATIONAL 10th April - AFirst Britons settle in South Africa
	1821	TRADE Britain adopts gold standard
HATTON GARDEN Hatton Garden	1822	LONDON 23rd January - PN Johnson signs lease for 79 Hatton Garden
HATTON GARDEN Hatton Garden	1824	LONDON Described as 'an esteemed situation for the gentry'
HATTON GARDEN Farringdon	1826	LONDON 20th November - Market opens replacing Fleet Market
LONDON Sir Robert Peel founds Met Police	1829	
HATTON GARDEN Ely Palace		LONDON Catholic Emancipation Act permits St Etheldreda's to be used for Catholic worship again
HATTON GARDEN Hatton Garden	1836	LONDON Mazzini, Italian patriot, lived at No. 2 Hatton Garden
TRADE 15th July - Official opening of the new Goldsmiths Hall	1835	
	1836	LONDON PN Johnson had 13 workers in precious metal
		LONDON First passenger steam train from Deptford to Bermondsey
NATIONAL AND INTERNATIONAL Queen Victoria takes throne	1837	
	1840	NATIONAL AND INTERNATIONAL New Zealand founded

	YEAR	
HATTON GARDEN Field Lane	1841	LONDON 7th November - Andrew Provan, foundation of Ragged Schools, Field Lane School
NATIONAL AND INTERNATIONAL Britain occupies Hong Kong		
HATTON GARDEN Hatton Garden	1842	LONDON Police Court leaves Hatton Garden
LONDON 10th June - New Oxford Street opened to carriages, via St Giles rookeries	1845	
	1848	TRADE 24th January - Discovery of gold in California
HATTON GARDEN Hatton Garden		LONDON 30th May - Prudential founded in Hatton Garden
	1850	TRADE 6th April - Koh-i-noor leaves India
TRADE 17th July - Sydney Herald 'Gold nuggets found in Australia'	1851	
HATTON GARDEN Hatton Garden		LONDON 18th September - George Matthey joins Mr Johnson
	1852	TRADE 15th October - Gold discovered in New Zealand
TRADE 9ct, 13ct and 15ct introduced	1854	LONDON Cholera epidemic kills more than 10,000 Londoners
HATTON GARDEN Holborn	1855	LONDON Holborn District formally established
		TRADE Gold wedding rings now need to be hallmarked
LONDON Thames is now a sewer	1858	
LONDON London divided into postal districts		
	1860	TRADE 18th April - $250 paid by De Beers Bros for their new farm

	YEAR	
HATTON GARDEN Farringdon	1863	LONDON 10th January - Metropolitan Railway official opening
HATTON GARDEN St Peter's Church established	1866	HATTON GARDEN Holborn Viaduct constructed
LONDON Only one diamond cutter in London	1867	
	1869	HATTON GARDEN 6th November - Opening of Holborn Viaduct
TRADE Diamonds arrive from South Africa	1870s	
LONDON Street names regulated – odds on one side, evens on the other (too late for Hatton Garden)	1871	TRADE 19th October - De Beers Bros sell their farm for £6,300
	1873	TRADE 5th June - Kimberley, South Africa, named
HATTON GARDEN Holborn Circus	1874	LONDON Unveiling of statue of Prince Albert
	1876	LONDON Alexander Graham Bell makes first telephone call from Brown's Hotel
LONDON Clerkenwell Road opens	1878	
HATTON GARDEN Holborn		LONDON AW Gamage starts his business
HATTON GARDEN St Etheldreda's	1879	LONDON Restored as Catholic after 350 years
HATTON GARDEN Hatton Garden	1881	LONDON 16th November - Post Office raided
HATTON GARDEN Hatton Garden	1883	LONDON Sir Hiram Maxim, inventor of machine gun, lived at 57 HG

	YEAR	
HATTON GARDEN Hatton Garden	1885	LONDON 25th May - Robbery 'The Mysterious Affair'
HATTON GARDEN Hatton Garden		LONDON 67 Diamond merchants
HATTON GARDEN Sir Moses Montefiore dies at 56 Hatton Garden		
	1886	HATTON GARDEN Plaster removed from Staple Inn to reveal original timber-framed structure
NATIONAL AND INTERNATIONAL French Court decides to sell off the Crown Jewels	1887	
	1888	TRADE 13th March - De Beers formed
LONDON 21st March - LCC begins	1889	
	1893	TRADE 30th June - The Excelsior diamond found, then the largest in the world
HATTON GARDEN Hatton Garden	1895	LONDON February - First movie to be seen in UK
TRADE 14th June - Barney Barnato lost at sea, captain's log of Scott	1896	
	1897	TRADE 17th July - The Excelsior arrives in San Francisco with miners from the Yukon
HATTON GARDEN Holborn		LONDON Old Bell Inn demolished
LONDON 25 diamond cutters in London	1900	
HATTON GARDEN Holborn		LONDON 6th November - First meeting of Holborn Council
HATTON GARDEN Chancery Lane		LONDON Central Line opens
HATTON GARDEN Holborn	1901	LONDON Black Bull Inn demolished

	YEAR	
	1902	TRADE 26th March - Cecil Rhodes dies
NATIONAL AND INTERNATIONAL First powered flight, by Wright Brothers	1903	
	1905	TRADE 26th January - Cullinan diamond found
TRADE 10th February - Mr J Asscher cleaves the Cullinan	1908	NATIONAL AND INTERNATIONAL Ford model T invented
	1909	NATIONAL AND INTERNATIONAL First flight across the English Channel, by Louis Bleriot
TRADE White gold invented	1912	LONDON 18th June - Cheapside Hoard discovered
HATTON GARDEN Hatton Garden	1913	LONDON 17th November - Great Pearl Robbery of Hatton Garden
NATIONAL AND INTERNATIONAL 28th July - Start of First World War	1914	
	1915	NATIONAL AND INTERNATIONAL Zeppelins begin to bomb London
NATIONAL AND INTERNATIONAL 11th November - End of First World War	1918	
HATTON GARDEN Hatton Garden	1920	LONDON 1st July - De Beers adopt the metric carat
TRADE Mikimoto produces first round cultured pearls	1921	
HATTON GARDEN Farringdon	1922	LONDON 26th January - New building for Farringdon and High Holborn Station opened
NATIONAL AND INTERNATIONAL First commercial flight from London to Paris	1924	
HATTON GARDEN Hatton Garden	1925	LONDON Formation of LCCI Laboratory

	YEAR	
	1926	NATIONAL AND INTERNATIONAL General Strike
NATIONAL AND INTERNATIONAL October - Wall Street Crash	1929	
	1930s	NATIONAL AND INTERNATIONAL Further European migration
LONDON St Andrew's National School	1930	TRADE Formation of the London Diamond Syndicate
	1931	TRADE 15th January - GIA founded
TRADE 12 and 15ct gold standards cancelled and replaced with 14ct	1932	
	1933	TRADE June - Diamond Trading Company formed
HATTON GARDEN 21st April - Farringdon Station renamed	1936	
	1939	NATIONAL AND INTERNATIONAL 1st September - Start of Second World War
NATIONAL AND INTERNATIONAL 10th May - Italy declares war on Britain – Italians interned	1940	LONDON 7th September - Blitz begins
HATTON GARDEN Hatton Garden		LONDON London Diamond Bourse formed
		NATIONAL AND INTERNATIONAL 21st October - Purchase Tax introduced
HATTON GARDEN Ely Place		LONDON 7th November - London Diamond Club established in Ely Place
HATTON GARDEN St Andrew's	1941	LONDON 16th April - Hit by an incendiary bomb
HATTON GARDEN Holborn Circus		LONDON 16th April - Thomas Wallis store destroyed in Blitz
HATTON GARDEN Hatton Garden		LONDON 10th May - 8 Charterhouse Street destroyed. Home of Diamond Trading Company

	YEAR	
HATTON GARDEN St Etheldreda's	1941	LONDON 11th May - Roof and glass destroyed by German bomb
HATTON GARDEN Holborn		LONDON 15th May - Negretti & Zambra bombed
	1942	TRADE Provision of Supplies limits wedding rings to 9ct gold of 3.11 grams or less
HATTON GARDEN Holborn	1944	LONDON 24th August - Staple Inn hit by a flying bomb
HATTON GARDEN Farringdon	1945	LONDON 9th March - Market hit by V2 rocket
		NATIONAL AND INTERNATIONAL 2nd September - End of Second World War
HATTON GARDEN Hatton Garden	1949	LONDON 24th October - Opening of Hatton Garden Safe Deposit
NATIONAL AND INTERNATIONAL Petrol rationing ends	1950	
HATTON GARDEN Hatton Garden	1950s	LONDON Hatton Garden is trade only
HATTON GARDEN Farringdon	1954	LONDON 22nd May - Three people killed when a lorry went off the bridge and landed on the tracks
HATTON GARDEN Holborn	1955	LONDON Staple Inn restored
LONDON London Gold Market reopens after 15 years	1956	
	1957	LONDON London's first parking meters
HATTON GARDEN Only 3 shops in Hatton Garden	1960s	

	YEAR	
	1962	LONDON 8th May - Last trolley buses in London
LONDON Holborn becomes part of Camden	1965	
NATIONAL AND INTERNATIONAL House of Commons votes to join EEC NATIONAL AND INTERNATIONAL 15th February - Decimal coinage introduced	1971	NATIONAL AND INTERNATIONAL 16th January - Start of two-month Post Office strike NATIONAL AND INTERNATIONAL USA leaves gold standard
HATTON GARDEN Holborn	1972	LONDON Gamages closes
NATIONAL AND INTERNATIONAL UK joins EEC LONDON IRA bombs explode in London	1973	TRADE New Hallmarking Act proposed to replace all earlier ones NATIONAL AND INTERNATIONAL 2nd April - VAT replaces Purchase Tax
NATIONAL AND INTERNATIONAL January - Three-day working week lasts until March	1974	NATIONAL AND INTERNATIONAL 1st January - New Year's Day a public holiday
	1975	TRADE 2nd January - 1973 Hallmarking Act comes into force
NATIONAL AND INTERNATIONAL 1st May - May Day Bank Holiday introduced TRADE Rap List introduced	1978	
	1979	NATIONAL AND INTERNATIONAL 31st January - Dustmen's strike
LONDON January - New postcodes introduced	1980	NATIONAL AND INTERNATIONAL 27th March- Silver price crashes
LONDON IRA bomb Harrods, killing six	1983	NATIONAL AND INTERNATIONAL 26th November- Brink's-Mat Robbery
	1990	LONDON 6th May - London phone codes changed from 01 to 07

	YEAR	
TRADE Merger of Bourse and Club	1990	NATIONAL AND INTERNATIONAL Tim Berners-Lee invents worldwide web
	1996	LONDON Canary Wharf bombed by IRA
TRADE Ekati diamond mine, Canada, officially opened	1998	
	2005	LONDON 7th July - 52 killed in London bomb attacks by Islamist suicide killers
HATTON GARDEN Assay Office opens in Greville Street	2006	
	2008	NATIONAL AND INTERNATIONAL October - Credit Crunch – government bails out banks
TRADE 22nd July - Palladium hallmarked for the first time	2009	
HATTON GARDEN Hatton Garden	2015	LONDON April - Safe Deposit Burglary
NATIONAL AND INTERNATIONAL June - Vote in referendum to leave EU	2016	
	2017	NATIONAL AND INTERNATIONAL 6th January - HM Queen celebrates Sapphire Wedding Anniversary
NATIONAL AND INTERNATIONAL 31st October - Brexit	2019	
NATIONAL AND INTERNATIONAL 31st January - Britain leaves the EU	2020	NATIONAL AND INTERNATIONAL Coronavirus, Covid-19 means lock down for businesses and families
	2022	NATIONAL AND INTERNATIONAL Platinum Jubilee of Queen Elizabeth II

STREET VIEW

A LEGEND OF BLEEDING HEART YARD

The story of Sir Christopher Hatton's rise to fame and fortune is captured well in *The Ingoldsby Legends* by Richard Barham (aka Thomas Ingoldsby). He tells the story of how Lady Elizabeth Hatton, wife and socialite of her day, was murdered in 1626. Her body was found in what became known as Bleeding Heart Yard, the morning after the lavish party held by her at Hatton House on 26–27 January.

For convenience, the relevant sections are shown in black and the most pertinent part in bold.

THE HOUSE-WARMING!!

Sir Christopher Hatton he danced with grace,
He'd a very fine form and a very fine face,
And his cloak and his doublet were guarded with lace,
And the rest of his clothes,
As you well may suppose,
In taste were by no means inferior to those;
He'd a yellow-starched ruff,
And his gloves were of buff,
On each of his shoes a red heel and a rose,
And nice little moustache under his nose;
Then everyone knows
How he turned out his toes,
And a very great way that accomplishment goes,
In a Court where it's thought, in a lord or duke, a
Disgrace to fall short in 'the Brawls' – (their Cachoucas)

So, what with his form, and what with his face,
And what with his velvet cloak guarded with lace,
And what with his elegant dancing and grace,
His dress and address
So tickled Queen Bess
That her Majesty gave him a very snug place;
And seeing, moreover, at one single peep, her
Advisers were, few of them, sharper or deeper,
(Old Burleigh excepted), she made him Lord Keeper

I've heard, I confess with no little surprise,
English history called a farrago of lies,
And a certain Divine,
A connexion of mine,
Who ought to know better, as some folks opine,
Is apt to declare,
Leaning back in his chair,
With a sort of a smirking, self-satisfied, air,
That 'all that's recorded in Hume, and elsewhere,
Of our early "Annales"
A trumpery tale is,
Like the "Bold Captain Smith's," and "the luckless Miss Bayley's"–
That old Roger Hoveden, and Ralph de Diceto,
And others (whose names should I try to repeat o-
ver, well I'm assured you would put in your veto),
Though all holy friars,
Were very great liars,
And raised stories faster than Grissel and Peto –
That Harold escaped with the loss of a 'glim'–
– That the shaft which killed Rufus ne'er glanced from a limb
Of a tree, as they say, but was aimed slap at him,– 'That Fair Rosamond never was poisoned or spitted,
But outlived Queen Nell, who was much to be pitied;–
That Nelly her namesake, Ned Longshanks's wife,
Ne'er went Crusading at all in her life,
Nor suck'd the wound made by the poison-tipped knife!
For as she,
O'er the sea,
Towards far Galilee
Never, even in fancy, march'd carcass or shook shanks,
Of course she could no more suck Longshanks than Cruikshanks,
But, leaving her spindle-legged liege-lord to roam,
Staid behind, and suck'd something much better at home,–
That it's quite as absurd

To say Edward the Third,
In reviving the Garter, afforded a handle
For any Court-gossip, detraction, or scandal,
As 'twould be to say,
That at Court 'tother day,
At the fête which the newspapers say was so gay,
His Great Representative then stole away
Lady Salisbury's garters as part of the play.–
– That as to Prince Hal's being taken to jail,
By the London Police, without mainprize or bail,
For cuffing a judge,
It's a regular fudge;
And that Chief-Justice Gascoigne, it's very well known,
Was kicked out the moment he came to the throne.–
– Then that Richard the Third was a 'marvellous proper man'–
Never killed, injured, or wrong'd of a copper, man!–
Ne'er wished to smother
The sons of his brother,–
Nor ever stuck Harry the Sixth, who, instead
Of being squabashed, as in Shakspeare we've read,
Caught a bad influenza, and died in his bed,
In the Tower, not far from the room where the Guard is
(The octagon one that adjoins Duffus Hardy's).
– That, in short, all the 'facts' in the Decem Scriptores,
Are nothing at all but sheer humbugging stories.'

Then if, as he vows, both this country and France in,
Historians thus gave themselves up to romancing,
Notwithstanding what most of them join in advancing
Respecting Sir Christopher's capering and prancing,
'Twill cause no surprise
If we find that his rise
Is not to be solely ascribed to his dancing!
The fact is, Sir Christopher, early in life,
As all bachelors should do, had taken a wife,
A Fanshawe by family,– one of a house,
Well descended, but boasting less 'nobles' than nous;
Though e'en as to purse
He might have done worse,
For I find, on perusing her Grandfather's will, it is
Clear she had 'good gifts beside possibilities,'
Owches and rings,
And such sort of things,

Orellana shares (then the American Stocks),
Jewell'd stomachers, coifs, ruffs, stilk-stockings with clocks,
Point-lace, cambric handkerchiefs, nightcaps, and – socks –
(Recondite apparel contained in her box),
– Then the height of her breeding
And depth of her reading
Might captivate any gay youth, and, in leading
Him on to 'propose,' well excuse the proceeding:
Truth to tell, as to 'reading,' the Lady was thought to do
More than she should, and know more than she ought to do;
Her maid, it was said,
Declared that she read
(A custom all staid folks discourage) in bed;
And that often, o' nights,
Odd noises and sights
In her mistress's chamber had giv'n her sad frights,
After all in the mansion had put out their lights,
And she verily thought that hobgoblins and sprites
Were there, kicking up all sorts of devil's delights;–
Miss Alice, in short, was supposed to 'collogue'– I
Don't much like the word – with the subtle old rogue, I
've heard call'd by so many names – one of them's 'Bogy'–
Indeed 'twas conceived,
And by most folks believed,
– A thing at which all of her well-wishers griev'd –
That should she incline to play such a vagary,
Like sage Lady Branxholm, her contempo-rary,
(Excuse the false quantity, reader, I pray),
She could turn a knight into a waggon of hay,
Or two nice little boys into puppies at play,
Raison de plus, not a doubt could exist of her
Pow'r to turn 'Kit Hatton' into 'Sir Christopher;'
But what 'mighty magic,' or strong 'conjuration,'
Whether love-powder, philtre, or other potation
She used, I confess,
I'm unable to guess,–
Much less to express
By what skill and address
She 'cut and contrived' with such signal success,
As we Londoners say, to 'inwiggle' Queen Bess,
Inasmuch as I lack heart
To study the Black Art;
Be that as it may,– it's as clear as the sun,
That, however she did it, 'twas certainly done!

Now, they're all very well, titles, honour, and rank,
Still we can't but admit, if we choose to be frank,
There's no harm in a snug little sum in the Bank!
An old proverb says,
'Pudding still before praise!'
An adage well known I've no doubt in those days,
And George Colman, the Younger, in one of his plays,
Makes one of his characters loudly declare
That 'a Lord without money,'– I quote from his 'Heir-
At-Law'–"s but a poor wishy-washy affair!'–
In her subsequent conduct I think we can see a
Strong proof the Dame entertain'd some such idea,
For, once in the palace,
We find Lady Alice
Again playing tricks with her Majesty's chalice
In the way that the jocose, in
Our days, term 'hocussing;'
The liquor she used, as I've said, she kept close,
But, whatever it was, she now doubled the dose!
(So true is the saying,
'We never can stay, in
Our progress, when once with the foul fiend we league us.')
– She 'doctor'd' the punch, and she 'doctor'd' the negus,
Taking care not to put in sufficient to flavour it,
Till, at every fresh sip
That moisten'd her lip,
The Virgin Queen grew more attach'd to her Favourite.
'No end' now he commands
Of money and lands,
And, as George Robins says, when he's writing about houses,
'Messuages, tenements, crofts, tofts, and outhouses,'
Parks, manors, chases, She 'gives and she grants,
To him and his heirs, and his uncles and aunts;'
Whatever he wants, he has only to ask it,
And all other suitors are 'left in the basket,'
Till Dudley, and Rawleigh
Began to look squally,
While even grave Cecil, the famous Lord Burleigh,
Himself, 'shook his head,' and grew snappish and surly.
All this was fine sport,
As our authors report,
To dame Alice, become a great Lady at Court,
Where none than her Ladyship's husband look'd bigger,
Who 'led the brawls' still with the same grace and vigour,

Though losing a little in slimness and figure;
For eating and drinking all day of the best
Of viands well drest,
With 'Burgess's Zest,'
Is apt, by degrees, to enlarge a man's vest;
And, what in Sir Christopher went to increase it, he
'd always been rather inclined to obesity;
– Few men in those times were found to grow thinner
With beefsteaks for breakfast, and pork-pie for dinner.

Now it's really a difficult problem to say
How long matters might have gone on in this way,
If it had not unluckily happened one day
That Nick,– who, because
He'd the gout in his claws,
And his hoofs – (he's by no means so young as he was,
And is subject of late to a sort of rheumatic
attack that partakes both of gout and sciatica,)–
All the night long had twisted and grinn'd,
His pains much increased by an easterly wind,
Which always compels him to hobble and limp,
Was strongly advised by his Medical Imp
To lie by a little, and give over work,
For he'd lately been slaving away like a Turk,
On the Guinea-coast, helping to open a brave trade
In Niggers, with Hawkins who founded the slave-trade,
So he call'd for his ledger, the constant resource
Of your mercantile folk, when they're 'not in full force;'
– If a cold or catarrh makes them husky and hoarse,
Or a touch of gout keeps them away from 'the Bourse,'
They look over their books as a matter of course.
Now scarce had Nick turn'd over one page, or two,
Ere a prominent item attracted his view,
A Bill!– that had now been some days overdue,
From one Alice Hatton, née Fanshawe – a name
Which you'll recognise, reader, at once as the same
With that borne by Sir Christopher's erudite dame!
The signature – much more prononcée than pink,
Seem'd written in blood – but it might be red ink –
While the rest of the deed
He proceeded to read,
Like ev'ry 'bill, bond, or acquittance' whose date is
Three hundred years old, ran in Latin,–'Sciatis
(Diaboli?) omnes ad quos hæc pervenient –'

– But courage, dear Reader, I mean to be lenient,
And scorn to inflict on you half the 'Law-reading'
I picked up 'umquhile' in three days' special-pleading,
Which cost me – a theme I'll not pause to digress on –
Just thirty-three pounds six-and-eightpence a lesson –
'As I'm stout, I'll be merciful,' therefore, and sparing
All these technicalities, end by declaring
The Deed so correct
As to make one suspect,
(Were it possible any such person could go there)
Old Nick had a Special Attorney below there:
'Twas so framed and express'd no tribunal could shake it,
And firm as red wax and black ferret could make it.

By the roll of his eye
As Old Nick put it by,
It was clear he had made up his mind what to do
In respect to the course he should have to pursue,
When his hoof would allow him to put on a shoe!!

No, although the Lord Keeper held under the crown, house
And land in the country – he'd never a Town-house,
And, as we have seen,
His course always had been,
When he wanted a thing, to solicit the Queen,
So now, in the hope of a fresh acquisition,
He danced off to Court with his 'Humble Petition.'

'Please your Majesty's Grace,
I have not a place,
I can well put my head in, to dine, sup, or sleep!
Your Grace's Lord Keeper has nowhere to keep,
So I beg and intreat,
At your Majesty's feet,
That your Grace will be graciously pleas'd for to say,
With as little delay
As your Majesty may,
Where your Majesty's Grace's Lord Keeper's to stay –
– And your Grace's Petitioner ever will pray!'

The Queen, when she heard
This petition preferr'd,
Gave ear to Sir Christopher's suit at a word;–
'Odds Bobs, my good Lord!' was her gracious reply,

I don't know, not I,
Any good reason why
A Lord Keeper, like you, should not always be nigh
To advise – and devise – and revise – our supply –
A House! we're surprised that the thing did not strike
Us before – Yes!– of course!– Pray, whose House would you like!
When I do things of this kind, I do them genteelly,
A House?– let me see! there's the Bishop of Ely!
A capital mansion, I'm told, the proud knave is in,
Up there in Holborn, just opposite Thavies' Inn –
Where the Strawberries grow so fine and so big,
Which our Grandmother's Uncle tucked in like a pig,
King Richard the Third, which you all must have read of –
The day,– don't you know?– he cut Hastings' head off –
And mark me, proud Prelate!– I'm speaking to you,
Bishop Heaton!– you need not, my lord, look so blue –
Give it up on the instant! I don't mean to shock you,
Or else by –! (The Bishop was shocked!) – I'll unfrock you!!'

The Queen turns abruptly her back on the group,
The Courtiers all bow as she passes, and stoop
To kiss, as she goes, the hind flounce of her hoop,
And Sir Christopher, having thus danced to some tune,
Skips away with much glee in his best rigadoon!
While poor Bishop Heaton,
Who found himself beaten,
In serious alarm at the Queen's contumelious
And menacing tone, at once gave him up Ely House
With every appurtenance thereto belonging,
Including the strawberry beds 'twas so strong in;
Politely he bow'd to the gratified minion,
And said, 'There can be, my good lord, in opinion
No difference betwixt yours
And mine as to fixtures,
And tables, and chairs –
We need no survey'rs –
Take them just as you find them, without reservation,
Grates, coppers, and all, at your own valuation!'

Well! the object is gain'd!
A good town-house obtained,
The next thing to be thought of, is now
The 'house-warming' party – the when and the how –

The Court ladies call,
One and all, great and small,
For an elegant 'Spread,' and more elegant Ball,
So, Sir Christopher, vain as we know of his capering,
No sooner had finished his painting and papering,
Than he sat down and wrote,
A nice little pink note
To every great Lord, whom he knew, and his spouse,
From our poor place on Holborn-hill (late Ely House),
Lord Keeper and Dame Alice Hatton request,
Lord So-and-so's (name, style, or title exprest)
Good company on
The next Eve of St. John,
Viz: Friday week, June 24th, as their guest,
To partake of pot-luck,
And taste a fat buck.
N.B. Venison on table exactly at 3,
Quadrilles in the afternoon.
R. S. V. P.

For my good Lord of So-and-so these, and his wife;
Ride! ride! for thy life! for thy life! for thy life!'
Thus, courtiers were wont to indorse their expresses
In Harry the VIIIth's time, and also Queen Bess's.
The Dame, for her part, too, took order that cards
Should be sent to the mess-rooms of all the Hussards,
The Household troops, Train-bands, and horse and foot Guards.

Well, the day for the rout
At length came about,
And the bells of St. Andrew's rang merrily out,
As horse-litter, coach, and pad-nag, with its pillion,
(The mode of conveyance then used by 'the Million,')
All gallant and grand,
Defiled from the Strand,
Some through Chancery (then an unpaved and much wetter) Lane,
Others through Shoe (which was not a whit better) Lane,
Others through Fewtar's (corrupted to Fetter) Lane;
Some from Cheapside, and St. Mary-le-Bow,
From Bishopsgate Street, Dowgate Hill, and Budge Row,
They come and they go,
Squire and Dame, Belle and Beau,
Down Snore Hill (which we have since whitewashed to Snow),

All eager to see the magnificent show,
And sport what some call 'a fantastical toe;'
In silk and in satin,
To batten and fatten
Upon the good cheer of Sir Christopher Hatton,

A flourish, trumpets! – sound again! –
He comes, bold Drake, the chief who made a
Fine hash of all the pow'rs of Spain,
And so serv'd out their Grand Armada:
With him come Frobisher and Hawkins,
In yellow ruffs, rosettes, and stockings.

Room for my Lord! – proud Leicester's Earl
Retires a while from courtly cares,
Who took his wife, poor hapless girl!
And pitch'd her neck and heel down stairs;
Proving, in hopes to wed a richer,
If not her 'friend,' at least her 'pitcher.'

A flourish, trumpets! strike the drums!
Will Shakspeare, never of his pen sick,
Is here – next Doctor Masters comes,
Renown'd afar for curing men sick,–
Queen's Serjeant Barham with his bums
And tipstaves, coif, and wig forensic;
(He lost, unless Sir Richard lies, his
Life at the famous 'Black Assizes.')
Room! Room! for great Cecil! – place, place, for his Dame! –
Room! Room! for Southampton – for Sidney, whose name
As a Preux Chevalier, in the records of Fame
'Beats Banagher'– e'en now his praises, we all sing 'em,
Knight, Poet, Gentleman! – Room for sage Walsingham!

Room for Lord Hunsdon! – for Sussex!– for Rawleigh!–
For Ingoldsby!! Oh! it's enough to appal ye!
Dear me! how they call!
How they squall! how they bawl!
This dame has lost her shoe – that one her shawl –
My lord's got a tumble – my lady a fall!
Now a Hall! a Hall!
A Brawl! a Brawl!
Here's my Lord Keeper Hatton, so stately and tall,
Has led out Lady Hunsdon to open the Ball!

Fiddlers! Fiddlers! fiddle away!
Resin your catgut! fiddle and play!
A roundelay!
Fiddle away!
Obey! obey! – hear what they all say!
Hip! – Music! – Nosey!!– play up there! – play!'
Never was any thing half so gay
As Sir Christopher Hatton's grand holiday!

The clock strikes twelve!– Who cares for the clock?
Who cares for – Hark!– What a loud Single-knock!
Dear me! dear me!
Who can it be?–
Why, who can be coming at this time of night,
With a knock like that honest folk to affright?–
'Affright?'– yes, affright!– there are many who mock
At fear, and in danger stand firm as a rock,
Whom the roar of the battle-field never could shock,
Yet quail at the sound of a vile 'Single-knock!'
Hark?– what can the Porter be thinking of?– What!–
If the booby has not let him in I'll be shot!–
Dear me! how hot
The room's all at once got!–
And what rings through the roof?–
It's the sound of a hoof!–
It's some donkey a-coming upstairs at full trot!
Stay!– the folding-doors open! the leaves are thrown back,
And in dances a tall Figurant – ALL IN BLACK!!

Gracious me what an entrechat! Oh, what a bound!
Then with what an a-plomb he comes down to the ground!
Look there! look there!
Now he's up in the air!
Now he's here!– now he's there – now he's no one knows where!–
See! see!– he's kick'd over a table and chair!
There they go!– all the strawberries, flowers, and sweet herbs,
Turn'd o'er and o'er,
Down on the floor,
Ev'ry caper he cuts oversets or disturbs
All the 'Keen's Seedlings' and 'Wilmot's Superbs!'
There's a pirouette!– we're
All a great deal too near!
A ring!– give him room or he'll 'shin' you – stand clear!
There's a spring again!– oh! 'tis quite frightful! – oh dear!

His toe's broke the top of the glass chandelier!!

Now he's down again!– look at the congees and bows
And salaams which he makes to the Dame of the House,
Lady Alice, the noble Lord Treasurer's spouse!
Come, now we shall view
A grand pas de deux
Perform'd in the very first style by these two
– But no!– she recoils – she could scarce look more pale if
Instead of a Beau's 'twas the bow of a Bailiff!–
He holds out his hand – she declines it, and draws
Back her own – see!– he grasps it with horrid black claws,
Like the short, sharp, strong nails of a Polar Bear's paws!!

Then she 'scream'd such a scream!'
Such another, I deem,
As, long after, Miss Mary Brown scream'd in her dream,
Well she might! for 'twas shrewdly remark'd by her Page,
A sharp little boy about twelve years of age,
Who was standing close by
When she utter'd her cry,
That the whole of her arm shrivell'd up, and grew dry,
While the fingers and thumb of the hand he had got
In his clutches became on the instant RED HOT!!

Now he whirls and he twirls
Through the girls in their curls
And their rouge, and their feathers, and diamonds, and pearls;
Now high,– now low,–
Now fast, and now slow,
In terrible circumgyration they go;
The flame-coloured Belle and her coffee-faced Beau!
Up they go once! and up they go twice!–
Round the hall!– round the hall!– and now up they go thrice!
Now one grand pirouette, the performance to crown!
Now again they go up!!– and they NEVER COME DOWN!!!

***

The thunder roars!
And the rain it pours!
And the lightning comes in through the windows and doors!
Then more calling, and bawling,

And squalling, and falling,
Oh! what a fearful 'stramash' they are all in!
Out they all sally,
The whole corps de ballet –
Some dash down Holborn-hill into the valley,
Where stagnates Fleet Ditch at the end of Harp Alley,
Some t'other way, with a speed quite amazing,
Nor pause to take breath till they get beyond Gray's Inn.
In every sense of the word, such a rout of it,
Never was made in London, or out of it!

When they came the next day to examine the scene,
There was scarcely a vestige of all that had been;
The beautiful tapestry, blue, red, and green,
Was all blacken'd and scorch'd, and look'd dirty and mean.
All the crockery broken, dish, plate, and tureen!
While those who look'd up could perceive in the roof,
One very large hole in the shape of a hoof!

Of poor Lady Hatton, it's needless to say,
No traces have ever been found to this day,
Or the terrible dancer who whisk'd her away;
But out in the court-yard – and just in that part
Where the pump stands – lay bleeding a LARGE HUMAN HEART!
And sundry large stains
Of blood and of brains,
Which had not been wash'd off notwithstanding the rains,
Appear'd on the wood, and the handle, and chains,
As if somebody's head with a very hard thump,
Had been recently knock'd on the top of the pump.
That pump is no more!– that of which you've just read,–
But they've put a new iron one up in its stead,
And still, it is said,
At that 'small hour' so dread,
When all sober people are cosey in bed,
There may sometimes be seen on a moonshiny night,
Standing close by the new pump, a Lady in White,
Who keeps pumping away with, 'twould seem, all her might,
Though never a drop comes her pains to requite!
And hence many passengers now are debarr'd
From proceeding at nightfall through Bleeding Heart Yard!

MORAL.

Fair ladies attend!
And if you've a 'friend
At Court,' don't attempt to bamboozle or trick her!
– Don't meddle with negus, or any mix'd liquor!–
Don't dabble in 'Magic!' my story has shown,
How wrong 'tis to use any charms but your own!

Young Gentlemen, too, may, I think, take a hint,
Of the same kind, from what I've here ventured to print,
All Conjuring's bad! they may get in a scrape,
Before they're aware, and whatever its shape,
They may find it no easy affair to escape.
It's not every body that comes off so well
From leger-de-main tricks as Mr. Brunel.

Don't dance with a Stranger who looks like a Guy,
And when dancing don't cut your capers too high!
Depend on't the fault's in
Your method of waltzing,
If ever you kick out the candles – don't try!

At a ball or a play,
Or any soirée,
When a petit souper constitutes the 'Après,'
If strawb'ries and cream with CHAMPAGNE form a part,
Take care of your HEAD!– and take care of your HEART!

If you want a new house
For yourself and your spouse,
Buy, or build one,– and honestly pay, every brick, for it!
Don't be so green as to go to old Nick for it –
– Go to George Robins – he'll find you 'a perch,'
(Dulce domum's his word,) without robbing the Church!

The last piece of advice which I'd have you regard
Is, 'don't go of a night into Bleeding Heart Yard,'
It's a dark, little, dirty, black, ill-looking square,
With queer people about, and unless you take care,
You may find when your pocket's clean'd out and left bare,
That the iron one is not the only 'PUMP' there?

BIBLIOGRAPHY

There are many books that would be of interest to anyone wanting to look further into the history of London and specifically Hatton Garden. The list shown here are those titles that I found helpful in my research and could commend for further study.

Author	Title	Year
Ackroyd, Peter	*The Clerkenwell Tales*	2003
Allbutt, Robert	*Rambles in Dickens' Land*	1899
Allen, Tudor	*Little Italy: The Story of London's Italian Quarter*	2008
Arkell, Reginald	*Green Fingers*	1934
Baker, H Barton	*Stories of the Streets of London (reprint)*	2017
Barron, Caroline	*The Parish of St Andrew*	1979
Bartholomew	*Reference Atlas of Greater London*	1957
Barton, Nicholas	*The Lost Rivers of London*	1960
Bell, Walter	*The Great Plague in 1665*	1924
Bolitho & Peel	*Without the City Wall*	1952
Bowers, Gordon	*The Great Diamond Heist*	
Brett-James, Norman	*The Growth of Stuart London*	1935
Brewer, HW	*Old London Illustrated*	1940
Brewer, HW	*Old London Illustrated*	1962
Burke, Thomas	*The Streets of London*	1949
Bush, Arthur	*Portraits of London*	1950
Chandlery, PJ	*The Tower to Tyburn*	1924
Clarkson, Wensley	*Sexy Beasts*	2016
Crosby, Molly Caldwell	*The Great Pearl Heist*	2012
Cunningham, Peter	*Hand Book of London*	1850
Davies, Philip	*Lost London*	2009
Deacon, Malcolm	*The Courtier and the Queen*	2008
De Loriol	*The London Book of Days*	2013
Denford & Hellings	*Streets of Old Holborn*	1999
Dennett, Laurie	*A Sense of Security*	1998
Dickens, Charles	*Little Dorrit*	
Dutton, Ralph	*London Homes*	1952

Ehrlich, Blake	*London on Thames*	1966
Fitzgerald, Michael	*Ragged London The Life of London's Poor*	2011
Forbes, JS	*Hallmark*	1998
George, M Dorothy	*London Life in the 18th Century*	1925
Girling, Brian	*Holborn, Bloomsbury and Clerkenwell*	1999
Green, Benny	*The Streets of London*	1985
Grew, ES	*The Foundling Hospital*	
HMSO	*Historical Monuments of West Cambridgeshire*	1968
Hobson, Oscar	*How the City Works*	1954
Home, Gordon	*Roman London*	1926
Hoh-Cheung & Mui, Lorna H	*Shops & Shopkeeping in 18th Century England*	1989
Humphreys, Christmas	*The Great Pearl Robbery of 1913*	
Inglis, Lucy	*Georgian London – into the Streets*	2013
Ingoldsby, Thomas	*The Ingoldsby Legends*	1869
Jackson, Peter	*London Explorer*	-
Jackson, Peter	*Walks in Old London*	1993
Jarvis, Stephen	*A History of Ely Place*	-
Jowett, Judy	*The Warning Carriers*	2005
Keefe, HJ	*A Century in Print – The Story of Hazell's 1839–1939*	1939
Kerr & Duncan	*The Portledge Papers 1687–1697*	1928
Lamprey, L	*The Days of the Guilds*	1927
Lehmann, John	*Holborn*	1970
Lenzen, Dr G	*The History of Diamond Production and the Diamond Trade*	
Lichtenstein, Rachel	*Diamond Street*	2012
Linnane, Fergus	*London, The Wicked City*	2003
London Topog. Soc.	*The A–Z of Georgian London*	1982
Marryat & Broadbent	*The Romance of Hatton Garden*	1930
McCarthy, James	*Fire and Earth*	
McDonald, Donald	*The Johnsons of Maiden Lane*	1964
McDonald, Donald	*Percival Norton Johnson*	1951
Morton, HV	*Ghosts of London*	1939
Morton, HV	*The Spell of London*	1926
Murray, John	*Handbook of London*	1850
Newton, Douglas	*London West of the Bars*	1951
Nicolas, Sir Harris	*Memoirs of Sir Christopher Hatton*	1848
Norsworthy, Laura	*The Lady of Bleeding Heart Yard*	1936
Ogilvy, James S	*Relics & Memorials of London City*	1910
Palmer, Arnold	*Straphangers*	1927
Parry-Crooke, Charlotte	*Mr Gamages Great Toy Bazaar*	1982
Passingham, WJ	*London's Markets*	
Patterson, James	*Heist*	
Pearce, David	*The Great Houses of London*	1986
Pettifer & Sommerfield	*One Last Job*	2016
Porter, Roy	*London: A Social History*	1994
Pudney, John	*Hatton Garden*	
Pugh, E	*Hughson's History of London Vol I & Vol IV*	1805
Pugh, Gillian	*London's Forgotten Children*	2007
Richardson, John	*A History of Camden*	1999
Ross & Clark	*London The Illustrated History*	2008
Sanitt, Leonard	*On Parade: Memoirs of a Jewish Sergeant-Major in World War II*	1990
Saunders, Ann	*London Topographical Record. Vol 25*	1985
Silliman, Benjamin	*Journal of Travels*	1812
Sleigh, Linwood	*St Etheldreda's and Ely Place*	1952
Smith, Anthony	*Machine Gun*	2002
Stapleton, Alan	*London Alleys, Byways & Courts*	
Stapleton, Alan	*London Lanes*	1930
Stow, John	*Survey of London 1598*	1842
Tait, Arthur	*A Story of Staple Inn on Holborn Hill*	2001

Taylor, Gladys	*Old London Gardens*	1953
Thackeray, William M	*The New Comers*	1900
The Foundling Museum	*The Foundling Museum*	
Thornbury, Walter	*Old London Charterhouse to Holborn*	1987
Times Books	*The Times History of London*	
Tindall, Gillian	*The Man who Drew London*	1988
Trench and Hillman	*London under London*	1993
Troke, Margaret	*A Medieval Legacy*	
Tyler, David	*Thomas Gainsborough's Days in Hatton Garden*	
Unwin, George	*The Gilds and Companies of London*	1938
V & A Museum	*The Panelled Rooms Part V. The Hatton Garden Room*	
Vines, Alice Gilmore	*Neither Fire nor Steel – Sir Christopher Hatton*	1978
Waller, Maureen	*1700 Scenes from London Life*	1988
Ward, Laurence	*LCC Bomb Damage Maps*	2015
Waugh, Maureen	*Memories of Holborn*	1986
Weymouth, Anthony	*Of London and Londoners*	1951
Williams, E	*Early Holborn and the Legal Quarter of London*	1927
Williams, Montague QC	*Leaves of a Life*	1890
	A Guide to St Andrew Holborn	
	Camden History Review 15	
	The Foundling Museum	1988
	HOLBORN Official Guide	
	Prudential in Pictures	1998
	St Etheldreda's Ely Place (A Pitkin Guide)	
	The Post Office Directory	1957
	Old and New London	
	The Field Lane Story	

WEBSITES

http://hidden-london.com/nuggets/bleeding-heart-yard
http://libcom.org/library/reds-green-short-tour-clerkenwell-radicalism
http://lndn.blogspot.com/2005_08_01_archive.html
www.a2a.org.uk
www.Britainfromabove.org.uk
www.british-history.ac.uk/old-new-london
www.britishnewspaperarchive.co.uk
www.britishpathe.com
www.cityoflondon.gov.uk/lma
www.collage.cityoflondon.gov.uk
www.debeers.com
www.dickensmuseum.com
www.flickeringlamps.com
www.gracesguide.co.uk
www.hatton-garden.net/heritage4.html
www.hidden-london.com/littleitaly.html
www.historicengland.org.uk
www.history.ac.uk/gh
www.islington.gov.uk/heritage
www.italianchurch.org.uk
www.londonlives.org
www.maryevans.com
www.maryflanagan.com
www.matthey.com
www.movinghere.org.uk
www.museumoflondon.org.uk
www.nationalarchives.gov.uk
www.romanticlondon.org
www.smithandharris.com
www.stetheldreda.com
www.thesilvervaults.com
www.tudorplace.com.ar/Bios/ChristopherHatton.htm
www.visionofbritain.org.uk

THANKS

Special thanks to a few of the many without whom this story could not have been told.

Adrian Klein	
Alan Cohen	London Diamond Bourse
Alan Gard	
Alison Hardwick	Born in Hatton Garden
Barry Sullivan	Jewellery Advisory Services
Bill Timms	
Carole Parker	IPG
Charles Bonas	Bonas & Co.
Charles Evans	
Christopher Klean	
Clive Baxter	Artist: Street Profile
Daniel Caspi	Davril
David Callaghan	
David Halperin	Val d'Or
David Kaye	
David Pearl	Pearl & Coutts
David Strassman	
Dorit Gordon	Georges: HGSD
Eleni Bide	Goldsmiths Company Library
Fiona Roberts	Ely Place
Gareth Harris	Smith & Harris
Gary Williams	Presman
Harold Cox	Slee, Son & Carden
Harry Levy	Levy Gems
Ian Thomson	
Jack Ogden	
Jack Yakutiel	
James Riley	
Jan Hajioff	Jongems
Janice Devitt	Ely Place
Jason Holt	Holts
Joe Ullmann	Andrew R Ullmann
John Padgett	Barnard Silversmiths
John Kessler	
John Taylor	Charles Matthews
John Watson	PJ Watson
Jonathan Kendal	De Beers
Jonathan Weissbart	S Weissbart
Joseph Ullmann	Andrew Ullmann
Judith Norman	Ye Olde Mitre
Kurt Eichner	
Lionel Wiffen	
Mandy Bennett	
Martin Kutock	Apollo
Martin Vainer	M Vainer
Michael Ferraro	TH March
Michael Landsberg	
Mr Stellman	S Stellman: Original designs from 1930s and '40s
Nicholas Hills	St Andrew's Church
Nilesh Shah	RM Shah
Paul Podolsky	Wartime memories
Peter Vokes	
Richard Cornelius	E Wolfe
Robert Wilson	Bleeding Heart
Roy Huddlestone	
Sarah Parker	Historian: Access to Carole Parker's research
Stephen Wright	BKT
Sue Johns	St Andrew's Church
The Ullmann Family	Andrew R Ullmann
Tony Dellow	House of Hatton
Tracey Skeggs	PJ Watson
Trevor Tyler	Trevor Tyler
Tudor Allen	Senior Archivist: London Borough of Camden
Vartkess Knadjian	Backes & Strauss
Vaughan Segal	

CONTACT

PJ Watson Ltd
Chesham House
Church Lane
Berkhamsted
HP4 2AX
United Kingdom

01442 200030
vwatson@pjwatson.co.uk

We would love to hear from you if you feel you could have contributed to this story.
Any additional material would be most welcome. Perhaps you would like to offer an anecdote or maybe you have some old photos or a memory you could share. Please don't hesitate to get in touch, however small you think your offering may be.

PICTURE CREDITS

Great care has been taken to diligently seek any copyright permissions for images within this publication. All other images are courtesy of The Diamond Trust.

The author expresses his thanks to The Worshipful Company of Goldsmiths for their encouragement and support, without which this book may not have been published.

A Arlidge: p. 38
Alamy: p. 22; Sir C Hatton, pp. 129; 147; 194; NJ Hill advertisement, p. 200; G Mazzini School, p. 208; Rowlands advertisement, p. 237; Leather Lane c. 1954, p. 240; p. 246; Angela Rogers, p. 7

BKT: pp. 43; 369; 370; 371; 372

Camden Local Studies and Archives Centre: pp. 53; 57; 74; 98; 170; 176; 179; 180; 195; 196; 197; 232; 235; 246
Carole Parker: pp. 278; 297

E Wolfe: p. 331

Getty Images Inc.: p. 49 Hulton Deutsch; Corbis Historical Collection, p. 75; Fox Photos, Hulton Archive, p. 85; Phillips, Hulton Archive, p. 145; Topical Press Agency, Hulton Archive, p. 158; Popperfoto, Topical Press Agency, Hulton Archive, p. 197

Guildhall Art Gallery, p. 156

Harry Levy: p. 334
Historic England Archive, Aerofilms Collection: p. 71
Historic England Archive: pp. 103; 142; 161; 196; 197; 213; 219; 238; 239
HMSO: p. 118
Hudson family: pp. 323; 324
HW Brewer: p. 18

Imperial War Museum: p. 69

James S Ogilvy: pp. 33; 178
Jason Holt: p. 336

London Evening Standard: p. 78 (JAK), p. 84
London Picture Archive (© London Metropolitan Archives): p. 28, ref: 5927; p. 46, ref: 72573; p. 63, ref: 72522, P91. ref: 10048, p. 93, ref: 2742; p. 94, ref: 24424; p. 100, ref. 427; p. 101, ref. 429; p. 117, ref. 8146; p. 120, ref. 314732; p. 148, ref. 318661; p. 193, ref. 72560; p. 200, ref. 72500; p. 204, ref. 72582; p. 205, ref. 72521; p. 209, ref. 72502; p. 211, ref. 72581; p. 214, ref. 72543; p. 221, ref. 72493; p. 222, ref. 72492, p. 224, ref. 72587; p. 225, ref. 72503; p. 230, ref. 72518; p. 250, ref. 318825; p. 253, ref. 314582; p. 254, ref. 314574; p. 293, ref. 72499
LMA: p. 72; p. 73
Lost Rivers of London, p. 96

Monnickendam, p. 366
Mrs Gordon: p. 224; safe deposit, p. 333
M Vainer: front cover; the Vainer briolette, pp. 349, 350

National Portrait Gallery: front cover; Sir Christopher Hatton, pp. 21, 23, 107, 194, 260

Parish of St. Andrew's, The: p. 171
PJ Watson: front cover; emerald and diamond ring, pp. 353; 354; 355

Steve Duncan: p. 92

The Bleeding Heart: p. 178
The Builder: p. 116
TH March: p. 271
Tom O'Donogue: p. 306

Ullmann family: p. 322

Vokes family: p.67

Weissbart family: p. 304